D1058180

Corporate Financial Distress and Bankruptcy

Founded in 1807, John Wiley & Sons is the oldest independent publishing company in the United States. With offices in North America, Europe, Australia, and Asia, Wiley is globally committed to developing and marketing print and electronic products and services for our customers' professional and personal knowledge and understanding.

The Wiley Finance series contains books written specifically for finance and investment professionals as well as sophisticated individual investors and their financial advisors. Book topics range from portfolio management to e-commerce, risk management, financial engineering, valuation, and financial instrument analysis, as well as much more.

For a list of available titles, visit our Web site at www.WileyFinance.com.

Corporate Financial Distress and Bankruptcy

Predict and Avoid Bankruptcy,
Analyze and Invest in Distressed Debt

Third Edition

EDWARD I. ALTMAN
EDITH HOTCHKISS

John Wiley & Sons, Inc.

Copyright © 2006 by Edward I. Altman and Edith Hotchkiss. All rights reserved.

Published by John Wiley & Sons, Inc., Hoboken, New Jersey.
Published simultaneously in Canada.

No part of this publication may be reproduced, stored in a retrieval system, or transmitted in any form or by any means, electronic, mechanical, photocopying, recording, scanning, or otherwise, except as permitted under Section 107 or 108 of the 1976 United States Copyright Act, without either the prior written permission of the Publisher, or authorization through payment of the appropriate per-copy fee to the Copyright Clearance Center, Inc., 222 Rosewood Drive, Danvers, MA 01923, (978) 750-8400, fax (978) 646-8600, or on the web at www.copyright.com. Requests to the Publisher for permission should be addressed to the Permissions Department, John Wiley & Sons, Inc., 111 River Street, Hoboken, NJ 07030, (201) 748-6011, fax (201) 748-6008, or online at http://www.wiley.com/go/permissions.

Limit of Liability/Disclaimer of Warranty: While the publisher and author have used their best efforts in preparing this book, they make no representations or warranties with respect to the accuracy or completeness of the contents of this book and specifically disclaim any implied warranties of merchantability or fitness for a particular purpose. No warranty may be created or extended by sales representatives or written sales materials. The advice and strategies contained herein may not be suitable for your situation. You should consult with a professional where appropriate. Neither the publisher nor author shall be liable for any loss of profit or any other commercial damages, including but not limited to special, incidental, consequential, or other damages.

For general information on our other products and services or for technical support, please contact our Customer Care Department within the United States at (800) 762-2974, outside the United States at (317) 572-3993 or fax (317) 572-4002.

Designations used by companies to distinguish their products are often claimed by trademarks. In all instances where the author or publisher is aware of a claim, the product names appear in Initial Capital letters. Readers, however, should contact the appropriate companies for more complete information regarding trademarks and registration.

Wiley also publishes its books in a variety of electronic formats. Some content that appears in print may not be available in electronic books. For more information about Wiley products, visit our web site at www.wiley.com.

Library of Congress Cataloging-in-Publication Data:

Altman, Edward I., 1941–
    Corporate financial distress and bankruptcy : predict and avoid
bankruptcy, analyze and invest in distressed debt / Edward I. Altman,
Edith Hotchkiss. — 3rd ed.
        p.   cm. — (Wiley finance series)
    Includes bibliographical references and index.
    ISBN-13: 978-0-471-69189-1 (cloth)
    ISBN-10: 0-471-69189-5 (cloth)
    1. Bankruptcy—United States.   I. Hotchkiss, Edith, 1961– .
II. Title.   III. Series.
HG3766.A66 2006
658.15—dc22

                                                        2005017835

Printed in the United States of America.

10 9 8 7 6 5 4 3

Contents

Preface   vii

Acknowledgments   xi

About the Authors   xiii

PART ONE

The Legal, Economic, and Investment Dimensions of Corporate
Bankruptcy and Distressed Restructurings

CHAPTER 1
Corporate Distress: Introduction and Statistical Background   3

CHAPTER 2
Evolution of the Bankruptcy Process in the United States and
International Comparisons   21

CHAPTER 3
Post–Chapter 11 Performance   79

CHAPTER 4
The Costs of Bankruptcy   93

CHAPTER 5
Distressed Firm Valuation   103

CHAPTER 6
Firm Valuation and Corporate Leveraged Restructuring   121

CHAPTER 7
The High Yield Bond Market: Risks and Returns for Investors
and Analysts   145

CHAPTER 8
Investing in Distressed Securities   183

CHAPTER 9
Risk-Return Performance of Defaulted Bonds and Bank Loans   203

CHAPTER 10
Corporate Governance in Distressed Firms   219

PART TWO

**Techniques for the Classification and Prediction of Corporate
Financial Distress and Their Applications**

CHAPTER 11
Corporate Credit Scoring—Insolvency Risk Models   233

CHAPTER 12
An Emerging Market Credit Scoring System for Corporates   265

CHAPTER 13
Application of Distress Prediction Models   281

CHAPTER 14
**Distress Prediction Models: Catalysts for Constructive Change—
Managing a Financial Turnaround**   297

CHAPTER 15
Estimating Recovery Rates on Defaulted Debt   307

References   331

Author Index   347

Subject Index   350

Preface

In looking back over the first two editions of *Corporate Financial Distress and Bankruptcy* (1983 and 1993), we note that on both occasions of their publication the incidence and importance of corporate bankruptcy in the United States had risen to ever more prominence. The number of professionals dealing with the uniqueness of corporate death in this country was increasing so much that it could have perhaps been called a "bankruptcy industry." There is absolutely no question now in 2005 that we can call it an industry. The field has become even more popular in the past 10 to 15 years, and this has been accompanied by an increase in the number of academics specializing in the corporate distress area. These academics provide the serious analytical research that is warranted in this field. Indeed, there is nothing more important in attracting rigorous and thoughtful research than data! With this increased theoretical and especially empirical interest, Edith Hotchkiss has joined the original author of the first two editions to produce this volume.

It is now quite obvious that the bankruptcy business is big-business. While no one has done an extensive analysis of the number of people who deal with corporate distress on a regular basis, we would venture a guess that it is at least 40,000 globally, with the vast majority in the United States but a growing number abroad. We include turnaround managers (mostly consultants); bankruptcy and restructuring lawyers; bankruptcy judges and other court personnel; accountants, bankers, and other financial advisers who specialize in working with distressed debtors; distressed debt investors, sometimes referred to as "vultures"; and, of course, researchers. Indeed, the prestigious Turnaround Management Association (www.turnaround.org) numbered more than 7,000 members in 2005.

The reason for the large number of professionals working with organizations in various stages of financial distress is the increasing number of large and complex bankruptcy cases. In the United States in the three-year period 2001–2003, 100 companies with liabilities greater than $1 billion filed for protection under Chapter 11 of the Bankruptcy Code. These "billion-dollar babies" are listed in the appendix to Chapter 1. Over the past 35 years (1970–2005), there have been at least 228 of these large firm bankruptcies in the United States. On the eve of the publication of this book, two of the nation's major airlines, Delta and Northwest, have filed for bankruptcy protection. Chapter 1 of this book presents some relevant definitions and statistics on corporate distress and highlights the increasing reality that size is no longer a proxy for corporate health.

The planning for this book began long before its completion in mid-2005, and we were unaware that the eventual passing of the new Bankruptcy Abuse Prevention and Consumer Protection Act of 2005 (BAPCPA) would coincide with the timing of our completion. Most observers were commenting on the implications of the new Act for consumer (personal) bankruptcies, but as the details of the new Act became evident, it was clear that the implications for corporations and the reorganization process are also quite important. We attempt to treat many of these new provisions in Chapter 2 when we explore the evolution of the bankruptcy process in the United States with comparisons to many other countries.

With this background in place, the remaining chapters in the first section of the book address a number of key issues central to our understanding of the restructuring process. In Chapter 3, we explore the success of the bankruptcy reorganization process, especially with respect to the post-bankruptcy performance of firms emerging from Chapter 11. In a disturbing number of instances, these emerging firms have sustained recurring operating and financial problems, sometimes resulting in a second filing, unofficially called a "Chapter 22." Indeed, we are aware of at least 157 of these two-time filers over the period 1980–2004, and seven three-time filers (Chapter 33s). If we include filings prior to the 1978 Bankruptcy Reform Act, there is even one Chapter 44 (TransTexas Gas Corporation)! Despite the numbers of bankruptcy repeaters, many firms reduce the burden of their debt and go on to achieve success, especially if the core business is solid and can be managed more effectively with less debt.

As bankruptcy cases have become larger and more complex, there is a need for professionals with increasingly specialized skills. For example, with the sales of pieces of or entire businesses becoming more common in the recent wave of bankruptcies, there is a need for professionals skilled in managing the mergers and acquisitions (M&A) process. With the growth in the number and size of cases has come increased scrutiny of bankruptcy costs. Chapter 4 summarizes the extensive amount of academic research that has helped us to understand the nature of these costs. For larger firms, the dollar magnitude of these costs may be tremendous; for smaller firms, these costs may be prohibitive and ultimately lead to liquidation.

Chapters 5 and 6 explore the importance and analytics of the distressed firm valuation process from theoretical and pragmatic standpoints. In essence, the most important determinants of the fate of the distressed firm are (1) whether it is worth more dead than alive and (2) if worth more alive, what its value is relative to the claims against the assets. Chapter 5 provides a careful discussion of valuation models for distressed firms, and explains why we observe seemingly wide disagreements over the reorganized firm's value between different parties in the bankruptcy negotiation process. Chapter 6 concentrates on the highly leveraged restructuring, the relevant valuation and capital structure theories, and empirical results.

Chapters 7 through 9 explore, in great depth, the two relevant capital markets most important to risky and distressed firms. Chapter 7 explores the development and risk-return aspects of the U.S. high yield bond and bank loan markets. Since high yield or "junk" bonds are the raw material for future possible distressed debt situations, it is important to investigate their properties. Among the most relevant statistics to investors in this market are the default rate as well as the recovery rate once the firm defaults. The high yield corporate bond market approached $1 trillion outstanding in 2005, and topped $1 trillion when General Motors' and Ford's bonds were downgraded to non–investment grade status in May 2005.

Chapters 8 and 9 go on to examine the size and development of the distressed and defaulted debt market. This market was actually larger than the high yield market in 2002 when the face value of distressed debt (public and private) was almost $950 billion—at that time greater in size than the gross domestic products (GDPs) of all but seven of the world's countries! As the default rate subsequently decreased from record high levels in 2002, the size receded somewhat but still was relatively large in 2005 so that the distressed and defaulted debt market is now generally thought of as a unique asset class itself and perhaps the fastest growing segment in the hedge fund sector. As such, we explore its size, growth, risk-reward dimensions, and investment strategies.

Rounding out the first major section of this book is Chapter 10 on corporate governance in the distressed firm. Virtually every aspect of a firm's governance can change in some way when a firm undergoes a distressed restructuring. Management turnover rates for firms that emerge from Chapter 11 reach 90 percent. Board size declines as firms become distressed, and the board often changes in its entirety at reorganization. Most importantly, many restructurings ultimately involve a change in control of the company.

The second section of this book deals with the development and implications of models built to classify and predict corporate distress. The estimation of the probability of default in the United States (Chapter 11) and for emerging markets (Chapter 12) and the loss given default (Chapter 15) are explored in depth. Emphasis is on estimation procedures and their relevance to the new features of Basel II's capital adequacy requirements for banks and other financial institutions.

In an appendix to Chapter 11 of this book, we present a bibliography of the development and application of distress prediction models in more than 20 countries outside the United States. This highlights the incredible explosion in interest in the corporate bankruptcy phenomenon all over the world. As illustrated earlier in Chapter 2 and further documented in Chapter 12, corporate distress is a global phenomenon and, as such, deserves careful analysis and constructive commentary and legislation.

Models for estimating default probabilities are discussed in Chapters 11 and 12 followed in Chapter 13 by their applications to many different scenarios, including credit risk management, distressed debt investing, turnaround management and other advisory capacities, and legal issues. This chapter, in addition, comments on the leading practitioner firms in these functions.

With respect to the turnaround management arena, Chapter 14 further explores the possibility of using distressed firm predictive models, for example our Z-Score approaches, for assisting the management of the distressed firm itself in order to manage a return to financial health. We illustrate this via an actual case study discussed in Chapter 14—the GTI Corporation and its rise from near extinction.

EDWARD I. ALTMAN
EDITH HOTCHKISS

New York, New York
Chestnut Hill, Massachusetts
October 2005

Acknowledgments

We would like to acknowledge an impressive group of practitioners and academics who have assisted us in the researching and writing of this book. We are enormously grateful to all of these persons for helping us to shape our analysis and commentary in our writings and in our classes at the New York University Stern School of Business and Boston College.

Among the practitioners, Ed Altman would like to thank Amit Arora, John Beiter, Maria Boyarzny, Brooks Brady, Bruce Buchanan, Michael Embler, Ken Emery, Holly Etlin, John Fenn, Jerry Foms, Martin Fridson, Rich Gere, Geoffrey Gold, Shelly Greenhaus, Harvey Gross, Robert Grossman, David Hamilton, Loretta Hennessey, Max Holmes, Shubin Jha, Sau-Man Kam, D. L. Kao, David Keisman, Al Koch, Martha Kopacz, Pat LaGrange, Markus Lahrkamp, E. Bruce Leonard, Bill Lutz, Judge Robert Martin, Chris McHugh, Robert Miller, Steven Miller, Wilson Miranda, David Newman, Mark Patterson, Gabriella Petrucci, Robert Raskin, Barry Ridings, Wilbur Ross, Til Scheurmann, Mark Shenkman, Dennis Smith, Christopher Stuttard, Ronald Sussman, Matt Venturi, Mariarosa Verde, Robert Waldman, Lionel Wallace, Jeffrey Werbalofsky, Bettina Whyte, David Winters, and Steven Zelin. And extra special thanks to his two ex-students, Allan Brown and Marti Murray. Edie Hotchkiss would like to thank William Derrough, Joseph Guzinski, Melissa Hager, Gregory Horowitz, Isaac Lee, Brett Miller, and Barry Ridings for their helpful discussions.

Ed Altman would also like to thank the many graduate assistants at the NYU Salomon Center over the years and the wonderful staff at the Center, including Mary Jaffier, Anita Lall, Robyn Vanterpool, and especially Lourdes Tanglao. The authors also thank Kimberly Thomas for her assistance with this manuscript. The editorial assistance of Mary Daniello, Bill Falloon, and Laura Walsh of John Wiley & Sons is also appreciated by the authors.

Edie Hotchkiss and Ed Altman would like to acknowledge the many contributions to the literature and field of corporate distress by academics, especially the more than 20 scholars who make up the Academic Advisory Council to the Turnaround Management Association and the many coauthors on their academic research papers.

Finally, Ed Altman would like to thank his wife and longtime companion, Elaine Altman, and son Gregory, for enduring his perverse enthusiasm for various degrees of corporate distress. Edie Hotchkiss would like to thank Ed for first introducing her to this field as her Ph.D. dissertation adviser, and for inviting her to collaborate on this project. She would also like to thank her husband Steven and daughter Jenny for their loving support.

E.I.A.

E.H.

About the Authors

Edward I. Altman is the Max L. Heine Professor of Finance at the Stern School of Business, New York University, and director of the Credit and Fixed Income Research Program at the NYU Salomon Center.

Dr. Altman has an international reputation as an expert on corporate bankruptcy, high yield bonds, distressed debt, and credit risk analysis. He was named Laureate 1984 by the Hautes Etudes Commerciales Foundation in Paris for his accumulated works on corporate distress prediction models and procedures for firm financial rehabilitation, and he was awarded the Graham and Dodd Scroll for 1985 by the Financial Analysts Federation for his work on default rates and high yield corporate debt.

He was inducted into the Fixed Income Analysts Society Hall of Fame in 2001 and elected president of the Financial Management Association (2003) and a Fellow of the FMA in 2004. He was honored by *Treasury and Risk Management* magazine as one of the 100 most influential people in finance (June 2005).

Dr. Altman is an adviser to many financial institutions, including Citigroup, Concordia Advisors, Droege & Company, Investcorp, Miller-Mathis, the New York State Common Retirement Fund, and SERASA, S.A.; he is on the boards of the Franklin Mutual Series Funds, Automated Trading Desk L.L.C., and the Ascend Group, and is chairman of the Academic Advisory Council to the Turnaround Management Association; and he has testified before federal and state legislative bodies.

Edith Hotchkiss is an Associate Professor of Finance at the Carroll School of Management at Boston College. She received her Ph.D. in Finance from the Stern School of Business at New York University and her B.A. from Dartmouth College. Prior to entering academics, she worked in consulting and for the Financial Institutions Group of Standard & Poor's Corporation.

Dr. Hotchkiss's research covers such topics as corporate financial distress and restructuring, the efficiency of Chapter 11 bankruptcy, and trading in corporate debt markets. Her work has been published in journals including the *Journal of Finance*, *Journal of Financial Economics*, *Journal of Financial Intermediation*, and *Review of Financial Studies*. She has served on the national board of the Turnaround Management Association, and as a consultant to the National Association of Securities Dealers (NASD) on trading in corporate bond markets.

The Legal, Economic, and Investment Dimensions of Corporate Bankruptcy and Distressed Restructurings

Corporate Distress: Introduction and Statistical Background

Corporate distress, including the legal processes of corporate bankruptcy reorganization (Chapter 11 of the Bankruptcy Code) and liquidation (Chapter 7), is a sobering economic reality reflecting the uniqueness of the American way of corporate "death." The business failure phenomenon received some exposure during the 1970s, more during the recession years of 1980 to 1982, heightened attention during the explosion of defaults and large firm bankruptcies in the 1989–1991 period, and an unprecedented interest in the 2001–2002 corporate debacle and distressed years. In the 1989–1991 period, 34 corporations with liabilities greater than $1 billion filed for protection under Chapter 11 of the Bankruptcy Code, and in the three-year period 2001–2003 as many as 100 so-called billion-dollar babies, including the top five, filed for protection under the Code (see Appendix 1.1).

The lineup of major corporate bankruptcies was capped by the mammoth filings of Conseco ($56.6 billion in liabilities), WorldCom ($46.0 billion), and Enron ($31.2 billion—actually almost double this amount once you add in the enormous amount of off-balance liabilities, making it the largest bankruptcy in the United States). Two of these three largest bankruptcies were fraud-related (see our discussion of corporate governance issues in distressed companies in Chapter 10). Incidentally, we believe that it is more relevant to list and discuss the size of bankruptcies in terms of liabilities at the time of filing rather than assets. For example, WorldCom had about $104 billion in book value of assets but its market value at the time of filing was probably less than one-fifth of that number. It is the claims against the bankruptcy estate, as well as the going-concern value of the assets, that are most relevant in a bankrupt company. We list the largest corporate bankruptcies in the United States over the period 1970–2005 (Q1) in Appendix 1.1—the so-called billion-dollar babies. Actually, only two of the

228 entries in this list were from the 1970–1979 decade—Penn Central (1970) and W. T. Grant (1975)—and only 21 occurred in the 1980s. The majority of the largest bankruptcies in the 1970–2004 period were from the first four years of the new millennium. Even adjusting for inflation, it is clear that size is no longer a proxy for corporate health, and there is little evidence, except in very rare circumstances, of the old adage "too big to fail." Lately, that question has been asked about General Motors and Ford.

The unsuccessful business enterprise has been defined in numerous ways in attempts to depict the formal process confronting the firm and/or to categorize the economic problems involved. Four generic terms that are commonly found in the literature are *failure, insolvency, default*, and *bankruptcy*. Although these terms are sometimes used interchangeably, they are distinctly different in their formal usage.

Failure, by economic criteria, means that the realized rate of return on invested capital, with allowances for risk consideration, is significantly and continually lower than prevailing rates on similar investments. Somewhat different economic criteria have also been utilized, including insufficient revenues to cover costs and where the average return on investment is continually below the firm's cost of capital. These economic situations make no statements about the existence or discontinuance of the entity. Normative decisions to discontinue operations are based on expected returns and the ability of the firm to cover its variable costs. It should be noted that a company may be an economic failure for many years, yet never fail to meet its current obligations because of the absence or near absence of legally enforceable debt. When the company can no longer meet the legally enforceable demands of its creditors, it is sometimes called a legal failure. The term *legal* is somewhat misleading because the condition, as just described, may exist without formal court involvement.

The term *business failure* was adopted by Dun & Bradstreet (D&B), which for many years until recently supplied relevant statistics on businesses to describe various unsatisfactory business conditions. According to D&B, business failures included "businesses that cease operation following assignment or bankruptcy; those that cease with loss to creditors after such actions or execution, foreclosure, or attachment; those that voluntarily withdraw, leaving unpaid obligations, or those that have been involved in court actions such as receivership, bankruptcy reorganization, or arrangement; and those that voluntarily compromise with creditors."[1]

---

[1]In the prior editions of this book (Altman 1983 and 1993) we used the D&B "failure rate" definition to explore the macro and micro determinants of failure. Since D&B has discontinued its business failure coverage, we no longer will focus on this statistic.

Insolvency is another term depicting negative firm performance and is generally used in a more technical fashion. *Technical insolvency* exists when a firm cannot meet its current obligations, signifying a lack of liquidity. Walter (1957) discussed the measurement of technical insolvency and advanced the theory that net cash flows relative to current liabilities should be the primary criterion used to describe technical insolvency, not the traditional working capital measurement. Technical insolvency may be a temporary condition, although it often is the immediate cause of formal bankruptcy declaration.

Insolvency in a bankruptcy sense is more critical and usually indicates a chronic rather than temporary condition. A firm finds itself in this situation when its total liabilities exceed a fair valuation of its total assets. The real net worth of the firm is, therefore, negative. Technical insolvency is easily detectable, whereas the more serious bankruptcy insolvency condition requires a comprehensive valuation analysis, which is usually not undertaken until asset liquidation is contemplated. Finally, a relatively recent concept that has appeared in judicial courts concerns the condition known as *deepening insolvency*. This involves an eventually bankrupt company that is alleged to be kept alive unnecessarily and to the detriment of the estate, especially the creditors. This concept is explored in Chapter 13 of this book.

Another corporate condition that is inescapably associated with distress is *default*. Defaults can be technical and/or legal and always involve the relationship between the debtor firm and a creditor class. *Technical default* takes place when the debtor violates a condition of an agreement with a creditor and can be the grounds for legal action. For example, the violation of a loan covenant, such as the current ratio or debt ratio of the debtor, is the basis for a technical default. In reality, such defaults are usually renegotiated and are used to signal deteriorating firm performance. Rarely are these violations the catalyst for a more formal default or bankruptcy proceeding.

When a firm misses a scheduled loan or bond payment, usually the periodic interest obligation, a legal default is more likely, although it is not always the result in the case of a loan. Interest payments can be missed and accrue to the lender in a private transaction, such as a bank loan, without a formal default being declared. For publicly held bonds, however, when a firm misses an interest payment or principal repayment, and the problem is not cured within the grace period, usually 30 days, the security is then in default. The firm may continue to operate while it attempts to work out a *distressed restructuring* with creditors and avoid a formal bankruptcy declaration and filing. It is even possible to agree upon a restructuring with a sufficient number and amount of claimants and then legally file for bankruptcy. This is called a *prepackaged Chapter 11* (discussed in Chapter 2).

Defaults on publicly held indebtedness have become a commonplace event, especially in the two major default periods, 1989–1991 and 2001–2002. Indeed, in 1990 and again in 1991, over $18 billion of publicly held corporate bonds defaulted each year involving about 150 different entities. And in 2002, defaults soared to an almost unbelievable level of close to $100 billion! Table 1.1 shows the history of U.S. public bond de-

TABLE 1.1 Historical Default Rates—Straight Bonds Only Excluding Defaulted Issues from Par Value Outstanding, 1971–2004 ($Millions)

Year	Par Value Outstanding[a]	Par Value Defaults	Default Rates
2004	$933,100	$11,657	1.249%
2003	825,000	38,451	4.661
2002	757,000	96,858	12.795
2001	649,000	63,609	9.801
2000	597,200	30,295	5.073
1999	567,400	23,532	4.147
1998	465,500	7,464	1.603
1997	335,400	4,200	1.252
1996	271,000	3,336	1.231
1995	240,000	4,551	1.896
1994	235,000	3,418	1.454
1993	206,907	2,287	1.105
1992	163,000	5,545	3.402
1991	183,600	18,862	10.273
1990	181,000	18,354	10.140
1989	189,258	8,110	4.285
1988	148,187	3,944	2.662
1987	129,557	7,486	5.778
1986	90,243	3,156	3.497
1985	58,088	992	1.708
1984	40,939	344	0.840
1983	27,492	301	1.095
1982	18,109	577	3.186
1981	17,115	27	0.158
1980	14,935	224	1.500
1979	10,356	20	0.193
1978	8,946	119	1.330
1977	8,157	381	4.671
1976	7,735	30	0.388
1975	7,471	204	2.731
1974	10,894	123	1.129
1973	7,824	49	0.626
1972	6,928	193	2.786
1971	6,602	82	1.242

TABLE 1.1 *(Continued)*

			Standard Deviation
Arithmetic Average Default Rate	1971 to 2004	3.232%	3.134%
	1978 to 2004	3.567	3.361
	1985 to 2004	4.401	3.501
Weighted Average Default Rate[b]	1971 to 2004	4.836%	
	1978 to 2004	4.858	
	1985 to 2004	4.929	
Median Annual Default Rate	1971 to 2004	1.802%	

[a]As of midyear.
[b]Weighted by par value of amount outstanding for each year.
Source: Authors' compilations.

faults from 1971 to 2004, including the dollar amounts and the amounts as a percentage of total high yield bonds outstanding—the so-called junk bond default rate. Default rates are also calculated on leveraged loans, which are the private debt market's equivalent to speculative grade bond defaults (see Chapter 7 of this book).

Finally, we come to *bankruptcy* itself. One type of bankruptcy was described earlier and refers to the net worth position of an enterprise. A second, more observable type is a firm's formal declaration of bankruptcy in a federal district court, accompanied by a petition either to liquidate its assets (filing Chapter 7) or attempt a recovery program (filing Chapter 11). The latter procedure is legally referred to as a *bankruptcy reorganization*. The judicial reorganization is a formal procedure that is usually the last measure in a series of attempted remedies. We will study the bankruptcy process in depth and the evolution of bankruptcy laws in the United States in the next chapter.

BANKRUPTCY AND REORGANIZATION THEORY

In an economic system, the continuous entrance and exit of productive entities are natural components. Since there are costs to society inherent in the failure of these entities, laws and procedures have been established (1) to protect the contractual rights of interested parties, (2) to provide for the orderly liquidation of unproductive assets, and (3) when deemed desirable, to provide for a moratorium on certain claims in order to give the debtor time to become rehabilitated and to emerge from the process as a continuing entity. Both liquidation and reorganization are available courses of action in most countries of the world and are based on the following premise: If an entity's intrinsic or economic value is greater than its current liquidation value, then from both a public policy and the entity ownership viewpoints, the firm should be permitted to attempt to reorganize and continue. If, however, the firm's assets are "worth more dead than alive"—that is, if liquidation value exceeds the economic going-concern value—liquidation is the preferable alternative.

The theory of reorganization in bankruptcy is basically sound and has potential economic and social benefits. The process is designed to enable the financially troubled firm to continue in existence and maintain whatever goodwill it still possesses, rather than to liquidate its assets for the benefit of its creditors. Justification of this attempt is found in the belief that continued existence will result in a healthy going concern worth more than the value of its assets sold in the marketplace. Since this rehabilitation process often requires several years, the time value of money should be considered explicitly through a discounted cash flow procedure. If, in fact, economically productive assets continue to contribute to society's supply of goods and services above and beyond their opportunity costs, the process of reorganization has been of benefit, to say nothing of the continued employment of the firm's employees, revenues for its suppliers, and taxes paid on profits. These benefits should be weighed against the costs of bankruptcy to the firm and to society. We will explore further those costs in Chapters 4 and 6.

The primary groups of interested parties are the firm's creditors and owners. The experience of these parties is of paramount importance in the evaluation of the bankruptcy reorganization process, although the laws governing reorganization reflect the legislators' concern for overall societal welfare. The primary immediate responsibility of the reorganization process is to relieve the burden of the debtor's liabilities and restructure the firm's assets and capital structure so that financial and operating problems will not recur in the foreseeable future.

BANKRUPTCY FILINGS

The two broad categories of bankruptcy filings are business and consumer filings. Although the vast majority are consumer bankruptcies, with close to 98 percent of the total filings in recent years (e.g., 97.9 percent in 2004), this book deals almost exclusively with large business filings, primarily Chapter 11. Table 1.2a and b and Figure 1.1 list the bankruptcy filings for business and nonbusiness entities from 1980 to 2004. Our focus will be on the larger firm Chapter 11 proceedings. Note that while the absolute num-

TABLE 1.2a Bankruptcy Filings by Type, 1980–2004

Year	Business	Nonbusiness	Total	Nonbusiness Percent of Total
2004	34,317	1,563,145	1,597,462	97.85%
2003	35,037	1,625,208	1,660,245	97.89
2002	38,540	1,539,111	1,577,651	97.56
2001	40,099	1,452,030	1,492,129	97.31
2000	35,472	1,217,972	1,253,444	97.17
1995	51,959	874,642	926,601	94.39
1990	64,853	718,107	782,960	91.72
1985	71,277	341,233	412,510	82.72
1980	43,694	287,570	331,264	86.81

Source: Bankruptcydata.com, www.abiworld.org/stats.

TABLE 1.2b Bankruptcy Filings by Bankruptcy Chapter, 2000–2004

Year	Chapter 7	Chapter 11	Chapter 12	Chapter 13
2004	1,137,958	10,132	108	449,129
2003	1,176,905	9,404	712	473,137
2002	1,109,923	11,270	485	455,877
2001	1,054,975	11,424	383	425,292
2000	859,220	9,884	407	383,894

Source: Bankruptcydata.com, www.abiworld.org/stats.

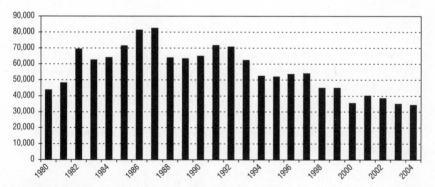

FIGURE 1.1 Business Bankruptcy Filings, 1980–2004
Source: Bankruptcydata.com.

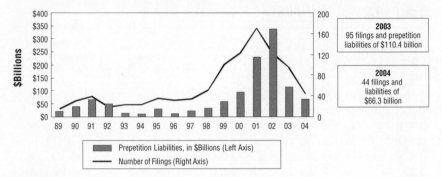

FIGURE 1.2 Filings for Chapter 11: Number of Filings and Prepetition Liabilities of Public Companies, 1989–2004
Note: Minimum $100 million in liabilities.
Source: New York University Salomon Center Bankruptcy Filings Database.

bers of business filings have receded to between 35,000 and 40,000 per year in 2000–2004, the size in terms of total liabilities at the time of filing rose to record levels, especially in 2002 when more than $330 billion of liabilities were impacted. Certainly, the massive fraud-related bankruptcies had an important influence on the 2001–2002 numbers, but it is also fair to say that no longer does the term *bankruptcy* have the same ultranegative connotation that it once did for larger companies.

Some observations are worth mentioning. First, the incredible increase in nonbusiness (consumer) bankruptcies is apparent, reflecting the huge increase in personal indebtedness in the United States. These personal bankruptcies have increased almost fivefold over the past 25 years. With the tougher conditions for consumers under the Bankruptcy Abuse Prevention and Consumer Protection Act of 2005 (see Chapter 2), most observers are expecting a significant decrease after the new Act goes into effect on October 17, 2005. Second, the number of business filings has actually decreased since the peak period of 1991–1992 (see Figure 1.1). Third, despite the decrease in the number of filings since the early 1990s, total liabilities of the larger business bankruptcies have swollen to record levels in the 2000–2004 period, especially in 2001 and 2002 (see Figure 1.2).[2] These trends have fed the distressed debt investment sector and have given unprecedented importance to this new alternative asset class (see our discussion in Chapters 8 and 9).

---

[2]Figure 1.2 shows the time series of total liabilities of Chapter 11 bankruptcies from 1989 to 2004. These statistics are restricted to bankruptcies with a minimum of $100 million in liabilities.

THE BANKRUPTCY INDUSTRY PLAYERS

The fact that corporate bankruptcy in the United States is a major industry can be documented by the size and scope of activities that are associated with bankruptcy and distress. While the sheer volume of corporate bankruptcy filings peaked in the early 1990s, bankruptcies now (2005) attract a record number of practitioners and researchers. Perhaps the main reason is the size of the entities in recent years that have found it necessary to file for bankruptcy. As noted earlier, firms with liabilities and assets of at least $1 billion are now fairly commonplace. And, just as important to strategists and researchers, is the availability of data on distressed firms from many sources. The major players in the bankruptcy and related distressed firm industry are:

- Bankrupt and failed firms—the debtors.
- Bankruptcy legal system (judges, trustees, etc.).
- Bankruptcy law specialists.
- Bankruptcy-insolvency accountants and tax specialists.
- Bankrupt firm creditors and committees.
- Distressed firm securities traders and analysts.
- Distressed firm turnaround specialists.
- Financial restructuring advisers.
- Public relations firms specializing in troubled firms.
- Bankruptcy and workout publications.

Most of these bankruptcy and distressed firm players are discussed in Chapter 13 of this book.

THE DEBTORS

As we discussed in prior versions of this book, during the 1970s, about 29,000 to 35,000 business entities filed for protection to either liquidate or reorganize under the bankruptcy laws of the United States each year. As shown earlier in Table 1.2a and b and Figures 1.1 and 1.2, under the Bankruptcy Code that went into effect in October 1979 and was recently amended in 2005, the number of business bankruptcy filings increased to nearly 44,000 in 1980, were well over 60,000 per year from 1982 to 1993, then receded to between 35,000 and 55,000 from 1993 to 2004.

Although the amendments to the Bankruptcy Code in 2005, the Bankruptcy Abuse Prevention and Consumer Protection Act of 2005 (BAPCPA), dramatically changed the provisions dealing with individuals, we do not focus on consumer bankruptcies in this book. The new Act in 2005 also did change some important corporate provisions, which we review in the next chapter.

CHAPTER 22 DEBTORS AND BANKRUPTCY SUCCESS

The bankruptcy reorganization process is, unfortunately, not always successful even if the firm emerges as a continuing entity. It is certainly possible for the emerged firm to fail again and file a second time (or even a third time and so on) for protection under the code. We first coined the term *Chapter 22* (Altman 1983) to illustrate those companies that have filed twice. These Chapter 22s were saddled with too much debt and/or the business outlook was overly optimistic at the time of emergence the first time. We will explore the postbankruptcy performance of firms in Chapter 3 of this volume in much greater depth. Table 1.3 lists the esti-

TABLE 1.3   Chapter 22s and 33s in the United States, 1984–2004

Year	Number of Chapter 22s	Number of Chapter 33s
1984	2	0
1985	2	0
1986	4	0
1987	1	0
1988	5	0
1989	4	0
1990	10	0
1991	9	0
1992	6	0
1993	8	0
1994	5	0
1995	9	0
1996	12	2
1997	5	0
1998	2	1
1999	10	0
2000	12	1
2001	17	2
2002	11	0
2003	17	1
2004	6	0
Total:	157	7

Source: E. Hotchkiss, Boston College, and the *Bankruptcy Almanac*, annually, Boston: New Generation Research.

mated number of Chapter 22s and 33s each year since 1984. As one can observe, the totals are nontrivial and indicate some problems in our distressed restructuring process. We argue later in Chapter 13 for some further tests to increase the probability of a firm's successful emergence from Chapter 11.

REASONS FOR CORPORATE FAILURES

Without question, the most pervasive reason for a firm's distress and possible failure is some type of managerial incompetence. In its earlier annual publication of *The Failure Record* (no longer published), D&B itemized the many reasons for failure, and those related to management invariably totaled about 90 percent. Of course, most firms fail for multiple reasons, but management inadequacies are usually at the core of the problems. The ultimate cause of failure is usually simply running out of cash, but there are a variety of means-related reasons that contribute to the high number of bankruptcies and other distressed conditions in which firms find themselves.

These reasons include:

- Chronically sick industries (e.g., agriculture, textiles, department stores).
- Deregulation of key industries (i.e., airlines, financial services, health care, energy).
- High real interest rates in certain periods.
- International competition.
- Overcapacity within an industry.
- Increased leveraging of corporate America.
- Relatively high new business formation rates in certain periods.

Several of these reasons are obvious (e.g., high interest rates, overleveraging, and competition).

Deregulation removes the protective cover of a regulated industry and fosters larger numbers of entering and exiting firms. Competition is far greater in a deregulated environment, such as the airline industry. Hence, airline failures multiplied in the 1980s following deregulation at the end of the 1970s and have continued virtually unabated since. New business formation is usually based on optimism about the future. But new businesses fail with far greater frequency than do more seasoned entities, and the failure rate can be expected to increase in the years immediately following a surge in new business activity. The aggregate new business formation determinant of business failures, as well as other macroeconomic factors, was modeled in an earlier edition of this book (Altman 1983) in a distributed-lag econometric framework.

THE JUDICIAL SYSTEM

The legal structure whereby businesses of all sizes and in most economic sectors settle their financial difficulties and in many cases attempt to reorganize is our nation's federal bankruptcy courts. The intricate and sometimes complex evolution of the bankruptcy laws and the courts that administer them is discussed in detail in Chapter 2. The bankruptcy laws are designed either to rehabilitate a distressed debtor or to liquidate its assets for distribution to claimants.

At the end of 2004, there were about 360 bankruptcy judge positions nationwide authorized to guide the debtors and their various creditors through the bankruptcy process. These are federal judges who serve in 90 judicial districts encompassing the 50 states, Puerto Rico, and the District of Columbia. No district includes more than one state, although several districts can be found in the same state. Bankruptcy statistics, gathered by the Administrative Office of the U.S. Courts, Bankruptcy Division, in Washington, D.C., are assembled by district and then aggregated. Bankruptcy judges are assisted by U.S. trustees who play a major role in the scheduling of hearings and record keeping of the huge flow of cases in the system. Trustees are appointed by the U.S. attorney general's office. This trusteeship function should not be confused with either the old bankruptcy trustees under Chapter X of the previous bankruptcy law (1938), whereby individuals were appointed by bankruptcy judges to both manage the bankrupt debtor and propose a plan of reorganizing, or the new (2005) law's stipulation that a Chapter 11 trustee may be appointed by the court if incompetence, gross mismanagement, fraud, or dishonesty by current management is found (not just suspected).

Finally, the nation's large core of bankruptcy lawyers make up an important constituency in the bankruptcy process. These lawyer-consultants represent the many stakeholders in the process, including the debtor, creditors, equity holders, employees, and even tax authorities. An educated guess as to the number of practicing bankruptcy lawyers in recent years (e.g., 2002–2005) is at least 5,000, especially during periods when the number of large firm failures is at a peak. Martinsdale.com lists 4,991 bankruptcy lawyers in 2005 (see www.martinsdale.com). Some of the larger firms with specialization in the bankruptcy area are Weil Gotshal, Stroock, Stroock and Lavan; Kirkland & Ellis; Skadden, Arps, Slate, Meagher & Flom; Davis Polk & Wardell; and Wilkie-Farr, among others.

We now turn to the nation's bankruptcy laws themselves and how they have evolved over the years.

APPENDIX 1.1   Bankrupt Companies—$1 Billion in Liabilities or More, 1970–2005 (Q1)

Company	Liabilities ($MM)	Date
1 Conseco Inc.	$56,639.30	Dec-02
2 WorldCom Inc.	45,984.00	Jul-02
3 Enron Corp.	31,237.00	Dec-01
4 Pacific Gas & Electric Co.	25,717.00	Apr-01
5 UAL Corporation	22,164.00	Dec-02
6 Texaco (incl. subsidiaries)	21,603.00	Apr-87
7 Conseco Finance Corp.	20,278.50	Dec-02
8 Olympia & York (I)	19,800.00	May-92
9 Adelphia Communications Corp.	17,349.10	Jun-02
10 Mirant Corp.	16,460.00	Jul-03
11 Global Crossing, Ltd.	14,639.00	Jan-02
12 Executive Life Insurance	14,577.00	Apr-91
13 NTL, Inc.	14,134.00	May-02
14 Mutual Benefit Life	13,500.00	Jul-91
15 Reliance Group Holdings, Inc.	12,877.47	Jun-01
16 Finova Group, Inc.	11,822.21	Mar-01
17 Swissair	11,704.50	Oct-01
18 NRG Energy, Inc.	11,579.89	May-03
19 US Airways Group (I)	10,640.00	Aug-02
20 Kmart Corp.	10,263.00	Jan-02
21 United Pan-Europe Communications Nv	10,086.40	Dec-02
22 Campeau (Allied & Federated)	9,947.00	Jan-90
23 First Capital Holdings	9,291.00	May-91
24 Home Holdings, Inc.	9,132.00	Jan-98
25 Baldwin United	9,000.00	Sep-83
26 PG&E National Energy Group, Inc.	8,908.00	Jul-03
27 USAir Inc. (II)	8,383.00	Sep-04
28 Federal Mogul Corp.	8,232.70	Oct-01
29 Owens Corning	7,375.00	Oct-00
30 Williams Communications Group, Inc.	7,153.80	Apr-02
31 Comdisco, Inc.	6,742.00	Jul-01
32 ANC Rental Corp.	6,252.40	Nov-01
33 Continental Airlines (II)	6,200.00	Dec-90
34 Air Canada	6,182.00	Apr-03
35 Lomas Financial (I)	6,127.00	Sep-89
36 XO Communications, Inc.	5,851.06	Jun-02
37 Penncorp Financial Group, Inc.	5,595.46	Jan-00
38 Macy's	5,320.00	Jan-92
39 Montgomery Ward (II)	5,067.00	Dec-00
40 Trenwick Group Ltd.	5,017.19	Aug-03
41 Olympia & York Cos. (II)	5,000.00	Oct-95

(Continued)

APPENDIX 1.1 *(Continued)*

Company	Liabilities ($MM)	Date
42 Columbia Gas	$4,998.00	Jul-91
43 LTV (incl. LTV Int'l NV (I)	4,700.00	Jul-86
44 LTV Corp. (II)	4,669.00	Dec-00
45 PSInet, Inc.	4,599.30	May-01
46 Exodus Communications, Inc.	4,446.00	Sep-01
47 Bethlehem Steel Corp.	4,420.00	Oct-01
48 McLeodUSA, Inc.	4,419.20	Jan-02
49 Winstar Communications, Inc.	4,379.20	Apr-01
50 Laidlaw, Inc.	4,377.10	Jun-01
51 Budget Group	4,333.61	Aug-02
52 Montgomery Ward & Co. (I)	4,271.00	Jul-97
53 Maxwell Communication	4,100.00	Dec-91
54 Integrated Health Services, Inc.	4,061.16	Feb-00
55 Metromedia Fiber Network, Inc.	4,007.00	May-02
56 Nextwave Personal Communications, Inc.	3,773.00	Jun-98
57 Loewen Group, Inc.	3,768.47	Jun-99
58 Touch America Holdings, Inc.	3,765.77	Jun-03
59 RCN Corp.	3,668.24	May-04
60 Solutia, Inc.	3,591.00	Dec-03
61 Armstrong World Industries, Inc.	3,485.30	Dec-00
62 TWA (I)	3,470.00	Jan-92
63 Dow Corning	3,450.00	May-95
64 Southland	3,380.00	Oct-90
65 Globalstar, LP	3,328.40	Feb-02
66 Penn Central Transportation	3,300.00	Jun-70
67 Amerco	3,274.35	Jun-03
68 Iridium LLC/Capital Corp.	3,261.73	Aug-99
69 Sunbeam Corp.	3,201.51	Feb-01
70 Eastern Airlines	3,196.00	Mar-89
71 Fleming	3,156.00	Apr-03
72 Safety-Kleen Corp.	3,141.32	Jun-00
73 Kaiser Aluminum Corp.	3,129.40	Feb-02
74 ICH Corp. (Southwestern Life)	3,111.00	Oct-95
75 Genuity Inc.	3,102.00	Nov-02
76 USG Corp. (I)	3,100.00	Mar-93
77 Warnaco Group, Inc.	3,078.35	Jun-01
78 Loral Space & Communications Ltd.	3,047.03	Jul-03
79 Flag Telecom Holdings, Ltd.	3,046.74	Apr-02
80 Covanta Energy Corp.	3,031.40	Apr-02
81 Nextel International Inc.	3,000.00	May-02
82 Pan Am World Airlines	3,000.00	Jan-91
83 Drexel Burnham Lambert	3,000.00	Feb-90

APPENDIX 1.1 *(Continued)*

Company	Liabilities ($MM)	Date
84 Washington Group International, Inc.	$2,914.50	May-01
85 360Networks, Inc.	2,806.00	Jun-01
86 Petroleum Geo-Services ASA	2,777.90	Jul-03
87 Global Telesystems, Inc.	2,760.20	Nov-01
88 Northwestern Corp.	2,748.41	Sep-03
89 AEI Resources, Inc.	2,746.20	Feb-02
90 CHS Electronics, Inc.	2,723.63	Apr-00
91 USG Corp. (II)	2,700.00	Jun-01
92 Viatel, Inc.	2,683.00	May-01
93 TWA (III)	2,659.00	Jun-95
94 Hayes Lemmerz International, Inc.	2,655.70	Dec-01
95 Mariner Post-Acute Network, Inc.	2,639.64	Jan-00
96 Flagstar Companies	2,639.00	Apr-97
97 Tower Automotive Inc.	2,621.00	Feb-05
98 W. R. Grace & Co.	2,574.89	Apr-01
99 Exide Technologies, Inc.	2,524.20	Apr-02
100 Spectrasite Holdings, Inc.	2,482.20	Nov-02
101 Leap Wireless International, Inc	2,469.00	Apr-03
102 Trans World Airlines, Inc. (II)	2,384.47	Jan-01
103 Farmland Industries	2,351.50	May-02
104 ICG Communications Corp.	2,345.16	Nov-00
105 Westpoint Acquisition	2,340.00	Jun-92
106 Archibald Candy Corp.	2,312.14	Jan-04
107 Regal Cinemas	2,293.98	Oct-01
108 Harnischfeger Industries, Inc.	2,276.06	Jun-99
109 Genesis Health Ventures	2,254.00	Jun-00
110 Century Communications Corp.	2,229.60	Jun-02
111 Interco	2,213.00	May-90
112 Paging Network, Inc.	2,212.39	Jul-00
113 Charter Medical Corporation	2,150.00	Jun-92
114 West Point Stevens, Inc.	2,147.20	Jun-03
115 Sun Healthcare Group, Inc.	2,142.40	Oct-99
116 National Steel Corp.	2,118.90	Mar-02
117 E-II Holdings	2,050.00	Jul-92
118 Arch Wireless, Inc.	2,045.40	Dec-01
119 Transamerica Energy Corp.	2,041.00	Apr-99
120 Grand Union (and G.U. Capital) (I)	2,039.00	Jan-95
121 Stelco, Inc. (Canada)	2,027.00	Jan-04
122 Trump Hotels & Casino Resorts, Inc.	2,026.00	Nov-04
123 Firstplus Financial Group, Inc.	2,017.06	Mar-99
124 Pathmark Stores, Inc.	2,005.42	Jul-00

(Continued)

APPENDIX 1.1 *(Continued)*

Company	Liabilities ($MM)	Date
125 Laventhol & Horwath	$2,000.00	Nov-90
126 Wickes	2,000.00	Apr-82
127 Highlands Insurance Group, Inc.	1,978.70	Nov-02
128 Canadian Airlines Corp.	1,931.80	Mar-00
129 Pegasus Communications Corp.	1,929.42	Jun-04
130 NVR	1,911.00	Apr-92
131 Semi-Tech Corporation	1,888.60	Sep-99
132 Ameriserve Foods, Inc.	1,886.24	Jan-00
133 Asia Global Crossing Ltd.	1,868.80	Nov-02
134 Chiquita Brands International, Inc.	1,823.00	Nov-01
135 Dade Behring Holdings Inc.	1,808.60	Aug-02
136 Cardinal	1,800.00	Aug-92
137 Global Marine	1,800.00	Jan-86
138 JWP	1,780.00	Dec-93
139 Fruit of the Loom, Inc.	1,740.90	Dec-99
140 Encompass Services Corporation	1,725.30	Nov-02
141 Penn Traffic Company	1,723.40	Mar-99
142 Metropolitan Mortgage & Securities Co., Inc.	1,713.84	Feb-04
143 Memorex Telex, N.V. (I)	1,700.00	Jan-92
144 Public Service, New Hampshire	1,700.00	Jan-88
145 Itel	1,700.00	Jan-81
146 Ames Department Stores (II)	1,687.57	Aug-01
147 Spiegel Inc.	1,675.00	Mar-03
148 Continental Information Systems	1,669.00	Jan-89
149 Adelphia Business Solutions, Inc.	1,654.30	Mar-02
150 Covad Communications Group, Inc.	1,652.53	Aug-01
151 Breed Technologies, Inc.	1,649.95	Sep-99
152 Teligent, Inc.	1,649.40	May-01
153 Polaroid	1,634.40	Oct-01
154 Service Merchandise	1,614.96	Mar-99
155 Integrated Resources	1,600.00	Feb-90
156 Zale Corporation	1,594.00	Jan-92
157 Republic Technologies International Holdings, LLC	1,578.75	Apr-01
158 Philip Services Corp.	1,540.81	Jun-99
159 Wilshire Financial Services Group, Inc.	1,529.39	Mar-99
160 Magellan Health Services	1,506.00	Mar-03
161 Loews Cineplex Entertainment Corp.	1,505.65	Feb-01
162 Revco	1,500.00	Jul-88
163 Placid Oil	1,488.00	Apr-85
164 At Home Corp.	1,468.20	Sep-01
165 Atlas Air Worldwide Holdings, Inc.	1,467.83	Jan-04
166 Acterna Corporation	1,451.30	May-03

APPENDIX 1.1 *(Continued)*

Company	Liabilities ($MM)	Date
167 Ames Department Stores (I)	$1,440.00	Apr-90
168 DVI Inc.	1,438.99	Aug-03
169 Criimi Mae, Inc.	1,428.30	Oct-98
170 Vencor, Inc.	1,404.65	Sep-99
171 Pillowtex Corp.	1,402.10	Nov-00
172 Allegiance Telecom. Inc.	1,397.49	May-03
173 Southmark	1,395.00	Jul-89
174 Carter Hawley Hale Stores	1,385.00	Feb-91
175 Best Products	1,367.00	Jan-91
176 Memorex Telex, N.V. (II)	1,363.00	Feb-94
177 Weirton Steel Corp.	1,361.00	May-03
178 US Office Products Co.	1,352.00	Mar-01
179 Venture Holdings Co. LLC	1,345.82	Apr-03
180 National Gypsum (Aancor)	1,345.00	Oct-90
181 El Paso Electric	1,344.00	Jan-92
182 Hechinger Co.	1,338.50	Jun-99
183 Zonic Corp.	1,327.03	Jun-01
184 GST Telecommunications, Inc.	1,326.30	May-00
185 Interstate Bakeries	1,322.00	Sep-04
186 Mobilemedia Communications	1,322.00	Jan-97
187 Wang	1,320.00	Aug-92
188 Royal Mortgage Partners, LP	1,312.33	Aug-00
189 Unicapital Corp.	1,310.60	Dec-00
190 Gentek	1,307.03	Oct-02
191 Alterra Healthcare Corporation	1,300.00	Jan-03
192 Rockefeller Ctr. Props.	1,300.00	May-95
193 America West	1,280.00	Jun-91
194 McLean Industries	1,270.00	Nov-86
195 AMF Bowling Worldwide, Inc.	1,265.61	Jul-01
196 Sterling Chemicals Holdings, Inc.	1,228.92	Jul-01
197 Impsat Fiber Networks, Inc.	1,216.00	Jun-02
198 Grand Union Co. (II)	1,214.00	Jun-98
199 Aurora Foods, Inc.	1,211.00	Dec-03
200 Hillsborough Holdings (Jim Walter)	1,204.00	Dec-89
201 Bell National	1,203.00	Aug-85
202 Boston Chicken, Inc.	1,202.00	Oct-98
203 Alphastar Insurance Group Ltd.	1,201.66	Dec-03
204 Hills Dept. Stores	1,200.00	Jan-91
205 LJ Hooker	1,200.00	Aug-89
206 GHR Energy	1,200.00	Jan-83
207 Nationsrent, Inc.	1,197.40	Dec-01

(Continued)

APPENDIX 1.1   *(Continued)*

Company	Liabilities ($MM)	Date
208 ICO Global Communications Services Corp.	$1,184.29	Aug-99
209 Lomas Financial (Lomas Mort.) (II)	1,167.00	Oct-95
210 Wheeling-Pittsburgh Corp. (1)	1,160.00	Nov-00
211 Bruno's Inc.	1,121.60	Feb-98
212 Manville	1,116.00	Aug-82
213 e.spire Communications, Inc.	1,111.18	Mar-01
214 Choice One Communication	1,100.00	Oct-04
215 Circle K	1,100.00	May-90
216 Continental Airlines (I)	1,100.00	Sep-83
217 Braniff Airlines (I)	1,100.00	May-82
218 The IT Group, Inc.	1,086.55	Jan-02
219 American Business Financial Services Inc.	1,072.00	Jan-05
220 Envirodyne Industries	1,070.00	Jan-93
221 EOTT Energy Partners	1,062.40	Oct-02
222 Payless Cashways, Inc.	1,050.00	Jul-97
223 Levitz Furniture, Inc.	1,029.54	Sep-97
224 Wheeling-Pittsburgh (1)	1,010.60	Apr-85
225 WKI Holding Company, Inc.	1,002.35	May-02
226 Fox Meyer	1,000.00	Aug-96
227 Thermadyne Industries	1,000.00	Dec-93
228 WT Grant	1,000.00	Oct-75

Source: E. Altman and the New York University Salomon Center Bankruptcy Filings Database.

CHAPTER **2**

Evolution of the Bankruptcy Process in the United States and International Comparisons

The Constitution empowers the U.S. Congress to establish uniform laws regulating bankruptcy. By virtue of this authority, various acts and amendments have been passed, starting with the Bankruptcy Act of 1898. Several bankruptcy acts have been passed since; in 1938, the Chandler Act replaced the inadequate earlier statute, and in 1978 Congress enacted the Bankruptcy Reform Act of 1978, which was the standard until the new bankruptcy reform act, the Bankruptcy Abuse Prevention and Consumer Protection Act (BAPCPA), was signed into law on April 30, 2005. To appreciate the bankruptcy process, it is helpful to review the previous statutes and codes that have helped to form the present system. The U.S. bankruptcy laws were enacted in 1898, in 1938, and again in 1978. So, it had seemed we receive a new bankruptcy act every 40 years, whether we need it or not! With this pattern, we would have expected a new Act in 2018, but Congress surprised us with one in 2005.

EQUITY RECEIVERSHIPS

The Bankruptcy Act of 1898 provided only for a company's liquidation and contained no provisions allowing corporations to reorganize and thereby remain in existence. Reorganization could be effected, however, through equity receiverships. Although the basic theory of corporate reorganization is sound, the equity receivership procedure proved to be ineffective. It was developed to prevent disruptive seizures of property by dissatisfied creditors who were able to obtain liens on specific properties of the financially troubled concern. Receivers were appointed by the courts to manage the corporate property during financial reorganization. The procedure presented serious problems, however, and essentially was replaced by provisions of the temporary bankruptcy acts of 1933 and 1934. Receivership in equity is not the same as receivership in bankruptcy. In the latter case, a receiver is a court agency that administers the bankrupt's assets until a trustee is appointed. Equity receivership was extremely time-consuming and costly, as well as being susceptible to severe injustices. The courts had little control over the reorganization plan, and the committees set up to protect security holders were usually made up of powerful corporate insiders who used the process to further their own interests. The initiative for equity receivership was usually taken by the company in conjunction with some friendly creditor. There was no provision made for independent, objective review of the plans that were invariably drawn up by a biased committee or friendly receiver. Since ratification required majority creditor support, it usually meant that companies offered cash payoffs to powerful dissenters to gain their support. This led to long delays and charges of unfairness. Because of these disadvantages, the procedure was ineffective, especially when the number of receiverships skyrocketed during the Depression years.

THE CHANDLER ACT OF 1938

In 1933, a new bankruptcy act with a special Section 77 (for railroad reorganizations) was hastily drawn up and enacted. The following year Section 77B was enacted, to provide for general corporate reorganizations. The Act was short-lived: in 1938 it underwent a comprehensive revision and was thereafter known as the Chandler Act. This legislation was the result of the joint efforts of the National Bankruptcy Conference; the Securities and Exchange Commission (SEC), which had embarked on its own study of reorganization practices; and various other interested committees and associations.

For our purposes, the two most relevant chapters of the Chandler Act were those related to corporate bankruptcy and to subsequent attempts at reorganization. Chapter XI arrangements applied only to the unsecured creditors of corporations and removed the necessity to get all creditor types to agree on a plan of action. A Chapter XI arrangement was a voluntary proceeding that could be initiated by corporate or noncorporate entities or persons. The court had the power to appoint an independent trustee or receiver to manage the corporate property or, in many instances, to permit the old management team to continue its control during the proceedings. The debtor's petition for reorganization usually contained a preliminary plan for financial relief. The prospect of continued management control and reduced financial obligations made Chapter XI particularly attractive to present management. During the proceedings, a referee called the creditors together to go over the proposed plan and any new amendments that had been proposed. If a majority in number and amount of each class of unsecured creditors consented to the plan, the court could confirm the arrangement and make it binding on all creditors. Usually, the plan provided for a scaled-down creditor claim, composition of claims, and/or extension of payment over time. New financial instruments could be issued to creditors in lieu of their old claims.

In addition to these advantages, Chapter XI placed the bankrupt's assets strictly in the custody of the court and made them free from any prior pending court proceeding. Also, the debtor could borrow new funds that had preference over all unsecured indebtedness (essentially debtor-in-possession financing—see discussion later in this chapter). Although the interest rate on such new credit was expectedly high, it still enabled the embarrassed firm to secure an important new source of financing. As in all corporate reorganizations, the assets were protected by the court during these proceedings. The Chapter XI arrangements, if successful, were of relatively short duration compared to the more complex Chapter X reorganization cases, since administrative expenses were a function of time. Chapter XI was usually less costly than proceedings that involved all security holders. Successful out-of-court settlements, however, were usually even less costly. Finally, the arrangement was binding in all states of the country.

The least common but most important type of corporate bankruptcy reorganization was the Chapter X proceeding. The importance of this bankruptcy form is clearly illustrated by the dollar amount of liabilities involved, the size and importance of the petitioning companies, and the fact that most of the empirical data of that time utilized in bankruptcy analysis and research involved Chapter X bankrupts. Chapter X proceedings applied to publicly held corporations, except railroads, and to those that had secured as well as unsecured creditors. This bankruptcy process could be initiated voluntarily by the debtor or involuntarily by three or more creditors with total claims of $5,000 or more. The bankruptcy petition had to contain a statement of why adequate relief could not be obtained under Chapter XI. The aim of this requirement was to make Chapter X proceeding unavailable to corporations having simple debt and capital structures. However, the court had the right (and exercised it on several occasions) to refuse to allow a Chapter XI proceeding and to require that a reorganization be processed under Chapter X, usually when a substantial public interest was involved.

In most cases, a Chapter XI was preferred by the debtor because Chapter X automatically provided for the appointment of an independent, disinterested trustee or trustees to assume control of the company for the duration of the bankruptcy proceeding. Although the Chandler Act provided for the appointment of the independent trustee in every case in which indebtedness amounted to $250,000 or more, there were numerous examples where the courts permitted Chapter XI arrangements to continue even in large liability cases. Where the indebtedness was less than $250,000, the judge could either continue the debtor in possession or appoint a disinterested trustee. The only prescribed qualification of the trustee, in addition to disinterestedness, was competence to perform the duties.

The independent trustee was charged with the development and submission of a reorganization plan that was "fair and feasible" to all the parties involved. The Interstate Commerce Commission (ICC) was charged with this task in the case of railroad bankruptcies. Invariably, this plan involved all the creditors as well as the preferred and common stockholders. This important task was in addition to the day-to-day management responsibilities, although the trustee usually delegated the latter authority to the old management or to a new management team. New management was often installed, since management incompetence, in one form or another, was by far the most common cause of corporate failure. In most Chapter X bankruptcies, the trustee was aided by various experts in the development and presentation of reorganization plans, as well as by committees representing the various creditors and stockholders. At the outset, the creditors, indenture trustees, and stockholders were permitted to file answers controverting the allegations of a voluntary or involuntary petition. While bankruptcy initiation action was curtailed by the 1938 Act, the ability to answer was enhanced.

Another important participant in Chapter X proceedings was the SEC. (This was not the case under the changes in the 1978 Act, which all but eliminated the role of the SEC.) Although the commission did not possess any decision-making authority, its involvement, via the SEC advisory reports, was a powerful objective force in the entire process. The SEC was charged with rendering its advisory report if the debtor's liabilities exceeded $3 million, but the court could ask for SEC assistance regardless of liability size. The advisory reports usually took the form of a critical evaluation of the reorganization plan submitted by the trustee and an opinion on the fairness and feasibility of the plan. This involved a comprehensive valuation of the debtor's existing assets in comparison with the various claims against the assets. In the event of a discrepancy between the SEC evaluation and that of the trustee, the former usually suggested alternative guidelines. Ultimately, the decisions on (1) whether the firm was permitted to reorganize and (2) the submission of the plan for final acceptance rested with the federal judge (and with the new bankruptcy judge under the 1978 Bankruptcy Reform Act).

The Chandler Act provided that the Chapter X reorganization plan, after approval by the court, be submitted to each class of creditor and stockholder for final approval. Final ratification required approval of at least two-thirds in dollar amounts and one-half in number (majority in the case of Chapter XI) of each class of creditor and stockholder (unless total liabilities exceed total asset value). If the plan, as accepted by the court, completely eliminated a particular class, such as the common stockholders, this excluded group had no vote in the final ratification, although it could always file suits on its own behalf. Common stockholders were eliminated when the firm was deemed insolvent in a bankruptcy sense—that is, when the liabilities exceeded a fair valuation of the assets. Regardless of whether the old stockholders were permitted to participate in the reorganized enterprise, the plan invariably entailed a restructuring of the old capital accounts as well as plans for improving the productivity of the debtor.

Liquidation

When, through either a court petition or a trustee decision, it is deemed that there is no hope for rehabilitation or if prospects are so poor as to make it unreasonable to invest further efforts, costs, and time, the only alternative remaining is liquidation. Economically, liquidation is justified when the value of the assets sold individually exceeds the capitalized value of the assets in the marketplace. Usually, the key variables are time and risk. For instance, it may be estimated that the absolute economic value of the firm will exceed the liquidation value but the realization of the economic benefits is subject to uncertainty because of time and subjective probability estimates, resulting in a lower discounted value. In this case, final liquidation may take the form of an assignment or a formal bankruptcy liquidation under Chapter 7 of the Bankruptcy Code.

An assignment is a private method whereby assets are assigned to a trustee, usually selected by the creditors, to be liquidated by him or her. The net liquidation value realized is equal to the funds received less the creditor claims against the company. Rarely are the funds sufficient to pay off all creditors in full. All creditors must agree to the settlement. Since the assignment is generally handled in good faith, it is customary for the creditors to release the debtor from further liability. This process is usually faster and less costly than the more rigid bankruptcy procedure, but is not feasible if the debtor has a complicated liability and capital structure.

The expanded Chandler Act (1938) continued to provide for the orderly liquidation of an insolvent debtor under court supervision. Regardless of who filed the petition, liquidations were handled by referees who oversaw the operation until a trustee was appointed. The latter liquidated the assets, made a final accounting, and paid the liquidating dividends—all subject to referee approval. Payments of receipts usually entailed the so-called absolute priority doctrine, under which claims with priority must be paid in full before less prior, or subordinated, claims can receive any funds at all.

The liquidation fate is primarily observed in the small firm. The large bankrupt firm is more likely to attempt a reorganization and/or a merger with another entity. Sometimes, however, the basis for merger terms while a corporation is in bankruptcy is the net liquidating value of the company, not its capitalized income value. This was precisely the basis for negotiation in the ICC hearings on the Penn Central–New York, New Haven & Hartford Railroad merger in 1968.

Although larger firms usually attempted to reorganize or merge in bankruptcy, the result was often not successful, and liquidation eventually occurred. In the cases prior to 1970, a large percentage of firms were not successfully reorganized and as many as 56 percent of the cases resulted in a total loss to common stockholders (Altman 1971).[1] A glaring example of a failure to reorganize successfully was the billion-dollar W. T. Grant case. The firm filed under Chapter XI in 1975 and attempted to reorganize, but was forced to liquidate several months later in 1976. This is in contrast to several other large, successful reorganizations, including the billion-dollar (in assets) United Merchants & Manufacturing (UMM) Chapter XI proceeding in July 1977. The firm was reorganized and emerged as a going concern in less than one year. Unfortunately, the UMM reorganization was not as successful as first thought and resulted in a Chapter 22 in 1993 (and a Chapter 33 in 1996)!

BANKRUPTCY REFORM ACT OF 1978

Forty years after the passage of the Chandler Act, Congress created the Bankruptcy Reform Act of 1978, which revised the administrative and, to some extent, the procedural, legal, and economic aspects of corporate and personal bankruptcy filings in the United States. The following four reasons were presented in 1970 in a joint Congressional resolution to create a commission to look into the nation's bankruptcy laws.

1. In the 30 years since the last major revision, there had probably been even greater change in the social and economic conditions of the country than in the 40 years prior to the enactment of the 1938 Act.

---

[1]We will comprehensively review the historical evidence of the success of Chapter 11 cases under the 1978 code in Chapter 3 of this book.

2. Population had increased by 70 million people, while installment credit had skyrocketed from about $4 billion to $80 billion. The number of total bankruptcies had risen to an annual rate of more than 200,000 from a rate of 110,000 in 1960. By far, the major increase had been in personal bankruptcies (sounds similar to the reason for the 2005 Bankruptcy Act).
3. More than one-quarter of the referees in bankruptcy had problems in the administration of their duties and had made suggestions for substantial improvement in the 1938 Act.
4. There was little understanding by the federal government and the commercial community in evaluating the need to update the technical aspects in the 1938 Act.

In 1978, the problems under the old act were even more acute. The long-term worldwide problems of inflation and recession had further increased the number of bankruptcy filings in the U.S. court system. Transitions in credit policies—for example, greater reticence to delay default proceedings in large corporations, and other not so definable changes—had contributed to making the old bankruptcy laws awkward and the 1978 code desirable.

The new act, which went into effect on October 1, 1979, was divided into four titles, with Title I containing the substantive and much of the procedural law of bankruptcy. This part, known as "the code," was divided into eight chapters: 1, 3, 5, 7, 9, 11, 13, 15. Chapter 1 (General Provisions), Chapter 3 (Case Administration), and Chapter 5 (Creditors, the Debtor, and the Estate) apply generally to all cases, and Chapter 7 (Liquidation), Chapter 9 (Adjustment of Municipality Debt), Chapter 11 (Reorganization), Chapter 13 (Adjustment of Debts of Individuals with Regular Income), and Chapter 15 (U.S. Trustee Program) apply to specific debtors and procedures. The major provisions of the 1978 Act are discussed next.

Bankruptcy Filings under the 1978 and 2005 Acts

The debtor must reside or have a domicile or place of business or property in the United States. This was a controversial issue in the Yukos bankruptcy petition in 2004, where the U.S. courts ruled against the claim by the Russian debtor and some of its U.S. creditors that the firm had operations in the United States and therefore was subject to our bankruptcy laws. A foreign bank or foreign insurance company that is not engaged in business in the United States but does have assets here may become a debtor under the code, but an involuntary petition cannot be filed against a foreign bank even if it has property here. The debtor may file a petition for liquidation or reorganization. The filing of the petition constitutes what is known as "an order for relief." An involuntary case may be commenced only under Chapter 7, dealing with liquidation, or Chapter 11, dealing with reorganization. This route is not permitted for municipalities under Chapter 9, nor in Chapter 13 small business cases. An involuntary petition is prohibited against farmers, ranchers, and charitable institutions.

Chapter 9—Municipal Bankruptcies

Chapter 9 of the Bankruptcy Code deals with municipalities that commence a case by filing a petition within the municipality's judicial district. A Chapter 9 proceeding must be voluntary, and notice of its filing must be published in at least two newspapers for three weeks. The Bankruptcy Code sets forth five criteria for municipality eligibility. One of these criteria stipulates that the debtor be insolvent. This was interpreted in Bridgeport, Connecticut's attempted bankruptcy (June 1991) as meaning its inability to pay its obligations as they came due. Since, technically, Bridgeport did have sufficient cash and securities to meet its current obligations, the bankruptcy petition was dismissed by the court in August 1991. In this case, the court ruled against the state's objection to Bridgeport's authority to seek protection under the code but ruled that the city was not insolvent.

It is beyond the scope of this book to go into detail about Chapter 9 municipality bankruptcies, but for those interested, see discussions by Cohen, Golden, Kennedy, Spiotto, and Cook et al. in *Turnarounds & Workouts*, 1992.

Insolvency Issues under Chapter 11

In numerous Chapter 11 cases since the 1978 code went into effect, courts have permitted bankruptcy petitions without any reference to the debtor's insolvency, either in the ability to pay debts as they come due or in terms of a fair valuation of its assets relative to liabilities, as we described in Chapter 1. In some cases, contingent events that could cause insolvency have been argued successfully as reasons for protection under the new code. Examples of these contingent events are Johns Manville Corp. (1982), Continental Airlines (1983), A. H. Robins (1985), and Texaco (1987). In each of these cases, the debtor was able to meet its cash commitments as they came due, although Texaco claimed that a $10 billion-plus lawsuit escrow account payment was not feasible. The major point to be made here is that insolvency, in almost any sense, does not appear to be a necessary criterion today for bankruptcy reorganization. The vast majority of filing debtors, however, are insolvent *in some sense*.

Leases in Bankruptcy

Under the Bankruptcy Reform Act of 1978, a lessor was entitled to a claim on unpaid rents of a maximum of one year of lease or rental payments in a straight bankruptcy liquidation and a maximum of three years in a reorganization. In essence, the claim for damages resulting from the termination of a lease of real property was now the greater of one year of payments or 15 percent, not to exceed three years, of the remaining term of the lease, plus any unpaid rent due under such lease. Such terms started the earlier of (1) the petition date or (2) the date on which the lessor repossessed the leased property, or the lessee surrendered it. See our discussion, at a later point, on the changes regarding leases under the new Bankruptcy Code of 2005.

Section 365 of the code dealt with executory contracts and unexpired leases and specified under what provisions a trustee, or the court, could assume continuance of a lease while in reorganization. Essentially, the code specified that lessors must be cured or compensated for their claims or that adequate assurance of prompt compensation be given. The trustee must assume a lease or executory contract within 60 days of the petition date unless an extension is permitted.

A lessee-debtor had the power under Section 365(a) of the Bankruptcy Code to reject or assume an unexpired residential or personal property lease anytime before the reorganization plan confirmation. If the lease had expired before the filing, the estate had no claim to it. For leases of nonresidential real property, for example a factory, the debtor had 60 days to reject or assume the lease.

The debtor or trustee had the right to assign a lease to a third party, without permission from the lessor, and garner any revenues from this new lessee. The lease could, therefore, become a valuable asset, especially if market values change and the asset's purchase becomes prohibitive. It was argued that the destruction of this potentially valuable asset would leave creditors worse off. Some leases, such as in personal services, could not be assigned.

Employee Claim Priority

The concept of provability of claims, apparently troublesome under the previous Act before 1978, was discarded in favor of simple sections (501–503) dealing with the allowance of claims. Among other things, these sections required that contingent or unliquidated claims be estimated. Many of the familiar priorities for claims remained, but significant changes were made to protect employees. The 1978 Act expanded and increased the wage priority. The amount entitled to priority was raised from $600 to

$2,000 and later to over $4,000. Under the 2005 Act, this amount is increased to $10,000. The priority was expanded to cover fringe benefits.

Trading Claims

When the 1978 code went into effect, the only claims that were routinely traded in the financial marketplace were publicly owned debt securities. The market expanded dramatically in the 1980s. What was not in evidence at the beginning of the 1980s was the active trading and valuation of private claims of bankrupt firms—both the private bank and trade debt. These two emerging claims markets have grown to encompass a large and still growing investment vehicle estimated to involve as much as $425 billion outstanding in March 2005, although only a small fraction actually trades among sellers and investors. Perhaps 15 percent ($64 billion) of that is trade debt, with the bulk being bank loans.

The private distressed market has attracted enough attention that several large broker-dealers are making regular markets in bank and trade debt. These markets were discussed first in Altman (1990, 1991, 1992) and in Chapters 8 and 9 of this book. Trade claims were also discussed in law journals (e.g., Fortgang and Mayer, 1991). Indeed, so prominent are these new markets that the purchase of bank debt and other claims, combined with a cash equity infusion tender offer, has been used fairly regularly to gain control of the bankruptcy reorganization process and eventually lead to control of the debtor upon emergence from Chapter 11. This was the case when Japonica Partners gained control of Allegheny International in 1990; see Fortgang and Mayer (1991) for an in-depth description of the Allegheny case.[2] LTV Corporation and Bethlehem Steel in 2002 and 2003 came under the control of W. L. Ross (an active-control distressed debt fund).

On August 1, 1991, the bankruptcy rules with respect to trading of claims (rule 3001[e]) were amended, in essence making it easier to purchase claims without judicial court interference. These rules, drafted by a 13-member advisory committee to the U.S. Judicial Conference, apply to all claims—public and private, including trade debt. Judges become involved only if there is an objection lodged. Also, the amount paid for a claim and any other terms of the transfer do not have to be disclosed.

Some analysts consider these changes to be extremely permissive, enabling investors to gain control of the confirmation process by buying only the right to vote on a reorganization plan. These changes, in effect, re-

---

[2]For a lively description of many of these high-profile distressed debt ventures, see Rosenberg (1992, rev. ed. 2000).

versed the rulings of bankruptcy judges in such cases as *Allegheny International* (1988), *Chateaugay* (1988), and *Revere Copper & Brass* (1985)—all cases where written estimates of the value or the exact price of the transfer were required. Notwithstanding these rules, it is still possible for a court that perceives a claims transfer as unfair to other creditors to find other reasons to nullify the transfer. On the other hand, the increasing number of trade and bank claims traded through brokers provides a record of market values for others to consider in their assessment of future trades. Since these trades are over-the-counter, the dissemination of information on prices is not complete, but it helps to counteract the increased secrecy emerging from the 1991 ruling.

Bank Setoffs

Banks could specify that, in the event of bankruptcy, all existing balances of the debtor would be set-off against the outstanding claim of the bank and the balance of the loan would be included among general creditor claims. One can argue that this was unfair to the debtor (and to other creditors), since under normal circumstances once a loan is made the proceeds can be used in any manner that borrower chooses. The banks can argue, on the other hand, that the balances are a type of security against repayment of the loan. The 1978 Act provided for the continuation of setoffs, but the court had to ratify them in a manner that was more formal than in the past. The right of setoff was unaffected except when the creditor's claim was disallowed by the court or the creditor had acquired the claim, other than from the debtor, during a 90-day period preceding the case at a time when the debtor was insolvent. An exception to the right of setoff was the automatic stay provided for in Section 362 of the code. The automatic stay refers to an injunction against the creditor and prohibits any action to further set-off the loan after the petition is filed.

The 1978 code contained an additional limitation on the rights of creditors who have offset a mutual debt on or within 90 days before the filing of a petition. This is considered a preferential payment. For example, assume that a debtor owes a bank $150,000 and has $50,000 on deposit 90 days prior to the filing. If the bank exercises its right of setoff 30 days before filing, when the debtor owes $75,000, the bank will recover all but $75,000 of the amount owed to it by the debtor; if the bank had set off the amount 90 days before bankruptcy, in contrast, it would have received $50,000. Thus, by waiting 60 days before exercising its right of setoff, the bank recovered an additional $25,000 and therefore improved its position by that amount. This $25,000 is the amount that the trustee may recover for the debtor.

The setoff section operates only in the case of prefiling setoffs, thus encouraging creditors to work with the debtor rather than attempting to recover as much as appears possible at the time. In any case, a default must exist before there is a setoff right. Still, we can expect that financial institutions and others will continue the practice and it will be up to the trustee to recover the funds.

Chapter 11 Reorganizations

An extremely important change in the 1978 code involved the new Chapter 11, which is a consolidated chapter for business rehabilitations. It adopted much of the older Chapter XI arrangements and incorporated a good portion of the public protection of the old Chapter X and also a major part of Chapter XII real property arrangements. All of these provisions also continue under the 2005 Act. Under Chapter 11, the debtor continues to operate the business unless the court orders a disinterested trustee for cause shown, or if it would be in the best interests of the creditors and/or the owners. Cause includes fraud, dishonesty, incompetence, or gross mismanagement, either before or after commencement of the case. The newer 2005 Act retains these trustee appointments by the Chapter 11 U.S. trustee.

Creditors Committee

After the petition for a Chapter 11 rehabilitation has been filed, the court, or a U.S. trustee where available, appoints a committee of unsecured creditors. Chapter 11 is permitted to affect secured debts and equity security holders and, upon request of a party in interest, the court may order the appointment of additional committees of creditors or of equity security holders. Ordinarily, committees consist of the holders of the seven largest claims or interests to be represented, if they are willing to serve. The number of members can exceed seven, especially in large, complex cases. The code permits continuation of a committee selected before the case is filed if the committee is fairly chosen and is representative of the different kinds of claims to be represented. A designated committee of equity security holders ordinarily consists of the persons willing to serve who hold the seven largest amounts of shares of the debtor. On the request of a party in interest, the court is authorized to change the size of membership of the creditors or the equity security holders' committee if the membership is not representative of the different claims or interests.

Reorganization Plan Filing

The essence of the reorganization process is the plan of reorganization for financial and operating rehabilitation. The 1978 code gave the debtor, or its trustee if appointed, the exclusive right for 120 days to file a plan. The debtor has up to 180 days after the reorganization petition is filed to receive the requisite consents from the various creditors and owners (if relevant). The court, however, is given the power to increase or reduce the 120- and 180-day periods. If the debtor fails to meet either of these deadlines or others established by the court, creditors and other interested parties may file a plan for approval. The exclusivity period and the routine granting of extensions prompted the writers of the 2005 Act to limit the length of the exclusivity to a maximum of 18 months, plus two months for confirmation.

Role of the Securities and Exchange Commission

Under the 1978 code and the 2005 Act, the SEC may raise objections and be heard on any issue but may not appeal any judgment order or decree. Greater expediency for completing the reorganization and alleged uneven performance of the SEC in past cases are reasons that were given for the virtual exclusion of the SEC after 1978. Although any interested party can still petition the courts and appeal any perceived inequities, the role of the SEC as the public's representative has been greatly diminished. For example, the SEC had often petitioned to change a Chapter XI arrangement to a Chapter X reorganization. Despite the criticism of the SEC's performance in Chapter X cases, in our opinion it had issued some excellent commentary and suggestions in its reorganization reports, particularly on the valuation process.

Reorganization Valuation

The reorganization plan has as its centerpiece the valuation of the debtor as a continuing entity. Traditionally, valuation is based on the capitalization of future earnings flows, which involves a forecast of expected after-tax earnings and free cash flows, and the attachment of an appropriate capitalization rate (discount rate). The capitalized value can then be adjusted for excess working capital, tax loss carryforwards, and other considerations. If the resulting value is greater than the liquidation value of the assets, reorganization is justified; otherwise a liquidation is usually preferred. If the value is less than the allowed claims, the firm is insolvent in a bankruptcy sense and the old shareholders are usually eliminated under absolute priority rules. Typically, the creditors become the new shareholders along with anyone purchasing shares.

Absolute Priority Claims

Since the inception of the bankruptcy laws, most reorganization plans have been guided by the absolute priority doctrine. This doctrine stipulates that creditors should be compensated for their claims in a certain hierarchical order and that most senior claims must be paid in full before a less senior claim can receive anything. In fact, however, plans are often based on a combination of absolute and relative priorities whereby lesser claimants receive partial payment even though a claim that is more senior is "not made whole" (not paid off completely). This arrangement is often expedient and it permits compromise with creditors who are likely to vote against the plan unless some satisfactory payment to them is forthcoming.

Violations of the absolute priority doctrine are increasingly common and are guided by a "best interest of creditors test" whereby no impaired creditor class receives less value than would have been the case in a Chapter 7 (or 11) liquidation. Most liquidations come under the auspices of Chapter 7. In essence, absolute priority is a guideline in a Chapter 11 plan and not a necessary policy. So-called violations of absolute priority have been carefully documented by Weiss (1990), Eberhart et al. (1990), Betker (1991), and Franks and Torous (1989 and 1992). Weiss found that 29 of 37 large Chapter 11 cases studied violated the doctrine. Eberhart et al. found that the average violation gave 7 percent of the total value of the reorganized firm to junior creditors and to the old owners where strict adherence to absolute priority would have eliminated these interests. Betker finds that deviations from absolute priority in favor of equity are lower the more insolvent the firm and higher the greater percentage of bank and secured debt. And Franks and Torous (1989) conclude that, after analyzing 41 large firms' experience in Chapter 11, almost $900 million was given to creditors who did not deserve it, based on absolute priority. So-called undeserving shareholders received about one-third of that amount.

Our own evaluation of the absolute priority doctrine is that it should be adhered to in liquidation (as it is) but that since the valuation process is at best an inexact science, some form of contingent security, like stock warrants, for junior claimants is justified in many cases. If a sufficient number (one-half) and amount (two-thirds) of the creditors in each impaired class sanction the violation, then the best interest test takes precedent and the plan is "crammed down" those who object to the plan (see discussion shortly on cram-down).

The objective of the reorganization plan is to provide for a fair and feasible rehabilitation. The term *fair* refers to the priority of claims, and *feasible* implies that the recapitalized company will be structured so that the new fixed cost burden will realistically be met without a recurrence of default. The reorganization plan must therefore provide the cash flow analysis necessary to make that assessment. The costs involved with negotiations for restructuring—both in bankruptcy and in what takes place out of reorganization, that is, a quasi-reorganization—are referred to as agency costs and represent a deadweight loss to the firm (i.e., a loss that is not someone else's gain in society).

Priorities are spelled out in Section 507 of the code. Expenses and claims have priority in the following order:

1. Administration expenses of the bankruptcy, such as legal, accounting, and trustee fees.
2. Unsecured claims arising in the ordinary course of the debtor's business or financial affairs after the commencement of the case, for example, supplier claims on goods delivered and accepted, with some exceptions as spelled out in Section 502(f).
3. Unsecured claims for wages, salaries, or commissions, including vacation, severance, and sick leave pay earned by an individual within 90 days before the filing of the petition or the date of the cessation of the debtor's business but only to the extent of $2,000 (now $10,000) per individual.
4. Unsecured claims for contributions to employee benefit plans, with the same limitations noted in item 3.
5. Unsecured claims to individuals up to $900 arising from the deposit, before bankruptcy, of money in connection with the future use of goods or services from the debtor.
6. Unsecured claims of governmental units (e.g., taxes on income, property, and employment, and excise and tax penalties).
7. Secured debts—that is, debt that has specific assets as collateral—has priority over the funds received in the liquidation of that asset. To the extent that the funds received are insufficient to cover the entire allowed claim, the balance is owed by the debtor and is considered part of the remaining unsecured claims.
8. Senior debt has priority over all debt that is specified as subordinated to that debt but has equal priority with all other unsecured debt. The terms of most loan agreements spell out these priorities.
9. Remaining unsecured claims.
10. After the unsecured claims are satisfied, the remaining claimants are the equity holders of the firm—preferred and common stockholders, in that order. As noted earlier, these individuals should not receive any payment or securities in the new firm if the value of the firm's assets is less than the allowed claims.

Postpetition Interest

In the event of a secured claim's collateral having a liquidation value greater than the amount of the claim, postpetition interest is routinely allowed by the courts. For example, in the first LTV bankruptcy (1986), while the unsecured creditors' claims were valued in the single digits (i.e., under $100 per $1,000 face value), secured claimants' claims were valued at well above face value (e.g., the Youngstown Sheet and Tube Corp. public secured bonds). Payments to secured creditors are covered under the adequate protection clause that enables the debtor to utilize the collateral for its benefit during reorganization.

In other cases, the value of the debtor may be deemed sufficient to grant unsecured claimants interest in the postpetition period. For example, in *Wilson Foods* (1983) and *Johns Manville* (1982), unsecured bank creditors ultimately received these payments. Any impaired creditor can appeal these allocations, however.

Equitable Subordination and Fraudulent Conveyance

One of the more intriguing aspects of a Chapter 11 proceeding is the possible change in priority of claims as the case unfolds. While not a common occurrence, there have been some examples of a senior or even a secured claimant seeing their claim subordinated to a junior unsecured creditor. At the request of those unsecured creditors, bankruptcy judges have at times changed the usual order of priority. Judges have the latitude to change priorities under the code if the senior creditors have misused their knowledge and influence over the debtor and junior creditors, or otherwise acted unfairly.

One example of equitable subordination involves a fraudulent conveyance claim that is upheld by the court. Plaintiffs can argue that certain knowledgeable creditors, like banks, unfairly benefit from highly leveraged transactions such as leveraged buyouts (LBOs) that eventually fail, resulting in losses to junior creditors. The centerpiece of the claim is that banks and other insiders knew or should have known that the restructuring would likely result in a failure to meet the debtors' liabilities but went along with the deal to derive its own benefit from up-front fees, priority payments, and so on.

In other cases, equitable subordination cases are filed to force secured creditors into a settlement that is more favorable to unsecured creditors. For example, a bankruptcy judge in Philadelphia ruled in June 1991 that a secured lender, MNC Commercial Corp. of Baltimore, had stopped making loans to a certain debtor, M. Paolella & Sons, a tobacco and candy distributor, based on "surreptitious and misleading methods." This contributed, in part, according to the judge, to the eventual failure of the company. In the interest of fairness, the judge moved $1.9 million of unsecured creditor claims above MNC's.

Finally, in another case, one involving Clark Pipe & Supply, a federal appeals court in New Orleans ruled that equitable subordination applied only where the secured lender engaged in "inequitable conduct such as fraud, misrepresentation, or oppressive control over the debtor's decision making." This latter ruling may give secured creditors some solace in their concern that bankruptcy judges will utilize different standards for determining inequitable conduct and fairness.

Execution of the Plan

A plan must provide adequate means for its execution. It may provide for the satisfaction or modification of any lien, the waiver of any default, and the merger or consolidation of the debtor with one or more entities. The issuance of nonvoting equity securities is prohibited, and the plan must provide for distribution of voting powers among the various classes of equity securities. It may impair, or leave unimpaired, a class of claims, secured or unsecured; provide for the assumption or rejection of executory contracts or unexpired leases not previously rejected; and propose the sale of all or substantially all of the estate property and the distribution of the proceeds among creditors and equity security holders, making it a liquidating plan.

Confirmation of the Plan

A plan may insert a claim in a particular class if such claim is substantially similar to other claims of the class. Confirmation of a plan requires that every claimant or holder of an interest accept the plan, or, if it is not accepted by all classes, the creditors must receive or retain under the plan an amount that is not less than the amount that they would receive or retain if the debtor were liquidated on the date of the plan. At least one class of creditors must accept the plan. Thus, for example, if the only class affected by the plan comprises a mortgagee, the plan cannot be confirmed without the mortgagee's consent. A plan is deemed accepted by a class of creditors if at least two-thirds in amount and more than one-half in number of the allowed claims of the class that are voted are cast in favor of the plan. Shareholders are deemed to have accepted the plan if at least two-thirds in dollar amount of the outstanding shares actually voted are cast for the plan.

Cram-Down Provision

The 1978 code dealt with the impairment of claims, which was a new concept. A plan may be confirmed over the dissent of a class of creditors. If all the requirements for confirmation of the plan are satisfied, except that a class of impaired claimants or shareholders has not accepted it, the court may nevertheless confirm the plan if the plan does not discriminate unfairly and is "fair and equitable" with respect to each class of claims or interests impaired.

This is the code's version of the "cram-down" clause, which appeared in Chapters X and XII. The test for what is fair and equitable with regard to a class of secured claimants impaired under a plan is met, in general, if the plan provides (1) that said class will retain its lien on the property whether the property is retained by the debtor or transferred, (2) that the property will be sold and the lien transferred and the secured creditor will receive deferred cash payments of at least the allowed amount of the claims of the value on the date of confirmation, and (3) that the secured class will realize the "indubitable equivalent" of its claims under the plan. If a class of unsecured claims that are impaired under the plan will receive property or payment equal to the allowed amount of the claims, or if the holders of the claims junior to such class will receive nothing under the plan, the plan has met the "fair and equitable" test of the code.

While "cram-down" is always a possibility, the threat to impaired creditors is perhaps more illusory than real, especially in single-asset real estate bankruptcies. This argument, however, rests on the relatively low probability that a small firm Chapter 11 case will result in a successful reorganization. Indeed, Flynn (1989) estimated that as little as 10 to 12 percent of all Chapter 11 cases are confirmed successfully. Provisions regarding confirmation and cram-down are extremely complicated. With the occurrence, however, of so many large firm bankruptcies involving considerable tangible assets, the likelihood of a successful culmination to Chapter 11 is much higher than with small one-asset or no-asset cases. Cram-down, therefore, is a more likely result in highly contentious cases.

Reorganization Time in Bankruptcy

One of the important goals of the 1978 code (and also the 2005 Act) is to reduce the time it takes for a firm to go through the reorganization process and devise a plan for restructuring its capital financing and rehabilitating its operations. The requirement that the debtor submit a reorganization plan within 120 days was instituted in 1979 to speed up the initial process. As we have often argued, granting routine extensions to the 120-day requirement should be avoided as much as possible and the burden of proof as to why the firm should not be liquidated be placed squarely on the debtor's shoulders. The 2005 Act limits the extensions to a maximum of 18 months, which is, perhaps not by coincidence, close to the average time in bankruptcy (20 months).

Judiciary Procedure

The 1978 code created a U.S. bankruptcy court in each of the districts where there was a U.S. district court. The new court system was established April 1, 1984. Bankruptcy judges are appointed by the President, with the advice and consent of the Senate, for a term of 14 years. The code eliminated the jurisdictional dichotomy between summary and plenary jurisdiction. The bankruptcy court was given exclusive jurisdiction over the property of the debtor wherever it is located. All cases under the code and all civil actions and proceedings arising from its enforcement are held before the bankruptcy judge unless he or she decides to abstain from hearing a particular proceeding that is already pending in the state court or in another court that is believed to be more appropriate. Appeals from the bankruptcy judge go to the district judge, unless the circuit counsel of the circuit court orders the chief judge of the circuit to designate panels of three bankruptcy judges to hear appeals in the bankruptcy court. The panel may not hear an appeal from an order entered by a panel member. An appeal from the panel will go directly to the U.S. Court of Appeals.

U.S. Trustee Program

To aid bankruptcy judges in avoiding involvement in many administrative functions and to allow them to devote more time to the area of judicial determination, the code established a U.S. trustees system. The U.S. trustees serve the bankruptcy courts either as assistants to the bankruptcy judges or as arms of the court, but are under the supervision of the Attorney General, who will appoint them.

SOME BANKRUPTCY TAX AND ACCOUNTING ISSUES

The Bankruptcy Reform Act of 1978 completely rewrote the laws that govern bankruptcy procedures and principles but was essentially silent with respect to tax considerations. In bankruptcy proceedings, the government acts both as a creditor and as a force to aid in the rehabilitation of an entity. The two roles are not easy to reconcile and the tax laws that are relevant present considerable problems and are the subject of much debate. A proposed tax bill contemporaneous with the new bankruptcy code was so controversial, for solvent as well as nonsolvent firms, that it never was voted on by Congress; instead, the Bankruptcy Tax Bill of 1980 (H.R. 5043) was evaluated by the House Ways and Means Committee and passed by the House of Representatives on March 24, 1980. As a consequence, the nation was governed for a period of time by a bankruptcy code that had no relevant tax law. The Bankruptcy Tax Bill of 1980 was finally passed and went into effect in early 1981.

Discharge of Indebtedness

In Public Law 95-598, Congress repealed provisions of the old bankruptcy act governing income tax treatment of a discharge of indebtedness in bankruptcy for cases filed on or after October 1, 1979. The Bankruptcy Tax Bill of 1980 filled this vacuum by providing that no amount of debt discharge was to be included in income for federal income tax purposes if the debtor is insolvent. Instead, the amount of debt reduction can be applied at the debtor's election first to reduce the debtor's depreciable asset basis. This policy can, however, affect reported income in the future, and the government will eventually be rewarded for its generosity if the firm becomes a profitable, going concern. In essence, the government is helping to provide a fresh start but is not totally forgiving the benefits for all time.

If the debtor did not choose to apply the reduction to depreciable assets, the amount is applied to reduce the taxpayer's tax attributes in the following order:

1. New operating losses and carryovers.
2. Carryovers of investment tax credits and other tax credits.
3. Capital losses and carryovers.
4. The basis of the taxpayer's assets.

The reduction in each category of carryovers is made in the order of taxable years in which the items would be used, with the order based on the year of discharge and the taxes that would have been paid. After reduction of the specified carryover, any remaining debt discharge is applied to reduce the debtor's asset basis, but not below the amount of the taxpayer's remaining undischarged liabilities. Finally, any remaining debt discharge is disregarded.

Direct Bankruptcy Costs

Much has been made of the sometimes considerable costs incurred by debtors that involve major outside legal, accounting, and consulting costs as well as internal legal costs. While these costs can be sizable, for those firms that emerged from the Chapter 11 process and were able to utilize their tax-loss benefits, the tax deductibility aspect of direct costs softened their impact. But a May 1991 Internal Revenue Service (IRS) ruling released in early 1992 (Technical Advice Memo 9204001) on an unidentified debtor held that such costs are not deductible as current business expenses if they stem from the overall proceeding and are tied to the long-term benefit of the company. In these cases, the costs must be capitalized and deducted only if and when the company is sold or liquidated. Prior to this recent ruling, the direct costs of bankruptcy were usually immediately deductible. If the debtor can show that costs are connected with liability claims, then they can be deductible. Also, this ruling is appealable in court. We discuss bankruptcy costs in depth in Chapters 4 and 6 of this book.

Discharge of Debt

Some IRS and court rulings with respect to discharge of all or a portion of a debtor's liabilities, whether in an out-of-court distressed restructuring or a legal Chapter 11 proceeding, have disadvantaged both the debtor and investors. The former must report any reduction of debt, arrived at through negotiation, as taxable income. However, upon emergence, the debtor can utilize the now higher asset values and depreciate them, thereby garnering higher tax-deductible write-offs. The write-offs can offset the taxable gain from discarding debt.

Fresh Start Rule

An accounting rule in 1991, known as the "fresh start rule," enabled emerging Chapter 11 companies that distribute more than 50 percent of their stock to the old creditors to treat the company as a new business. Assets can be written up to market value rather than carried at historical cost. The valuation process is somewhat complex, especially the determination of the market value upon emergence. A market value is determined based on future cash flow estimates. As much as possible of this value is assigned to tangible assets, like plant and equipment. The remainder is a new asset called "reorganization value in excess of amounts allocable to identifiable assets," such as goodwill. The reorganization thereby creates an entity with immediate positive equity. For example, Allegheny International's emergence as Sunbeam-Oster (1989) resulted in assets valued at $686 million compared to $561 million before reorganization. Such measures as the debt-to-equity ratio can be vastly improved under the "fresh start" format.

Tax Loss Carryforwards and Firm Valuation

Tax loss carryforwards are an extremely important element in any reorganization, especially if the value of the new firm is relevant, as it almost always is. Tax loss questions are irrelevant, of course, in a straight liquidation. Theoretically, the value of a firm is equal to the discounted present value of its future earnings after taxes. Since tax loss carrybacks or carryforwards will affect taxes paid, they have a potentially powerful impact on the earnings to be discounted. An alternative procedure is to discount the expected after-tax earnings projection and then add the present value of tax loss carryforwards to arrive at the net overall value.

Under the old Chapter X, tax-free transfers of corporate assets to a successor corporation were generally provided for. But no reference was made to the carryover of tax losses, and this caused considerable confusion. Certain cases established the clean-slate rule, which held that a firm emerging from bankruptcy that had discharged its old debts was precluded from using losses from the "old" business. Other cases ruled on the so-called continuity of business doctrine, and allowed carryovers of losses when there was a continuity of interest and of the business. When the principal purpose of a merger (in or out of bankruptcy) was tax avoidance, carryovers were disallowed (see Section 269 of the Internal Revenue Code). In practice, this has come to mean that the tax loss carryover is not allowed when a greater than 50 percent change in ownership, or a change in business, occurs after the transfer of assets. This highly subjective test probably has not been very effective in curbing takeovers for tax purposes. In addition, the debtor or creditor could petition for a favorable IRS ruling in a bankruptcy-merger reorganization plan that was the only feasible alternative to liquidation.

The 1978 bill introduced a category of tax-free reorganization, known as a "G" reorganization, which is more flexible than other types and is, in the belief of the Congress, a means to facilitate the rehabilitation of a problem firm. For instance, a "G" does not require a statutory merger (type A), nor does it require that the financially distressed corporation receive solely stock of the acquiring corporation in exchange for its assets (type C), and former shareholders do not have to be in control of a split off company (type D). This new type of reorganization is intended to facilitate the reorganization of bankrupt companies. In light of the debt discharge rules of the bill, which adjust tax attributes of a reorganized corporation to reflect changes in debt structure, the statutory rule regarding loss carryovers will apply in "G" reorganizations.

Since "G" reorganizations are subject to the same rules on security exchanges for shareholders and other security holders that apply generally to reorganizations, any party receiving new securities whose principal value is greater than that of the securities surrendered is taxed on the excess, and vice versa. Money or other property received in a "G" will be subject to the dividend equivalency tests (as to whether the property is a return on capital), which apply to reorganizations generally. Likewise, securities transferred to creditors based on claims attributable to accrued or unpaid interest on securities surrendered will be subject to tax as if interest income were received. In general, the use of tax loss carryforwards in Chapter 11 cases was severely restricted by the Tax Act of 1986, including provisions dealing with change in control, remaining in a similar line of business, forgiveness of indebtedness, and other tests.

THE ROLE OF DIRECTORS IN BANKRUPTCY AND INSOLVENCY

The board of directors of a corporation is charged to make decisions in the best interests of the entity's owners. Senior managers, who are typically also members of the board, act as agents of owners along with other directors. When a firm's condition changes, however, and it becomes distressed and is in the "zone of insolvency," and certainly when it files for bankruptcy, the board's role changes. In bankruptcy, a director's fiduciary responsibility shifts to one of a trustee, conserving assets for the estate to pay creditors, with the interests of existing owners as a residual one at best. This shift is often hard to do for directors who were selected under more positive conditions, and it is no wonder that, as Gilson (1990) finds, 54 percent of board members leave the firm before plan confirmation. The role of the board and other insiders is discussed in Chapter 10 of this book as well as within the concept of the "zone of deepening insolvency" in Chapter 13 of this book.

The role of directors in firms that face insolvency and are in distress is not as clear as the so-called bright-line responsibility in bankruptcy. A court ruling in 1991 by Judge William Allen of the Delaware Chancery Court would appear to give some strength to the theory that in distress the board of directors should weigh the risks of corporate decisions and decide in favor of the trusteeship allegiance over that of the owners' agency role. Judge Allen (for many years now an academic colleague at the New York University Stern School of Business) ruled that creditors of Pathe Communications Corporation could exercise their voting privilege and oust existing directors of Pathe if the management-owner violated a certain pact. This agreement was crafted earlier while the firm was reorganizing under Chapter 11 in the aftermath of its disastrous November 1990 buyout of MGM/UA Communications Co. The creditor, Credit Lyonnais Bank, Nederland, then went to court to affirm its actions, thereby receiving Judge Allen's verdict.

Judge Allen ruled in favor of the creditors who had become directors and then refused to grant permission to sell some assets that MGM's largest shareholder had decided to sell. Allen concluded that these directors had the obligation to consider the "community of interest that sustained the corporation" and not just the owner's interest. As long as the board gave due consideration to the owner's position, they were free to reject it in favor of others, primarily creditors. While this decision was made in a case where the directors were in place to protect creditor claims due to a prior agreement, the general question of director responsibilities in distress situations would seem to be less clear and certainly more difficult. Indeed, in some other countries of the world, such as Australia and the United Kingdom, a director is always personally at risk when a company fails and creditors routinely sue to recover damages. This is not just a possible court occurrence, it is the law! In the Australian case, directors' clear responsibility shifts to creditors in times of distress. And certainly the introduction of Sarbanes-Oxley has heightened the responsibility and liability of directors of bankrupt companies (e.g., in the WorldCom case in 2004).

DEBTOR-IN-POSSESSION FINANCING

Debtor-in-possession (DIP) financing is obtained by a debtor that has filed for bankruptcy and under Section 364 of the Bankruptcy Code receives permission to arrange for debt financing, primarily to (1) pay for professionals to assist in the reorganization process, (2) operate the business by acquiring the necessary working capital, and (3) finance capital expenditures and/or necessary maintenance and repairs on existing assets. DIP lenders receive superior seniority and enhanced security that typically supersedes any claims that existed prior to filing for bankruptcy.[3] In addition, the company cannot exit Chapter 11 until the DIP facility is completely repaid. The theory of DIP financing is that it enables the debtor to remain liquid during the most difficult days after filing and to invest in positive net present value (NPV) projects that would not have been possible without the additional credit. This will, it is argued, decrease the time in bankruptcy and increase

---

[3]Sections 364(a) and (b) provide lenders with seniority on a par with administrative expenses such as legal fees. Subsection 364(c) provides enhanced priority on unencumbered assets, and 364(d) allows a priming lien even on assets that had an existing lien already in place.

the chances of a successful reorganization. Detractors of this type of financing might argue that it leads to overinvestment giving managers the incentive and means to accept extremely risky or negative NPV projects.

To obtain DIP financing, the debtor must file a motion under Federal Rule of Bankruptcy Procedure 4001c(1). This motion is served to the trustees and any creditor committees and must be accompanied by a copy of the agreement. After this, there is a 15-day waiting period before the court commences a final hearing on this motion. In the interim, the court may authorize an immediate borrowing limited to the needs of the company pending a final hearing. At the final hearing, the court may authorize permanent financing up to the full amount of DIP borrowings requested. In order to secure the financing, a debtor must (1) develop a business plan, (2) project cash flows, (3) value the firm's assets, (4) provide evidence that the DIP financing is sustainable, and (5) secure a lender. The financing plan and its estimated repayment schedule must be approved by the court. The valuation plan must show that there is value added from the DIP facility.

Since DIP financing is very common in large Chapter 11s and since a valuation plan must be presented to the court and other interested parties, it seems to us that there is little reason for the excuse that the debtor's situation is so complex that it needs multiple extensions to the exclusivity period of 120 days after filing. The new Bankruptcy Act of 2005 limits these extensions to a total of 18 months after filing plus two months for confirmation—still, in our estimation, too long in most cases, but an important motivation to speed up the process.

DIP Financing Terms

DIP terms vary by lender, industry, and risk profile of the debtor. Loans are typically floating rate based on either the London Interbank Offered Rate (LIBOR) or prime plus. Lenders can charge points, exit fees, monitoring fees, unused line fees, and so on, and typically total costs of the loan range from 10 to 20 percent. The loans usually take the form of revolving lines of credit, accompanied by a term loan or letter of credit. The tenure of the loan is typically short-term, rarely exceeding two years. An average DIP line ranges from 6 to 18 months, suggesting that the funds are intended to match cash flow cycles and provide working capital and usually are not for capital expenditures. Some DIP loans also restrict the use of funds to operating expenses. Repayment schedules vary, and lenders may also require equity kickers such as warrants. Drawing on the DIP line is usually based on a detailed budget and contingent on certain covenants. DIP covenants reinstate the monitoring and maintenance provisions of prepetition debt. Affirmative covenants include performance objectives—for example, cash balances; earnings before interest, taxes, depreciation, and amortization

(EBITDA); cash flow ratios—with which a firm must comply. The firm must also allow the DIP lender access to financial statements and physical inventory. The firm's commitment to close monitoring is viewed as a positive signal to lenders. Negative covenants restrict certain operating decisions such as operating expenses and disposition of assets. Most of these terms provide greater protection to the DIP lender.

DIP Lenders

The prepetition lender gains an advantage by leading the DIP financing, as it can control collateral and be in the best position to recover as much of its prebankruptcy exposure as possible. This category generally provides the lowest-cost financing. Often a lender is also a prepetition creditor. In these cases, the lender may ask for waivers from the debtor covering possible lender liability issues including conflicts of interest such as preferences or fraudulent transfers. Other lenders are specialists in distressed debt financing and potential acquirers.

Specialists include traditional bank and asset-backed lenders, such as J. P. Morgan Chase and Citigroup. Specialists in asset-based lending, who are also experienced in monitoring cash, can offer flexible loan structures to suit the needs of customers. These asset-backed lenders can monitor the collateral very well, which enables the turnaround specialist, if there is one in place, to have better access to capital and financial information. The lenders are usually skilled at understanding the cyclical and seasonal nature of the business. See our discussion on turnaround managers in Chapter 13.

Potential acquirers of a bankrupt company may provide DIP financing with the ulterior motive of positioning themselves as the front runner to purchase company assets. They attempt to structure the loan in a way that gives them flexibility to purchase the company while increasing the cost to other potential suitors. For example, a DIP lender may have the option to convert its debt to equity, while another party that is interested in acquiring the company would be required to repay 100 percent of the debt immediately. Overall, Section 364 provides the DIP lender with superpriority status to induce lenders to financially distressed firms through the reorganization period. Despite this enhanced security, DIP lenders are subject to potential loss, albeit with a very low probability. If the debtor fails to reorganize in a reasonably timely manner, losses can result from conversion to Chapter 7 liquidation where only administrative expenses of liquidation take priority over DIP financing.

Risk in DIP Lending

While lending to a distressed firm appears to be quite risky, in fact DIP lending is remarkably *not* a very risky endeavor. The number of problem DIP loans made over the past 16 years (1988–2004) is so few you could probably count them on one hand. The most publicized DIP loan that resulted in a loss to the lender was WinStar (2001 bankruptcy). Since there have been more than 500 DIP facilities over the period 1988–2004, the loss rate has been minuscule. Is there a better risk-return trade-off in financial markets?

DIP Lending and Performance

Chapter 3 discusses the relationship between DIP lending and debtor performance. Studies have shown a positive stock market reaction to the announcement that a DIP facility was secured and that this positive abnormal stock movement is associated with both a prepackaged Chapter 11 and the successful acquisition of a DIP loan facility. A number of studies have documented that DIP financing has a positive correlation with the eventual success of a reorganization, that it is also correlated with a shorter reorganization period, and that firms that obtain DIP financing from existing lenders tend to have reduced time in bankruptcy. The latter may be because of the inside information and the enhanced monitoring role of the DIP original lender.

DIP loans have been so successful in the United States since their inception in the late 1980s that a number of foreign governments now provide for equivalent financing (e.g., Japan) and many others are considering revising their bankruptcy codes to include DIP financing.

BANKRUPTCY ACT OF 2005

The U.S. Congress enacted a revised Bankruptcy Act on April 20, 2005, called the Bankruptcy Abuse Prevention and Consumer Protection Act of 2005 (BAPCPA). Although the most sensational, controversial, and publicized aspects of the Act impact consumer (personal) bankruptcies by making the laws significantly less debtor friendly, the new Act also has many important provisions that impact corporate bankruptcies. In general, as with consumers, the new Act is more favorable for creditors of a bankrupt company and could have a profound impact on the ability of firms to reorganize successfully. Table 2.1 lists many of the more important provisions.[4]

---

[4]Many of the important law firms produced summaries of the new Act that were very informative, for example, "New Bankruptcy Law Amendments: A Creeping Repeal of Chapter 11" (Skadden, Arps, Slate, Meagher & Flom and affiliates, March 2005) and "Immediately Effective Bankruptcy Code Amendments" (Davis Polk & Wardell, April 30, 2005). Many of the Skadden Arps' summaries are included in our discussion.

TABLE 2.1   Some Changes in the Bankruptcy Act of 2005

Limit Rights of Insiders	■ Reduces use of key employee retention plans (KERP; e.g., bonuses) unless employee is essential and has competing job offer; limits on severance.
Expedite Cases	■ Maximum exclusively limited to 18 months (plus two extra months to permit solicitation).
Creditor Access to Information	■ Official committee must provide access to information to creditors represented by that committee and solicit and receive input from such creditors.
Professional Adviser Retentions	■ Reduces disinterested requirements; increases ability for large investment banks to enter restructuring advisory market by repealing a measure prohibiting an investment bank from advising a bankrupt company if the debtor had been an underwriting client within three years before its Chapter filing.
Payment for Deliveries of Goods/Reclamation	■ Automatic 20-day reclamation period (no preference defense); 45-day reclamation period upon receipt of goods.
Prepackaged Plans	■ Permits solicitation to continue after the Chapter 11 filing as long as it started before.
Other Provisions	■ U.S. trustee must seek appointment of Chapter 11 trustee if there are reasonable grounds to suspect fraud, dishonesty, or criminal conduct. ■ Two-year fraudulent conveyance lookback. ■ No stay of investigations by self-regulatory bodies. ■ Employee priority increased to $10,000. ■ Limitations on time to assume/reject leases (one extension for 90 days).

Source: Author's compilation and Blackstone Investment Bank (New York).

Most of these provisions go into effect six months after the Act was passed (i.e., on October 17, 2005).

Key Employee Retention Plans and Executive Compensation

The new Act makes it more difficult to pay bonuses or other perks to retain old management or directors. These managers must show proof of a competing job offer at the same or greater compensation and it is deemed that their continued participation is essential for the successful rehabilitation of the firm. BAPCPA limits the amounts even if it is deemed essential to retain them. The language also contains a limitation on severance payments, and these must be available to all full-time employees and cannot exceed 10 times the mean severance given to nonmanagement employees in the same year. The ambiguity of some of the clauses related to compensation will make for some lively and divisive debates as the Act gets implemented. Practically, however, is it likely that a competent manager who receives a competing offer, at the same or greater compensation, will remain with the debtor? We do not think so.

Appointment of a Trustee

Like the 1978 code, the new Act affords the possibility of an appointment of a bankruptcy trustee by the U.S. trustee if there are "reasonable grounds to suspect" that the debtor's current CEO, CFO, or board members (or board members who appointed the CEO or CFO) participated in "actual fraud, dishonesty, or criminal conduct in the management of the debtor or the debtor's public financial reporting." In essence, however, as with the old code, the court must find cause for the appointment of the trustee even though the language of "reasonably suspect" is also present. Also, the appointment should be in the interests of creditors, stockholders, and other interests of the estate. This provision will increase the likelihood of litigation costs in the early stages of many cases, especially where the filing is associated with fraudulent reporting, and boards of directors will almost certainly be motivated to act before the bankruptcy petition to remove officers who may be involved so as to avoid the disruption of a trustee being appointed postpetition.

Exclusivity Period

We have already commented that bankruptcy reorganization cases are unnecessarily protracted under the current code due to numerous extensions to the exclusivity period granted by judges. The new Act tries to limit these extensions by specifying a maximum of 18 months for the exclusivity period to produce a reorganization plan by existing management (plus two months to permit solicitation). While this is a step in the right direction, it seems somewhat counterproductive if the rule will lead to most extensions for the full 18 months, which coincidentally was about the average time for a Chapter 11 reorganization under the last two bankruptcy acts. Frankly we were disappointed not to see a provision with respect to showing clear and convincing arguments that the firm's going-concern value should at least be greater than its liquidation value at a fairly early stage in the bankruptcy process—say four to six months. This would avoid long-drawn-out proceedings that result in a failed reorganization and a transfer to a Chapter 7 liquidation or a subsequent quick Chapter 22 filing after the original case has been completed.

Creditor Access to Information

BAPCPA requires that an official creditors committee and other committees share confidential information with noncommittee creditors, which will subject the debtor to provide reports or disclosures to those noncommittee creditors. The committees will also be required to solicit and receive comments from their constituents. The latter point will probably slow down the process and many of the noncommittee creditors will not be interested, anyway, if this restricts their ability to trade.

While increasing access to confidential information is a positive change to induce a more effective process and possibly motivate an increased number of bids on the sale of the debtor in bankruptcy, it is unclear that the old system materially inhibited interested parties from stepping up and making a bid. Certainly, the number of active-control investors in bankruptcies increased in the years leading up to the new Bankruptcy Act of 2005 (see Chapters 8 and 9 of this book).

Professional Adviser Retentions

Under the old 1978 Bankruptcy Code, most of the large investment banks that participated in continuous underwritings of stocks and bonds for corporations were essentially prohibited from advising debtors that file for bankruptcy protection. This was due to the "disinterestedness rule" regarding any prior activities for three years before the filing for the debtor, regardless of whether such securities are still outstanding. Due to the successful lobbying by several of these large banks, under BAPCPA there will be reduced disinterestedness standards because the old rule is repealed, although the judge can still rule that a bank is conflicted due to past activity if found that an entity has an interest adverse to the interests of the estate or any class of creditors or equity holders by reason of any relationship to or interest in the debtor. This leaves open the disinterestedness rule for a current or former underwriter.

It will be interesting to observe whether the competitive landscape, including fees charged by financial and legal advisers, will change under the new Act. Certainly, smaller restructuring firms would seem to be attractive acquisition targets for the larger investment banks that decide to enter the distressed firm market.

Prepackaged Reorganization Plans

One of the more important innovations under the old 1978 Bankruptcy Code was the possibility to combine the time- and cost-saving attributes of an out-of-court distressed restructuring with the more lenient voting conditions of a formal Chapter 11 proceeding. This is known as a *prepackaged* arrangement where the key element is the elimination of the minority hold-out problem in that only two-thirds of the voting creditors from each class in amount and more than 50 percent in number need to sanction a plan. A successful out-of-court restructuring prior to bankruptcy requires virtually 100 percent of the creditors to agree. This is not to minimize the necessity in a prepackaged Chapter 11 to still reach a consensus from a reasonable number of creditors. Under Section 11, U.S.C. 1126(b) of the old code, debtors were permitted to negotiate with creditors prior to a filing and to accept prepetition votes with proper disclosure (i.e., adequate disclosure and a reasonable time for analysis and discussion and vote). The confirmation period after the filing still takes from 30 to 180 days, so usually a reasonable time period for analysis has not been an issue.

Under the old code, a few dissenting creditors could effectively stall or stop a prepackaged arrangement, however. This could happen if a bankruptcy petition was filed either voluntarily by the debtor to enjoy the "automatic stay" conditions, or involuntarily by a group of creditors attempting to disrupt the vote solicitation process. In either case, the vote solicitation process had to cease and the prepackaged attempt would be ended. Under BAPCPA, however, vote solicitation is permitted to continue after the filing of the petition as long as it began before and the process complies with applicable nonbankruptcy law, usually the relevant securities laws. Thus, dissenting creditors will now need to file their involuntary petition before solicitation begins and the tactic of forcing a voluntary filing by aggressive actions by dissidents will no longer interfere with the solicitation of acceptance of a "prepack."

In addition, to expedite the prepack where adequate disclosure is deemed to have occurred, the court may enter that a Section 341 meeting of creditors not be held. This reduces the ability of the U.S. trustee to object to a plan without the 341 meeting.

Advantages and Ingredients of a Prepackaged Chapter 11

A debtor who negotiates a prepackaged Chapter 11 has the advantage of a clearly defined exit strategy from the bankruptcy and has dramatically increased its chances of emerging as a going concern. While it still may take many months to emerge even after a prefiling plan is agreed upon, the average time in bankruptcy of these cases is far less than the almost two years average of all Chapter 11s.

According to Salerno and Hansen (1991), there are four essential ingredients to a successful prepackaged reorganization:

1. Foresight of the debtor to realistically assess the magnitude of its financial problems.
2. Willingness and ability to incur professional fees necessary to implement the prepackaged strategy.
3. Formulation of a viable exit strategy and a going-forward business plan.
4. One or more creditor groups that are willing to negotiate the prepackaged plan and that find the business plan and exit strategy (i.e., new capital structure) acceptable.

While the last ingredient is necessary for success, the first three are prerequisites to the plan's acceptance. An additional key ingredient to a successful large firm prepackaged deal reflects the debtor's ability to raise new equity capital. New equity is important even when there is a viable core business and the main problem appears to be too much debt. This was critical in the Southland Corporation case and many others. (The Southland case involved an unsuccessful first effort to prepackage a deal, and it took six months to finally conclude a plan. Its final confirmation was mainly based on the new equity's role.) New equity infusion by existing or new investors signals to the market that real economic value exists in the firm's assets. While capital can also be raised via DIP financings, the superpriority status of these investors is not as clear a signal as the willingness for investors to contribute equity—the lowest-priority type of capital.

Prepackaged Plan Risks and Costs

A prepackaged plan is not without its disadvantages and costs. Again, Salerno and Hansen list these as:

- Requiring cash to pay the necessary fees.
- Informing the business community of the firm's problems.
- Providing creditors time to undertake collection efforts in anticipation of a bankruptcy.

The first requirement is obvious since there is little chance that an adviser will work toward a prepackaged filing unless there is sufficient cash set aside to cover the newly incurred costs. The second item is probably not too important since the debtor's problems are probably already known to the industry. While the third item is likely refutable through voidable preference payments, the process of dealing with panicked and difficult creditors is unpleasant at best and certainly costly in time as well as resources spent. In addition, there is always the possibility that what was thought to be a successfully negotiated prepetition plan will prove to be rejected once the Chapter 11 confirmation process begins. This can be caused by a change in the business outlook for the debtor and/or a recalcitrant major creditor who changes his or her mind. A prominent example of a misfired prepackage that took much longer than planned to accomplish in Chapter 11 is Resorts International in 1994.

Preferences

Under the old code, challenges to creditors who received payments from a debtor within 90 days of the filing could defend such payments by showing that (1) the payment was a debt incurred and paid in the ordinary course of business of both parties and (2) the payment was made according to ordinary business terms. Both provisions had to be met to retain the payments. BAPCPA will require the creditor to show only one of these conditions instead of both. So, payments will be allowed if they meet industry standards regardless of whether they were in the ordinary course of that business.

While the preference rule is relaxed for the receiving creditor, it will probably mean that other creditors will receive less. In essence, if the value of the debtor is less than the total claims against it, then preference payment changes are a zero-sum game. Also, the probability of litigation is increased, which is always more costly.

Other changes in preference are related to time. For example:

- The fraudulent conveyance lookback is extended to two years.
- Creditors will have 30 days, instead of 20, after the debtor receives possession of an asset where a lien is given. For all other collateral, a creditor will be insulated from preference attacks if it perfects its lien within 30 days, rather than 10 days.

Priorities and Timing

Allowed unsecured claims—for example, claims by employees for unpaid earnings—are now increased to $10,000 for earnings from up to 180 days prior to the filing (or cessation of the debtor's business, whichever occurs first), instead of $4,925 within 90 days.

Substantial additional rights to those who sell goods and services to the debtor before bankruptcy will be effected. For example, claims for goods or services received by the debtor within 20 days of the filing will receive priority status for the "value of the goods" rather than being just a low-priority general unsecured claim. This leaves open the possibility of a debtor sequencing receipt of goods or services from what it considers a critical vendor to the detriment of those not considered critical. Creditors can also protect themselves by giving a written reclamation demand to the debtor within 45 days after the debtor receives the goods or within 20 days after the bankruptcy, whichever is later. For example, the financial burden to a debtor could be increased as administrative expenses must be paid in full as a condition of the plan's confirmation. Finally, the administrative burden of setting up a system to monitor reclamation demands could be very difficult for some debtors, especially smaller, less liquid ones.

Lease Rejections

While lease rejections by debtors will be retained, there will be a limitation of time to do so with only one possible extension for 90 days.

Taxes

BAPCPA makes extensive changes in the taxation of debtors and provides substantial protections for property tax claimants, usually local municipalities. While too technical and time-consuming for this discussion, these changes include such areas as (1) payment of back taxes under a Chapter 11 plan, (2) interest on tax claims to be based on applicable nonbankruptcy law, and (3) ability of tax refunds to the debtor to be offset against any taxes owed to the taxing agency (this was not under the old law due to the automatic stay clause).

Other Provisions

Other provisions in the new Act that make substantive changes in bankruptcy proceedings involve (1) appointment of official committee members, (2) utility services, (3) retiree benefits, (4) single-asset real estate debtors, (5) automatic stay on pension plan loans, and (6) notices. We suggest the interested reader contact legal counsel or go to the new Act itself for details.

INTERNATIONALIZING BANKRUPTCIES AND DIFFERING BANKRUPTCY REGIMES

As the economic world evolved into a global community, it was inevitable that large corporate holdings of assets across national geographic boundaries would, on occasion, become internationally distressed. Since nations' bankruptcy laws differ dramatically, corporates can often file in the environment most conducive to preserving their assets and if possible to avoid liquidation. Most countries outside the United States have more restrictive bankruptcy laws favoring creditors, and the usual result of a bankruptcy in these areas is liquidation. On the other hand, very large firms can often depend on some type of government or quasi-government bailout in order to preserve employment and reduce economic friction.

The British Commonwealth system is a case in point. Countries in the Commonwealth, such as England, Canada, and Australia, work under a system whereby a debtor that cannot meet its obligations as they fall due is assigned to a receiver (of the assets), whose job is either to recommend a "scheme of arrangement" to continue the business or to liquidate the assets and pay off the creditors according to their seniority. In most cases, the receiver is an accounting firm executive and the usual result is liquidation, especially if the creditors reject any plan for "trading-on" (i.e., a rehabilitation attempt).

Even with the changes in the U.S. Bankruptcy Act of 2005, there is little doubt that the U.S. bankruptcy laws are friendlier and more flexible to the debtor and, as a result, firms will usually opt for a U.S. filing, or at least a filing in two countries if the debtor has significant business in the United States and its headquarters abroad. An example of this dual filing was the mammoth Olympia & York Development Company filing on May 14, 1992. Another example was the recent filing of Parmalat in Italy (December 2003) and in the United States in early 2004. Interestingly, since Parmalat was so large and complex relative to most Italian firms, the Italian government had to enact new legislation to deal with the cross-border issues, while the U.S. subsidiary sailed through the bankruptcy courts here and emerged in early 2005.

The differences in bankruptcy systems globally are beginning to get the attention of international scholars, regulators, and institutes. For example, the International Insolvency Institute was instrumental in working with the United Nations Commission on International Trade Law (UNCITRAL) and the U.S. Congress to enact the UNCITRAL Model Law on Cross-Border Insolvency, which was substantively adopted as a new Chapter 15 to the 2005 Bankruptcy Code. We will discuss this new chapter in a moment.

In Appendix 2.1, we summarize a report from Tilley (2004) on the major issues of reorganization and bankruptcy from 10 countries, including the United States. These issues deal with such items as the current bankruptcy act in each country, bankruptcy triggers, standards of judgment, director duties and liabilities in bankruptcy, executing contracts, automatic stay, exit mechanisms, and priority rankings. Davydenko and Franks (2004) review the different bankruptcy regimes in the United Kingdom, Germany, and France and discuss their impact on creditor recoveries and reorganization results in those countries. They find that due to the new creditor-unfriendly bankruptcy laws in those countries, banks adjust their lending and reorganization practices to mitigate the expected unfriendly aspects of their new laws. For example, French banks require more collateral, especially on small and medium-size firm loans. Still, median bank recovery rates were relatively high, especially in the United Kingdom (92 percent), with lower levels in Germany (67 percent) and France (56 percent).

Eckbo and Thornburn (2004) analyze the results of bankruptcies in Sweden and conclude that the auction system of insolvent companies in that country appears to be more efficient than the formal bankruptcy system, resulting in very high recoveries for creditors. Acharya, Sundaram, and John (2005) conducted a theoretical and empirical study of the impact of bankruptcy codes on firms' capital structure choices. In their theoretical framework, costs of financial distress are endogenously determined as a function of the bankruptcy code and anticipated liquidation values are assigned a key role in the capital structure–bankruptcy code link.

UNCITRAL Model Law on Cross-Border Insolvency

As just noted, the new law on cross-border insolvencies was enacted as part of the Bankruptcy Act of 2005 (BAPCPA) under the new Chapter 15 of the Act. Like most of the other new chapters, it became effective on October 17, 2005. The United Nations Commission on International Trade Law (UNCITRAL) produced this new Model Law, which was adopted by the U.S. Congress.[5] The new Chapter 15 is the successor to Section 304 of the 1978 Bankruptcy Code. The objective of the Model Law is to establish a set of uniform principles to deal with the requirements that a corporate entity would need to meet in order to have access to the courts of other countries in cross-border cases.[6]

Foreign insolvency proceedings in the Model Law are divided into two categories—"main" and "nonmain" proceedings. A main proceeding is one that takes place in the country where a debtor has its primary operations. Once the proceeding is recognized as a main one, the Model Law provides an automatic stay by creditors against the debtor's right to transfer, encumber, or otherwise transfer its assets. Normal requirements of that country's bankruptcy law then proceed. The Model Law suggests a high level of cooperation between courts in different countries. The main country court can appoint someone to communicate between the relevant courts and coordinate the administration of the debtor's assets and affairs in the main and nonmain jurisdictions. Among other benefits of the Model Act, it is expected that the greater certainty in matters of creditor and debtor rights will assist international trade, commerce, and the availability of capital in less-developed countries. If, though, there were prejudicial treatment for creditors in one country over those in other countries, where the claims are of equal priority, then international trade and capital movement would suffer. For example, if a domestic proceeding is commenced after an application for recognition of the foreign proceeding, the domestic court must review the relief sought by the foreign representative and must modify that relief if it is inconsistent with the domestic proceeding. Specifically, Article 13(2) of the Model Law states that the claims of foreign creditors must not be ranked lower than the claims of general domestic creditors.

In the development of the Model Law on Cross-Border Insolvencies, more than 70 countries and international organizations participated. The law had been passed by Japan, Mexico, Poland, Romania, and Spain, as well as the United States in mid-2005. Enabling legislation in the United Kingdom has been passed, and recommendations for the passing of such a law have been introduced in such countries as Australia, Canada, and New Zealand. It was expected that the formal enactment of Chapter 15 in the United States would influence other countries that were also considering its adoption.

---

[5]UNCITRAL is an important United Nations entity, headquartered in Vienna, Austria, which conducts major studies on international trade laws and has produced a number of international conventions and model laws, which have been widely adopted around the world.

[6]The official text of the Model Law on Cross-Border Insolvency is available on UNCITRAL's web site www.uncitral.org. A summary of Chapter 15 can be found from the International Insolvency Institute at info@iiiglobal.org.

APPENDIX 2.1 Matrix of Reorganization and Bankruptcy Issues in Major Jurisdictions

This document must be used as a guide only. Any actions should only be made after competent legal advice in each jurisdiction.

	United States	United Kingdom
Main Defining Legislation	U.S. Bankruptcy Code	Insolvency Act 1986 Companies Act 1985 and 1989 Company Directors Disqualification Act 1986 Enterprise Act 2002
Practical Clarifying Aspects	Federal law governs bankruptcy but claimant rights may be subject to state law. Debtor in possession with management running day to day operations is not mirrored in European legislation. U.S. law is the most debtor friendly regime and most responsive for preservation of enterprise value. The only regime where chief restructuring officer concept has general acceptance.	Reorganizations are governed by company law. Significant changes regarding the rights of floating charge debenture holders and removing state debt preference became law 15/9/93 with the Enterprise Act aimed at aiding restructuring within administration. Out-of-court voluntary reorganizations may occur on a consensual basis using the informal "London Approach." In court Creditor Voluntary Arrangements are possible but there is no "stay" and it is difficult to manage small creditors. All-in Court Administration or Liquidation is performed by licensed insolvency practitioners, normally qualified accountants. Management has influence over the initial appointment but thereafter has no influence. Most administrations end in piecemeal sales of assets or business sectors and final liquidation.

APPENDIX 2.1 *(Continued)*

	United States	United Kingdom
Bankruptcy Triggers	Insolvency is not required for validity of voluntary filing. Failure to generally pay debts as they become due or general assignment for the benefit of creditors required for involuntary filing.	Insolvency—Liabilities exceed assets. Illiquidity—Unable to meet debts as they fall due in ordinary course of business. A court judgment is unsatisfied.
Standards of Judgment	Application for Chapter 11 protection does not require evidence of insolvency. There exist uncertainties as to the applicable formulation of insolvency and the standards to which directors of an insolvent company will be held. In principle an officer should act in good faith to shareholders and creditors to avoid impairment to assets that would be available to creditors as the company enters deeper the zone of insolvency.	Liability to creditors for wrongful trading can accrue when, but only when, there is no reasonable prospect of the company's avoiding insolvent liquidation. There is a fiduciary responsibility to cause a company to continue to trade if there is still a possible solution to avoiding potential loss to creditors, which leaves this a fine balanced judgment. In practice if an officer has acted in good faith to prevent solvency and has current and accurate information on the company's financial situation he has a reasonable defense against potential "wrongful trading" claims. Although insolvency is when liabilities exceed assets, this is a vague concept and not one that alone would determine need to file.
Directors' Duties and Liabilities		
Solvent	Fiduciary duties of care and loyalty.	Fiduciary duties of care and loyalty.
Insolvent	Duty to creditors and then shareholders, to resolve conflicts in good faith and avoid self-dealing.	"Fraudulent" trading—Intent to defraud. "Wrongful" trading—Trading after insolvent. Transactions at undervalue or preference.

(Continued)

APPENDIX 2.1 *(Continued)*

	United States	United Kingdom
Liabilities	Civil action for recovery of breach.	Fraudulent trading both criminal and civil and punishable by fine, jail, and recovery including punitive compensation. Other infractions are civil. Liability is to restore position.
Forms of Administration	**Chapter 11 Debtor in Possession** Existing management manages day-to-day transactions essentially with powers of a trustee to preserve and protect debtor's estate. On motion and for cause the court may order a trustee appointment. Transactions beyond ordinary course of business require court approval. Creditors committees monitor the operation of the business and consult on decisions requiring court approval.	**Company Voluntary Arrangement (CVA)** Agreement with creditors (75% in value) for composition. Made via nominee who is an insolvency practitioner. No automatic stay and difficult in practice to arrange so little used. **Sec 425 Scheme of Arrangement** Agreement with creditors (75% in value) for composition. Made through an insolvency practitioner with much court involvement and is little used as there is no stay and it is time-consuming. **Administrative Receivership** Forced by charge holder (normally banks) to recover assets. Destroys value and will be constrained by Enterprise Act 2002 for new security charges entered post–15/9/03. **Administration** Court ordered on application where value will be enhanced and run by administrator who is an insolvency practitioner. Automatic stay and some flexibility to void executory contracts. No debtor in possession and usually reduces enterprise value through loss of confidence of customers and suppliers.

APPENDIX 2.1 *(Continued)*

	United States	United Kingdom
Key Administration Processes		
Funding	DIP funding available with superpriority status secured on unencumbered assets or junior status on encumbered property.	Not freely available in practice.
Executory Contracts	Contracts that are material to performance remain enforceable. Debtor authorized to assume or reject any contract or lease subject to court approval. Contracts or leases cannot be expired or terminated.	Onerous contracts can be disclaimed.
Automatic Stay	Available against unsecureds. Secureds may apply to court for relief from stay for cause if risk of security erosion.	Available in court-approved administration or administrative receivership but not for CVA or Section 425 schemes of arrangement without specific court approval. Creditors have the right of prepetition setoff. Retention of title claims is permissible.
Exit Mechanisms	Upon acceptance by creditors of a plan of reorganization and court approval. Cram-down available.	CVAs and Section 424 schemes end on payment to creditors. Administrations end usually when the ongoing assets or businesses have been sold, final distributions made, and the residual company liquidated or struck off.
Security and Rankings	• Administrative claims in priority • Secureds • Prepetition unsecureds • Subordinated debt • Equity	• Secureds • Administration expenses • Preference holders • Employees to low ceiling • State taxes VAT and social security • Unsecureds • Subordinated debt • Equity Note that post–15/9/03 Enterprise Act State preference is waived in favor of unsecureds.

(Continued)

APPENDIX 2.1 *(Continued)*

	Germany	France
Main Defining Legislation	Insolvency Act 1999 (*Insolvenzordnung*)	The 1985 Law—Insolvency proceedings The 1984/94 Law—Voluntary arrangements A 2004 draft amendment adds a further process to reorganization—*reglement amiable* becomes *Conciliation and Procedure de Sauvegarde*. Court-supervised consensual restructurings.
Practical Clarifying Aspects	The German insolvency law now provides for reorganization within administration under an *Insolvenzplan* but this is not Chapter 11, there being no debtor in possession. The process is run by a court-appointed administrator who may or may not utilize management. In practice the profession has been slow and reluctant to adopt the process, which is still subject to an apparent harsh regime of personal penalties and liabilities. In certain circumstances by a *Finanzplan* management can restructure a balance sheet when overindebted if the company is liquid and the plan is sound and all parties in interest are in compliance. This is rare in practice but has applications for subsidiary companies in global restructurings. Administrators are court-appointed legal practitioners. Management has no influence over appointments.	This new law will become effective in 2005/6. The Law for Voluntary Arrangements is designed to facilitate reorganizations with a prime aim of job preservation. The three processes of administration: *Procedure d'alerte*—early warning *Mandataire ad hoc*—informal voluntary *Reglement amiable*—formal are all supervised by Commercial Court (*Tribunal de Commerce*)-appointed administrators with assistance from management but no management authority. The system is flexible in its structure but bureaucratic in execution and court approvals are heavily "social plan" influenced. If after four months in *reglement amiable* no consensual agreement is reached insolvency proceedings begin under a court-appointed administrator. Administrators are legal practitioners. Most administrations end in a formal liquidation after piecemeal asset or business sector sales.

APPENDIX 2.1 *(Continued)*

	Germany	France
Bankruptcy Triggers	Insolvency—Overindebtedness. Illiquidity—Unable to meet debts as they fall due in ordinary course of business.	Insolvency—When a company cannot meet its debts from available assets. Rather vague and complex and in retrospect the date can be determined by the court. **New 2005 law will clarify** *periode suspect.*
Standards of Judgment	The standards of judgment are more stringently interpreted in Germany than in the "case law" countries by both insolvency lawyers and officers. In particular this applies to the 21-day filing requirement. The main area of uncertainty applies to overindebtedness definition. The delay is precise, the valuation of assets and liabilities less so. Provision exists for the assessment of hidden reserves such as property valuations and the adoption of a reasonable *Finanzplan* to restore equity to 50% of share capital of a viable and liquid enterprise. In practice a German board mindful of both civil and criminal personal liabilities will deem filing to be necessary before a comparable situation in the United States, United Kingdom, Netherlands, France, or Italy.	The key decision is to file within 15 days of insolvency but this in itself is as vague as the definition of insolvency. Accordingly personal liability is rather a case-by-case interpretation of reasoned decision making based on accurate record keeping and the avoidance of preference or personal gain. There is more latitude to seek protection in suspension of payments than in Germany and the flexibility of the system allows time for restructuring providing liquidity and viability maintained. **In 2005 law** *Soutien Abusif* (lender liability) no longer is an issue in **Conciliation.** Note also that a company has a statutory duty to restore net capital to above 50% of issued capital in the event of a deficit, within certain time scales. Subordinated debt can substitute for equity and in groups intercompany debt is often used in this context.
Directors' Duties and Liabilities Solvent	Specific duties for record keeping, account preparation, tax and social security payment, and preservation of share capital and intellectual property. General duty of diligent management.	Fiduciary duty of care and diligent management.

(Continued)

APPENDIX 2.1 *(Continued)*

	Germany	France
Insolvent	Calling shareholders meeting and filing in 21 days from commencement of insolvency.	A wide range of officers and de facto directors can be at risk of prosecution from the court, the administrator, creditors, or the public prosecutor in the case of management fault and a deficit of assets.
Liabilities	Failure to file or putting creditors at risk, or granting preferences are criminal offenses. The insolvency receiver and creditors will scrutinize to consider personal liability. The possibility exists that there may be grounds for criminal prosecution. However, reimbursement does not apply if payments after insolvency were made with normal business diligence. Liability does not occur in the case of wrongful trading and for the full amount of the liability entered into post the date insolvency should have been filed. The managing director is personally liable for unpaid taxes including employee income tax deducted at source and employees' social security but not employers'.	Fault must be proven and then will be joint and several for all officers "*comblement du passif.*" Fault encompasses poor decisions, failure to keep proper records or supervise, acts of personal gain, and failure to file for suspension of payments when insolvent. Fault must also be precise and not merely incompetence. Fault can cover a wide range of operational and investment decisions. The definition varies from court to court. Where fault, however casual the link to the deficiency, can be proven personal liability may accrue to the extent of the deficiency, the onus on the creditor as plaintiff to prove.
Forms of Administration	**Insolvency Plan** (*Insolvenzplan*) Court-appointed administrator (legal background) runs company. Initial period of three months in which with management a structuring plan may be submitted to the court. Plan needs approval of creditors by class in a majority.	*Mandataire Ad Hoc* A court-appointed expert who seeks an informal and voluntary arrangement. No automatic stay in law but in practice normally effective. Expert works with management and has no formal powers. The duration is determined by the court and the final arrangements are normally approved by the court.

APPENDIX 2.1   *(Continued)*

	Germany	France
Forms of Administration *(Continued)*	State pays employees for initial three-month period after which it becomes liability of the company and administrator. In practice it is difficult to get a plan approved in three months and although extensions are permitted with court approval the three-month hurdle is a barrier that makes liquidation and break-up a more popular and less risky course.	***Reglement Amiable*** A court-appointed mediator who seeks a composition agreement with creditors. Four-month duration with automatic stay. The composition agreement is consensual and contractual between the parties. ***Redressement Judiciare*** If the court considers there is a viable business the court appoints an administrator who manages the business through an observation period normally ending in piecemeal disposal. There is no time limit to this period. Assuming the company itself is not continued, the process moves to liquidation. ***Liquidation Judiciare*** Activities cease and the business is wound up under court supervision.
Key Administration Processes **Funding**	If available would have priority over unsecured ranking subsidiary only to administrator fees.	Junior to post proceeding employee claims, administration costs, pari passu to postpetition executory contracts, and senior to all other postpetition claims. In practice not freely available other than on factored receivables.
Executory Contracts	Administrator may terminate prepetition contracts. Employment contracts need three months notice of termination. Lessors may not terminate lease or rental contracts on the grounds of prepetition nonpayment.	Contracts that are material to performance remain enforceable. Administrator is authorized to assume or reject any lease.

(Continued)

APPENDIX 2.1 *(Continued)*

	Germany	France
Automatic Stay	In the first instance on filing a preliminary administrator is appointed without automatic stay if supervisory only. Specific grant of stay can be granted by court. Retention of title permissible. Creditors have the right of prepetition setoff.	Only on specific order of court. Retention of title permissible. Creditors have the right of prepetition setoff.
Exit Mechanisms	Insolvency plans are deemed to have been accepted if the majority of classes have a majority by value and number and dissenting classes do not receive less than they would without the plan. In practice no cram-down is available as any creditor can block a plan if he receives less than he would without the plan.	Reorganizations are formally concluded when the parties have agreed to the plan. Court approval is not compulsory but usually is requested for grounds of completeness and comfort. In the event of a *reglement amiable* the conclusion is at the end of the four-month period or on consensual agreement if earlier. As the process is consensual no cram-down applies.
Security and Rankings	• Secureds • State preferred debt • Administration expenses • Unsecureds • Subordinated debt • Equity	• Employee claims up to 60 days • 13 months social security unemployment pay less 60-day claim above • Administrative expense • Postpetition claims • Prepetition secureds • Prepetition unsecureds • Subordinated debt • Equity

APPENDIX 2.1 *(Continued)*

	Italy	Netherlands
Main Defining Legislation	The Civil Code Article 2221 The Insolvency Act 1942 "Large Company in Crisis" legislation 1999 ("New Prodi Law") This has been amended following the Parmalat insolvency ("Law Marzano").	Bankruptcy Act *(Faillissementswet)*
Practical Clarifying Aspects	Current procedure is pro creditor and court-based and supervised with difficult interaction with management. Law 80/2005 of 5/05 introduces new measures of creditors composition and changes to clawback. The Large Company (200+ people) process was pre–80/2005 the only practical rescue process. Following Parmalat companies of 500+ people can appoint a Restructuring Officer who has 270 days to file a Restructuring Plan. "*Concordata Preventivo*" or Composition Arrangement with creditors (minimum 100% of secureds and 40% unsecureds) can work in a "prepack" for part of the business but is bureaucratic and normally ends in liquidation. "*Amministrazione Controllata*" or Judicial Moritorium is rarely used with success, being costly, interest bearing on debt, and requiring full settlement of debts albeit over a two-year period. Out-of-court settlements are possible under a restructuring adviser but require full Bank of Italy support and compliant banks.	The framework provides for either bankruptcy or suspension of payments. Suspension involves a court-appointed administrator who acts in concert with management to propose a plan with secureds and preferreds paid in full and others voting 75% (value) and 66.6% (number). A reasonably friendly restructuring process with limited court supervision and some management influence. Two-month stay process. Often used with a prepack where a viable ongoing business exists.

(Continued)

APPENDIX 2.1 *(Continued)*

	Italy	Netherlands
Bankruptcy Triggers	Insolvency—Where a company is incapable of fulfilling its obligations in a timely manner by the utilization of normal means of payment or where the statutory minimum share capital is lost and there is no provision to increase it.	Insolvency—The debtor has ceased to pay its debts.
Standards of Judgment	Civil actions against the directors are the same in insolvency as may be brought when in good standing. There is no clear-cut definition of wrongful trading, and acting in good faith while taking all reasonable steps to avoid insolvency while not impairing creditors would be reasonable action.	Mismanagement and impairment of creditors are risk areas. However, where officers are acting in good faith to preserve the value of the company, premature insolvency filing should be avoided.
Directors' Duties and Liabilities Solvent	Duty to uphold the law and the company's articles.	Duty of care (creditors' claims against mismanagement relate to actions up to three years preceding bankruptcy).
Insolvent	Duty to avoid trading in a way detrimental to financial position, to avoid preferential payments, and if share capital is below statutory minimum not to enter new transactions.	Duty to creditors.
Liabilities	Liability is to the creditors for failure to preserve assets. In the case of fraudulent bankruptcy there is a criminal sanction of 5 to 10 years jail. Criminal penalties may occur for undue filing delay that increases liabilities or if there is a failure to keep proper books.	Managing directors may be liable to the trustee for the deficit if caused by reckless or careless management practices detrimental to the creditors.

APPENDIX 2.1 *(Continued)*

	Italy	Netherlands
Forms of Administration	*Concordata Preventivo* Court appoints an administrator who runs company, usually after dismissing officers. The proposal must satisfy the court to full settlement of secureds and preferreds and minimum 40% of unsecureds. The plan must show adequate liquidity after stay. The process is closely monitored by the court and is time-consuming and generally destroys the enterprise value. *Amministrazione Controllata* Court appoints an administrator who runs company, usually after dismissing officers. There is an automatic stay. The court must be satisfied that plan is viable and that the company is only in temporary difficulty and has potential to exit within two years with full satisfaction including accrued interest. The process requires approval of the creditors as a majority but including 66.6% of the unsecureds. In practice needs major creditor prepack and is rarely used. *Amministrazione Straordinaria* Special process for large companies with recovery potential and debts less than 66.6% of assets. A judicial commissioner is appointed to run company as directors' powers are suspended. Commissioner prepares plan of restructuring. Automatic stay with priority for administrative claims.	Suspension of Payments The court appoints an administrator who acts in close concert with management to structure an exit plan usually involving nonsecureds and nonpreferreds. There is usually a two-month stay period. State debt may be reduced to increase unsecured dividend. The plan must be approved by a majority of unsecured creditors (75% value/66% number) and approved by the court.

(Continued)

APPENDIX 2.1 *(Continued)*

	Italy	Netherlands
Key Administration Processes		
Funding	Not freely available.	Where available and with administrator's consent can be secured against unpledged assets.
Executory Contracts	Executory contracts may be terminated at administrator's discretion.	Executory contracts may be terminated. All contracts remain enforceable by the commissioner.
Automatic Stay	Automatic stay granted but creditors have the right of setoff. No retention of title.	During a suspension of payments only secureds and preferreds can pursue claims unless there is a moratorium. Limited retention of title rights. Creditors have the right of prepetition setoff.
Exit Mechanisms	Reorganizations conclude upon satisfaction of creditors. In practice a *concordata preventivo* can drift on for many years, the 40% unsecureds not being met on payout and the court moving the company into bankruptcy. In an *amministrazione controllata* the exit follows first the agreement of the creditors to the moratorium and secondly the satisfaction of the moratorium terms or the expiration of two years. Cram-down is not applicable.	Suspension of payments need creditor approval (66.6% in number/75% in value) followed by court approval. Secureds and preferreds are expected to be paid in full unless there is a prepack to the contrary. An unsecured majority in value but short of 75% will permit a second vote. There is no provision for cram-down.
Security and Rankings	• Administration expenses, wages, and taxes • Indirect taxes • Secureds • Subordinated debt • Equity	• Secureds • Preferred (state may waive some rights) • Unsecureds • Subordinated debt • Equity

APPENDIX 2.1   *(Continued)*

	Switzerland	Belgium
Main Defining Legislation	Federal Debt Collection & Bankruptcy Act 1889 amended through 1997	Law on Bankruptcies 1997 Law on Judicial Compositions 1997
Practical Clarifying Aspects	The regime in Switzerland is not conducive to restructuring, and while there is provision for a moratorium and court-supervised restructuring this is rare in practice for four main reasons for international groups operating with a Swiss sub:	New judicial composition legislation has seen some court-supervised restructuring.
	Swiss boards consist of a majority of Swiss nationalists who if nonexec are very risk-averse.	This is not Chapter 11 style, it being court-supervised through an administrator with no DIP.
	In a bankruptcy the public prosecutor will actively investigate for criminal liability.	Most restructurings result in piecemeal asset or business sector sales and subsequent liquidation of the rump of the business.
	Swiss debt collection is very strict and suppliers are quick to force bankruptcy.	Apparent harsh criminal penalty for failure to file in a timely fashion may result in premature management action.
	Bankruptcy law prima facie favors civil action against directors.	
Bankruptcy Triggers	Insolvency—Excess of liabilities over assets.	Insolvency—Erosion of half share capital value.
	Illiquidity—Failure to satisfy a creditor claim.	Illiquidity—Unable to pay debts as they fall due.
Standards of Judgment	Switzerland does not have a restructuring culture and for the reasons mentioned above the standards of judgment applied leave little latitude for interpretation of insolvency.	Belgian law gives reasonable flexibility in interpreting insolvency and allows for a two-month delay in calling a shareholders meeting after the 50% rule is breached and thereupon submission of a plan to improve the financial position within a reasonable period.
	In reality there have been only a small number of court decisions holding directors liable.	
	Thus there is a conflict between an apparently harsh regime and actual experience.	Belgian law is not unduly onerous in the interpretation of directors' liability except in the case of fraudulent or wrongful trading.
	Overindebtedness requires a bankruptcy filing to avoid criminal penalties.	

(Continued)

APPENDIX 2.1 *(Continued)*

	Switzerland	Belgium
Directors' Duties and Liabilities		
Solvent	Duty of care to the company, shareholders, and creditors and liability to the above for damages caused by willful or negligent violation of duties.	Duty of care to shareholders and the company.
Insolvent	As above.	Duty to creditors.
Liabilities	To be held liable for damages, a breach of duty, actual damages, willful neglect, or negligent conduct and a causal connection between the breach and the damage must be proven. Criminal liability may occur in the event of fraudulent diminution of assets. It may also be applied to "acts of management" such as excess, hazardous speculation, negligence, fraudulent preference, and trading while overindebted.	Criminal liability for failure to file when insolvent but much latitude in the event of balance sheet insolvency to restructure. Civil liability in the event of mismanagement or fraudulent preference. Mismanagement is obvious or serious violation of normal standards. Criminal liability for acts of personal preference or failure to restructure balance sheet insolvency.
Forms of Administration	**A Composition** Subject to a majority of creditors and district court approval and under a commissioner's supervision. A draft plan is presented to the court and under the commissioner, usually in four to six months but exceptionally 12 to 24, a composition is proposed requiring 66.6% creditor approval and court sanction. Compositions are rare.	**Judicial Compositions** In situations of "temporary illiquidity" that can be cured and there is a real expectation of recovery and the directors are acting in good faith. On request of the debtor and within 15 days the court will appoint a commissioner and invoke a suspension of payments for a six-month observation period during which due interest must be kept current. During the observation period a restructuring plan is prepared requiring 50% of creditor approval in value and number. This includes secureds only if they are affected by the plan.

APPENDIX 2.1 *(Continued)*

	Switzerland	Belgium
Forms of Administration *(Continued)*		Restructuring plans often involve whole or partial business sales that require creditor and court approval and can be over 24 months. Management is closely supervised by the commissioner and actions are restricted to current business activity and ordinary business.
Key Administration Processes **Funding**	Not available.	Not available.
Executory Contracts **Automatic Stay**	Automatic stay. Retention of title rights. Creditors have setoff rights. Two-thirds of creditors voting in favor and court approval.	Automatic stay assuming interest is paid current on prepetition interest-bearing debt. Retention of title rights. Creditors have setoff rights. Majority of affected creditors in value and number in favor plus court approval.
Exit Mechanisms	No cram-down.	No cram-down.
Security and Rankings	• Secureds • Preferreds • Unsecureds—Employee claims up to six months • Other unsecureds • Subordinated debt • Equity	• Secureds • Administration expenses • Government priority claims—Taxes • Nongovernment priority claims—Rent • Unsecureds • Subordinated debt • Equity

(Continued)

APPENDIX 2.1 *(Continued)*

	Spain	Sweden
Main Defining Legislation	Insolvency Act 2003 *Ley Concursal* Companies Act 1989 and 1995	Bankruptcy Act 1987 Reorganization of Business Act 1996
Practical Clarifying Aspects	The new Spanish Insolvency legislation has come into force on September 1, 2004. Replacing outdated legislation dating as far back as the nineteenth century, its main features are: 1. It unifies all prior bankruptcy and insolvency proceedings in one single insolvency process. 2. New Commercial Courts are created, with wide and overreaching powers in all matters pertaining to insolvency proceedings (including corporate, commercial, and labor dispute matters). 3. Commercial Courts reviewing any insolvency file may determine whether the insolvent company's management are to keep their posts or the court-appointed insolvency administrators are not only to oversee but to actually manage the insolvent company during the process. 4. Liability for individuals acting as directors or de facto managers of insolvent companies is severely toughened. 5. Court-appointed insolvency administrators are normally three: an economist-CPA, a lawyer, and a creditor. 6. Debts owed to parent or group companies, related parties are subordinated and relegated.	Business reorganizations are not common. Recent trends are to improving the climate for reorganizations. However, the concept of floating charge still exists, which gives banks a strong influence over the process and prefers bankruptcy to reorganization. Legislation is in consideration to change rights of priority to abolish priority of rental claims and reduce floating charges to 50% of the value of the assets in order to facilitate business reorganizations. The business reorganization process is supervised by an administrator so is unlike Chapter 11 debtor in possession.

APPENDIX 2.1 *(Continued)*

	Spain	Sweden
Bankruptcy Triggers	Insolvency—Defined as the situation where debtor cannot fulfill regularly its obligations, regardless of whether it has sufficient assets to cover its liabilities.	Insolvency—Erosion of 50% of share capital. Illiquidity—Unable to pay debts as they fall due and such inability is not merely temporary.
Standards of Judgment	Latitude afforded to directors has been reduced on account of the severity of liability sanctions set out by the new legislation: Directors are obliged to file for court proceedings within two months of insolvency; otherwise they may be held liable for company debts and not be allowed to serve as directors or officers in any other company from 2 to 15 years. Furthermore, the new legislation provides some guidance and sets out instances where insolvency is deemed to be occurring: 1. Where creditors with a court sentence are not able to seize debtor's assets for collection. 2. Where a debtor undergoes a generalized seizure of its assets by claimant creditors. 3. Generalized breach of due payment commitments by debtor. 4. Three months running failure to make recurring tax payments, social security contributions, and pay workforce payroll. 5. Where there is evidence of quick or undervalued disposal of assets by debtor.	Directors have a responsibility when they believe that the net worth is less than 50% of the share capital to cause an audit of the balance sheet under special valuation rules. The company at shareholders meeting has to resolve to file or if it resolves to continue has eight months to restore share capital in full. Failure to comply to the above exposes the directors to personal liability.
Directors' Duties and Liabilities **Solvent**	Fiduciary duties of care and loyalty.	Duty of care to shareholders and company.

(Continued)

APPENDIX 2.1 *(Continued)*

	Spain	Sweden
Insolvent	Directors are obliged to file for proceedings within two months of insolvency.	Duty to shareholders, company, and creditors.
Liabilities	Standard directors' civil and criminal liability statutes remain in force and applicable to insolvency scenarios. Additionally, the new insolvency legislation sets out specific insolvency-related liabilities that may be imposed on formal or de facto directors, managers, or liquidators of insolvent companies under certain circumstances, which may entail holding them liable for company debts (to the extent that they are not covered by its assets) and may ban them from holding any corporate directorship or office anywhere from 2 to 15 years. Furthermore, the new insolvency courts are given wide latitude to seize directors' personal assets at any time to cover eventual liabilities.	Personally liable for debts if the 50% of capital erosion process is not followed effectively. Liability extends to unpaid state debts in the event of negligence and to unlawful dividends. Criminal liability is restricted to gross negligence or fraud. In general Swedish courts and Swedish practice are not onerous for directors acting with reasonable care.
Forms of Administration	**Court-Appointed Insolvency Administrators** Normally made up of three members: an economist-CPA, a lawyer, and a creditor (who may, in turn, appoint a professional practitioner). Decisions are taken by majority voting. On small size insolvency classes, court may decide to appoint only one administrator. Administrator fees are based on a government-approved fee schedule and cleared by court.	**Business Reorganizations** Board resolution needed to file an application for court-supervised business reorganization under an appointed administrator where there is reasonable possibility of achievement. The administrator in consultation with the debtor forms a plan, which is sent to the creditors and court for informal agreement.

APPENDIX 2.1 *(Continued)*

	Spain	Sweden
Forms of Administration *(Continued)*	Insolvency administrators, as the court may decide, will be in charge of: 1. Reviewing and clearing all actions to be performed by the ongoing management; or 2. Replacing ongoing management, and taking direct management responsibility. Insolvency administrators are also charged with preparing a report outlining the reasons leading to insolvency, the financial situation of the company, and the value of its assets, and to value the restructuring plans there may be, if any. When the insolvency proceedings are geared to the liquidation of the company, the insolvency administrators act as liquidators.	In the event of nonacceptance the debtor can apply for public composition. In this case the assumption is that the plan covers all secureds and preferreds in full and is put to a vote of the unsecureds for majority vote. Final court approval of the plan is required.
Key Administration Processes **Funding**	If available, junior only to (1) prepetition 30 days employees' salaries, and (2) postpetition incurred credits of prior due date.	Not available.
Executory Contracts	Court may unilaterally terminate these contracts, setting out the corresponding refunds and compensations accordingly.	Not voidable.
Automatic Stay	Automatic and indefinite stay for unsecured credits. Automatic one-year stay for enforcement of secured credits. Creditors have setoff rights if available by operation of law regardless of insolvency status. Interest on debts stop accruing during insolvency proceedings.	Available against unsecureds. Setoff and counterclaims three months prior to application for reorganization allowed. Determined by creditors' acceptance and ratified by court.

(Continued)

APPENDIX 2.1 *(Continued)*

	Spain	Sweden
Exit Mechanisms	**Creditor Composition** Based on a viability plan to be put forward by company advisers, it requires the approval of 1. 50% ordinary unsecured creditor value for the forgiveness of up to 50% of debts and/or up to five years payment extension. 2. Favorable majority of creditors attending the composition-approval meeting agreeing upon immediate payment with 20% discount or three-year extension. **Liquidation** Sale of business as productive going-concern asset or piecemeal asset sales possible.	
Security and Rankings	• Prepetition employees' 30 days salaries • Insolvency proceeding and administration costs • Postpetition company debts • Asset-secureds (mortgages and pledges) • Generally secureds • Ordinary unsecureds • Subordinated claims (including parent/sister company loans and credits) • Equity	• Maritime and aircraft liens • Landlord's claim for three months' rent • Claims secured by floating charge • Secured claims • Auditing and tax claims • Employees' claims • Unsecureds • Subordinated claims • Equity

Source: Glass & Associates (Allan Tilley, 2004), current through August 2005. Spain reviewed by Noraction (September 2004).

CHAPTER 3

Post–Chapter 11 Performance

A key goal of Chapter 11 is to provide economically viable firms an opportunity to reorganize, while liquidating those that are not viable. There has been considerable debate as to whether the current bankruptcy code strikes the right balance between reorganization and liquidation, or whether it is biased toward allowing inefficient firms to reorganize. The number of failures following a Chapter 11 reorganization, as seen in the significant number of Chapter 22 filings, might be taken as evidence of a problem with the structure of Chapter 11. At the same time, we have seen some spectacular success stories upon emergence from bankruptcy, at least from the perspective of equity holders in the reorganized company. For example, Kmart's common stock traded at under $14 per share when the firm emerged from Chapter 11 in May 2003, but rose to over $100 per share by late 2004. National Gypsum's stock increased almost 300 percent in the 18 months after exiting Chapter 11 in July 1993.

There are several ways in which one might evaluate the success of Chapter 11. The first requirement of a successful restructuring is for the firm to in fact emerge from the process. For firms that do emerge, we can track postbankruptcy success based on either operating performance or stock performance. This chapter describes recent evidence on postbankruptcy performance and its relevance to the debate over the efficiency of Chapter 11.

OUTCOMES OF CHAPTER 11 CASES

Arguably, the simplest measure of a successful Chapter 11 case is whether the firm is reorganized in some form. It is important to understand that only a portion of firms that enter Chapter 11 emerge as independent companies. The Executive Office for United States Trustees provides comprehensive national analysis of reorganization plan confirmation rates for Chapter 11 cases, and

TABLE 3.1   National Chapter 11 Filing and Confirmation Figures
(Excluding North Carolina and Alabama) by Year since 1990

Year Filed	Total Cases Filed	Total Confirmed	Percent Confirmed
1990	20,493	5,398	26.3%
1991	23,899	6,605	27.6
1992	22,772	6,512	28.6
1993	19,055	5,313	27.9
1994	14,708	4,145	28.2
1995	12,716	3,886	30.6
1996	11,683	3,664	31.4
1997	10,517	3,075	29.2
1998	8,224	2,486	30.2
1999	9,176	4,125	45.0
2000	9,849	4,365	44.3
2001	11,102	4,244	38.2
2002	10,973	4,238	38.6
2003	9,152	2,783[a]	30.4

[a]As of January 2005.
Source: Executive Office for United States Trustees.

has periodically published analyses of case outcomes.[1] The most striking facts
emerging from their analysis are:

- A large proportion of cases are closed without confirmation, or closed
  as a no-asset Chapter 7 case.
- Estimated confirmation rates for cases do not exceed 45 percent (and
  are likely substantially less) in any year since 1990.
- Many confirmed plans are liquidating plans.
- There is a strong correlation between the amount of assets listed by the
  debtor and the confirmation rate.

Confirmation rates for all national Chapter 11 cases since 1990 are provided in Table 3.1. These figures include all national filings (except North
Carolina and Alabama), not only those of publicly registered companies. A
caveat in interpreting these figures, however, is that large companies entering
Chapter 11 often file a number of bankruptcy petitions for the various entities within the firm, and each individual case is treated as a separate observation in this analysis. For example, in early 2004, Footstar Inc. filed in the
Southern District of New York. This case included approximately 2,510 sep-

---

[1]Statistics are available at www.usdoj.gov/ust.

TABLE 3.2 Outcomes of Chapter 11 Cases for 1,400 Public Companies Filing from 1979 to 2002

Liquidated or Dissolved	21.5%
Merged with Another Operating Company	7.6
Emerged, but Not Publicly Registered	26.6
Emerged as a Publicly Registered Company	44.3

arate filings—about 20 percent of all of the Chapter 11 cases expected to be filed nationwide that year. This was by far the largest number of related cases ever to be filed. While the number of related cases is generally not nearly as extreme as for Footstar, this problem does lead to an overstatement of confirmation rates, particularly since 1999, since bigger cases with a number of related filings are more likely than average to reach confirmation. Still, it is clear that at least 55 to 60 percent of cases are closed without confirmation.

Among public companies, the likelihood that the case will be closed and that the firm will emerge as an independently reorganized company is substantially higher. The difficulty in assessing the outcomes for public companies, however, is that these statistics are not readily available and must be compiled by researchers using various sources including news services.

Hotchkiss and Mooradian (2004) study a comprehensive sample of 1,770 public companies that filed for Chapter 11 between 1979 and 2002. This sample consists of all public companies listed by the Securities and Exchange Commission (SEC) as having filed for Chapter 11 since the 1978 Bankruptcy Reform Act, as well as cases listed by New Generation Research.[2] Hotchkiss and Mooradian are able to determine some publicly cited resolution of the case by June 2004 for 79 percent of the firms studied. The remaining 21 percent are either still in bankruptcy as of June 2004 or else have likely ended in liquidation.

The outcomes of the 1,400 Chapter 11 cases that could be determined are described in Table 3.2. These statistics are fairly similar to those reported by Hotchkiss (1995) for the subset of firms filing between 1979 and 1988. Firms that are liquidated or dissolved include firms that convert from Chapter 11 to Chapter 7, as well as lengthier liquidating Chapter 11 plans. The firms that convert to Chapter 7 after failed efforts to reorganize are typically smaller firms, but do include some well-known large failures such as Eastern Airlines in 1991, retailer Merry-Go-Round in 1996, and Tower Air in 2001.

---

[2]Until 1993, the SEC published quarterly listings of Chapter 11 cases with SEC involvement, covering most public companies filing for Chapter 11. Subsequently, more limited information appears in SEC annual reports. New Generation Research publishes listings of Chapter 11 filings for firms with greater than $50 million in liabilities at filing.

These firms spend on average over one year in Chapter 11 before they move to Chapter 7. A relatively small number of firms appear to merge with another operating company under a plan of reorganization. Hotchkiss and Mooradian (1998) examine these transactions, and suggest that one explanation for the relatively low number of mergers is that the structure of Chapter 11 discourages such acquisitions, since they cannot occur without creditor and management support. Still, Hotchkiss and Mooradian find that mergers are an effective mechanism for redeploying the assets of Chapter 11 firms, in the sense that the combined cash flows of the merged company after Chapter 11 increase by more than is observed for similar nonbankrupt transactions (see Chapter 10 for further discussion).

A large proportion of public companies do emerge from Chapter 11, though not all remain as publicly registered companies. Several researchers have tried to identify factors that are related to the probability a firm will successfully emerge from Chapter 11. One of the first such attempts was Hotchkiss (1993). The overwhelmingly most important firm characteristic related to whether firms successfully reorganized rather than liquidated was firm size, measured by the prepetition assets of the company. Hotchkiss shows that many of the emerging firms considerably downsize while in Chapter 11, so that the ability to divest assets and use the proceeds to fund remaining operations is likely to be important in understanding why these firms are more likely to survive Chapter 11.

More recently, Dahiya et al. (2003) argue that the availability of debtor-in-possession (DIP) financing to large companies is an important determinant of the reorganization versus liquidation outcome. Under Section 364 of the Bankruptcy Code, special status is granted to these postpetition loans; in particular, the DIP loans can receive superior priority relative to prepetition claims and enhanced security. The size of the DIP financing market grew dramatically with the wave of bankruptcies in the early 1990s. Firms typically file a motion for authorization of this financing simultaneously with the filing of a Chapter 11 petition or shortly thereafter. Access to DIP financing is particularly important to firms such as retailers whose suppliers might otherwise discontinue business with the bankrupt firm without this source of funding. Consistent with Hotchkiss (1993), using a sample of 538 public companies filing for Chapter 11 between 1988 and 1997, Dahiya et al. find that larger firms are much more likely to reorganize. However, they also show that firms that have received DIP financing have a greater probability of reorganizing rather than liquidating.

For the group of firms that survive Chapter 11 as publicly registered companies, we can examine various aspects of postbankruptcy performance for the emerging firm. Existing studies of firms that emerged from Chapter 11 are summarized in Table 3.3, and described in the remainder of this chapter.

TABLE 3.3 Academic Studies of Postbankruptcy Performance

	Operating Performance	Ability to Meet Cash Flow Projections	Stock Performance	Sample
Hotchkiss (1995)	✓	✓		197 firms emerging by 1989
Hotchkiss & Mooradian (2004)	✓		✓	620 firms emerging by 2004
Maksimovic & Phillips (1998)	✓			Plant-level data for 302 manufacturing firms in Chapter 11 1978–1989
Alderson & Betker (1999)	✓			89 firms emerging from Chapter 11 1983–1993 (includes 62 emerging 1990–1993)
Hotchkiss & Mooradian (1997)	✓			288 firms defaulting on public debt 1980–1993 (166 are reorganized in Chapter 11)
McHugh, Michel, & Shaked (1998)		✓		35 firms emerging from Chapter 11 1990–1994
Betker, Ferris, & Lawless (1999)		✓		69 firms emerging from Chapter 11 1984–1994
Aggarwal, Altman, & Eberhart (1999)			✓	131 firms emerging from Chapter 11 1980–1993
Goyal, Kahl, & Torous (2003)			✓	Firms distressed between 1980 and 1983; 35 firms in first year after resolution of distress to 25 firms five years after

POSTBANKRUPTCY OPERATING PERFORMANCE

If Chapter 11 does in fact suffer from economically important biases toward continuation of unprofitable firms, poor investment decisions will be reflected in the postbankruptcy operating performance of firms emerging from the process. Therefore, researchers have found it useful to examine several dimensions of postemergence performance for the group of firms surviving as publicly registered companies:

- Accounting measures of profitability.
- Ability to meet cash flow projections on which the reorganization plan is based.
- Incidence of subsequent distressed restructurings, including Chapter 22 filings.

Accounting Measures of Profitability

The most comprehensive analysis of postbankruptcy operating performance to date is reported by Hotchkiss (1995), who examines firms that emerged as public companies from Chapter 11 by 1989. These firms had an average book value of assets prior to filing of $285 million, were generally insolvent at the time of filing, and spent on average 1.7 years in bankruptcy. The financial performance of each firm was traced for up to five years following the time of emergence from bankruptcy.

This analysis produced some striking results. Over 40 percent of the firms emerging from bankruptcy continued to experience operating losses in the three years following bankruptcy. Based on accounting ratios such as return on assets and profit margins, performance was substantially lower than for matched groups of firms in similar industries. For example, in the year following emergence from Chapter 11, almost three-quarters of the sample firms had a ratio of operating income to sales that was lower than observed for nonbankrupt firms in the same industry. The firms showed some positive growth in revenues, assets, and number of employees in the postbankruptcy period, but showed little improvement in profitability, especially in comparison to industry groups. Performance varied little over the five-year postbankruptcy period, which suggests the firms did not simply need more time to recover.

This analysis has been confirmed for a more recent time period by Hotchkiss and Mooradian (2004). The most significant difference from the earlier study is that larger firms, which become more prominent in later sample years, have somewhat better performance based on these accounting measures. Still, for even the larger firms in the updated sample, more than two-thirds of the firms underperform industry peers for up to five years following bankruptcy, and over 18 percent of the sample firms have negative operating income in the year following emergence. This behavior is consistent with the continued high incidence of Chapter 22 bankruptcy filings, discussed in Chapter 1 and later in this chapter.

An important concern in interpreting any analysis of postbankruptcy performance based only on firms that survive Chapter 11 is the fact that a firm's asset composition changes significantly before and during bankruptcy. Maksimovic and Phillips (1998) examine this issue by studying plant-level operating data for manufacturing firms in Chapter 11 between 1978 and 1989. They examine measures of productivity of capital, as well as operating cash flow, for 1,195 plants of 302 bankrupt firms, as well as plants of nonbankrupt counterparts. Since they are able to track the productivity of individual plants, regardless of whether these plants are redeployed to new owners or are closed, Maksimovic and Phillips are able to examine asset performance even for firms that are liquidated or emerge as private companies from Chapter 11, thus avoiding survivorship bias.

For the manufacturing firms they study, changes in bankrupt firms' performance can be explained for the most part by asset sales and closures, not by changes in the efficiency of retained assets. Bankrupt firms in high-growth industries are more likely to sell assets than bankrupt firms in declining industries. The plants that are not sold by these firms have lower productivity compared to those that are sold off. In contrast, for nonbankrupt firms in the same industry, plants retained have significantly higher productivity than those sold. This result provides an alternative explanation as to why operating performance of emerging firms does not improve from prebankruptcy levels, namely that some firms have retained their least profitable assets. Further, in high-growth industries, the productivity of the assets sold increases under new ownership. This evidence is consistent with the efficient redeployment of assets to more productive uses.

A key insight of the Maksimovic and Phillips study is that industry conditions are an important determinant not just of the frequency of bankruptcy, but of economic decisions such as asset redeployment in bankruptcy. In contrast to higher-growth industries, in declining industries the productivity of plants in Chapter 11 and subsequent to emerging does not significantly differ from their industry counterparts. This finding remains even when controlling for the changing asset composition of bankrupt firms as they make decisions to retain, sell, or close plants.

Even if the change in asset composition can explain some firms' poor postbankruptcy operating performance, the question remains whether the reorganization plan for the remaining assets of the emerging firm is viable. Theoretically, another useful benchmark against which to assess postbankruptcy performance is the return that could have been earned by liquidating the firm's remaining assets and placing the proceeds in an alternative investment. This idea is examined by Alderson and Betker (1999) for a sample of 89 firms emerging from bankruptcy between 1983 and 1993 (62 of these firms—70 percent—emerged between 1990 and 1993). The authors of this study compute the annualized return earned by the reorganized firm, relative to the value that would have been received in liquidation. The annualized return is calculated by comparing the firm's estimated terminal value five years after emergence to an estimated liquidation value at emergence, and an excess return is computed as the difference between this measure and the annualized return on the S&P 500 index over the same period. Terminal value is estimated as the sum of net cash flows paid to any claim holders over the five-year postbankruptcy period (compounded by reinvesting in the S&P 500) plus the market value of the firm five years after emergence. The liquidation value at emergence is estimated as either the liquidation value presented with the plan of reorganization (a lower bound) or the plan's estimated market value for the firm at emergence.

While this approach directly addresses the key theoretical question as to whether the firm should have been allowed to reorganize, the difficulty in implementing this approach arises in the estimation of values. Liquidation values are likely to be understated, while estimated plan values suffer from biases in either direction (see Chapter 5). Terminal values can be calculated only for firms whose stock price is available following emergence, again biasing toward more successful companies. Still, Alderson and Betker estimate that firms on average neither underperform nor outperform following Chapter 11. In light of the potential sample biases, a useful interpretation of this study is that, based on cash flow returns, emerging firms at best perform as well as the market overall.

A final issue in evaluating whether firms return to profitability after Chapter 11 concerns the ownership and governance of the postbankruptcy firm. Hotchkiss and Mooradian (1997) find that the involvement of vulture investors, which has risen dramatically since the early 1990s (see Chapter 10), is strongly related to postbankruptcy success. Their study is based on a sample of 288 firms that defaulted on public debt between 1980 and 1993. The percentage of firms experiencing negative operating income in the year following bankruptcy is 31.9 percent for firms with no evidence of vulture involvement, versus 11.7 percent when a vulture has been involved in the restructuring.

Strikingly, when the vulture remains active in the governance of the firm post–Chapter 11, the percentage of firms experiencing operating problems drops to 8.1 percent. Improvements in performance relative to predefault levels are greater when a vulture joins the board, becomes the CEO or chairman, or gains control of the firm. When there is evidence of vulture involvement but the vulture is not subsequently active in the restructured company, performance appears no better than for those firms with no evidence of vulture involvement. Thus, the presence of these investors in the governance of the restructured firm is strongly related to postbankruptcy success for the sample studied. There have been a number of more recent cases where firms have been successfully returned to profitability under the control of distressed debt investors (see Chapter 10). As described earlier, Kmart produced tremendous returns for its shareholders based on operating gains after emerging from Chapter 11 under the control of Edward S. Lampert (ESL Investments). International Steel Group (ISG), formed in 2002 by investor Wilbur L. Ross, has put together a successful and profitable group of steel companies by purchasing steelmakers in Chapter 11, including LTV Corporation and Bethlehem Steel Corporation.

Ability to Meet Cash Flow Projections

In order for a plan of reorganization to be confirmed by the court, the debtor must show that the plan is feasible. To meet this requirement, many firms provide cash flow forecasts, generally prepared by management or their financial advisers, when the plan is submitted to creditors and the court. The ability to meet these projections provides another measure of postbankruptcy success.

Cash flow projections are typically provided in the firm's disclosure statement, as part of the effort to gain creditor approval of the reorganization plan. Although the court has reviewed and approved these statements, it can still be difficult for outsiders to assess the validity of projections. First, the quantity and quality of financial information produced for firms in Chapter 11 may be reduced relative to prebankruptcy levels. For example, security analysts have often reduced coverage of these firms, and some firms cease to report audited financial statements. Weiss and Wruck (1998) cite the lack of credible information as one of the reasons creditors were not able to identify the downward spiral of Eastern Airlines during its Chapter 11. Second, the various constituencies involved in the case, including management and various creditor groups, can have divergent interests; the cash flow forecasts and the values they imply can arise either from negotiations among these parties or from the group that largely controls the process.

Ex post comparisons of projected versus realized cash flows have been examined by several researchers, each of whom finds that on average firms fail to achieve their projections. In her study of postbankruptcy performance, Hotchkiss (1995) shows that projections are on average overly optimistic. For example, operating income is lower than projected for 75 percent of the 72 sample firms for which cash flow projections are available. However, there is a difference in the magnitude of the negative forecast error depending on who is in control of the firm when the projections are made: When prebankruptcy managers are still in office at the time the plan is submitted, the shortfall between projected and actual performance is significantly greater. If management is concerned with the firm's survival, they may need to convince creditors and the court that the firm value is high enough to justify reorganization rather than liquidation. A shareholder-oriented management might also overstate forecasts in order to justify giving a greater share of the reorganized stock to prepetition equity holders.

Further evidence demonstrating that firms on average are unable to meet cash flow projections is provided by McHugh, Michel, and Shaked (1998), who find that failures to meet projections tend to outnumber cases where projections are satisfied. Their analysis is based on a sample of firms completing a Chapter 11 reorganization between 1984 and 1994, but largely in the early 1990s, extending the time period examined by Hotchkiss. Betker, Ferris, and Lawless (1999) examine the quality of financial projections included in disclosure statements for a similar sample of 69 firms emerging between 1984 and 1994. By the second year following reorganization, the cumulative error for earnings before interest and taxes (EBIT) is more than 70 percent of its mean projected value. That is, the sum of the errors in forecasted EBIT for the first two years following reorganization is equivalent to 70 percent of the average annual EBIT forecast in the disclosure statement. By the fourth year, the mean percent cumulative error is nearly 180 percent of the average annual projected EBIT. They conclude that these forecasts have a systematic, optimistic, and inaccurate bias in favor of reorganization.

Incidence of Subsequent Distressed Restructurings

Studies of postbankruptcy performance also find a striking number of cases where the reorganized business needs to restructure again through a private workout or second bankruptcy. For example, Hotchkiss (1995) finds that 32 percent of her sample firms restructure again either through a private workout, a second bankruptcy, or an out-of-court liquidation. The group of firms in her sample that file twice (Chapter 22s) includes some large, well-known companies such as Continental Airlines. The reasons cited by management at the time of the second filing or restructuring are varied and often similar to those at the time of the first filing. While some firms claim they have emerged with too much debt, approximately half of these firms cite operating problems as the primary reason for the second filing, suggesting they had not made adequate corrective changes in corporate policy in the earlier restructuring. The high rate of subsequent failures occurred despite requirements under the Bankruptcy Code that, in order for a reorganization plan to be confirmed, the company must demonstrate that further reorganization is not likely to be needed.[3]

Several other studies find a similar rate of recidivism. Among the earliest, LoPucki and Whitford (1993), in their study of 43 large Chapter 11 cases (assets greater than $100 million at filing) confirmed by March 1988, find that 32 percent of the firms studied reenter Chapter 11 within four years. More recent statistics for the incidence of Chapter 22 filings show that this pattern has continued (see Chapter 1).

There are several potential explanations for this high rate of subsequent failures. One possibility is that firms have not sufficiently reduced their debt under the restructuring plan. Supporting this idea, Gilson (1997) finds that firms remain highly levered after emerging from Chapter 11, though leverage is not as high as for those firms that complete an out-of-court restructuring: The median ratio of long-term debt to the sum of long-term debt and common shareholders' equity is 0.47. Another potential explanation is that management is overly optimistic about the prospects for the reorganized firm. In addition to the evidence on failure to achieve cash flow forecasts, Hotchkiss (1995) shows that the continued involvement of the original management in the restructuring process is strongly associated with the likelihood of postbankruptcy failure. Finally, researchers have suggested that the pro-debtor orientation of the Bankruptcy Code and/or courts permits inefficient firms to reorganize; some commentators have in particular criticized the Southern District of New York and Delaware courts in this light. Combined, it is likely that all these factors play a significant role in understanding the frequency of failure for firms subsequent to Chapter 11.

As shown in Chapter 1, the high rate of Chapter 22 filings is not a new phenomenon, and has persisted since the early years of Chapter 11. A number of the repeat filers first entered bankruptcy in the wave of the early 1990s, and reentered in the more recent wave of 2000 and later. There have also been strong industry factors related to many second filings: For example,

---

[3]According to §1129(a)(11) of the code, the reorganization plan described by the disclosure statement must be feasible. The statute specifically requires the bankruptcy judge to find that approval of the reorganization plan "is not likely to be followed by the liquidation or the need for further financial reorganization of the debtor."

from among the 157 Chapter 22 or 33 filers traced by Hotchkiss, there are a number of airline, steel, and textile companies, clearly reflecting their difficult industry conditions. Of particular interest to critics of Chapter 11, however, is the fact that several of the repeat filers entered their second restructuring within a relatively short time period after exiting bankruptcy. For example, former Fortune 500 company Pillowtex (manufacturer of Fieldcrest sheets and towels) reorganized and emerged from its first bankruptcy in May 2002, then refiled for Chapter 11 in July 2003, and immediately announced it would liquidate. The firm quickly failed to meet the operating projections that the first bankruptcy's reorganization plan was based on, and it became clear that the reorganized firm was not viable. There has in fact been one "Chapter 44" case, though the initial filing occurred prior to the 1978 Bankruptcy Reform Act: TransTexas Gas Corporation emerged from bankruptcy in 1980, 1987, 2000, and 2003, and following its most recent restructuring continued to operate as a private company.

POSTBANKRUPTCY STOCK PERFORMANCE

While only a portion of firms entering Chapter 11 emerge as independent, publicly registered companies, an even smaller fraction of these firms successfully relist their stock following emergence. For example, of the 197 emerging firms studied by Hotchkiss (1995), only 60 percent had their stock relisted on the New York Stock Exchange (NYSE), the American Stock Exchange (Amex), or Nasdaq following emergence. She finds positive unadjusted but negative market-adjusted stock returns for the year following emergence from bankruptcy. Similar statistics are reported by Hotchkiss and Mooradian (2004) for a more recent sample of emerging firms. A large proportion of emerging firm stocks trade only on the Over-the-Counter (OTC) Bulletin Board or Pink Sheets, and so are not reflected in these studies. If the ability to relist the company's stock is a reflection of its postbankruptcy success, this might bias studies of postbankruptcy stock performance toward better-performing firms.

Still, studying the performance of this group of stocks is interesting for several reasons. Most generally, it allows us to test the efficiency of the market for stocks of emerging firms, and is of particular interest to potential investors. More specific to our evaluation of the Chapter 11 process, it allows us to assess the accuracy of valuations of firms as projected in reorganization plans (see Chapter 5), by comparing the plan-based valuation to the actual traded market value of the emerging firm. Further, creditors who receive stock as part of a reorganization plan but do not plan to hold the stock for the long term have a need to understand this market.

TABLE 3.4   Abnormal Returns for Postbankruptcy Stock Performance

Event Period	Average Cumulative Abnormal Return	Wealth Relative	Median Cumulative Abnormal Return
(1,2)	0.038***	1.038	0.000
	(0.059)		(0.184)
(1,200)	0.246*	1.249	0.063**
	(0.004)		(0.025)

Source: Taken with permission from *The Journal of Finance*, Blackwell Publishing, Aggarwal, Altman, and Eberhart, 1999, "The Equity Performance of Firms Emerging from Bankruptcy," Vol. 54, No. 5. *, **, and *** indicate significant difference from zero at the 1, 5, and 10 percent levels, respectively. The wealth relative is the average of the daily compounded actual rate of return divided by the daily compounded expected rate of return. *P*-values are shown in parentheses.

The only published academic study to date of the equity performance of firms emerging from bankruptcy is Aggarwal, Altman, and Eberhart (AAE, 1999).[4] Examining a sample of 131 firms emerging from Chapter 11 between 1980 and 1993, their key result is that there are large positive excess returns in the 200 days following emergence. A key issue in estimating these returns is the benchmark comparison or expected return from which to calculate abnormal performance. However, their results are robust with respect to different methods of estimating expected returns. A fairly comprehensive industry study by Lee (2004) of J. P. Morgan reaches similar conclusions to that of AAE.

Table 3.4 shows the most conservative estimates from AAE (1999), where the benchmark return is a sample of nonbankrupt firms matched on industry according to two-digit Standard Industrial Classification (SIC) code and on size (equity capitalization). Based on these estimates, the average cumulative abnormal return over the first 200 days following emergence is 24.6 percent (median is 6.3 percent). Using an alternative measure of expected returns, their study reports that the long-term cumulative abnormal return is as high as 138.8 percent. Overall, they conclude that

---

[4]Goyal, Kahl, and Torous (2003 working paper) study postdistress stock performance for a small sample (falling from 35 firms in the first year following bankruptcy to 25 after five years). They find that initially, mean abnormal returns are positive but insignificant. The returns fall and approximate zero (3.04 percent) after five years using a value-weighted reference portfolio, or become significantly negative (−50.93 percent) using a size and book-to-market reference portfolio.

while returns in the first two days following emergence are not clearly significant, there are large positive and significant abnormal returns in the year following emergence.

AAE further find that the positive excess returns are not concentrated in low-priced stocks, firms that change their line of business, or prepackaged bankruptcies. They also find some weak evidence that when institutional investors accept only equity in return for their claims, the long-term returns are higher. This result suggests the type of securities accepted by informed investors may reflect information on the stock's intrinsic value that is not fully reflected in the stock price upon emergence from Chapter 11. Finally, AAE find that there are significant positive excess returns in response to earnings announcements after emergence, indicating that the market is being surprised by the postemergence performance.

While the results of this study are clearly of interest to potential investors in these securities, the implications for evaluating Chapter 11 are less clear. Direct comparison with studies of operating performance such as Hotchkiss (1995) are difficult because only some firms emerge with stock trading on the NYSE, AMEX, or Nasdaq. Regardless, in contrast to studies showing poor operating performance, the stock performance indicates that firms do better than the market had expected at the time of emergence. These results may also be related to management incentives to issue relatively low firm valuations as part of the plan confirmation process (see Chapter 5 for a discussion of these biases).

IMPLICATIONS FOR CHAPTER 11

Critics of the Chapter 11 process have primarily argued that the current U.S. bankruptcy system is biased toward allowing inefficient firms to reorganize. These critics have focused either on specific provisions of the Bankruptcy Code that are characterized as pro-debtor (such as management's ability to remain in control and initially propose a plan of reorganization), or on the behavior of particular courts that have been characterized as too pro-debtor (for example, through extensions to exclusive periods to file a reorganization plan and other rulings). The high incidence of failures subsequent to leaving Chapter 11, described in detail in this chapter, is certainly consistent with this view. The cause of this poor performance, however, is more open to debate. Further, the research described here demonstrates that the governance structure of the emerging firm is importantly related to postbankruptcy performance. Purely from an investment perspective, the traded securities of certain firms emerging from the process present unusual opportunities.

CHAPTER 4

The Costs of Bankruptcy

The costs of financial distress and legal proceedings under the Bankruptcy Code are important for obvious practical reasons. For small firms, the costs involved in a reorganization can often exceed any remaining firm value, explaining why so many smaller cases end with the firm being dissolved. For larger firms, the dollar magnitude of professional fees has become a concern, particularly in many of the recent multibillion-dollar Chapter 11 cases. For example, fees paid to advisers in the Enron bankruptcy case are ultimately expected to exceed $1 billion.

Distress costs have also been recognized as an important determinant of the pricing of a firm's debt and of its capital structure. There has been some debate, however, as to how significant their impact might be. Haugen and Senbet (1978) were among the first to argue that bankruptcy costs should not be significant because claimants in financial distress should be able to negotiate outside of court without affecting the value of the underlying firm. More recent scholars, however, such as Jensen (1991) note that not only the conflicts between creditor groups, but also the influence of certain bankruptcy court decisions have had a negative impact on firms' ability to renegotiate their claims out of court. When a firm is unable to complete an out-of-court reorganization, it may be unable to avoid a more costly court-supervised bankruptcy proceeding. Regardless, it is clear that if distress costs are in fact significant, the optimal leverage for a company may be lower. A number of researchers discuss the bankruptcy cost issue within the framework of capital structure and cost of capital assessment (see Chapter 6).

The costs of financial distress are typically classified as either direct or indirect. Direct costs include out-of-pocket expenses for lawyers, accountants, restructuring advisers, turnaround specialists, expert witnesses, and other professionals. Indirect costs include a wide range of unobservable opportunity costs. For example, many firms suffer from lost sales and profits caused by customers choosing not to deal with a firm that may enter bankruptcy. They may also suffer from increased costs of doing business, such as higher debt costs or poorer terms with suppliers while in a financially vulnerable position. Indirect costs also include the loss of key employees, or lost opportunities due to management's diversion from running the business.

While direct costs are relatively easy to identify, it has not been easy for researchers to obtain the information needed to study these costs in a systematic way. The various estimates that have been constructed over time are described in this chapter. Indirect costs are not directly observable, but there have also been several recent studies that provide useful estimates of their potential magnitude and determinants. (See Table 4.1.)

DIRECT COSTS

The difficulty in measuring direct costs is that there is no centralized source listing all firms filing for bankruptcy (with the notable exception of the Administrative Office of the U.S. Courts and Executive Office for the U.S. Trustees, which does not make information publicly available), let alone information on costs in bankruptcy cases. The only way to compile this information has been to obtain documents from individual federal bankruptcy courts scattered throughout the country. Studies of direct costs therefore have been based on samplings of cases, often for larger firms, filed in one or more jurisdictions. A listing of these studies and summaries of their findings are presented in Table 4.1.

One of the earliest attempts to measure direct costs is by Warner (1977). He examines payments for legal fees, professional services, trustees' fees, and filing fees for 11 bankrupt railroads filing under Section 77 of the Bankruptcy Act between 1933 and 1955. These cases took on average 13 years to settle, and the direct costs are estimated to average 4 percent of the market value of the firm one year prior to default.

More recently, Weiss (1990) obtained documents from seven bankruptcy courts, including the Southern District of New York. Based on his examination of 37 cases between 1980 and 1986, all of which were NYSE or AMEX firms, he estimates that direct costs of bankruptcy average 3.1 percent of the book value of debt plus the market value of equity at the fiscal year-end prior to the bankruptcy filing, with a range from 1 percent to 6.6 percent. Weiss interprets these figures as relatively low direct costs, which would be expected to have little or no impact on the pricing of claims prior to bankruptcy.

Several other studies report mean direct costs estimates in the range of Weiss's study. These include Ang, Chua, and McConnell (1982) (7.5

TABLE 4.1 Estimates of Direct and Indirect Costs of Distress

Study	Sample Used to Calculate Costs	Time Period	Estimated Costs
Direct Costs			
Altman (1984)	19 Chapter 11 cases; mean assets $110 million before filing	1974–1978	Mean 4% (median 1.7%) of firm value just prior to bankruptcy for 12 retailers; 9.8% (6.4%) for 7 industrial firms
Ang, Chua, & McConnell (1982)	86 liquidations, Western District of Oklahoma; estimated mean prebankruptcy assets of $615,516	1963–1979	Mean 7.5% (median 1.7%) of total liquidating value of assets
Betker (1997)	75 traditional Chapter 11 cases; 48 prepackaged Chapter 11 cases; 29 exchange offers; mean assets FYE before restructuring $675 million	1986–1993	Prepackaged bankruptcies—mean 2.85% (median 2.38%) of prebankruptcy total assets; traditional Chapter 11s—mean 3.93% (median 3.37%); exchange offers—2.51% (1.98%)
Bris, Welch, & Zhu (2004)	Over 300 Arizona and SDNY Chapter 11 (mean prebankruptcy assets $19.8 million) and Chapter 7 cases (mean prebankruptcy assets $501,866)	1995–2001	Chapter 7: mean 8.1%, median 2.5% of prebankruptcy assets Chapter 11: mean 9.5%, median 2%
Gilson, John, & Lang (1990)	18 exchange offers (from a sample of 169 distressed firm restructurings)	1978–1987	0.65% average offer costs as a percentage of book value of assets (max 3.4%)
Lawless & Ferris (1997)	98 Chapter 7 cases from 6 bankruptcy courts; median total assets $107,603	1991–1995	Average 6.1% of total assets at filing (median 1.1%)
LoPucki & Doherty (2004)	48 Delaware & SDNY Chapter 11 cases; mean assets at filing $480 million	1998–2002	Mean professional fees equal 1.4% of assets at beginning of case

(Continued)

95

TABLE 4.1 *(Continued)*

Study	Sample Used to Calculate Costs	Time Period	Estimated Costs
Lubben (2000)	22 Chapter 11 cases; median assets $50 million	1994	Cost of professional fees in Chapter 11 averages 1.8% (median 0.9%) of total assets at beginning of case; 2.5% excluding prepacks
Tashjian, Lease, & McConnell (1996)	39 prepackaged Chapter 11 cases; mean book value assets FYE before filing $570 million	1986–1993	Mean 1.85%, median 1.45% of book value of assets at fiscal year-end preceding filing
Warner (1977)	11 bankrupt railroads; estimated mean market value $50 million at filing	1933–1955	Mean 4% of market value of firm one year prior to default
Weiss (1990)	37 Chapter 11 cases from 7 bankruptcy courts; average total assets before filing $230 million	1980–1986	Mean 3.1% (median 2.6%) of firm value prior to filing
Indirect Costs			
Altman (1984)	19 Chapter 11 cases	1974–1978	10.5% of firm value measured just prior to bankruptcy
Andrade & Kaplan (1998)	31 highly leveraged transactions that subsequently became distressed	1987–1992	10% to 20% of firm value
Maksimovic & Phillips (1998)	302 Chapter 11 cases (owning 1,195 plants)	1978–1989	
Opler & Titman (1994)	Distressed industries	1974–1990	Financial distress costs are positive and significant
Pulvino (1999)	27 U.S. airlines, 8 of which are in Chapter 7 or 11	1978–1992	Prices received for sales of used aircraft by bankrupt airlines are lower than prices received by distressed but nonbankrupt firms

percent of total liquidating value); Altman (1984) (6.1 percent of firm value for his full sample); and Betker (1997) (3.93 percent of prebankruptcy total assets for nonprepackaged bankruptcies). Finally, two recent studies report professional fees for relatively large public companies in Chapter 11. Lubben (2000) reports, for 22 firms filing in 1994, that the cost of professional fees in Chapter 11 is 1.8 percent of the distressed firm's total assets, with some cases reaching 5 percent. LoPucki and Doherty (2004) find professional fees equal to 1.4 percent of debtor's total assets at the beginning of the bankruptcy case for 48 Delaware and New York cases. In comparison to the earlier studies, their findings suggest that there may be substantial fixed costs associated with the bankruptcy process, and therefore economies of scale with respect to bankruptcy costs.

One notable study examining bankruptcy costs is Bris, Welch, and Zhu (2004). They examine over 300 cases from two bankruptcy courts, Arizona and the Southern District of New York. These courts were selected because electronic documents are available dating back to 1995. What distinguishes their study from prior research, however, is that they look at both Chapter 7 and Chapter 11 cases. Further, in contrast to most of the previous studies, which look exclusively at large public companies, their study considers primarily smaller nonpublic firms. For Chapter 7 cases, direct bankruptcy expenses are estimated to have a mean of 8.1 percent of prebankruptcy assets (median of 2.5 percent). However, bankruptcy professionals (attorneys, accountants, and trustees) regularly end up with most of the postbankruptcy firm value in Chapter 7 cases. Based on their estimates of postbankruptcy remaining value, in 68 percent of the Chapter 7 cases the bankruptcy fees "ate" the entire estate. This figure is in line with statistics reported by the U.S. Trustee's office, which also show that after paying these expenses, many Chapter 7 cases have no remaining distributable value. The only other published study to consider smaller Chapter 7 cases is Lawless and Ferris (1997), who find fees in these cases average 6.1 percent of total assets. For Chapter 11 cases, Bris et al. find that direct costs have a mean of 9.5 percent of prebankruptcy assets (median 2 percent).

Overall, several important facts emerge from these studies. First, there is likely to be an important scale effect. While much of the research on this question focuses on larger public companies, smaller firms may be unable to survive the reorganization process given the magnitude of fees relative to their assets. Second, the dollar amount of fees for large public companies can be tremendous, even though as a percentage of assets these fees are not large. Still, even when the percentage direct costs are low, indirect costs of financial distress may be significant. Third, as data becomes available in electronic form, our ability to measure and monitor these costs improves.

Before turning to studies of indirect costs, another important question is how direct costs of a formal bankruptcy proceeding compare to an out-of-court restructuring. Gilson, John, and Lang (1990) provide estimates of direct costs for a sample of firms completing exchange offers for distressed public debt, and find that these expenses are quite low (0.65 percent of assets). Betker (1997), however, reports costs averaging 2.51 percent for exchange offers. Interestingly, the development of prepackaged bankruptcies has given firms the ability to negotiate a Chapter 11 plan prior to filing, allowing firms to exit bankruptcy within months rather than years. A prepackaged bankruptcy calls for a firm to negotiate its reorganization plan and possibly solicit votes on the plan prior to filing a bankruptcy petition. The firm then simultaneously files its plan and its Chapter 11 petition. This allows firms to take advantage of voting rules and other provisions of the Bankruptcy Code, as well as tax advantages relative to an out-of-court restructuring, without incurring a lengthy and expensive stay in Chapter 11. In many ways, a prepackaged bankruptcy can be viewed as a hybrid of a more traditional Chapter 11 and an out-of-court restructuring. Crystal Oil (1986) and Southland (1991) are among the earliest examples of this type of bankruptcy. Betker finds that direct costs average 2.85 percent of prebankruptcy total assets for prepackaged bankruptcies; his figure is similar to traditional Chapter 11 cases, but includes restructuring expenses incurred prior to filing. Tashjian, Lease, and McConnell (1996) find that direct costs average 1.85 percent of the book value of assets at the fiscal year-end preceding Chapter 11, and 1.65 percent for the subsample of cases that are prevoted.

The relatively low direct costs of exchange offers, as well as the growth of the use of prepackaged bankruptcies, suggests that cost savings can be significant for firms that successfully restructure without entering a more traditional Chapter 11 case. Direct costs are also likely to increase with the length of time spent in bankruptcy. Franks and Torous (1989) report the time in bankruptcy for a sample of 30 firms entering Chapter 11 or its predecessor between 1970 and 1983. They find that the average time in bankruptcy is 3.7 years, but this length is largely due to several railroad bankruptcy proceedings. More recent estimates for nonprepackaged bankruptcies are typically close to two years; Weiss (1990) reports an average of 30 months in Chapter 11; Gilson et al. (1990) report an average of 20.4 months. Tashjian, Lease, and McConnell (1996) show that the average time in Chapter 11 for prepackaged bankruptcies is only 3.3 months, and is even shorter (1.9 months) when the plan has been voted on prior to filing. The short stay in Chapter 11 is associated with lower direct costs during the Chapter 11 period.

INDIRECT COSTS

In contrast to direct costs, indirect costs are not directly observable and are therefore difficult to specify and empirically measure. However, researchers have developed several different approaches used to infer the likely magnitude of these costs. The key measurement problem is that we cannot distinguish whether the poor performance of a firm is caused by the financial distress itself (and therefore is an indirect cost), or whether it is caused by the same economic factors that pushed the firm into financial distress in the first place. These studies therefore attempt to identify whether firm performance reflects the costs of financial distress, the costs of economic distress, or an interaction of the two.

Altman (1984) was the first to provide a proxy methodology for measuring indirect costs of bankruptcy. For a sample of firms entering Chapter 11, he compares expected profits to actual profits for the three years prior to bankruptcy (years –3 to –1); expected profits are based either on a comparison of each firm's sales and profit margin to industry levels prior to year –3, or on security analyst estimates. He finds that indirect costs average 10.5 percent of firm value measured just prior to bankruptcy. The combined direct and indirect costs average 16.7 percent of firm value, indicating that total bankruptcy costs are not trivial.

Subsequent to Altman's initial work, several other studies have attempted to isolate indirect distress costs, each using quite different methodologies and data sets. Their key insight is to recognize that it is important to separate the effects of financial versus economic distress. For example, while Altman documents large declines in profitability, he cannot distinguish them from negative operating shocks.

Andrade and Kaplan (1998), using methodology similar to that of Kaplan (1989 and 1994), examine 31 firms that have become distressed subsequent to a management buyout or leveraged recapitalization between 1980 and 1989. At the onset of distress, having recently completed a highly leveraged transaction, the firms in their sample are largely financially distressed but not economically distressed. Thus, their research design provides an opportunity to isolate the costs of pure financial distress.[1] Based on changes in firm value over time, they estimate the net costs of

---

[1]Cutler and Summers (1988) also attempt to isolate the effects of financial conflict from economic distress. They document significant wealth losses (over $3 billion) associated with the Texaco-Pennzoil litigation between 1985 and 1987. Although much of the costs they estimate are not directly related to Texaco's bankruptcy case, they do show that financial conflict can have substantial effects on productivity.

financial distress to be 10 to 20 percent of firm value; for firms that do not also experience an adverse economic shock, costs of financial distress are negligible. In addition, they find that distress costs are concentrated in the period after the firm becomes distressed, but before it enters Chapter 11, suggesting it is not Chapter 11 itself that contributes to indirect costs. Andrade and Kaplan also examine qualitative aspects of the behavior of distressed firms. A number of firms are forced to cut capital expenditures substantially, sell assets at depressed prices, or delay restructuring or filing for Chapter 11 in a way that appears to be costly. This evidence is consistent with Pulvino (1998 and 1999), who studies sales of aircraft by distressed versus nondistressed airlines. Pulvino finds that financially constrained airlines receive lower prices than their unconstrained rivals when selling used aircraft. In contrast to Andrade and Kaplan, however, he further finds that for airlines in either Chapter 7 or Chapter 11, the prices the bankrupt airlines receive for their used aircraft are generally lower than prices received by distressed but nonbankrupt firms.

While these studies each indicate that financial distress is costly, they differ in their conclusions as to how bankruptcy status, itself, influences these costs. The idea that financial distress, and not Chapter 11 per se, leads to a loss in value is further supported by Maksimovic and Phillips (1998). These authors use plant-level data, obtained from the U.S. Census Bureau, to examine the productivity and plant closure decisions of bankrupt firms. They find that Chapter 11 status is much less important than industry conditions in explaining the productivity, asset sales, and closure conditions of Chapter 11 bankrupt firms. In declining industries, the productivity of plants in Chapter 11 bankruptcy and subsequent to emerging does not significantly differ from that of their industry counterparts, nor does it decline during Chapter 11. This suggests that few real economic costs are attributable to Chapter 11 itself and that bankruptcy status is not important to indirect costs.

Opler and Titman (1994) also recognize the causality problem in studies that attempt to relate performance declines and financial distress. Their approach is to identify depressed industries that have experienced economic distress, based on negative industry sales growth and median stock returns below –30 percent. Within those industries, they investigate whether firms that are highly levered prior to the onset of the distressed period fare differently than their more conservatively financed counterparts. Their hypothesis is that if financial distress is costly, the more highly leveraged firms will have the greatest operating difficulties in a downturn. They find that highly leveraged firms lose market share and experience lower operating profits than their less-leveraged competitors. Although they do not provide specific estimates of the level of indirect costs, their tests minimize the reverse causality problem which made it difficult to interpret some of the previous work. They interpret their findings as being consistent with the view that the indirect costs of financial distress are significant and positive.

IMPLICATIONS OF RESEARCH ON BANKRUPTCY COSTS

In sum, this work suggests that while direct costs of bankruptcy are only a small percentage of firm value for large public companies, for smaller firms the costs may be prohibitive and lead to liquidation. Further, research shows that even for larger firms, the indirect costs of distress can be significant. It is also important to consider that indirect costs are not limited to firms that actually default or enter Chapter 11. At the same time, studies such as Andrade and Kaplan (1998) are also consistent with the idea there can be benefits to reaching financial distress, in that it can improve firm value by forcing managers to make difficult, value-maximizing choices that they would otherwise avoid (Jensen 1989).

Service	Investment Bankers	Crisis Managers	Accountants
M&A	●	◗	○
Capital Raising	●	◗	○
Valuation	●	◗	○
Debt Capacity/Capital Structuring	●	◗	○
Negotiation with Creditors	●	◐	○
Financial Modeling	●	◕	◕
Liquidation Analysis	●	◐	●
Bankruptcy Court Testimony	●	◐	◗
Strategic Business Analysis	◐	●	◗
Analysis of Financial Controls	○	●	●
Day-to-Day Business Analysis	○	●	◗
Audits	○	○	●
Pension Issues	○	○	●
Financial Reporting	○	○	●
SEC and Bankruptcy Court Operate Plants or Business	○	◔	○
Hire, Fire, or Manage Employees	○	●	○
Sell Company's Goods or Services/Collect Receivables	○	◗	○

FIGURE 4.1 Roles of Professionals in Chapter 11 Cases
Source: Lazard.

The recent trend toward increasing size and complexity of restructuring companies has contributed to the growth in bankruptcy costs. In addition to Enron, high-profile Chapter 11 cases in which fees have exceeded $100 million include WorldCom ($657 million), Pacific Gas & Electric ($462.5 million), LTV Corporation ($237 million), Global Crossing ($174 million), and Kmart ($135 million).[2] As the level of complexity rises, debtors have often hired increased numbers of professionals with specific skills. To provide an understanding of the need for these professionals in complex cases, Figure 4.1 outlines their typical roles in Chapter 11 cases. The role of financial advisers, including investment bankers in particular, has risen in recent years, especially as many large cases have involved sales of large portions of firms' assets.

Difficulties in restructuring complicated capital structures have also been evident from many recent Chapter 11 cases, and have contributed to these rising costs. For example, a number of cases have involved firms with multiple bank groups and bond issues at different levels in the capital structure, increasing the likelihood of conflicts between claimants. The size of creditor groups may render reaching a consensus difficult. Conflicts also occur between prebankruptcy and more recent entrants into the case, such as vulture investors, who may have purchased claims at prices substantially below par (see Chapter 8). When conflicts between claimants lead to increased difficulty in negotiating a restructuring, both direct and indirect costs of distress are likely to increase.

---

[2]*BusinessWeek*, March 25, 2005.

CHAPTER 5

Distressed Firm Valuation

The goal of Chapter 11 bankruptcy is to provide firms with an opportunity to reorganize when the going-concern value of the firm is greater than the value that would be realized in a liquidation. The reorganization plan must be premised on an estimate of value for the restructured firm. Thus, valuation becomes a central issue in the restructuring process. The firm's estimated value determines the size of the pie to be divided among prebankruptcy claimants, and drives projected payouts and recoveries. It is also critical in determining the feasibility of the plan and in determining an appropriate capital structure for the reorganized firm.

Bankruptcy in the United States is an administrative process, and the factors that lead to a reliable estimate of value in a market process are sometimes absent in bankruptcy. The structure of Chapter 11, under which incumbent management maintains significant control of the process, may discourage an active market for control of the assets of the bankrupt firm. Oversight from the capital markets is reduced because management has access to debtor-in-possession financing. The securities of bankrupt firms often trade infrequently (Hotchkiss and Mooradian 1997). Perhaps as a result, there is often limited analyst coverage. This absence of market forces makes valuation more complex and sometimes less precise.

The magnitude of valuation disputes that arise in Chapter 11 cases is striking. One well-known example is the case of National Gypsum Company, which filed for Chapter 11 in 1990. While the debtor's plan assumed an enterprise value of $200 million, junior creditors offered a plan based on a value well over $1 billion. When the firm emerged from bankruptcy, its market value was closer to $500 million, and the firm quickly experienced operating performance well exceeding its projections. Several additional examples demonstrating how the parties in a bankruptcy renegotiation can have vastly different estimates of value are described in Table 5.1. The outcome of these disputes has important consequences for

TABLE 5.1 Examples of Valuation Disagreements in Chapter 11

Company	Chapter 11 Date	Valuations
Storage Technology	October 1984	Debtor valued the firm between $500 and $600 million; creditors argued the firm was worth only about $250 million.
National Gypsum	October 1990	Debtor's plan valued the firm at $200 million; junior bondholders' competing plan assumed firm value over $1 billion.
E-II Holdings	July 1992	Debtor's plan valued the company at $824 million; Icahn, who owned large stakes in junior bonds, proposed competing plan valuing the firm at $1,345 million.
Exide Technologies	April 2002	Debtor's plan was based on a value of $950 to $1,050 million; unsecured creditors committee estimated value at $1.5 to $1.7 billion.
Mirant	July 2003	Debtor valued the firm between $7.7 and $9 billion; shareholders committee argued value was closer to $13 billion, alleging that earlier merger discussions by creditors showed the stand-alone value of the firm to be that amount.
WCI Steel Corporation	September 2003	Debtor valued the firm between $190 and $250 million. WCI note holders advanced a firm value between $300 and $350 million.

who will emerge holding the stock and possibly controlling the reorganized firm.

Since the intrinsic or true value of the firm is unobservable, we must rely on various methodologies that have been accepted as useful approaches to estimating value. An overview of these methods is provided in this chapter. We further examine evidence on the performance of these valuation models, and examine how estimates of value can be used strategically as part of the bankruptcy negotiation process.

VALUATION METHODOLOGIES

Unlike much of security analysis for nondistressed firms, the objective of valuation analysis in a distressed setting is typically not to value the equity, but rather to value the enterprise as a whole. The approaches described here are also used in mergers and acquisitions (M&A) and other corporate restructuring practices, but we emphasize concerns that are particular to distressed companies.

The two widely used approaches to valuation are relative valuation models (comparable company and comparable transactions value), where value is derived from the pricing of comparable assets, and discounted cash flow models.[1] For clarity in our discussion, we refer to the firm being valued as the target firm.

Relative Valuation Models: Comparable Companies and Comparable Transactions

The "comparable company" approach, sometimes also referred to as a "trading multiples" valuation, estimates the value of the target firm by applying the valuation multiples of peer firms to the target. The three steps involved are to (1) identify peer or comparable publicly traded firms, (2) observe how the comparable firms are valued by the market, and (3) apply that valuation to the target firm.

The most critical aspect of this analysis is the definition of a set of comparable companies. Selecting comparables, however, requires some judgment by the analyst. Fundamentally, comparable firms should match the target in terms of risk and growth prospects. A "pure play" peer firm would be an ideal comparable, but in most cases this exact match does not exist. Typically an industry screen, based for example on Standard Industrial Classification (SIC) codes, produces a set of possible comparable companies. From this set, comparability can be determined by comparing characteristics such as size, mix of businesses, bankruptcy status, profitability, leverage, cost structure, and so on. When the set of comparables has been defined, it is then useful to compare various financial performance measures for the comparable firms and target to understand both the degree of variability in these measures across the comparable firms as well as how well the target firm fits within this group. If the firms are in fact comparable, this analysis will show that financial ratios measuring performance, such as profitability ratios or asset utilization (turnover) ratios, should be similar.

---

[1]Overviews of valuation methodologies for bankrupt firms are also provided by Pantaleo and Ridings (2005) and Scarberry, Klee, Newton, and Nickles (1996).

Having defined the set of comparable companies, since each of the comparables is publicly traded, we can observe their current market value of equity. Our focus, however, is on total enterprise value (TEV) rather than equity value, where TEV is defined as the market value of equity plus total debt and preferred stock less cash and cash equivalents. The ratio of TEV to a particular cash flow or balance sheet measure for the firm yields a valuation multiple. For example, the ratio of TEV to earnings before interest, taxes, depreciation, and amortization (EBITDA) is the most commonly used metric when this type of analysis is used for restructuring companies, since EBITDA is likely to be highly correlated with firm value. Other multiples such as TEV/EBIT, TEV/revenues, or TEV/(EBITDA minus capital expenditures) are possible. Summary measures for these multiples (average, median, high, low) are typically used to describe the valuation multiples.

Finally, the valuation multiples obtained from the comparables are applied to produce an estimated range of values for the target firm. For example, one estimate of total enterprise value would be equal to the target EBITDA times the average TEV/EBITDA of the comparables. Applying multiples of several measures (such as EBITDA and revenues) or applying the range of multiples observed (high and low) produces a range of estimated values for the target. The application of the multiples is relatively straightforward if the target firm appears similar to the average comparable firm, or at least fits within the range of comparables. Additional subjective adjustments based on a belief that the comparables are fundamentally different from the target firm, however, can be difficult to support. As described by one of the leading valuation textbooks (Damodaran 1996, p. 304):

> *Even when a legitimate group of comparable firms can be constructed, differences will continue to persist in fundamentals between the firm being valued and this group. Adjusting for differences subjectively does not provide a satisfactory solution to this problem.*

Beyond potential difficulties in agreeing on comparables, one needs to be careful in how multiples are applied to firms undergoing a reorganization such as in Chapter 11. The usefulness of historical data for the target firm is limited when the firm undergoes significant asset restructuring. Therefore, it is typically more appropriate to apply the multiple to forecasted performance for the reorganized firm, using the cash flow forecasts provided to support the plan of reorganization. Further, cash flows immediately following the reorganization may not yet reflect normalized operations. For example, EBITDA could be temporarily low when a firm first emerges from bankruptcy, and applying a valuation multiple to this depressed number would understate the firm's long-run growth prospects. In this case, the multiple should be applied to the first projected year that represents normalized operations, though the future forecasted operating measure needs to be discounted back to present value. Using data from security analysts, projected performance for the comparables can be used to determine the valuation multiples. When forecasts for the comparables are not available, a multiple based on historical performance can still be used if it is valid to assume that the multiples would not significantly change over this time period.

An example of this analysis is given in Table 5.2 for WCI Steel Corporation, which filed for Chapter 11 in September 2003. The example is derived from a more detailed analysis filed with the court by the financial adviser to the WCI note holders.[2] The table shows multiples based on the last 12 months (LTM) as well as projected EBITDA. Since the historical (LTM) performance is based on WCI's time in bankruptcy, this produces a lower valuation ($104 million), which does not reflect the performance projected for the reorganized company. Using the comparables to determine median multiples of projected EBITDA produces a more realistic assessment of value of $292 million to $305 million for WCI.

The comparable company approach is widely used and relatively easy to implement. It is most useful when a large number of comparable firms trade in financial markets, and the market is, on average, pricing these firms correctly. Any relative valuation approach, however, will build in errors (overvaluation or undervaluation) that the market itself might be making in valuing these types of firms.

A second relative valuation model that is widely accepted is the "comparable M&A transaction" approach. The approach and its implementation are very similar to the comparable company approach, except the prices paid in recent acquisitions of companies comparable to the target are used to determine the valuation multiple. The greatest limitation to the comparable transaction approach is whether there have in fact been acquisitions of comparable firms recently enough under similar market conditions. In addition, the acquisition price paid for a comparable will typically reflect a control premium, leading to a somewhat higher estimate of value.

In using this analysis to determine the value of a firm emerging from bankruptcy, the comparable firm should not be a firm purchased in Chapter 11. Hotchkiss and Mooradian (1998) and Pulvino (1999) show that purchases of assets of firms in Chapter 11 typically occur at a discount to

---

[2]This information was filed with the bankruptcy court because there was in fact a disagreement over the value. We use this example only to illustrate the methodology, and do not comment on the choice of comparables, the validity of cash flow forecasts, or other factors affecting conclusions about value.

TABLE 5.2 WCI Steel Corporation—Comparable Company Analysis Based on EBITDA Multiple (*$Millions*)

Comparable Company	Market Value of Equity[a]	TEV	LTM EBITDA	2004P[b] EBITDA	2005P[b] EBITDA	LTM EBITDA Multiple	2004P EBITDA Multiple	2005P EBITDA Multiple
AK Steel Holding Corp.	$ 649	$ 1,643	$ 147	$ 335	$ 330	11.2x	4.9x	5.0x
Arcelor[c]	8,541	12,913	2,731	3,394	3,516	4.7x	3.8x	3.7x
Corus Group PLC[d]	1,829	2,804	305	589	665	9.2x	4.8x	4.2x
Dofasco, Inc.[e]	2,978	2,971	623	817	789	4.8x	3.6x	3.8x
International Steel Group	2,978	3,491	368	712	781	9.5x	4.9x	4.5x
Nucor Corporation	6,448	6,996	1,035	1,913	1,279	6.8x	3.7x	5.5x
Steel Dynamics, Inc.	1,514	2,045	297	603	429	6.9x	3.4x	4.8x
U.S. Steel	4,068	5,386	726	1,414	1,423	7.4x	3.8x	3.8x
Mean						7.6x	4.1x	4.4x
Median						7.2x	3.8x	4.3x
Low						4.7x	3.4x	3.7x
High						11.2x	4.9x	5.5x

	WCI Steel	Median Multiple	Implied Value Range
LTM EBITDA	15	7.2x	$104
2004P EBITDA	80	3.8x	$305
2005P EBITDA	67	4.3x	$292

[a]Equity Market Cap as of August 11, 2004.
[b]2004 and 2005 estimates are mean estimates from IBES Analysts' Earnings Estimates.
[c]Amounts in euros.
[d]Amounts in British pounds.
[e]Amounts in Canadian dollars.
Source: Based on analysis of CIBC World Markets, 8/16/2004 Valuation Report Update, as filed with the U.S. Bankruptcy Court, Northern District of Ohio. This example solely for illustration of methodology. Two additional comparables with incomplete data are excluded.

prices paid for similar nonbankrupt targets. This may limit the set of available comparables because, especially in the most recent wave of bankruptcies, there is often a large number of filings within the same industry, and sales of assets in bankruptcy have recently increased in frequency.

Discounted Cash Flow Methods

Discounted cash flow (DCF) is a forward-looking approach that estimates firm value as the discounted value of expected future cash flows. As such, it is sensitive to a number of assumptions used to derive the cash flows or discount rate. In contrast to the relative valuation models, however, this approach requires that the analyst be explicit about these important assumptions. DCF methods are considered by some to be the most useful measure of intrinsic value (Damodaran 2002).

The total enterprise value can be estimated from a DCF model as:

DCF value = Present value of cash flows during projection period
+ Present value of terminal value

This method requires detailed projections of the future operating performance of the reorganized company. The terminal value captures the value of the firm at the end of the projection period, and represents the value of all cash flows that would occur subsequent to the projection period.

The two important aspects of the DCF model are therefore the calculation of cash flows to be discounted, and the determination of a discount rate. The most commonly used DCF model is a free cash flow (FCF) approach. Here, the free cash flows are the total after-tax cash flows generated by the firm that are available to all providers of the company's capital, both creditors and shareholders. These cash flows are discounted at a rate that reflects all investors' (both debt and equity) opportunity cost for investing in assets of comparable risk, known as the weighted average cost of capital (WACC). The most important aspects of this approach, which parallels that taught in most business schools, are reviewed in this chapter.

There are several issues specific to valuation of firms in financial distress or bankruptcy that lead us to suggest a second DCF method that is based on an approach known as the adjusted present value (APV) method. The APV method is often easier to implement than the free cash flow approach when the firm's capital structure changes significantly during the forecast period, and is better suited for the complicated tax situations of firms in a distressed restructuring. Gilson, Hotchkiss, and Ruback (2000) implement this type of model for a sample of 63 companies emerging from Chapter 11 between 1984 and 1993. The key advantages of this alternative approach are also described in this chapter.

Free Cash Flow Valuation   Free cash flow (FCF) is defined as the sum of the cash flows generated by a firm that are available to all providers of capital, including common stockholders, bondholders, and preferred stockholders, and is calculated as:

$$
\begin{aligned}
\text{FCF} = {}& \text{EBIT}(1 - \text{Tax rate}) \\
& + \text{Depreciation and other noncash charges} \\
& - \text{Capital expenditures} \\
& - \Delta \text{ Net working capital}
\end{aligned}
$$

FCF excludes cash flow from nonoperating assets, which are generally valued separately. It can be thought of as the after-tax cash flow that would be available to the firm's shareholders if the firm had no debt. Free cash flow is before financing and therefore not affected by the company's financial structure. In other words, the tax benefits from the deductibility of interest on debt and other tax shields are not specifically included in the cash flows themselves, and tax payments are estimated as projected EBIT times the firm's marginal tax rate. While financial structure does not enter the cash flow calculation, it does affect the discount rate and therefore the estimated value.

The discount rate should reflect the rate of return required on assets of comparable risk. For free cash flows, which are flows to all providers of capital, the appropriate rate is a blend of the required rates of return on debt and equity, weighted by the contribution of those sources of capital to the firm's total market value. The resulting weighted average cost of capital is therefore:

$$
\text{WACC} = r_d(1-t) \times \frac{D}{V} + r_e \times \frac{E}{V}
$$

where r_d = expected yield on the firm's debt after the restructuring
t = marginal tax rate of the reorganized firm
D/V = proportion of market value of the reorganized firm financed with debt
r_e = cost of equity capital
E/V = proportion of market value of the reorganized firm financed with equity

A common approach to estimate the cost of equity capital, r_e, is to use the capital asset pricing model (CAPM):

$$
r_e = r_f + \beta_e \times (r_m - r_f)
$$

where r_f is the risk-free rate, β_e is the firm's equity beta, and $(r_m - r_f)$ is the market risk premium. Estimates of the market risk premium are available from published sources that provide data comparing returns on market indexes to those of Treasury securities over long historical periods.[3] Current Treasury bond yields are used for the risk-free rate.

To measure systematic or marketwide risk in nondistressed settings, an equity beta (β_e) is typically estimated using the firm's historical stock returns. In the case of bankrupt companies, such betas are generally not meaningful. Historical stock returns are generally negative as the debtor heads into financial distress, and they bear little resemblance to the returns that stockholders expect from a successfully reorganized debtor. Bankrupt firms also undergo substantial asset restructuring, making historical performance less relevant. Finally, these firms often do not have traded stock. The best alternative therefore is to use comparables, whose betas can be calculated from historical data or obtained from a number of public data providers. The equity beta obtained from comparables must be adjusted for differences in financial leverage between the comparables and target firm.[4]

An example of the WACC calculation is given in Table 5.3 for WCI Steel Corporation. The beta is estimated from comparables, and adjusted for the leverage of reorganized WCI (which is assumed in this example to be a debt-equity ratio of 1). This analysis produces a WACC of 12.3 percent for WCI.

The last important input to the free cash flow model is the calculation of terminal value. Two approaches are commonly used. The first is to determine the terminal value using a comparable company approach, for example applying a multiple of EBITDA to the projected cash flow immediately following the projection period (year $T + 1$ of a T-year cash flow projection period). The cash flow used in the terminal value should

---

[3]Ibbotson and Associates provides such estimates. Several recent academic studies suggest, however, that historical estimates of the equity risk premium overstate the equity risk premium that investors will require in the future; see Fama and French (2002).

[4]The equity beta is also known as the levered beta. The relationship between the levered and unlevered beta is given as:

$$\beta_{\text{Levered}} = \beta_{\text{Unlevered}} \times \left[1 + (1 - t)\frac{D}{E}\right]$$

where D and E are the market values of debt and equity and β_{Levered} is the average equity beta for the comparables. The unlevered beta for the comparables is a proxy for the unlevered beta of the target firm, and is then "relevered" at the expected D/E ratio for the reorganized firm. See Damodaran (2002) for further details.

TABLE 5.3 WCI Steel Corporation—*Example of Discount Rate (WACC) Derivation*

Inputs	Symbol	Value
Risk-Free Interest Rate (30-Year Government Bond Yield, 7/6/2004)	r_f	5.38%
Market Risk Premium[a]	r_m	10.10%
Mean Unlevered Beta of Comparables	$\beta_{Unlevered}$	0.91
Tax Rate	t	40%
Projected Equity to Value Ratio	E/V	50%
Projected Debt to Value Ratio	D/V	50%
Levered Equity Beta for Reorganized WCI $\{\beta_{Unlevered} * [1 + D/E * (1 - t)]\}$	β_e	1.46
Pretax Cost of Debt	r_d	7.7%
Cost of Equity = $r_f + \beta_e * (r_m - r_t)$	r_e	20.0%
Cost of Debt = $r_d * (1 - t)$		4.62%
WACC = $r_e * E/V + r_d(1 - t) * D/V$		12.3%

[a]From Ibbotson Associates 2004 Risk Premia over Time Report (includes micro-capitalization equity risk premium).
Based on analysis of CIBC World Markets, 7/6/2004 Valuation Report.

represent normalized operations expected to be sustained indefinitely. The second common approach is to use a growing perpetuity model:

$$\text{Terminal value} = \frac{FCF_{T+1}}{WACC - g}$$

Again, the free cash flow in year $T + 1$ should reflect normalized long-term operating performance. The key input to this model is g, the assumed long-term growth rate for cash flows. Detailed discussion of the assumptions behind the growing perpetuity approach is given by McKinsey & Company (2005, p. 277).

Using both the comparables and growing perpetuity model to determine the terminal value can sometimes produce useful information about the model assumptions. For example, for a given terminal value based on an EBITDA multiple, one can calculate an implied growth rate using the assumed WACC and projected FCF_{T+1}. These assumptions are particularly important because the terminal value can often account for a very large component of estimated total enterprise value. Gilson, Hotchkiss, and Ruback (2000) value 63 companies in Chapter 11 and find for the median firm in their sample that the terminal value accounts for 70.5 percent of total value. A small change in the assumed growth rate can have a significant impact on estimated value.

The free cash flow approach is used in Table 5.4 to value WCI Steel Corporation. Using a range of discount rates (see Table 5.3), and applying a range of EBITDA multiples from comparables to determine the terminal value, the estimated values range from $280 million to $335 million.

Adjusted Present Value The adjusted present value (APV) approach follows directly from the work of Modigliani and Miller; see Chapter 6 of this book and Bruner (2004, p. 268). The total enterprise value equals the sum of the values of the operating assets plus the present value of debt tax shields. Relating this to our discounted cash flow valuation model,

$$\text{Value}_{\text{Enterprise}} = \text{Value}_{\text{Enterprise, no debt}} + \text{Present value of debt tax shields}$$

$$= \sum \frac{\text{Free cash flow}}{1 + \text{WACC}_{\text{Unlevered}}} + \sum \frac{\text{Tax shields}}{1 + r_{\text{Tax shields}}}$$

Tax shields might equal interest expense times the tax rate, or can incorporate more complex tax shields such as those from net operating losses (NOLs).

A variant on this approach, known as the capital cash flow approach, uses the same discount rate for the unlevered firm cash flows and tax shields; see Ruback (1998):

$$\text{Value}_{\text{Enterprise}} = \sum \frac{\text{Capital cash flows}}{1 + \text{WACC}_{\text{Unlevered}}}$$

This approach assumes that debt is maintained as a fixed proportion of value, so that interest and other tax shields have the same risk as the firm.[5] During the projection period, capital cash flows are calculated using the formula:

$$
\begin{array}{l}
\quad \text{Net income} \\
+ \text{ Cash flow adjustments} \\
+ \text{ Cash and noncash interest} \\
\hline
= \text{ Capital cash flows}
\end{array}
$$

---

[5]Ruback (1998) shows that the capital cash flows approach is algebraically equivalent to discounting the firm's free cash flows by the WACC.

TABLE 5.4 WCI Steel Corporation—*Discounted Cash Flow Valuation (\$Thousands)*

	Four Months Ending Dec. 31, 2004	Fiscal Year Ending December 31			
		2005	2006	2007	2008
EBIT	$17,478	$37,382	$37,936	$21,493	$30,966
Less: Cash Taxes[a]	6,991	14,953	15,174	8,597	12,387
Net Operating Profit after Taxes	10,487	22,429	22,761	12,896	18,579
Plus: Depreciation and Amortization	6,524	22,422	24,222	25,222	27,022
Less: Capital Expenditures	(13,683)	(28,500)	(18,000)	(10,000)	(18,000)
Less: Change in Working Capital	39,285	(9,536)	4,803	2,858	1,208
Unlevered Free Cash Flow (FCF)	42,613	6,815	33,786	30,975	28,809
Example of Enterprise Value Calculation					
Discount rate	0.12				
Period	0.3	1.3	2.3	3.3	4.3
Pesent Value of FCF	41,033	5,859	25,936	21,230	17,630
Total Present Value of FCF	111,688				
Terminal Value Multiple	5.5×				
Terminal Year EBITDA					57,988
Terminal Value					318,934
Present Value of Terminal Value	195,174				
Enterprise Value	306,862				

Sensitivity to WACC and Terminal Value Multiple

		WACC:		
		11%	12%	13%
Terminal Value Multiple:	5%	$298,235	$289,119	$280,406
	5.5%	316,681	306,862	297,478
	6%	335,128	324,605	314,551

[a] Assumes a 40% effective tax rate.
Source: Based on analysis of CIBC World Markets, 7/6/2004 Valuation Report.

114

Cash flow adjustments include adding back depreciation, amortization, deferred taxes, and after-tax proceeds from asset sales, and subtracting working capital investment and capital expenditures. In contrast to the FCF model described in the previous section, capital cash flows are based on net income and therefore utilize the firm's own estimate of future tax payments. While the cash flows themselves incorporate direct forecasts of tax shields, the discount rate in this case is based on the unlevered firm. This can be done using the CAPM for the unlevered firm:[6]

$$WACC_{Unlevered} = r_f + \beta_{Unlevered} \times (r_m - r_f)$$

This approach is useful not only because the WACC does not need to be recomputed if the firm's capital structure changes over the forecast period, but because more complex tax shields are explicitly modeled in the cash flows and discounted. For example, Gilson, Hotchkiss, and Ruback (2000) find that the present value of tax shields from NOLs represents 5.7 percent of the median sample firm's estimated value and 9.9 percent on average.

FRESH START ACCOUNTING ESTIMATES OF VALUE

Financial Accounting Standards Board (FASB) Statement of Opinion (SOP) 90-7, *Financial Reporting by Entities in Reorganization under the Bankruptcy Code*, requires "fresh start accounting" for all firms that filed for Chapter 11 on or after January 1, 1991, or that had a plan of reorganization confirmed on or after July 1, 1991.[7] This directive requires some firms to restate their assets and liabilities at their going-concern values. Fresh start accounting must be adopted when (1) the going-concern value of the debtor's assets at reorganization is less than the value of all allowed

---

[6]The unlevered beta can be estimated using comparables and the following relationship:

$$\beta_{Unlevered} = \frac{(\beta_E \times E) + (\beta_D \times D)}{E + D}$$

where β_D is the beta of debt. Empirical estimates of debt betas of roughly 0.25 for highly levered companies are provided by Cornell and Green (1991) and Hotchkiss and Ronen (2002). Because the interest tax shields are assumed to have the same risk as the firm, the tax deductibility of interest does not alter the beta of the firm. As a result, no tax adjustment has to be made when calculating asset betas. See Ruback (1998) for further discussion.

[7]See Lehavy (1998) and Newton (1994) for discussions of fresh start accounting.

prepetition liabilities and postpetition claims, and (2) prepetition stock-holders retain less than 50 percent of the reorganized firm's voting common shares. Fresh start values are generally estimated using DCF and comparable company methods.[8]

Fresh start values are contemporary estimates of values that emerge from the administrative bankruptcy process. These values are produced by the accountants and managers, and as a result use information beyond the forecasts and incorporate the competing interests of the claimants (see later in this chapter).

LIQUIDATION VALUES

To emerge from bankruptcy, a firm must show that its reorganization plan is in the best interests of all claimants; that is, each creditor class must get at least as much as they would under the absolute priority rules in a Chapter 7 liquidation, according to Section 1129(a) of the Bankruptcy Code. Thus every firm must estimate what its assets would sell for in liquidation.

For a liquidation analysis, each asset on the balance sheet is assigned an estimate of the proceeds that would be received in a hypothetical conversion to Chapter 7. The amounts that can be recovered, net of fees and expenses, are available for distribution in priority order to the firm's claimants. Liquidation would result in additional costs including the compensation of a bankruptcy trustee to oversee the process, legal and other professional fees, asset disposition expenses, litigation costs, and claims arising from the operations of the debtor while the case is pending. Liquidation value will be low if asset specificity is high (i.e., value is low in any use other than the current one) or the secondary market for assets is thin.

If the objective of the firm is to reorganize under Chapter 11, which assumes that going-concern value is greater than liquidation value, there is clearly concern that the liquidation values presented with the plan will be understated. Aldersen and Betker (1995) examine projected liquidation values for 88 firms that completed reorganizations under Chapter 11. Comparing the estimated going-concern value to estimated liquidation value, they find that on average about one-third of going-concern value

---

[8]Disclosure statements rarely describe the assumptions used to generate fresh start estimates of value. In some cases they do not coincide exactly with assumptions given with management's cash flow projections in the same document.

would be lost in liquidation. Further, they find that firms with high liquidation costs choose lower debt levels at emergence, making future financial distress less likely.

SUMMARIZING VALUE FROM VARIOUS ESTIMATES

Each method will produce a different range of value for the target firm, so that overall value must be a weighting of the methods used. For any method, the valuation is only as good as the cash flow forecasts on which it is based. Sensitivity analysis and alternative projections based on different assumptions are often helpful; they are generally more useful than ad hoc adjustments to discount rates to account for additional unspecified risks because they force the analyst to be explicit about these risks.

How well do the models work? In a nondistressed M&A setting, Kaplan and Ruback (1995) find that the approaches described here yield relatively precise estimates of value for a sample of highly leveraged transactions. Valuation of distressed firms, however, may be more difficult for the reasons described earlier. Gilson, Hotchkiss, and Ruback (2000) examine the usefulness of these methods by applying them to cash flow forecasts provided with the plan of reorganization for a sample of firms emerging from Chapter 11. The accuracy of these valuations is evaluated by comparing estimated values from comparable companies and DCF models to the market value observed for the target company when it first trades following bankruptcy. They find that the estimated values are generally unbiased predictors of the realized market values, but they are not very precise. The sample ratio of estimated value to market value at emergence varies from less than 20 percent to greater than 250 percent. They argue that both the administrative rather than market-based process and the potential to use value estimates strategically in the renegotiation process explain the wide range of values.

STRATEGIC USE OF VALUATION IN BANKRUPTCY NEGOTIATIONS

One explanation for the lack of precision in estimated values and the large magnitude of disagreements over value is the strategic use of these values as part of the plan negotiation process. When the incentives of the parties involved in negotiations conflict, stated estimates of value can reflect the biases of these parties. Case studies described by Gilson, Hotchkiss, and Ruback (GHR, 2000) and the examples presented earlier in Table 5.1

strongly suggest that stated positions on the value of the bankrupt firm can be self-serving.

GHR suggest several factors they expect to be related to these biases: the relative bargaining strength of competing (senior versus junior) claimholders, management's equity ownership in the reorganized firm, the existence of outside bids to acquire or invest in the debtor, and senior management turnover. They develop empirical proxies for each of these factors, and show how these proxies are related to whether the firm is overvalued or undervalued relative to its market value at emergence from Chapter 11.

Senior versus junior claimholders often have conflicting interests in terms of establishing the reorganized firm's value. Provided that distributions under the plan approximately follow relative priority, basing the plan on a higher estimated value benefits junior classes by justifying a larger payout to their claims. Similarly, senior claimants benefit when the reorganization plan is premised on a low value. If firm value is low enough such that anyone below the senior claimholders is not entitled to any distribution, then typically the majority of the reorganized firm stock will be distributed to the senior claimants and those more junior will receive little or no distribution. If in fact the firm value after emerging is significantly higher than was assumed in the plan, there is a windfall to the senior claimants who received stock, who *ex post* may hold claims worth more than 100 percent of the value of their prebankruptcy claims. Any wealth gain that either group realizes *ex post* must come at the expense of the other group. GHR find that values estimated from cash flow projections provided with the plan are higher when an investor holding junior claims has gained control of the reorganized firm and lower when senior claimants gained control.

GHR also find that the distribution of stock and/or options in the reorganized firm is related to incentives to understate value. In Chapter 11, managers are often granted a fixed target number or percentage of outstanding shares, so that a low firm value makes managers' compensation appear lower. With stock option grants, a low firm value means that the estimated stock price for the reorganized firm is lower; since options are generally issued at-the-money, the option exercise price is therefore set lower. If in fact the firm is undervalued, this provides a windfall to managers when the firm emerges from bankruptcy.

Third-party equity investments are also fairly common as part of a reorganization plan. For the sample examined by GHR, these are typically "friendly" to incumbent management, in the sense that the incumbent management remains in office following emergence from bankruptcy. GHR find that the firm is more likely to be undervalued when an outside investor purchases equity in the firm as part of the reorganization plan. In these cases, the investors friendly to management successfully purchase equity at a significant discount.

Finally, Hotchkiss (1995) and others consistently find that managers whose tenure predates the bankruptcy filing issue overly optimistic forecasts for the reorganized firm. Consistent with this, firms are more likely to be overvalued when the prebankruptcy CEO is still in office when the reorganization plan is proposed.

Resolving debates over valuation remains a difficult issue. Typically, the parties that are able to maintain control over the process are more likely to be successful in promoting a plan based on a valuation that favors their interests. There have recently been, however, cases involving large public companies where confirmation of the reorganization plan is contested based on the value assigned to the reorganized firm, and the disputes are therefore resolved by the bankruptcy court. Interestingly, valuation disputes might also be resolved by issuing securities whose payoffs are explicitly tied to the firm's future market value (Bebchuk 1988; Hausch and Seward 1995). Such securities provide a hedge against mistakes in valuation and are often used in corporate mergers. Relatively few Chapter 11 cases to date have used this type of mechanism to reduce the potential for large valuation errors.

CHAPTER 6

Firm Valuation and Corporate Leveraged Restructuring

T he concept of corporate value, and how to maximize it, is perhaps the key element in the dynamics of corporate activity. While always central to the field of finance, corporate valuation issues have never been more relevant than they are today. This is because of the massive restructuring changes that took place in the United States in the 1980s and the explosion in corporate governance and capital structure issues in the United States and Europe since. Numerous texts and articles are constantly being written extolling the virtues of value-enhancing techniques.

The purpose of this chapter is to examine valuation from the perspective of the firm's capital structure. We analyze capital structure issues within the context of massive changes brought about by leveraged restructurings, particularly leveraged buyouts (LBOs). In doing so, we also address the question, Does debt matter and is there an optimal capital structure?

Our inquiry follows a decade of extraordinary activity in mergers and acquisitions (M&A) in the United States in the 1980s and the renewed interest in LBOs in 2004–2005. The transaction values of these restructurings rose in the earlier period as exceptionally high acquisition prices were offered due to the competitive interaction of numerous buyout funds. In turn, the debt amounts and proportions of the merged firms' capital structures also rose to levels never before seen in corporate America. Hence, both values and bankruptcy risks escalated in the mid and especially in the late 1980s.

This chapter is derived and updated from an article by E. Altman and R. Smith published in part in *Corporate Bankruptcy and Distressed Restructuring*, E. Altman, editor, Dow Jones–Irwin, Homewood, IL (1991a). Also see Altman and Smith (1991b).

We show that these high values can, in most cases, be sustained only if the levels of debt and distress risk are reduced very quickly after the initial restructuring. If this is not achieved, similar transactions will not be successful in attracting capital from the markets. In the case of leveraged restructurings that prove to be unsuccessful, debt levels will still be reduced through distressed exchange arrangements, or failing that, through Chapter 11 bankruptcy reorganizations. If all of these fail, the firm's assets will need to be liquidated. In these latter distressed situations, corporate values will decline sharply to levels significantly lower than if the firm had been able to reduce its debt as planned within a short time after the restructuring.

We first examine classical financial theories dealing with corporate valuation in terms of debt policy. These theories can help to explain not only why leveraged restructurings can change the valuation of firms, sometimes substantially, but also why these restructurings have met with the full spectrum of results, from great success to dismal failure. In essence, we share what we have learned, if anything, from the ill-fated and poorly structured leveraged restructurings in the past! In so doing, we hope to provide some insights into successful capital structure changes for future transactions.

CORPORATE RESTRUCTURINGS: DEFINITIONS AND OBJECTIVES

A corporate restructuring is any substantial change in a firm's asset portfolio or capital structure. Its objectives are usually to increase value to the owners, both old and new, by improving operating efficiency, exploiting debt capacity and tax benefits, and/or redeploying assets. In some cases, the objective is less strategic, in an operating sense, and not necessarily value maximizing, being directed simply to effect a change in corporate control or to defend against a loss of control—that is, to preserve independence. Independence of operation has long been important to boards of directors or principal shareholders of some corporations who have been accustomed to rule their firm's actions without full regard for the rights of public shareholders. Sometimes these actions are taken due to the fear of being taken over against management's will. In addition, senior management has often professed a goal to be independent of the influence that large lenders may exert on the operations of the firm. When highly leveraged restructurings are done in the name of corporate governance reasons, possibly to the detriment of shareholder value, then the "poison pill" may apply.

MERGERS AND ACQUISITIONS

The United States has gone through at least four distinct cycles of M&A activity. The latest one, in the 1980s, involved large corporate financial restructurings, often resulting in acquisition of control by another firm. Though this cycle has been completed in the United States, the forces behind it have also been seen in Europe, which saw its first major M&A movement in the 1980s. This movement is primarily a result of an overdue need for industrial restructurings and other influences. European M&A activity began after the 1985 European Community (EC) initiative to integrate all member country trade and capital market activities. Reduced barriers to cross-national firm mergers were the result of newly found confidence that deregulated, private sector markets could result in improved corporate performance compared to previous national income and protectionist policies. For more details on economic restructuring in Europe, see Smith and Walter (1990) and Altman and Smith (1991b). And, in the most recent years, 2004–2005, we have observed a distinct increase in private equity firm restructuring activity in Europe, specifically Germany.

LEVERAGED RESTRUCTURINGS

Corporations have also tried to increase value to shareholders by massive changes in leverage. These restructurings are mainly in the form of leveraged recapitalizations (recaps) or leveraged buyouts. The former involves some type of debt-for-equity swap, and the latter involves management acting either alone or as a partner with a third-party investment firm, purchasing all of the outstanding common stock so that the firm effectively becomes a private entity. The vehicle to buy back the equity is leverage—hence the name leveraged buyout (or leveraged buy-in when the firm remains public). We explore this mechanism in much greater depth and numerically after discussing the evolution of financial theory in valuation analysis and its relationship with a firm's capital structure.

Before we try to reconcile financial theories with corporate financial practice, it will be beneficial to define and discuss what has come to be known as the leveraged restructuring movement of the 1980s, particularly the late 1980s. The objectives of corporate restructurings are usually to do one or more of the following in order to increase the value of the firm—however one chooses to define value:

- Redeploy assets to change the mix of the business.
- Exploit leverage and other financial opportunities.
- Improve operational efficiency.

These objectives can be achieved by one or more of the following restructurings:

- Acquiring other companies or businesses.
- Leveraged buyouts.
- Recapitalizations, that is, stock repurchases or swaps of debt for equity.
- Major organizational, leadership, or corporate policy changes.

Leveraged Management Buyouts

A number of new techniques for increasing the value of firms were developed in the United States in the 1980s, usually involving several of the steps outlined earlier. The most visible, in many aspects, was the leveraged management buyout (LMBO) or leveraged buyout (LBO), in which control of a company was acquired in the market through a takeover bid, usually at a substantial premium over the market price of the shares (estimated at about 46 percent by Kaplan (1989) for LBOs in the early and mid-1980s and growing to even a greater premium, perhaps double, for the LBOs of the late 1980s). Often, the transaction was bitterly opposed by existing directors and managers if they were not part of the takeover team. As the premium grew, the new equity team had to rely more and more on borrowed capital from banks and the public. This resulted in a number of leverage excesses.

Management buyouts (MBOs) had been around for many years both in the United States and in Europe. The early transactions in the 1970s essentially involved the senior management of a company buying out all the outstanding shares and taking the firm private (if the firm was publicly held). A significant amount of the financing for the buyout was provided primarily by commercial bank loans, with the balance coming from the managers' equity investments. The transaction was a leveraged one but the size of the firm and the consequent amount of financing were relatively small. The resulting capital structure, while heavily leveraged, was quite simple with essentially one class of debt.

The type of firm most suitable for a management buyout was, and still is, one with relatively stable and predictable cash flows sufficient to easily repay the fixed costs from the additional interest and principal on the debt. The major motivation behind the buyout is that management will now directly benefit from their own efforts and reap the firm's profits in the form of equity returns, instead of a fixed or semifixed salary earned as managers. Indeed, it is often argued that the manager-owner will work more efficiently due to the added incentive built into ownership and control.

The LMBO or LBO differs from the MBO by the larger size and greater complexity of the transaction and the inclusion of a significant second ownership interest. Indeed, this second party, usually in the form of an investment private-equity company or partnership, provides and acquires the bulk of the equity capital, with at most 10 to 15 percent going to management. The greater complexity involves several layers of debt holders (some with deferred as well as current-pay interest payments in addition to equity participation features) and also several types of equity capital (preferred and common stock, sometimes including equity warrants and options).

A typical capital structure of a large LMBO in the United States in the 1987–1988 period is shown in Figure 6.1. Note that the senior debt from banks and insurance companies provided about 60 percent of the transaction value and amounted to about two-thirds of the total debt financing. These creditors were not willing to provide 100 percent of the debt financing, since the amounts were so large and the perceived risk so great. Indeed, many of these buyouts were greater than $1 billion, with the largest, by far, being the $25 billion RJR Nabisco buyout in 1989. Recently in 2005, we have seen the revival of the large LBO deals with the $11.5 billion SunGard deal and the €16 billion WIND telecom deal in Italy. A recent innovation has also been the equity ownership of these very large deals now being shared by several large private-equity buyout firms, that is, "club" transactions (e.g., SunGard).

Below the senior debt was the subordinated current-paying debt—that is, where interest payments commence immediately. This layer provided about 20 to 21 percent of the total financing. The primary innovation here was that this debt was, in many instances, sold directly to the public markets as part of the growing "junk bond" issuance. Using a concert-hall analogy, this debt is also known as "mezzanine" financing since its priority is below the "balcony" (senior debt) and above

1987	
Senior Bank Loans	47%
Other Senior Debt	13%
Subordinated Coupon	20%
Deferred Coupon	7%
Preferred Stock	3%
Common Stock	9%

1988	
Senior Bank Loans	40%
Other Senior Debt	19%
Subordinated Coupon	21%
Deferred Coupon	7%
Preferred Stock	3%
Common Stock	10%

FIGURE 6.1 Selected Capital Structures of LMBOs in 1987–1988
Source: Credit Suisse First Boston (CSFB) and author compilation.

the "orchestra" (equity financing). After 1986, the subordinated debt in the United States came mainly from publicly placed junk bonds. About 27 to 28 percent of the transaction price was provided by this source (including non-interest-paying subordinated debt). See our discussion of high-yield junk bonds in Chapter 7.

DIBs, PIKs, and Resets

Several new variants of subordinated debt were introduced in the late 1980s in order to reduce the initial cash interest payment burden of the transaction. These involved deferred-payment interest bonds (DIBs) and payment-in-kind (PIK) bonds. The latter paid whatever the coupon stated, not in interest but in additional bonds, so the liability and future interest payment grew over time. The former usually involved a period (e.g., three years) of no-coupon payments and then the start of interest coupon payments (e.g., in years four to maturity).

Another innovation pioneered by U.S. investment banks was reset notes, which guaranteed that the interest rate would be reset periodically so as to cause the bonds to sell at par value. This innovation, like so many of the others, ultimately operated adversely to the interests of the issuers as the junk bond market became more concerned with credit quality in 1989–1991. Such instruments can increase the likelihood of credit problems in the future. These deferred-payment debt instruments can be referred to as ticking time bombs if the debt itself is not redeemed before the cash-pay period begins or reset is necessary.

Role of Subordinated Debt and Equity

The subordinated debt in these restructurings played a pivotal role. Usually included as debt by those interested in total firm valuation, subordinate cash-pay and non-cash-pay debt nonetheless provided an important equity-like cushion from the standpoint of potential senior creditors. But, unlike the preferred stock financed mergers of the 1960s, subordinated debt provided important tax benefits.

Finally, below the multilayered debt structure came the preferred and equity financing, usually over 85 percent owned by the investment company with the residual owned by management. Despite the small percentage (12 to 15 percent) ownership for management, the sheer magnitude of the leveraged transactions could lead to extremely high returns to all of the equity owners—if the restructuring was successful.

Successful and Unsuccessful LBOs

A successful LBO from the standpoint of all parties concerned, including the old and new debt and equity holders, is one that:

- Results in relatively quick and successful repayment to the debt holders.
- Cashes out within three to seven years so that the equity holders recoup their investment and earn substantial profits.
- Does not cause any significant economic disruption of the acquired company, for example unemployment, resulting in some political reaction.

Operating efficiencies and asset sales (if necessary) should provide sufficient cash to the firm to repay a large portion of the senior debt within two years. After this period, even the increasing debt burden from the deferred interest junk bonds can be met without difficulty if the firm continues its substantial cash-flow generations. If, however, cash flows and asset sales are disappointing, then distress can set in and the LBO will, in many cases, fail.

Failed leveraged restructurings occurred in 1989–1991 to several of the large LMBOs and other highly leveraged transactions that resulted in critical bankruptcies and other distressed situations. These include the Campeau (Allied and Federated Stores) fiasco, Hillsborough Holdings, Southland, National Gypsum, and several others. In the United Kingdom, the Isosceles PLC buyout of Gateway Corporation was a distressed situation mainly due to disappointing asset sales and smaller than forecasted reductions in debt.

To cash out means that the firm is sold or recapitalized, either in part or as a whole, or the LBO goes public again by selling shares in the open market. In the case of partial firm sales, proceeds are often paid out to the new owners and debt refinanced, usually over a longer maturity period. Table 6.1 lists statistics on the average large firm LBOs that took place in the mid to late 1980s. The former period was prior to the leverage excesses of 1987–1989 that resulted in many failures. Note that the average premium paid to the original selling shareholders was 46 percent in the earlier period, resulting in average incremental debt of $400 million on a $524 million transaction. The initial debt-equity ratio was about 6:1. Successful LBOs netted the new owner returns of about 250 percent over three to five years, based on an average $100 million equity investment.

With respect to the leverage excesses and inflated prices paid in 1987–1988, results in Table 6.1 show how the average premium rose to 74

TABLE 6.1 Average Historical LBO Experience

	1982–1986 ($Millions)	1987–1988 ($Millions)
Prebuyout Value of Equity	$360	$1,023
Average Buyout Purchase Price	$524	$1,783
Average Gain to Prebuyout Shareholders	46%	74%
Equity as a Percent of Total Capital	15%	12%
Debt as a Percent of Total Capital	85%	88%
Debt-Equity Ratio	5.8:1	7.3:1
Incremental Debt	$400	$1,570
Postbuyout Sale of Firm	$750	n.a.
Postbuyout Gain from Sale (50%)	$250	n.a.
Return to New Equity Owners (Total)	250%	n.a.
Cash Flow Multiplier (Earnings after Taxes before Depreciation, Amortization, and Deferred Taxes)	6–8×	12×

Source: Kaplan (1989) and author compilation. Based on 46 completed LBOs in 1982–1986.

percent from the earlier 46 percent and the average cash flow multiplier rose to almost 12 times from the 6 to 8 times of the earlier period. Finally, the average size of larger firm transactions grew from $524 million to almost $1.8 billion in a relatively short period. The average postbuyout sale of the 1982–1986 deals resulted in a $750 million payment—a $250 million (50 percent) postbuyout gain from the sale. The actual gain to the equity holders was magnified, of course, as a result of the large amounts of leverage employed. Since their investment was only $100 million, the return on equity was 250 percent over an average period of three to four years. This is illustrative of how value was increased via the LBO.

Granted that the use of subordinated debt as tax-deductible "equity" helped to spark this dramatic increase, the main reason for the ultimate failure of many of these LBOs was the excessive price paid and the excessive amount of debt used. The bubble burst in late 1989.

Kaplan and Stein (1993) examined changes in the pricing and capital structure of large LBOs in the 1980s. They found that due to the intense competition for these highly leveraged restructurings (1) buyout price to cash flow ratios rose dramatically, (2) required bank principal payments accelerated, (3) private subordinated debt was replaced by public high-yield bonds, and (4) management teams and deal makers took more money out of transactions up front. In general, these overheating trends helped cause the meltdown starting in late 1989. Denis and Denis (1995) studied leveraged recapitalizations from 1985 to 1988 and found that 31 percent of these recaps subsequently encountered financial distress. The causes of distress involved (1) poor operating performance, (2) surprisingly low proceeds from sale of assets, and (3) negative stock price reactions associated with the demise of the market for highly leveraged transactions. They attributed the high rate of distress primarily to unexpected macroeconomic and regulatory developments.

Our own admittedly more casual analysis of the problems that followed several recap failures found factors similar to the ones that Denis and Denis found, but also that the deals were poorly structured, too high valuations were made, and far too much debt was used. A prime example of this was the Interco recap debacle of 1988, which resulted in a default in 1990 and bankruptcy soon thereafter.

LINKING CAPITAL STRUCTURE THEORY WITH LEVERAGED RESTRUCTURINGS

The relationship between a firm's capital structure and its true valuation has interested financial theorists for more than 40 years, but it was the works of Modigliani and Miller (M&M) (1958 and 1963) that catapulted the subject to center stage in the finance literature. In their classic 1958 article, M&M argued that the relationship between a firm's debt and equity had absolutely no impact on its overall value; the only variables that determined firm value were its future earning power (encompassed in expected cash flows) and the business risk-return class of the firm. In other words, how the firm packaged its financing had no material impact on value or the firm's overall weighted average cost of capital (WACC). Value was determined by what businesses a company was in and how well its managers ran it—nothing else. Their conclusion is represented by the horizontal line V in Figure 6.2.

Even though this theory rested upon a set of unrealistic assumptions (many of which were addressed in footnotes to their original 1958 article) and some rather simplistic empirical tests, the theory caused an immediate and strong response from the academic community. Miller (1989) argued, however, that "the view that capital structure is literally irrelevant or that 'nothing matters' in corporate finance, though still sometimes attributed to us, is far from what we ever actually said about real world applications of our theoretical propositions." One could infer that when M&M relax their restrictive assumptions (for example, no taxes and perfect information about earnings prospects), they, too, agree as to the value-enhancing power of debt. Indeed, Miller's comment on the rise in junk bonds to help bring

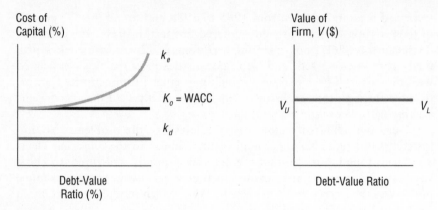

FIGURE 6.2 Original (1958) M&M Capital Structure Theory
Source: Modigliani and Miller (1958).

about leveraged restructurings was that he was puzzled why the use of such instruments took so long to develop.

In 1963, M&M published a correction article that stated that they had underestimated the important contribution to firm value from the tax subsidy on debt interest payments and the lower capitalization rate on these tax benefits. They reasoned that a firm could indeed lower its capitalization rate and increase its value by adding debt and receiving a bonus equal to the tax rate times the amount of debt (TD); see Figure 6.3. And it appeared that this increasing value of the leveraged firm (V_L)

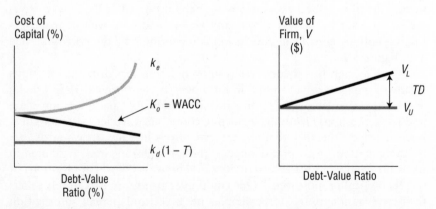

FIGURE 6.3 Effects of Leverage: M&M with Taxes (1963)
Source: Modigliani and Miller (1963) and author's compilation.

was evident *regardless* of the amount of debt. Could this have been the seminal work that guided the leveraged buyout movement that emerged in the United States more than 20 years later? Indeed, Dr. Modigliani was asked this very question soon after he had received the Nobel Prize in economics and after the LBO boom had begun. He vehemently denied this, citing other factors that might lower a firm's value as leverage increased.

A number of traditionalists opposed M&M's ideas. For example, Durand (1959) argued that the amount of debt did matter and that therefore there was an optimal debt-equity ratio represented by the minimum point on the WACC schedule in Figure 6.4. It was felt that a firm could lower its

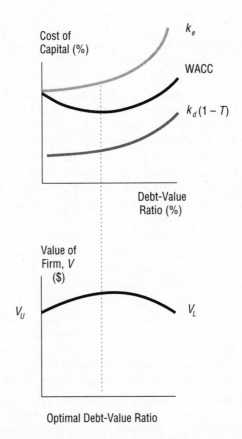

FIGURE 6.4 Effects of Leverage: Traditional Approach

WACC and at the same time increase its value (V_L) by adding a judicious amount of debt. The relatively low after-tax cost of debt, $K_d(1 - t)$, would bring down the overall cost despite the higher and rising cost of equity (K_e). At some point, however, the combination of increasing costs of debt and equity would begin to raise the overall cost (its capitalization rate) and lower the firm's value. And some empirical tests, notably by Weston (1963), showed that leverage did indeed impact the firm's overall cost of capital. Two and a half decades later, Weston (1989) again reflected on the M&M capital structure controversy. And of course, most corporate finance textbooks carry the important distinctions between M&M and traditional theory.

Finally, a combination of renewed traditional theory attempts and some new concepts dealing with financial distress costs (or bankruptcy costs) and "agency" conflicts (i.e., conflicts between decisions by managers as agents for owners and the owners' best interests) added both rigorous new theory and empirical tests to support the traditional view of an optimal capital structure that was not 100 percent debt. It was argued that as a firm's leverage increases, the probability of bankruptcy also increases, and if the costs of bankruptcy are significant, then a firm's value will fall when the marginal increase in the *expected* value of the tax benefits from debt is overwhelmed by the expected present value of distress costs (see Figure 6.5). After the break-even leverage point the overall cost of capital will rise beyond some optimum leverage proportion and the firm's value will fall.

Altman (1984) measured the costs of bankruptcy, not only in terms of the direct out-of-pocket costs to lawyers, accountants, and so on and the lost opportunities due to management's diversion from running the business, but the indirect costs as well. Indirect costs were defined as those lost sales and profits caused by customers choosing not to deal with a firm that was a high-potential bankrupt as well as increased costs of doing business (e.g., higher debt costs and poorer terms with suppliers) while in a financially vulnerable condition. We found that while the direct costs were consistent with Warner's (1977) earlier results, the indirect costs were quite significant and the overall distressed costs were in the 15 to 20 percent range of firm value. These percentages are consistent with those found by Andrade and Kaplan (1998). Of course, restructuring and recontracting may contribute to the financial rehabilitation of the firm, thereby lowering distress costs; see Chen, Weston, and Altman (1995). Bankruptcy costs are also reviewed, in depth, in Chapter 4 of this book.

Agency effects, first articulated by Jensen and Meckling (1976), argue that due to conflicts between debt and equity stockholders, indeed also between holders of different classes of debt (Bulow and Shoven 1978), a firm incurs real cost as the threat of bankruptcy grows. On the other hand,

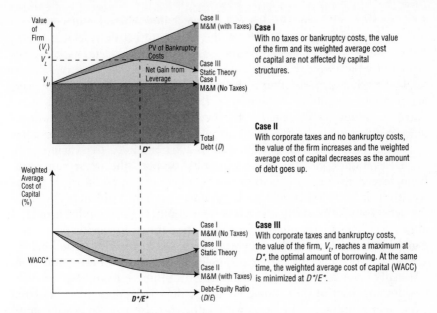

FIGURE 6.5   Net Effects of Leverage of Firm Value: M&M and Altman (1984)
Source: Modigliani and Miller (1958, 1963), Altman (1984), and author's compilation.

many have argued that the highly leveraged LBO, transforming the "manager-only" to a "manager-owner," has positive agency benefits by removing some manager-owner conflicts of interest.

Figure 6.5 shows that financial distress and agency costs are the major factors accounting for the difference between the so-called pure M&M value of the firm (with the tax subsidy) and the revised traditionalist value of the firm. The net result is an optimum point on the debt/value axis (D^*) at which the firm's value is maximized.

DELEVERAGING

As we postulated earlier, to be successful a highly leveraged restructured firm must reduce its debt substantially and usually within a short time after the restructuring transaction. The consequences of not achieving this deleveraging are apparent both in theory and in our observance of the substantial increase in highly leveraged, high-priced LBO situations of the late 1980s and the consequent increase in defaults. As we observed in Chapter

1 earlier and will discuss further in Chapter 7, junk bond defaults mounted to over $18 billion in both 1990 and 1991, resulting in a default rate of more than 10 percent in both years. Losses from these defaults, most but not all of which were the result of the restructurings, also increased due to the lower recovery rates, that is, lower prices just after defaults. The average recovery was about 25 percent in 1990 and 36 percent in 1991, compared to about 39 percent for the five-year period 1985–1989 and 40 percent for most of the history of defaults. Similar very low recovery rates were observed in the high-default years in 2001 and 2002 (see Chapter 15).

Deleveraging can be either voluntary or not—the latter can result from forced distressed exchange issues whereby the creditors of a distressed firm agree to accept a package of new securities in lieu of the existing debt. Invariably, this package contains equity in the troubled firm. The ability for firms to accomplish an equity-for-debt swap was severely hampered by the malaise in the equity markets, starting in the second half of 1990. Deleveraging can also be prompted by the fear of a crisis situation, especially prior to some trigger date such as an interest rate reset or cash-pay commencement date. Some voluntary debt reductions have occurred from debt repurchases by firms with sufficient cash to take advantage of the significant reduction in bond prices (e.g., in many usually successful highly leveraged firms starting in the summer of 1989). Deleveraging continued from debt repurchasing and expanded even more rapidly when the equity markets rebounded in 1992.

Two examples of major firm deleveraging efforts in the face of economic and financial uncertainties were the attempts by RJR Nabisco and Macy's—both large LBOs of the late 1980s. RJR Nabisco, bought by Kohlberg Kravis Roberts & Co. (KKR) in 1989, had already reduced debt by over $6 billion by mid-1990, but still found itself with about $20 billion of debt remaining. In the following year, facing an enormous increase in interest costs due to the impending reset event in April 1991, the firm redeemed another $2.4 billion of notes via an equity-for-debt swap. One might argue that the swap was prompted by the firm's perceived financial vulnerability; even so, its cash flow in 1990 was extremely positive, permitting partial bond paybacks and other deleveraging actions.

Macy's, an LBO with several large institutional stockholders, was attempting in 1990 to lessen its considerable debt burden. One strategic move was to reduce some of its $5.6 billion in debt through periodic repurchases financed by the sale of new convertible preferred stock to the public. The preferred stock sale was complemented by the sale of Macy's receivables and some real estate. These actions were precipitated primarily by the drastic reduction in market value of several of its outstanding debt issues and the perceived concern in the markets of the deterioration in credit quality of Macy's. These efforts were unsuccessful, however, and the firm filed for bankruptcy in January 1992.

LEVERAGED RESTRUCTURING AND VALUE—TWO EXAMPLES

We explore two scenarios whereby a restructuring of the permanent capital can be shown to increase firm value.

Example 1: Debt-for-Equity Swaps

The first scenario involves a classic debt-for-equity exchange, or swap, which is a type of leveraged recapitalization. Table 6.2 illustrates a situation whereby a firm in a 40 percent tax bracket swaps $3,000 of its equity for new debt. Before the transaction, the firm had $2,000 in debt at a before-tax cost of 8 percent and $4,032 in equity—the latter based on a

TABLE 6.2 Restructuring and Value Example 1: Leveraging Up—Debt-for-Equity Swap = $3,000

	Before	After	Change (Return %)
EBIT	$1,000	$1,000	—
Debt (BV)	$2,000	$5,000	$3,000
(MV)	$2,000	$4,600	$2,600
Cost of Debt:			
Before Tax	8.0%	10.0%	2.0%
After Tax	4.8%	6.0%	1.2%
Tc	40%	40%	—
Interest	$160	$460	$300
EAT	$504	$324	$180
Cost of Equity	12.5%	14.3%	1.8%
Equity Multiplier	8×	7×	−1×
Equity Value	$4,032	$2,268 ($3,000)	$1,236 = 31%
Total Firm Value	$6,032	$6,868	$836 = 14%
Cost of Capital	10.0%	8.7%	−1.3%

BV = Book Value
MV = Market Value
Tc = Marginal Tax Rate
EAT = Earnings after Taxes
Source: Author compilation.

price-earnings (P/E) ratio of 8 times after-tax earnings of $504. The total value of the firm's securities was therefore $6,032 and the weighted average cost of capital was 10 percent. The WACC is equal to the sum of the component after-tax costs of debt and equity, each multiplied by the amount of each as a proportion of total capital; that is, 10 percent = .048(2,000/6,032) + .125(4,032/6,032). The cost of equity is assumed to be the inverse of the P/E ratio.

After the swap, the cost of debt rises to, say, 10 percent, as the debt/total value ratio increases from 33 percent to 67 percent and the equity multiplier falls to 7 times due to the higher financial risk. But, since debt is now a greater proportion of total capital, although its after-tax cost has increased from 4.8 to 6.0 percent, the WACC decreases to 8.7 percent. The new equity value of $2,268 (7 times earnings of $324) plus $4,600 in debt (the old debt is now selling at a discount) raises the firm's total value by $836 to $6,868. This is a 14 percent increase. The break-even firm value point, comparing the "before" situation to "after" recapitalization, would manifest if the equity multiplier fell to about 4 times instead of 7 times. Note that if the firm's increase in value was equal to the tax benefits from the additional debt, the increase would be $1,200 (.4 × 3,000) instead of $836. We are therefore implicitly assuming bankruptcy and agency costs of $364. This increase in value was depicted earlier in our theoretical discussion and shown in both Figure 6.3 (M&M with taxes) and Figure 6.4 (traditional approach). Indeed, the value to the old equity holder has increased 31 percent, even more than the 14 percent increase in firm value. Based on a 7 times P/E ratio, the new equity value is $2,268 (7 × $324) plus the $3,000 derived in the swap, bringing the total value to the old equity holder to $5,268—a 31 percent increase over $4,032.

In addition to the tax benefits inherent in a debt-for-equity swap, there is evidence that a company's exchange offer is interpreted by the market as a signal about future cash flows. Copeland and Lee (1990) examined data on exchanges covering the period 1962–1984 and found evidence consistent with the signaling hypothesis. Also see McKinsey & Company (2005). They also found that leverage-increasing exchange offers result in decreases in systematic risk and increases in adjusted earnings, sales, and assets. Opposite results were found for leverage-decreasing exchange offers. We postulate that the vast majority of the firms in the Copeland and Lee sample had excess debt capacity.

Example 2: LBO Restructuring

The second scenario, illustrated in Table 6.3, involves the same initial condition as in Example 1, except now the swap is an extreme one with all of

TABLE 6.3 Restructuring and Value Example 2: LBO Financed by 90 Percent Debt and 10 Percent Equity

	Before	After	Change (Return %)
EBIT	$1,000	$1,000	—
Depreciation	$500	$500	—
Total Debt (BV)	$2,000	$7,080[a]	$5,080
(MV)	$2,000	$6,330	$4,330
Cost of Debt:			
Before Tax	8.0%	11.0%	3.0%
After Tax	4.8%	6.6%	1.8%
Interest	$160	$719	$559
Tax Rate	40%	40%	—
EAT	$504	$169	$335
Equity Multiplier	8×		
EBITD-Based Firm Multiplier		5.25	
Equity Value	$4,032	$1,545	
	(Investment = 0.10 × 5,645 = $565)		
Total Firm Value	$6,032	$7,875	$1,843 (31%)

[a]LBO purchased at a 40 percent equity premium = $5,645, new debt = $5,080.
BV = Book Value
MV = Market Value
EAT = Earnings after Taxes
Source: Author compilation.

the equity purchased through an LBO and the public firm becomes privately owned. The purchase of $4,032 in equity is accomplished by offering the old shareholders a 40 percent premium, or $5,654 (recall that 40 percent was about the average LBO premium in the period 1982–1986). The cost is financed by 90 percent debt and 10 percent equity, which increases the total book value of debt from $2,000 to $7,080. The dollar equity investment is $565 (10 percent of the cost),

After the buyout, the firm's cost of debt increases to, say, 11 percent (a 3 percent increase), which if publicly issued would no doubt be rated as a junk bond. And the market value of the old debt decreases proportionately. The after-tax cost of debt rises from 4.8 percent to 6.6 percent and the old debt's value falls from $2,000 to $1,250. Due to the high debt amount and increased cost, the interest expense is now $719 ($160 on the old and $559 on the new debt) and net earnings drops to $169. Since this is now a highly leveraged private firm, the P/E approach cannot be used directly to value the equity and the entire firm, although an estimate of value can be made by using P/E ratios of comparable highly leveraged firms that are publicly traded. Instead, a commonly used valuation practice in highly leveraged companies is the cash flow multiplier approach.

A typical range of total firm value to cash flow during the 1982–1986 period of LBOs was from 6 to 8 times. As the LBO movement in the United States heated up and exceptional profits were made, cash flow multipliers increased to 10 to 12 times and even higher. The firm in Example 2 has earnings before interest and taxes plus depreciation (EBITD) of $1,500. Assuming a more conservative multiplier of 5.25 times, the total firm value result is $7,875. Subtracting the market value of debt ($6,330) from total firm value results in an equity value of $1,545. Since the equity investment was only $565, the rather immediate returns to the new equity holders are estimated at 173 percent. At this point these returns are merely hypothetical. Total value of the firm also increases dramatically by 31 percent over the initial $6,032, reflecting the expected future benefits of the restructuring.

Note that we have not indicated any increase in EBITD from before to after—both are at $1,500. Most LBO and financial restructuring advocates, however, argue that a firm will usually become more efficient in its cost containment and productivity increases after it goes private. Indeed, Jensen (1989) argues for the "discipline of debt" as a positive motivation for increasing firm values—not to mention the tax benefits that we have seen in Examples 1 and 2. Evidence of sizable increases in cash flow can be observed in several articles from Amihud (e.g., 1989).

On the other hand, opponents of LBO restructurings argue that the enormous debt burden stifles new investment and puts the highly leveraged firm at a distinct long-term disadvantage vis-à-vis its less leveraged competitors. Further, optimistic forecasts of higher earnings and cash flows and successful asset sales do not always materialize and the suffocating amounts of debt cause perfectly good companies to falter. In these problem situations, both the new debt and equity holders could lose a significant proportion of their investment.

In the scenarios we have illustrated, the result described is dependent on our assumptions—ones we think are fairly realistic. The end result, regardless of the multipliers selected, shows the impact that financial structure can have on firm valuation.

LINKING BACK TO FINANCIAL THEORY

As we observed earlier, the value of an enterprise could be increased by an addition to debt, and the present value of that increase in value is equal to

TD (tax rate times the total amount of debt). Since an LBO is probably the extreme of a voluntary increase in debt, no doubt one of the motivations is to accrue these tax advantages. Hence, an ever-increasing debt-value ratio makes sense in a world of insignificant distress and agency costs. But these costs are not trivial, and the curve V_u in Figure 6.5 falls after some optimum debt amount (D^*).

In Altman (1984), we showed that a firm's optimum debt is where the expected bankruptcy (distress) costs are equal to the expected value of the tax benefits from debt:

$$P_{B,t}(\text{BCD}_t + \text{BCI}_t) \times (\text{PV})_t = (\text{PV}_t)\, T_c\, (Id_t) \times (1 - P_{B,t})$$

where $P_{B,t}$ = probability of bankruptcy estimated in period t
      BCD_t = direct bankruptcy costs estimated in t
      BCI_t = indirect bankruptcy costs estimated in t
      PV_t = present value adjustment to period t
      T_c = marginal tax bracket of the corporation
      $Id_{t \to \infty}$ = interest expenses from period t to infinity

Where the expected bankruptcy costs are lower than the expected tax benefits, increased leverage can be successfully undertaken.

BANKRUPTCY AND DISTRESSED FIRM COSTS

As mentioned earlier, distress costs can explain why firm values fall as leverage increases above critical levels (see Figure 6.5). Just how significant these distress costs are has been a subject of some debate and controversy for many years. Bankruptcy costs are discussed in depth in Chapter 4 of this book.

In our 1984 investigation of both direct and indirect costs of bankruptcy, we found evidence that total distressed firm costs are nontrivial. The firms examined included samples of 19 industrial and retail firms that went bankrupt in the 1970–1978 period and a second group of seven large industrial bankruptcies from the early 1980s. In many cases, the total bankruptcy costs exceeded 20 percent of the value of the firm measured just prior to bankruptcy and almost that level from up to three years prior. On average, bankruptcy costs ranged from 11 to 17 percent up to three years prior, when measured based on a regression technique constructed to capture the unexpected lost profits of a firm in distress. A second method used to estimate the indirect, lost-profits component was based on expert security analyst expectations of earnings versus actual earnings, and these results show even more dramatically that bankruptcy costs are significant.

THE CONCEPT OF TEMPORARY DEBT

The bankruptcy cost/tax benefit trade-off analysis rests on the assumption of fairly permanent, or at least long-term, debt. If, however, the initial burst of debt in an LBO is planned to be temporary, then the objective could, and in our opinion should, be to move back along the $V_L = V_U + TD$ function in Figure 6.5 to an optimal amount of debt (approximately D^*). While the expected value of the tax benefits is probably lower at this point than further out on the line, the probability of bankruptcy is also considerably lower. By leveraging up, the owners of an LBO can reap the initial increase in value and perhaps sustain that increase until they cash out. The new debt holders will benefit either by having their debt repurchased within, say, two years (especially the senior debt holders) or by continuing to receive the high yields on the subordinated debt (mezzanine or junk bonds) in highly leveraged restructurings.

If, however, the firm cannot move back successfully along the value line, then distress may grow to the point that the firm's value decreases sharply—perhaps to its liquidation value in extreme cases. This will occur when disappointing cash flows occur, lowering the unlevered value of the firm (V_U), and/or asset sales are disappointing or impossible (usually due to changed market conditions). Finally, another type of distress could occur when a seemingly healthy entity cannot refinance its existing debt. Theoretically, this should not occur as long as the intrinsic value of the assets exceeds the debt burden. But difficult conditions in the debt and equity capital markets can prevent refinancings, even for reasonably healthy but highly leveraged firms. This was the case in 1990, as markets lost confidence in highly leveraged transactions, the new issue junk bond market in the United States dried up, banks were increasingly hesitant to refinance the highly leveraged transactions, and equity markets were performing poorly.

EMPIRICAL EVIDENCE ON SUCCESSFUL LBOs AND DEBT PAYDOWN

We have examined some empirical evidence on successful and unsuccessful LBOs. In a study carried out in cooperation with the U.S. Controller of Currency, Moore (1990) investigated a sample of 11 successful and 9 unsuccessful LBOs. (See Table 6.4.) The latter are those that have failed,

TABLE 6.4 Successful versus Unsuccessful LBOs and Debt Paydown Experience

	Successful LBOs (Long-Term Debt/Total Assets Ratio) (%)							
Observation Number	LBO − 3	LBO − 2	LBO − 1	LBO Year	LBO + 1	LBO + 2	LBO + 3	LBO + 4
1		25.8	23.8	60.6	52.7	35.8	20.3	4.2
2	8.3	1.3	3.7	76.0	72.7	38.7	42.7	44.6
3				54.0	44.7	31.6	18.0	40.6
4					36.7	36.7	63.7	69.6
5	0.6	0.3	2.9	36.0	60.5			
6						38.5	26.4	52.2
7			2.2	59.8	59.3	56.9		
8	2.8	2.9	2.2	83.8	61.4	43.5	34.0	
9	30.4	45.1	34.5	49.5	62.6	58.3	82.0	85.0
10			9.7	64.2	44.5	27.7	31.1	
11				76.6	40.9	29.3	20.2	
Average	10.5	15.0	11.2	62.4	53.6	39.7	37.6	49.4
Number	4	5	7	9	10	10	9	6
Standard Deviation	11.8	17.7	11.8	14.2	10.9	10.0	20.6	25.2

(*Continued*)

TABLE 6.4 (Continued)

| | Unsuccessful LBOs (Long-Term Debt/Total Assets Ratio) (%) | | | | | | | |
Observation Number	LBO − 3	LBO − 2	LBO − 1	LBO Year	LBO + 1	LBO + 2	LBO + 3	LBO + 4
1		12.6	41.1	33.7	36.1	36.6	33.6	41.7
2			37.3	33.0	35.8	28.1	36.9	75.2
3	8.4	5.1	4.2	61.9	62.8	64.4	67.7	129.6
4				32.4	24.9	36.4	38.0	38.1
5	35.9	35.3	23.1	65.0				
6			21.3	41.1	34.2	46.1	64.1	
7			14.6	56.4	57.1	46.0	76.1	
8			19.5	43.9	49.6	57.0		
9	17.8	31.2	41.2	49.9	50.2			
Average	0.2	21.1	25.3	46.4	43.8	44.9	52.7	71.2
Number	3	4	8	9	8	7	6	4
Standard Deviation	11.3	12.5	12.5	11.8	12.1	11.6	16.9	36.7

Source: Moore (1990).

bonds have defaulted, or a distressed exchange issue was completed. Successful LBOs are those that were still in operation without disturbance for at least three years after the LBO and were considered healthy by the Controller of Currency.

The average long-term debt/total assets (LTD/TA) ratio was 62.4 percent for the successful sample, just after the LBO. This ratio fell to 53.6 percent, 39.7 percent, 37.6 percent, and 49.4 percent in the four post-LBO years. The unsuccessful LBOs, on the other hand, had a lower (46.4 percent) LTD/TA at the time of LBO, but saw the ratio rise to 71.2 percent in the fourth year after. Hence, we observe evidence of the correlation between debt paydown and successful LBOs. Admittedly, this is a small sample with a fair amount of variation, but the data seems quite compatible with our "temporary debt" thesis.

CONCLUSION

We have noted the increased importance of financial restructurings in corporate securities valuation. To the extent that different forms of financing, including subordinated debt, are available to firms to complement the traditional role played by banks, firm valuation can be raised by increasing the leverage in the capital structure. In the case of overleveraged companies with significant risk of distress and/or default, the opposite tonic is called for, namely deleveraging to a less-burdened capital structure. Thus, capital structure is shown to be one of the key variables in determining (and changing) corporate valuation.

CHAPTER 7

The High Yield Bond Market: Risks and Returns for Investors and Analysts

"**H**igh yield junk bonds, they are finished!" This was not an uncommon refrain heard from various pundits on Wall Street and in Washington in the wake of the corporate default surge in 1990 and 1991 and after the bankruptcy of the market's leading underwriter of these non-investment-grade bonds (Drexel Burnham Lambert) and the criminal indictment of the market's leading architect, Michael Milken. We argued then (Altman 1993), and in every other subsequent instance of a major domestic or international credit crisis, that high yield bonds are a legitimate and effective way for firms that have an uncertain credit future to raise money. One should expect periodic times of relatively high defaults commensurate with the risk premiums that firms need to offer investors to lend money (primarily the institutional investors, like mutual and pension funds, that seek higher fixed income returns than are available from safer corporate investment-grade and government bonds).

Figure 7.1 displays the rating hierarchy of credit and default risk from the leading bond and bank loan rating agencies—Fitch Ratings, Moody's Investors Service, and Standard & Poor's. Note the now familiar distinction between the relatively safe investment grade bonds (AAA to BBB– or Aaa to Baa3) and the more speculative, non-investment-grade, or high yield, securities (below BBB– or Baa3).

In 2004, more than a quarter of the total corporate bond market was comprised of lower-graded bonds. And the market for high yield bonds had grown dramatically to a total amount outstanding at year-end 2004 of almost $950 billion (see Figure 7.2). Note the consistent growth of the size of the market from 1996, when it totaled under $300 billion outstanding, to the impressive total in 2004. In 2004, a record annual amount of new issuance of al-

Moody's		S&P and Fitch
Aaa		AAA
Aa1		AA+
Aa2		AA
Aa3		AA–
A1		A+
A2	↑	A
A3		A–
Baa1		BBB+
Baa2		BBB
Baa3	**Investment- Grade**	BBB–
Ba1	**High Yield**	BB+
Ba2		BB
Ba3	↓	BB–
B1		B+
B2		B
B3		B–
Caa1		CCC+
Caa		CCC
Caa3		CCC–
Ca		CC
		C
C		D

FIGURE 7.1 Debt Ratings
Sources: Fitch Ratings, Moody's Investors Service, and Standard & Poor's.

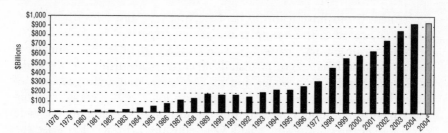

FIGURE 7.2   Size of U.S. High Yield Bond Market, 1978–2004 (Midyear U.S. $Billions)
[a]Year-end 2004.
Source: E. Altman, NYU Salomon Center, Stern School of Business.

most $150 billion was absorbed by the market at almost record low interest rate spreads over default-risk-free 10-year government bonds (i.e., a bit more than 3 percent over Treasuries).

The yields on various debt securities are determined by the market's assessment of three major risks in purchasing and holding a given issue: (1) its sensitivity to changes in interest rates, (2) its liquidity or lack thereof, and (3) its probability of default. Such yields are set by the market to provide investors with promised yields that increase with the level of these three risks. It is the third category of risk—the probability of default—that defines the high yield bond market and periodically has provided the raw-material securities that make up the distressed and defaulted debt market—another focus of this book.

High yield bonds are comprised of basically two types of issuing companies. About 25 to 30 percent of the market in recent years is made up of the so-called fallen angels—securities that at one time (usually at issuance) were investment grade, but, like most of us, get uglier as they age, and migrate down to non–investment grade or so-called junk level status. When the modern-age high yield market started in the late 1970s, just about 100 percent of the very small market was comprised of these fallen angels. Indeed, as we were writing this chapter, one of the icons of American industry, General Motors Corporation (GM), was being scrutinized by at least one of the major rating agencies as a possible fallen angel candidate. And, in May 2005, GM was downgraded to non–investment grade by S&P, soon to be followed by Fitch and then by Moody's. Ford Motor Company was also downgraded to high yield status by S&P at the same time.

The other source of high yield bonds is original-issue securities that receive a non–investment grade rating at birth. Today, all major investment banks have teams of bankers, analysts, and sales/trading personnel dedicated to this dynamic and growing speculative grade market. Since many investment banking divisions are part of larger commercial bank organizations, there is usually a close relationship between the low-grade bonds of an issuer and its corporate loan analogue, the so-called leveraged loan market. The latter are loans either issued by non-investment-grade companies or that require a risk premium, or yield spread, over the London Interbank Offered Rate (LIBOR) of at least 125 to 150 basis points.

The continuing growth of both the U.S. corporate high yield bond and the leveraged loan markets was punctuated by the record amount of new issuance in both markets in 2004: $265 billion of leveraged loans and $147 billion of high yield bonds. Those markets are much smaller in other parts of the world, but Europe has recently seen impressive growth in both. As we will now show clearly, the most important risk area, that of default, has seen a relatively large number of years when the rate of default has approached and even exceeded 10 percent. Yet the most recent high-default period of 2001–2002 has been shrugged off by the market with an impressive rebound in the following two years. Nobody was sounding serious alarms like they did about one decade earlier.

DEFAULTS AND DEFAULT RATES IN 2004 AND OVER THE PAST 25 YEARS

High yield bond defaults continued to fall in 2004, capped by just $3.04 billion in Q4-2004, the exact amount of Q4-2003, and just $11.7 billion for the entire year. This resulted in a 2004 default rate of 1.25 percent (see Table 7.1) and a 0.32 percent rate in Q4 (see Appendix 7.1). Quarterly default rates had been 0.41 percent or below since Q4-2003. We use a population base at midyear 2004 of $933.1 billion for our dollar-denominated (U.S. and Canadian) rate. Among the largest defaulting issuers (each with $500 million outstanding) were Level 3 Communications, Pegasus Communications, RCN Corp., Tricom, Trump Hotels & Casino Resorts, and USAir. One of our default definitions is a distressed restructuring (for example, Level 3 Communications) whereby creditors either accept lower interest rates, accept lower-priority securities (e.g., equity), or receive less than par at extinguishment or from an exchange of debt issues from the company. There were 79 defaulting issues from 39 issuers for the year 2004. This compares to 203 issues from 86 issuers in 2003 when the default rate was 3.5 times greater.

TABLE 7.1   Historical Default Rates—Straight Bonds Only Excluding Defaulted Issues from Par Value Outstanding, 1971–2004 ($Millions)

Year	Par Value Outstanding[a]	Par Value Defaults	Default Rates
2004	$933,100	$11,657	1.249%
2003	825,000	38,451	4.661
2002	757,000	96,858	12.795
2001	649,000	63,609	9.801
2000	597,200	30,295	5.073
1999	567,400	23,532	4.147
1998	465,500	7,464	1.603
1997	335,400	4,200	1.252
1996	271,000	3,336	1.231
1995	240,000	4,551	1.896
1994	235,000	3,418	1.454
1993	206,907	2,287	1.105
1992	163,000	5,545	3.402
1991	183,600	18,862	10.273
1990	181,000	18,354	10.140
1989	189,258	8,110	4.285
1988	148,187	3,944	2.662
1987	129,557	7,486	5.778
1986	90,243	3,156	3.497
1985	58,088	992	1.708
1984	40,939	344	0.840
1983	27,492	301	1.095
1982	18,109	577	3.186
1981	17,115	27	0.158
1980	14,935	224	1.500
1979	10,356	20	0.193
1978	8,946	119	1.330
1977	8,157	381	4.671
1976	7,735	30	0.388
1975	7,471	204	2.731
1974	10,894	123	1.129
1973	7,824	49	0.626
1972	6,928	193	2.786
1971	6,602	82	1.242

(Continued)

TABLE 7.1 *(Continued)*

			Standard Deviation
Arithmetic Average Default Rate	1971 to 2004	3.232%	3.134%
	1978 to 2004	3.567	3.361
	1985 to 2004	4.401	3.501
Weighted Average Default Rate[b]	1971 to 2004	4.836%	
	1978 to 2004	4.858	
	1985 to 2004	4.929	
Median Annual Default Rate	1971 to 2004	1.802%	

[a]As of midyear.
[b]Weighted by par value of amount outstanding for each year.
Source: Author compilations.

Default rates on leveraged loans also dropped to extremely low levels in 2004, as shown in Figure 7.3. Indeed, the 1 percent default rate for the second half of the year is reminiscent of the rate at the end of 1998. The default rate dropped to 1.01 percent at year-end 2004, down from 2.25 percent one year earlier. New leveraged loans soared by about 60 percent in 2004 to an impressive $265 billion. The U.S. component, by far the highest proportion (78 percent), was slightly greater than the amount borrowed in

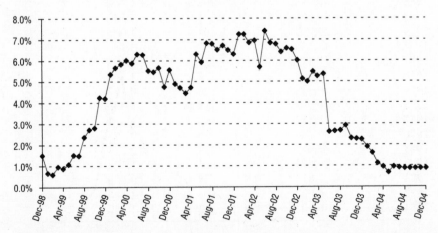

FIGURE 7.3 S&P Leveraged Loan Index 12-Month Moving Average Default Rate
Source: S&P, LPC Corp. Copyright © 2006, The McGraw-Hill Companies, Inc. Standard & Poor's including its subsidiary corporations ("S&P") is a division of The McGraw-Hill Companies, Inc. Reproduction of this chart in any form is prohibited without S&P's prior written permission.

1998, the previous record year (data goes back only to 1998). So there are several parallel results in 2004 with those of 1998, but 1998 was distinctive with some severe shocks to the credit markets in the latter part of the year (i.e., Russia's meltdown and the Long-Term Capital Management debacle).

Note from Table 7.1 that the annual arithmetic average default rate was 3.2 percent (4.8 percent weighted average by the amount outstanding each year) from 1971 to 2004 with a 3.1 percent standard deviation. So, the probability of a 10 percent year in the future is a bit more than 2.5 percent. Actually, however, over the past 35 years there have been four years (1990, 1991, 2002, and essentially 2001) when the default rate was about 10 percent or higher—a surprisingly high number of times.

DEFAULT RATES AND ECONOMIC ACTIVITY

The decline in the four-quarter (annual) default rate in 2004 is again consistent with a strong economic growth trend. Note the continuing drop in the quarterly and trailing four-quarter default rates in the present benign credit cycle (see Figure 7.4). Figure 7.5 shows the drop in default rates in 2003 to 2004 following, with a one-year lag, the end of the recession in 2001. The key question at year-end 2004 was how long the benign credit cycle would last and whether it would be similar to the long six-year cycle that occurred from 1993 to 1998. The market, in 2004, seemed to be betting that the cycle would continue for the foreseeable future, certainly at least for the next 12 to

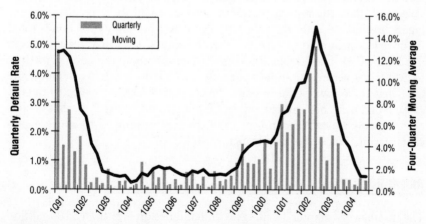

FIGURE 7.4 Quarterly Default Rate and Four-Quarter Moving Average, 1991–2004
Source: Authors' compilations.

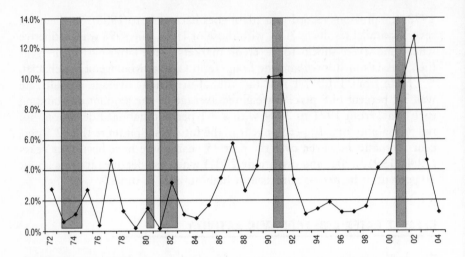

FIGURE 7.5 Historical Default Rates and Recession Periods in the U.S. High Yield Bond Market, 1972–2004
Periods of Recession: 11/73–3/75, 1/80–7/80, 7/81–11/82, 7/90–3/91, 4/01–12/01.
Source: E. Altman (NYU Salomon Center) and National Bureau of Economic Research.

24 months. We were concerned, however, that the easy credit cycle begun in 2003, with enormous amounts of low-rated new issue debt, would manifest in an upsurge in credit problems, perhaps as early as late 2005. It does not take much to shift the market from its seemingly ceaseless willingness to refinance shaky companies to a more restrictive credit posture. If this tolerance slackened, then the typical mortality pattern would drive credit problems higher. Indeed, in 2004 the proportion of new issue high yield bonds rated B– or below increased to 42.5 percent, the highest level in at least 15 years (see Figure 7.6). The level in 2003 was 31 percent, about the same as in 1999 to 2000, just before the surge in defaults in 2001 to 2002. We demonstrate later that these lower-quality bonds have relatively higher expected default rates. Note, from our earlier exhibits (Table 7.1 and Figure 7.4), that default rates actually started to climb in 1999 when rates jumped to above 4 percent, marking the end of that benign period.

BANKRUPTCIES

The number of Chapter 11 filings with liabilities greater than $100 million was 44 in 2004 with total liabilities of those firms of $66.3 billion. These levels are considerably lower than 2003's levels of 95 $100 million liabilities bankruptcies and $110 billion in total liabilities, and substantially less

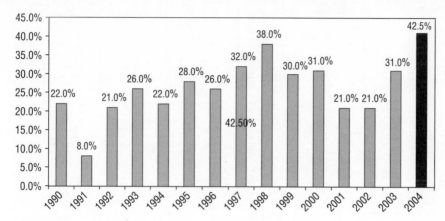

FIGURE 7.6   New High Yield Issues Rated B– or Below
Source: Standard & Poor's.

than the record totals of more than $330 billion in 2002 (see Figure 7.7). There were nine $1 billion mega-bankruptcies in 2004, led by Yukos, USAir, RCN Corp., Stelco, and Trump Hotels & Casino Resorts (all over $2 billion in liabilities). Recall that there were 100 of these mega-bankruptcies in the three-year period 2001 to 2003. For a complete list of $1 billion or more liabilities bankruptcies, see the appendix to Chapter 1.

INDUSTRY DEFAULTS

Table 7.2 shows that of the 39 issuers that defaulted in 2004, six were communications companies, three were retailers, and 23—the vast

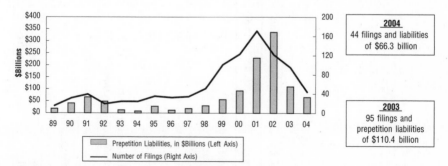

FIGURE 7.7   Total Liabilities (Minimum $100 Million) of Public Companies Filing for Chapter 11 Protection, 1989–2004
Source: NYU Salomon Center Bankruptcy Filings Database.

TABLE 7.2 Corporate Bond Defaults by Industry (Number of Companies)

Industry	1970–1982	1983	1984	1985	1986	1987	1988	1989	1990	1991	1992	1993	1994
Auto/Motor Carrier	3					1		3	3				
Conglomerates		3					3	1	1	3	3	3	
Energy	3	1	5	7	12	2	4	11	7	4	2	2	1
Financial Services	4		1	1			4	4	8	14	3	3	4
Leisure/Entertainment			1	2	6	2	4			2	4		3
General Manufacturing	9	1				3	3	1	5	8	8	7	
Health Care						1	2		2	1	1	1	
Miscellaneous Industries	3	1	2	6	3	1			4	4	3	1	1
Real Estate/Construction	7		1	1		1	1	3	7	5	1		
REITs	11	1									1		
Retailing	6	1					1	2	6	15	6	4	5
Communications	7	2	2	1	1	3	1		3	4	1	1	3
Transportation (Nonauto)	4	2		1	1	1		1	1	2			2
Utilities							1				1		
Total	57	12	12	19	23	15	24	26	47	62	34	22	19

TABLE 7.2 *(Continued)*

Industry	1995	1996	1997	1998	1999	2000	2001	2002	2003	2004	Total
Auto/Motor Carrier	1										12
Conglomerates					1			1	1	1	15
Energy	1			1	13	1		8	9	2	78
Financial Services	2	1	2	6	1	6	4	5	6		84
Leisure/Entertainment	3	1	5	5	8	9	6	5	6		79
General Manufacturing	8	6	7	6	16	23	43	22	13	17	218
Health Care	2			2	8	6	3	4	3		36
Miscellaneous Industries	1		3	3	16	34	38	25	16	6	171
Real Estate/Construction	2	1	2	1	4	6	4	3		2	52
REITs								1			14
Retailing	6	3	6	6	12	7	12	5	5	3	111
Communications	2	2	1	6	11	8	39	26	21	6	151
Transportation (Nonauto)			2	1	8	5	7	7	6	2	52
Utilities		1	1			1					6
Total	28	15	29	37	98	107	156	112	86	39	1,079

Source: E. Altman, NYU Salomon Center, Stern School of Business.

majority—were from either general manufacturing or miscellaneous industries. Five of the six communications firms were telecoms, and five of the miscellaneous firms were food related. A breakdown of defaults by industry from 1970 to 2004 is also listed in Table 7.2. As in 2004, communications and retailing lead the list of specific industries over the past 35 years.

AGE OF DEFAULTS

Table 7.3 shows that the pattern of our 39 defaulting issuers with 77 issues in 2004 of 10 years or less is seemingly atypical of the period 1989–2004, with the largest proportions coming in the fifth (13 percent), sixth (20 percent), and seventh (12 percent) years after issuance (i.e., issued in 1997–1999). Actually, that is not too surprising since those years had very high issuance of B– and below rated issues (see Figure 7.6, earlier). All other years from year 1 through 8 are around 10 percent of the total. And as much as 13 percent (five issuers with 10 issues) had bonds issued 10 years or more before default—an unusually high proportion. We expect that the more normal pattern of a higher proportion of earlier-year defaults will manifest in 2005–2006. The aging pattern of defaults will be discussed again later in our section on mortality rates.

FALLEN ANGEL DEFAULTS

Fallen angel defaults were relatively few in 2004 with only USAir and Foster Wheeler Corp. having original issue investment-grade defaults. These once investment-grade companies, however, accounted for 19 percent of all defaulting issues in 2004 (see Table 7.4), 17 percent of the defaulting dollars, but only 5 percent of all defaulting issuers. Actually, another fallen angel bankruptcy occurred in 2004, but it (Interstate Bakeries) had only rated loans and no public bonds outstanding. Since 1977, about 24 percent of all defaulting issues were investment grade at some point in their existence and the balance (76 percent) were always rated non–investment grade. We will explore shortly the impact of these fallen angel defaults on our default loss and recovery rate results.

Since there were only two fallen angel issuers that defaulted in 2004, the default rate for fallen angels was just 0.83 percent (issuer based), the lowest since 1995 when the rate was 0.25 percent (see Table 7.5). The average annual fallen angel default rate is below that of original issue high yield issuers, but the difference is not statistically significant.

TABLE 7.3 Distribution of Years to Default from Original Issuance Date (by Year of Default), 1989–2004

Years to Default	1989 No. of Issues	1989 % of Total	1990 No. of Issues	1990 % of Total	1991 No. of Issues	1991 % of Total	1992 No. of Issues	1992 % of Total	1993/1994 No. of Issues	1993/1994 % of Total	1995 No. of Issues	1995 % of Total	1996 No. of Issues	1996 % of Total	1997 No. of Issues	1997 % of Total
1	4	6	3	3	0	0	0	0	3	8	1	3	2	8	5	20
2	12	18	25	23	18	13	0	0	6	16	9	28	3	13	4	16
3	15	23	23	21	26	19	7	13	5	14	7	22	3	13	4	16
4	13	20	18	17	29	21	10	19	2	5	3	9	8	33	9	36
5	1	2	23	21	35	26	8	15	4	11	1	3	1	4	3	12
6	7	11	5	5	10	7	12	22	8	22	2	6	5	21	0	0
7	7	11	5	5	4	3	5	9	7	19	2	6	0	0	0	0
8	2	3	4	4	10	7	4	7	0	0	2	6	0	0	0	0
9	1	2	1	1	3	2	0	0	0	0	4	13	0	0	0	0
10	3	5	1	1	2	1	8	15	2	5	1	3	2	8	0	0
Total	65	100	108	100	137	100	54	100	37	100	32	100	24	100	25	100

(Continued)

TABLE 7.3 *(Continued)*

Years to Default	1998		1999		2000		2001		2002		2003		2004		1989–2004	
	No. of Issues	% of Total	No. of Issues	% of Total	No. of Issues	% of Total	No. of Issues	% of Total	No. of Issues	% of Total	No. of Issues	% of Total	No. of Issues	% of Total	No. of Issues	% of Total
1	2	6	32	25	19	10	40	12	29	8	18	9	8	10	166	9
2	5	15	37	30	51	28	69	21	51	15	30	15	7	9	327	18
3	10	30	15	12	56	31	87	26	61	18	26	13	8	10	353	20
4	3	10	14	11	14	8	65	19	56	16	23	11	6	8	273	15
5	10	30	7	6	13	7	27	8	45	13	40	20	10	13	228	13
6	2	6	8	6	5	3	14	4	21	6	20	10	16	21	135	8
7	1	3	10	8	12	6	21	6	8	2	25	12	9	12	116	7
8	0	0	2	2	4	2	5	2	7	2	3	1	6	8	49	3
9	0	0	0	0	3	2	4	1	12	3	5	2	1	1	34	2
10	0	0	0	0	6	3	3	1	54	16	13	6	6	8	101	6
Total	33	100	125	100	183	100	335	100	344	100	203	100	77	100	1,782	100

Source: Author compilations.

158

TABLE 7.4 Defaults by Original Rating (Investment Grade versus Non–Investment Grade) by Year

Year	Defaulted Issues[a]	% Originally Rated Investment Grade	% Originally Rated Non–Investment Grade
2004	79	19%	81%
2003	203	33	67
2002	322	39	61
2001	258	14	86
2000	142	16	84
1999	87	13	87
1998	39	31	69
1997	20	0	100
1996	24	13	88
1995	29	10	90
1994	16	0	100
1993	24	0	100
1992	59	25	75
1991	163	27	73
1990	117	16	84
1989	66	18	82
1988	64	42	58
1987	31	39	61
1986	55	15	85
1985	26	4	96
1984	14	21	79
1983	7	43	57
1982	20	55	45
1981	1	0	100
1980	4	25	75
1979	1	0	100
1978	1	100	0
1977	2	100	0
Total	1,874	24	76

[a]Where we could find an original rating from either S&P or Moody's.
Source: Author compilations from S&P and Moody's records.

DEFAULT LOSSES AND RECOVERIES

We calculate default loss rates to investors in high yield bonds based on the amount of principal lost (1 – Recovery rate at default) plus the loss of one semiannual coupon payment. The weighted average recovery rate (based on market prices just after defaults) on high yield bond defaults increased considerably to 57.7 percent (Table 7.6) from the 45.5 percent level of

TABLE 7.5 Fallen Angel versus Original Issue and All High Yield Default Rates (Issuer Based), 1985–2004

Year	Fallen Angel Average 12-Month Default Rate[a]	Original Issue Speculative Grade Default Rate[a]	All Speculative Grade Bond Default Rate[a]	Altman Dollar-Weighted Annual Default Rate
2004	0.83%	2.65%	2.29%	1.25%
2003	5.88	5.46	5.53	4.66
2002	6.59	8.55	8.32	12.79
2001	8.46	10.14	10.99	9.81
2000	7.01	7.10	7.03	5.07
1999	4.01	5.10	4.62	4.15
1998	3.31	2.75	2.23	1.60
1997	2.04	2.10	1.71	1.25
1996	1.38	2.00	1.71	1.23
1995	0.25	3.90	3.07	1.90
1994	0.00	2.31	1.70	1.45
1993	1.72	1.99	1.79	1.10
1992	4.50	5.48	5.45	3.40
1991	7.53	10.86	11.66	10.27
1990	5.77	8.30	8.20	10.14
1989	3.74	4.93	5.33	4.29
1988	4.25	3.39	3.95	2.66
1987	4.36	2.92	2.41	5.78
1986	2.46	6.29	4.78	3.50
1985	6.77	4.06	3.24	1.71
Arithmetic Average	4.04	5.01	4.80	4.40
Weighted Average (by Number of Issuers)	4.22	5.15	5.10	4.39
Standard Deviation	2.53	2.76	3.06	3.59

[a]Each year's figure is based on the one-year average of the 12 months for that year.
Source: Author compilation from Standard & Poor's Credit Pro Database and Table 7.1.

2003, substantially higher than the 25 to 27 percent range when default rates were extremely high in the early 2000 years. (See Table 7.7.)

The default loss rate in 2004, including the loss of six basis points from lost coupon payments, was 0.59 percent, significantly less than the 2.76 percent level of 2003 and the record loss of 10.15 percent in 2002 and also far below the historical average annual rate. The low default loss

TABLE 7.6 2004 Default Loss Rate

	Unadjusted for Fallen Angels	Only Fallen Angels	All Except Fallen Angels	Price Adjusted for Fallen Angels
Background Data				
Average Default Rate, 2004	1.249%	0.832%	1.322%	1.267%
Average Price at Default[a]	57.675	60.025	57.354	57.739
Average Price at Downgrade[a]		88.994		
Average Recovery	57.675	67.449	57.354	58.810
Average Loss of Principal	42.325	32.551	42.646	41.190
Average Coupon Payment	10.296	6.204	10.985	10.296
Default Loss Computation				
Default Rate	1.249%	0.832%	1.322%	1.267%
× Loss of Principal	42.325	32.551	42.646	41.190
Default Loss of Principal	0.529%	0.271%	0.564%	0.522%
Default Rate	1.249%	0.832%	1.322%	1.267%
× Loss of 1/2 Coupon	5.148	3.102	5.493	5.148
Default Loss of Coupon	0.064%	0.026%	0.073%	0.065%
Default Loss of Principal and Coupon	0.593%	0.297%	0.636%	0.587%

[a]If default date price is not available, end-of-month price is used.
Source: Author compilations and various dealer quotes.

TABLE 7.7 Default Rates and Losses[a] (1978–2004)

Year	Par Value Outstanding[a] ($MMs)	Par Value of Default ($MMs)	Default Rate (%)	Weighted Price After Default	Weighted Coupon (%)	Default Loss (%)
2004	$933,100	$11,657	1.25%	57.7	10.30%	0.59%[b]
2003	825,000	38,451	4.66	45.5	9.55	2.76[b]
2002	757,000	96,858	12.79	25.3	9.37	10.15[b]
2001	649,000	63,609	9.80	25.5	9.18	7.76
2000	597,200	30,295	5.07	26.4	8.54	3.95
1999	567,400	23,532	4.15	27.9	10.55	3.21
1998	465,500	7,464	1.60	35.9	9.46	1.10
1997	335,400	4,200	1.25	54.2	11.87	0.65
1996	271,000	3,336	1.23	51.9	8.92	0.65
1995	240,000	4,551	1.90	40.6	11.83	1.24
1994	235,000	3,418	1.45	39.4	10.25	0.96
1993	206,907	2,287	1.11	56.6	12.98	0.56
1992	163,000	5,545	3.40	50.1	12.32	1.91
1991	183,600	18,862	10.27	36.0	11.59	7.16
1990	181,000	18,354	10.14	23.4	12.94	8.42
1989	189,258	8,110	4.29	38.3	13.40	2.93
1988	148,187	3,944	2.66	43.6	11.91	1.66
1987	129,557	7,486	5.78	75.9	12.07	1.74
1986	90,243	3,156	3.50	34.5	10.61	2.48
1985	58,088	992	1.71	45.9	13.69	1.04
1984	40,939	344	0.84	48.6	12.23	0.48
1983	27,492	301	1.09	55.7	10.11	0.54
1982	18,109	577	3.19	38.6	9.61	2.11
1981	17,115	27	0.16	72.0	15.75	0.15
1980	14,935	224	1.50	21.1	8.43	1.25
1979	10,356	20	0.19	31.0	10.63	0.14
1978	8,946	119	1.33	60.0	8.38	0.59
Arithmetic Average 1978–2004			3.57%	$43.0	10.98%	2.45%
Weighted Average 1978–2004			4.86%			3.51%

[a]Excludes defaulted issues.
[b]Default loss rate adjusted for fallen angels is 9.3% in 2002, 1.82% in 2003, and 0.59% in 2004.
Source: Author compilations; Tables 7.1 and 7.6.

rate of 2004 was similar to the benign loss years of 1996 and 1997, when the recovery rate topped 50 percent. Over our 27-year sample period, the average annual loss rate of the high yield market was 2.45 percent per year (3.51 percent on a weighted average basis).

The loss rate in 2004 is unadjusted for fallen angel defaults. Since there were just two fallen angel defaults and the recovery rate on their defaulted debt was 67.4 percent, the adjusted default loss rate in 2004 is just slightly lower at 0.587 percent (last column in Table 7.6). Our adjustment calculation is based on the assumption that high yield investors purchase fallen angel bonds only after they have been downgraded to non–investment grade status at the price at that time. This low default loss rate in 2004 helped to fuel the better than expected return performance of high yield bonds, discussed later.

Table 7.8 lists the average recovery rates by seniority in 2004 and for the period 1978–2004. The usual hierarchy of recoveries by seniority held in 2004 with the weighted average recovery of senior secured bonds at 63.7 percent, the senior unsecured group at 56.8 percent, and senior subordinated at 37.4 percent. Discounted bonds did recover more than had been typical in the past. All seniority classes realized higher recovery rates than historic averages and medians. Note that over time, senior secured bonds (with many different types of collateral) recovered about 56 percent (median) of par value at default but somewhat higher (63 percent, not shown here) upon their ultimate recovery, senior unsecured bonds 42.5 percent (43 percent ultimate recovery), but lower for senior subordinated at 33 percent (31 percent ultimate) and junior subordinated 31 percent (30 percent ultimate).

Overall in 2004, an above average recovery rate of almost 58 percent is totally consistent with our expectations based on our univariate regression model forecasts found in Altman, Brady, Resti, and Sironi (2002, 2005). Indeed, our 2003 updated regressions, shown in Figure 7.8, predicted a recovery rate of about 50 percent in 2004, based on several of the univariate models and a 2004 default rate of 1.25 percent. This is somewhat below the actual recovery rate in 2004. A complete review of the literature on recovery rates and its association with the concurrent default rates can be found in Chapter 15 of this book as well as a book of readings by Altman, Resti, and Sironi (2005). Our estimates for recovery rates at default are based on a simple concept of supply and demand of the defaulted securities. When default rates are high, recovery rates are low (like in 2001 and 2002) and when rates are low, recoveries are high (like the situation in 2004).

TABLE 7.8 Weighted Average (by Issue) Recovery Rates on Defaulted Debt by Seniority per $100 Face Amount, 1978–2004

Default Year	Senior Secured		Senior Unsecured		Senior Subordinated		Subordinated		Discount and Zero Coupon		All Seniorities	
	No.	$	No.	$	No.	$	No.	$	No.	$	No.	$
2004	27	$63.67	33	$56.77	2	$37.44	0	$ 0.00	6	$40.66	68	$57.72
2003	57	53.51	108	45.40	29	35.98	1	38.00	8	32.27	203	45.78
2002	37	52.81	254	21.82	21	32.79	0	0.00	28	26.47	340	26.25
2001	9	40.95	187	28.84	48	18.37	0	0.00	37	15.05	281	25.62
2000	13	39.58	47	25.40	61	25.96	26	26.62	17	23.61	164	26.74
1999	14	26.90	60	42.54	40	23.56	2	13.88	11	17.30	127	32.20
1998	6	70.38	21	39.57	6	17.54	0	0.00	1	17.00	34	40.46
1997	4	74.90	12	70.94	6	31.89	1	60.00	2	19.00	25	57.61
1996	4	59.08	4	50.11	9	48.99	4	44.23	3	11.99	24	45.44
1995	5	44.64	9	50.50	17	39.01	1	20.00	1	17.50	33	41.77
1994	5	48.66	8	51.14	5	19.81	3	37.04	1	5.00	22	39.44
1993	2	55.75	7	33.38	10	51.50	9	28.38	4	31.75	32	38.83
1992	15	59.85	8	35.61	17	58.20	22	49.13	5	19.82	67	50.03
1991	4	44.12	69	55.84	37	31.91	38	24.30	9	27.89	157	40.67
1990	12	32.18	31	29.02	38	25.01	24	18.83	11	15.63	116	24.66

Year										
1989	9	82.69	16	53.70	21	19.60	30	23.95	76	35.97
1988	13	67.96	19	41.99	10	30.70	20	35.27	62	43.45
1987	4	90.68	17	72.02	6	56.24	4	35.25	31	66.63
1986	8	48.32	11	37.72	7	35.20	30	33.39	56	36.60
1985	2	74.25	3	34.81	7	36.18	15	41.45	27	41.78
1984	4	53.42	1	50.50	2	65.88	7	44.68	14	50.62
1983	1	71.00	3	67.72			4	41.79	8	55.17
1982			16	39.31			4	32.91	20	38.03
1981	1	72.00							1	72.00
1980			2	26.71			2	16.63	4	21.67
1979							1	31.00	1	31.00
1978			1	60.00					1	60.00
Total/Average	256	$54.15	947	$35.77	399	$30.17	248	$31.06	1,994	$35.43
Median		$55.75		$42.54		$32.79		$31.00		$40.67

Source: Author compilations from various dealer quotes.

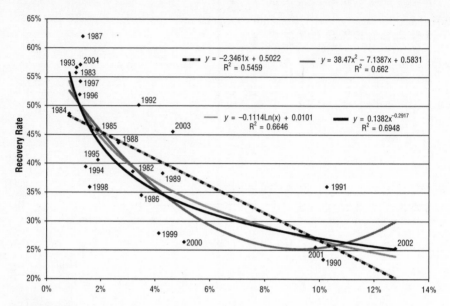

FIGURE 7.8 Recovery Rate/Default Rate Association: Altman Defaulted Bonds Data Set (1982–2004), Dollar-Weighted Average Recovery Rates to Dollar-Weighted Average Default Rates
Source: Update from Altman, Brady, Resti, and Sironi (2005).

RELATED RECOVERY RATE RESULTS

Table 7.9 shows the average recovery rate by original rating for over 1,800 bond issue defaults since 1971. Consistent with our earlier discussion on fallen angel default recoveries, we see that rates on AAA, AA, and A rated bonds are significantly higher than those rated BBB or below at issuance. Note that the non–investment grade original issues display essentially no difference in their recovery rates from BB down to CCC (high 20 percent to low 30 percent range).

Table 7.10 shows that the number of years that it takes a bond to default from the original issuance date has essentially no impact on the eventual recovery rate. So an early default is bad not only because the investor has not had time to collect many coupons, but also there is no benefit, in terms of recovery rates, to these early defaults.

TABLE 7.9   Average Price after Default by Original Bond Rating, 1971–2004

Rating	No. of Observations	Average Price	Weighted Average Price	Median Price	Standard Deviation	Minimum Price	Maximum Price
AAA	7	$68.34	$76.99	$71.88	$20.82	$32.00	$ 97.00
AA	23	61.33	76.20	54.50	27.04	17.80	99.88
A	118	53.97	47.87	55.32	27.54	2.00	100.00
BBB	318	41.78	32.67	41.00	23.88	1.00	103.00
BB	179	34.88	30.15	33.00	21.54	1.00	107.75
B	994	32.08	28.33	28.00	22.74	0.42	112.00
CCC	210	35.91	32.98	29.00	26.96	0.59	103.25
Total	1,849	$36.36	$31.44	$32.00	$24.66	$0.42	$112.00

Source: Author compilation.

TABLE 7.10   Average Price at Default by Number of Years after Issuance, 1971–2004

Years to Default	No. of Observations	Average Price
1	154	$30.29
2	322	32.08
3	378	30.36
4	288	35.60
5	224	34.73
6	180	42.13
7	125	37.72
8	62	35.69
9	39	38.37
10	105	37.10
All	1,877	$34.31

Source: Author compilation.

MORTALITY RATES AND LOSSES

The prior material on default rates and losses can be considered to be based on the traditional method for calculating the amount and impact of defaults for the entire high yield bond market. Similar techniques can be used for other assets, such as corporate loans. These metrics are useful for getting a snapshot impression of current or past default results, and journalists and analysts will find these helpful. Long-term average results, such as the weighted average default rate of 4.8 percent per year (Table 7.6), will also prove to be useful in assessing risk and return performance for the market as a whole over various periods of time (see our discussion of Table 7.15 shortly).

While the traditional approach is appropriate in some cases, it falls far short for measuring bonds or loans of a specific rating and says nothing about the aging effect and its impact on expected default rates. Indeed, one cannot be precise about the expected or unexpected default and loss rates of bonds or loans of a specific risk rating class—metrics that are critical to the inputs that banks, especially those conforming to the new (2004) capital requirements from the Bank for International Settlements (BIS) Basel II Accord, use when they apply their advanced internal-rate-based (IRB) approach to determine the amount of capital required from their credit asset portfolios. The Basel II Accord will be implemented by most large banks in 2007.

In order to be more precise about the expected default rate for a given credit rating, studies by Altman (1988, 1989); by Asquith, Mullins, and Wolff (1989); and then by Fons and Lucas (1990) and Standard & Poor's (1991) all identified the relevant cohort group for analysis as the bond rating at some point in time. As will be shown, however, our mortality measure examines bonds, separated by their *original* rating, for a period of up to 10 years after issuance. Moody's and Standard & Poor's assess default rates of all bonds of a given bond rating, regardless of their age. Moody's is of the view that macro phenomena are relevant as well as the vintage effects. It should also be noted that some rating agencies primarily use the issuer as the basic unit of account, while we use dollar amounts. Fitch Ratings also uses dollar amounts.

Altman (1989) retains the notion that default rates for individual periods—yearly, for example—are measured on the basis of defaults in the period relative to some base population at the start of that same period. The calculation, however, becomes more complex when we begin with a specific cohort group, such as a bond rating category, and track that group's performance for multiple time periods. Because the original population can change over time as a result of a number of different events, we consider mortalities in relation to a survival population and then input the defaults to calculate mortality rates. Bonds can exit from the original population because of at least four different kinds of events: defaults, calls, sinking funds and other redemptions, and maturities.

The individual mortality rate for each year—the marginal mortality rate (MMR)—is calculated using the equation:

$$MMR_t = \frac{\text{Total value of defaulting debt in year } t}{\text{Total value of population of bonds at start of year } t}$$

The cumulative mortality rate (CMR) is measured over a specific time period (1, 2, . . . , T years) by subtracting the product of the surviving populations of each of the previous years from one (1.0); that is,

$$CMR_T = 1 - \prod_{t=1}^{T} SR_t$$

where CMR_T = cumulative mortality rate in T
SR_t = survival rate in t; $1 - MMR_t$

The individual year marginal mortality rates for each bond rating are based on a compilation of that year's mortality measured from issuance. For example, all of the first-year mortalities are combined for the sample period to arrive at the year 1 rate; all of the second-year mortalities are combined to compute the year 2 rate, and so on.

The mortality rate is a value-weighted rate for the particular year after issuance rather than an unweighted average. If we were simply to average each of the year 1 rates, year 2 rates, and so on, our results would be susceptible to significant specific-year bias. If, for example, few new bonds were issued in a given year and the defaults emanating from that year were high in relation to the amount issued, the unweighted average could be improperly affected. Our weighted-average technique correctly biases the results toward the larger-issue years, especially the more recent ones.

Starting in 1988, we have measured and updated annually the corporate bond defaults and mortality rates from each of the major Standard & Poor's rating categories (AAA, AA, A, etc.) from 1971 to the present. Updated mortality statistics for 1971–2004 are reported in Tables 7.11 to 7.13. Table 7.11 shows the total amount of defaulting dollars by original bond rating. The dollar amount of defaults increases as the original rating decreases, except for the BBB original rating, which is greater than the BB amount ($74 billion versus $34 billion). The amounts again increased for

TABLE 7.11 Default Dollar Amount by Original Rating (Issues Defaulted from 1974 to 2004)

Rating	No.	Total (US$M)	Mean (US$M)	Standard Deviation	Median (US$M)
AAA	7	764.00	109.14	73.92	125.00
AA	23	3,777.40	164.23	175.59	75.00
A	117	13,751.58	117.53	175.45	60.00
BBB	322	73,528.77	228.35	425.17	125.00
BB	178	34,035.46	191.21	198.36	125.00
B	984	163,626.04	166.29	166.75	120.00
CCC	198	26,446.78	133.57	121.71	100.00
CC	8	1,223.30	152.91	88.60	132.25
C	3	615.97	205.32	207.68	195.00
NR	313	39,230.75	125.34	143.74	93.98
Total	2,153	357,000.1	165.80	224.50	110.00

Source: Author compilation.

B-rated issues. The BBB anomaly is due to the enormous amount of bonds issued by WorldCom in 2000, which defaulted two years later, as well as the greater number of BBB defaulting issues.

Table 7.12 shows the mortality rates for data through 2004. The results are generally lower than rates through 2003, as default rates continued to moderate. The exception is the slightly higher rates in the fifth and sixth years after issuance for lower-rated bonds. Lower rates in earlier years after issuance across the board can be observed. For example, the single-B rate in year 1 dropped to 2.85 percent in year 1 from 3.06 percent based on data through 2003 and to 6.85 percent in year 2, and BB-rated issues dropped to 1.19 percent (from 1.22 percent) and 2.48 percent in the first two years after issuance. We continue to observe a strong aging effort in the first three to four years after issuance. The exception is the BBB category, which has the usual (since 2002) anomalous result of a higher marginal mortality rate in year 2. Again, this is due to the WorldCom effect.

We should expect an aging effect on default rates since the first two years after issuance are marked by the firm's ability to make coupon payments both from the cash flows of the company as well as from the proceeds of the bond issue itself. After about two years, however, only the yearly cash flows are the primary source.

Mortality losses in Table 7.13 indicate a similar story to that of our mortality rate statistics. Losses are impacted by recoveries at default, lost

TABLE 7.12 Mortality Rates by Original Rating—All Rated Corporate Bonds,[a] 1971–2004

		Years after Issuance									
		1	2	3	4	5	6	7	8	9	10
AAA	Marginal	0.00%	0.00%	0.00%	0.00%	0.03%	0.00%	0.00%	0.00%	0.00%	0.00%
	Cumulative	0.00	0.00	0.00	0.00	0.03	0.03	0.03	0.03	0.03	0.03
AA	Marginal	0.00	0.00	0.32	0.16	0.03	0.03	0.00	0.00	0.03	0.02
	Cumulative	0.00	0.00	0.32	0.48	0.51	0.54	0.54	0.59	0.57	0.59
A	Marginal	0.01	0.10	0.02	0.09	0.06	0.11	0.06	0.21	0.11	0.06
	Cumulative	0.01	0.11	0.13	0.22	0.28	0.39	0.45	0.65	0.76	0.82
BBB	Marginal	0.36	3.22	1.43	1.28	0.77	0.45	0.20	0.20	0.14	0.40
	Cumulative	0.36	3.56	4.49	6.16	6.89	7.31	7.50	7.68	7.87	8.18
BB	Marginal	1.19	2.48	4.40	2.01	2.51	1.16	1.60	0.88	1.70	3.60
	Cumulative	1.19	3.64	7.88	9.74	12.00	12.93	14.36	15.07	16.52	19.60
B	Marginal	2.85	6.85	7.40	8.55	6.00	4.16	3.72	2.28	1.96	0.86
	Cumulative	2.85	9.51	16.20	23.37	27.94	30.96	33.46	34.97	36.25	36.80
CCC	Marginal	7.98	15.57	19.55	12.10	4.26	9.45	5.60	3.15	0.00	4.28
	Cumulative	7.98	22.31	37.50	45.06	47.37	52.35	55.01	56.43	56.43	58.30

[a]Rated by S&P at issuance based on 1,719 issues.
Source: Standard & Poor's and author compilation.

TABLE 7.13 Mortality Losses by Original Rating—All Rated Corporate Bonds,[a] 1971–2004

		Years after Issuance									
		1	2	3	4	5	6	7	8	9	10
AAA	Marginal	0.00%	0.00%	0.00%	0.00%	0.00%	0.00%	0.00%	0.00%	0.00%	0.00%
	Cumulative	0.00	0.00	0.00	0.00	0.00	0.00	0.00	0.00	0.00	0.00
AA	Marginal	0.00	0.00	0.05	0.05	0.01	0.01	0.00	0.00	0.03	0.02
	Cumulative	0.00	0.00	0.05	0.10	0.11	0.12	0.12	0.12	0.15	0.17
A	Marginal	0.00	0.03	0.01	0.04	0.03	0.06	0.02	0.04	0.08	0.00
	Cumulative	0.00	0.03	0.04	0.08	0.11	0.17	0.19	0.23	0.31	0.31
BBB	Marginal	0.25	2.25	1.10	0.77	0.46	0.27	0.10	0.11	0.07	0.24
	Cumulative	0.25	2.49	3.57	4.31	4.75	5.00	5.10	5.21	5.27	5.50
BB	Marginal	0.69	1.44	2.55	1.16	1.46	0.60	0.90	0.38	0.84	1.28
	Cumulative	0.69	2.13	4.62	5.72	7.10	7.66	8.48	9.83	9.60	10.76
B	Marginal	1.83	4.75	5.18	5.72	4.06	2.41	2.54	1.34	1.02	0.64
	Cumulative	1.83	6.50	11.34	14.41	19.80	21.73	23.72	24.75	25.51	25.99
CCC	Marginal	5.33	11.68	14.67	9.32	3.10	7.28	4.31	2.52	0.00	3.22
	Cumulative	5.33	16.39	28.65	35.31	37.31	41.88	44.38	45.78	45.78	47.53

[a]Rated by S&P at issuance based on 1,604 issues.
Source: Standard & Poor's and author compilation.

coupon payments, and, of course, the size of the cohort group. Due to lower default rates and higher recoveries in 2004, most mortality loss rates are lower than 2003's aggregated statistics.

COMPARING CUMULATIVE DEFAULT RATES ACROSS SOURCES

One can observe in Table 7.14 a marked difference in one-year default rates for many of the bond rating classes if you compare our mortality results with those cumulative default rates of the major rating agencies (Moody's and S&P). The different methodologies for computing marginal and cumulative rates can explain these seemingly confusing results. The differences can be explained by using:

- Dollar-weighted (Altman) versus issuer-weighted (rating agencies) data.
- Domestic straight debt only (Altman) versus domestic (or global) straight plus convertible (rating agencies).
- Original issuance ratings (Altman) versus grouping by rating regardless of age (rating agencies).
- Mortality approach (Altman) versus default rates based on original cohort size (agencies).
- Sample periods.

In our opinion, by far the most important reason is the third one, whereby we use the rating of an issue, and its size, when the bond was first issued. The rating agencies all use a basket of bonds, all with the same rating at a point in time, regardless of how long they have been outstanding and what the original rating was. So we observe substantially lower default rates in the first few years in the Altman mortality rate results than we do in the rating agency data. For example, the mortality rate for single-B rated issues in the first year is 2.85 percent while the one-year default rate for Moody's (5.7 percent) is substantially higher. Note that the differences usually persist until the fourth or fifth year, when the aging effect is diminished and all methods give fairly similar results.

These differences in results are immensely important for the bank or investor, who needs to estimate the one-year expected default rate for Basel II purposes (banks) or for expected defaults and loss reserves (all users). We believe that the age distribution of the portfolio under analysis should dictate the method used and the data referenced. Certainly, when making a new loan or investing in a newly issued bond, the mortality rate approach would be logical to use for estimating cash flows, net of defaults, and other

TABLE 7.14 Cumulative Default Rate Comparison (in Percent for Up to 10 Years)

	1	2	3	4	5	6	7	8	9	10
AAA/Aaa										
Altman	0.00	0.00	0.00	0.00	0.03	0.03	0.03	0.03	0.03	0.03
Moody's	0.00	0.00	0.00	0.04	0.12	0.21	0.30	0.41	0.52	0.63
S&P	0.00	0.00	0.03	0.06	0.10	0.17	0.24	0.36	0.41	0.45
AA/Aa										
Altman	0.00	0.00	0.32	0.48	0.51	0.54	0.54	0.59	0.57	0.59
Moody's	0.00	0.00	0.03	0.12	0.20	0.29	0.37	0.47	0.54	0.61
S&P	0.01	0.04	0.09	0.19	0.30	0.41	0.54	0.64	0.74	0.85
A/A										
Altman	0.01	0.11	0.13	0.22	0.28	0.39	0.45	0.65	0.76	0.82
Moody's	0.02	0.08	0.22	0.36	0.50	0.67	0.85	1.04	1.25	1.48
S&P	0.04	0.13	0.24	0.40	0.61	0.84	1.11	1.34	1.63	1.94
BBB/Baa										
Altman	0.36	3.56	4.49	6.16	6.89	7.31	7.50	7.68	7.87	8.18
Moody's	0.19	0.54	0.98	1.55	2.08	2.59	3.12	3.65	4.25	4.89
S&P	0.29	0.81	1.40	2.19	2.99	3.73	4.34	4.95	5.50	6.10

	1	2	3	4	5	6	7	8	9	10
BB/Ba										
Altman	1.19	3.64	7.88	9.74	12.00	12.93	14.36	15.07	16.52	19.60
Moody's	1.22	3.34	5.79	8.27	10.72	12.98	14.81	16.64	18.40	20.11
S&P	1.20	3.58	6.39	8.97	11.25	13.47	15.25	16.75	18.16	19.20
B/B										
Altman	2.85	9.51	16.20	23.37	27.94	30.96	33.46	34.97	36.25	36.80
Moody's	5.81	12.93	19.51	25.33	30.48	35.10	39.45	42.89	45.89	48.64
S&P	5.71	12.49	18.09	22.37	25.40	27.77	29.76	31.32	32.54	33.75
CCC/Caa										
Altman	7.98	22.31	37.50	45.06	47.37	52.35	55.01	56.43	56.43	58.30
Moody's	22.43	35.96	46.71	54.19	59.72	64.49	68.06	71.91	74.53	76.77
S&P	28.83	37.97	43.52	47.44	50.85	52.13	53.39	54.05	55.56	56.45

Source: Altman, Market value weights, by number of years from original Standard & Poor's issuances, 1971–2004, based on actual ratings.

Moody's, Issuer weighted, cohort analysis, 1971–2004, based on actual or implied senior unsecured ratings (Moody's Investors Service, 2005).

S&P, Issuer weighted, static-pool analysis, 1981–2004, based on actual or implied senior unsecured ratings (Standard & Poor's, 2005).

purposes. For more mature portfolios, there is perhaps more logic in the rating agencies' approach.

RETURNS AND SPREADS

Table 7.15 demonstrates the excellent relative return performance in 2004 for high yield bonds and for the entire sample period 1978–2004. While total returns on Citigroup's High Yield Bond Index registered a just below historical average absolute return of 10.79 percent, compared to the 11.37 percent historical average over the 27-year period 1978–2004, the outperforming return *spread* over 10-year U.S. Treasury bonds was an impressive 5.92 percent.

Results of 2004 increased the historic average annual spread for high yield bonds by 14 basis points to 2.36 percent per year (arithmetic average statistic) from the level in 2003. Over the sample period of our calculations, high yield bonds recorded a positive return spread over 10-year Treasuries in 17 of the 27 years and an absolute positive return in 22 of 27 years. A positive return spread, net of defaults, over the more liquid default-risk-free Treasury benchmark is necessary to attract investors and at least 2 percent per year would seem to be required to provide ample positive relative returns to compensate for higher *unexpected* losses as well as greater expected default losses.

Higher expected and unexpected losses result in positive (required by investors) yield spreads over Treasuries for high yield bonds. The historic 27-year average of 4.90 percent is indicative of these factors. Actually, the yield spread dropped to just 3.14 percent as of year-end 2004 (last column of Table 7.15), the lowest level since year-end 1984 (similar to 1996), indicating the market's expectation that the benign credit cycle would continue for some time in the future.

If one subtracts the average annual loss rate from defaults of 2.45 percent (Table 7.7) from the average annual yield spread of 4.90 percent, the resulting *expected return spread* of 2.45 percent per year is extremely close to the actual return spread of 2.36 percent per year (column 4 of Table 7.15). We are impressed by this observed rather simple, but reasonable, market trade-off that manifests in actual return spreads pretty much in line with expected results.

The year-end 2004 yield spread of just 3.14 percent implies that the market was expecting a far below average default rate in 2005. If the historic average return spread of 2.36 percent will be realized, assuming a 50 percent recovery rate (similar to the 2004 recovery) on a default rate of 1.25 percent and a year-end 2004 yield to maturity on high yield bonds of 7.35 percent, the resulting expected high yield return spread will be 2.39

TABLE 7.15   Annual Returns, Yields, and Spreads on 10-Year Treasury and High Yield Bonds,[a] 1978–2004

Year	Return (%) High Yield	Return (%) Treasury	Return (%) Spread	Promised Yield (%) High Yield	Promised Yield (%) Treasury	Promised Yield (%) Spread
2004	10.79	4.87	5.92	7.35	4.21	3.14
2003	30.62	1.25	29.37	8.00	4.26	3.74
2002	(1.53)	14.66	(16.19)	12.38	3.82	8.56
2001	5.44	4.01	1.43	12.31	5.04	7.27
2000	(5.68)	14.45	(20.13)	14.56	5.12	9.44
1999	1.73	(8.41)	10.14	11.41	6.44	4.97
1998	4.04	12.77	(8.73)	10.04	4.65	5.39
1997	14.27	11.16	3.11	9.20	5.75	3.45
1996	11.24	0.04	11.20	9.58	6.42	3.16
1995	22.40	23.58	(1.18)	9.76	5.58	4.18
1994	(2.55)	(8.29)	5.74	11.50	7.83	3.67
1993	18.33	12.08	6.25	9.08	5.80	3.28
1992	18.29	6.50	11.79	10.44	6.69	3.75
1991	43.23	17.18	26.05	12.56	6.70	5.86
1990	(8.46)	6.88	(15.34)	18.57	8.07	10.50
1989	1.98	16.72	(14.74)	15.17	7.93	7.24
1988	15.25	6.34	8.91	13.70	9.15	4.55
1987	4.57	(2.67)	7.24	13.89	8.83	5.06
1986	16.50	24.08	(7.58)	12.67	7.21	5.46
1985	26.08	31.54	(5.46)	13.50	8.99	4.51
1984	8.50	14.82	(6.32)	14.97	11.87	3.10
1983	21.80	2.23	19.57	15.74	10.70	5.04
1982	32.45	42.08	(9.63)	17.84	13.86	3.98
1981	7.56	0.48	7.08	15.97	12.08	3.89
1980	(1.00)	(2.96)	1.96	13.46	10.23	3.23
1979	3.69	(0.86)	4.55	12.07	9.13	2.94
1978	7.57	(1.11)	8.68	10.92	8.11	2.81
Arithmetic Annual Average 1978–2004	11.37	9.02	2.36	12.47	7.57	4.90
Standard Deviation	12.45	11.92	12.34	2.85	2.61	2.06
Compound Annual Average 1978–2004	11.16	8.76	2.41			

[a]End-of-year yields.
Source: Author compilation and Citigroup's High Yield Bond Index.

percent for 2005. This is derived from our own analytics (Altman and Bencivenga 1995) where:

$$BEY = \frac{R_f + \left[D_r(1 - RR) + D_r \dfrac{HYC}{2} \right]}{1 - D_r}$$

and

$$HYRS = HYY - BEY$$

where   BEY = break-even yield
       R_f = risk-free rate (10-year U.S. Treasury bonds)
       D_r = default rate (expected)
       RR = recovery rate (expected)
    HYC = high yield coupon rates
  HYRS = high yield return spread (expected)
   HYY = high yield yield to maturity

The idea of this formula is that the high yield investor earns the promised yield minus the default loss on the part of the market that does not default $(1 - D_r)$.

NEW ISSUE AND OTHER CHANGES IN THE MARKET

New high yield bond issue activity in 2004 reached a one-year record of $147.2 billion. Adjusting for refinancings, fallen angels, rising stars, and defaults, the size of the high yield bond market in the United States climbed to $940 billion compared to $886 billion at year-end 2003—a 6 percent net increase. The year's ratio of fallen angels ($34.1 billion) to rising stars ($28.2 billion) was a bit greater than 1.0. Typically, this ratio is considerably higher as it appears to be more likely that investment-grade bonds will be lowered to fallen angel status than the opposite—a rise to investment grade.

CONCLUSION

In conclusion, the high yield bond market in the United States is now a mature, universally accepted means of financing companies for a great variety of reasons, and its securities are a legitimate asset class. We will now explore the market for these securities, as well as loans to companies, when they become distressed or actually default.

APPENDIX 7.1 Quarterly Default Rate Comparison: Altman/NYU–SC versus Moody's High Yield Debt Market, 1990–2004

Quarter		Par Value Debt Outstanding ($Billions)	Debt Defaulted by Quarter ($Billions)	Quarterly Default Rates (%)	Altman/NYU-SC 12M Moving Average	Moody's 12M Issuer-Based Moving Average
1990	1Q	$185.00	$4.16	2.25%		6.51%
	2Q	185.00	2.51	1.36		7.93
	3Q	181.00	6.01	3.32		8.99
	4Q	181.00	5.67	3.13	10.14%	9.74
			$18.35			
1991	1Q	$182.00	$8.74	4.80%	12.67%	12.28%
	2Q	182.00	2.75	1.51	12.73	13.00
	3Q	183.00	5.01	2.74	12.18	11.97
	4Q	183.00	2.36	1.29	10.31	10.42
			$18.86			
1992	1Q	$183.20	$3.33	1.82%	7.35%	7.76%
	2Q	151.10	1.26	0.83	6.52	6.19
	3Q	163.00	0.37	0.23	4.84	5.58
	4Q	151.89	0.59	0.39	3.40	5.16
			$5.55			
1993	1Q	$193.23	$0.38	0.20%	1.71%	4.98%
	2Q	193.23	1.33	0.69	1.39	4.59
	3Q	206.91	0.05	0.03	1.22	4.23
	4Q	190.42	0.52	0.27	1.10	3.84
			$2.29			

(Continued)

APPENDIX 7.1 *(Continued)*

Quarter		Par Value Debt Outstanding ($Billions)	Debt Defaulted by Quarter ($Billions)	Quarterly Default Rates (%)	Altman/NYU-SC 12M Moving Average	Moody's 12M Issuer-Based Moving Average
1994	1Q	$232.60	$0.67	0.29%	1.35%	3.14%
	2Q	230.00	0.16	0.07	0.60	2.02
	3Q	235.00	0.41	0.17	0.76	2.33
	4Q	235.00	2.18	0.93	1.45	2.07
			$3.42			
1995	1Q	$240.00	$0.17	0.07%	1.24%	1.40%
	2Q	240.00	1.68	0.70	1.85	2.39
	3Q	240.00	0.98	0.41	2.09	2.70
	4Q	240.00	1.72	0.72	1.90	3.65
			$4.55			
1996	1Q	$255.00	$0.44	0.17%	2.01%	3.80%
	2Q	255.00	0.89	0.35	1.58	3.08
	3Q	271.00	0.41	0.15	1.36	2.29
	4Q	271.00	1.59	0.59	1.23	1.93
			$3.34			
1997	1Q	$296.00	$1.85	0.63%	1.75%	1.85%
	2Q	318.40	0.60	0.19	1.51	1.89
	3Q	335.40	1.48	0.44	1.74	2.40
	4Q	335.40	0.27	0.08	1.25	2.17
			$4.20			

1998	1Q	$379.00	$2.37	0.63%	1.41%	2.66%
	2Q	425.70	1.22	0.29	1.41	2.99
	3Q	465.50	1.62	0.35	1.29	2.75
	4Q	481.60	2.26	0.47	1.60	3.81
			$7.46			
1999	1Q	$515.00	$4.76	0.92%	2.05%	3.87%
	2Q	537.20	8.42	1.57	3.31	5.12
	3Q	567.40	5.24	0.92	3.85	5.91
	4Q	580.00	5.11	0.88	4.15	5.77
			$23.53			
2000	1Q	$584.00	$6.06	1.04%	4.28%	5.69%
	2Q	595.60	9.97	1.67	4.52	5.52
	3Q	597.50	4.32	0.72	4.27	5.23
	4Q	608.15	9.95	1.64	5.07	5.65
			$30.29			
2001	1Q	$613.20	$18.07	2.95%	6.96%	7.42%
	2Q	648.60	12.82	1.98	7.37	7.92
	3Q	649.00	14.65	2.26	8.56	9.17
	4Q	647.70	18.07	2.79	9.80	11.11
			$63.61			

(Continued)

APPENDIX 7.1 (Continued)

Quarter		Par Value Debt Outstanding ($Billions)	Debt Defaulted by Quarter ($Billions)	Quarterly Default Rates (%)	Altman/NYU-SC 12M Moving Average	Moody's 12M Issuer-Based Moving Average
2002	1Q	$669.00	$18.54	2.77%	9.89%	11.24%
	2Q	674.00	27.07	4.02	11.71	10.29
	3Q	757.00	37.48	4.95	15.01	9.01
	4Q	756.30	13.77	1.82	12.79	7.33
			$96.86			
2003	1Q	$750.00	$7.62	1.02%	11.36%	5.78%
	2Q	774.50	14.54	1.88	9.79	5.81
	3Q	825.00	13.25	1.61	6.56	5.67
	4Q	856.00	3.04	0.36	4.66	5.39
			$38.45			
2004	1Q	$886.00	$3.07	0.35%	3.96%	4.40%
	2Q	919.60	1.75	0.19	2.38	3.76
	3Q	933.10	3.80	0.41	1.27	2.73
	4Q	948.50	43.04	0.32	1.25	2.70
			$11.66			

Source: Author compilation, Citigroup, Moody's Investors Service, and NYU Salomon Center (NYU-SC) database.

CHAPTER 8

Investing in Distressed Securities

In the 1993 edition of this book, we wrote that the market for distressed firms' debt securities, the so-called vulture market, had captured the interest and imagination as never before. In 2005, more than a decade later, not only is this statement still true, but this market's size has grown more than fivefold since 1993 and the number of investment institutions dedicated to this asset class has more than doubled (see Appendix 8.1 for our list of distressed investors in June 2005). The market has also matured into what one can legitimately say is a genuine asset investment class. And we have been there every step of the way, watching it, documenting it, and nurturing its growth and maturity with statistics and analysis.[1] In addition to several articles and reports published on the market, there are several books related to the subject, including Ramaswami and Moeller (1990), Altman (1990, 1991, 1992, 1999, and 2002), Rosenberg (1992 and 2000), Branch and Ray (1992), Carlson and Fabozzi (1992), and Parker (2005).

SIZE OF THE MARKET

The purpose of the next two chapters is to document and analyze the distressed debt asset class in terms of both a descriptive anatomy of the market's major characteristics and participants as well as an analytical treatment of its pricing dynamics. Chapter 9 will explore its performance

---

[1]Indeed, the "Altman Report on the Investment Performance of the Defaulted and Distressed Debt Market" is an annual report published by both the NYU Salomon Center at the Stern School of Business and Citigroup. The most current version is Altman and Miranda (2005).

attributes, reviewing the 18-year period 1987–2004 with particular emphasis on the latter year's anatomy.

The large inventory years of 1989–1991 of distressed companies, following the highly leveraged restructuring movement in the United States in the 1980s, was the catalyst for our initial interest in this market and the writing of our first text in 1991. From Figure 8.1, we can see that the size of the defaulted and distressed debt market, public and private, was $300 billion (face value) and about $200 billion (market value) at year-end 1990. Returns to the niche investors in this market soared in 1991 to over 41 percent, as calculated by our newly developed, at that time, index of defaulted bond performance (see the Altman Foothill Reports on bonds (1990) and bank loans (1992) and our discussion later). The next great growth catalyst was the massive defaults and bankruptcy period of 2000–2002, when the market's size again surged, this time to a record $940 billion (face value) and more than $500 billion (market value) in 2002. The latest growth followed the benign credit cycle's impact on the reduced market size from 1993 to 1998. The number of distressed and defaulted companies grew to unprecedented levels following the combined factors of Russia's meltdown and Long-Term Capital Management's demise in 1998; massive fraud among large, heavily leveraged companies (like Enron, WorldCom, Adelphia, and Global Crossing, among others); the burst of the telecom bubble; and a host of bankruptcies in such industries as airlines, steel, health care, and retailers (see our bankrupt firm list in Appendix 1.1).

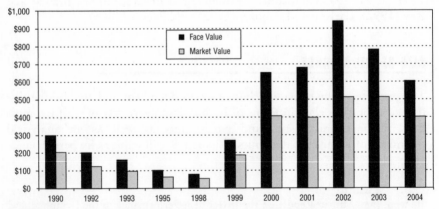

FIGURE 8.1 Size of the Defaulted and Distressed Debt Market, 1990–2004 ($Billions)
Source: E. Altman, NYU Salomon Center, Stern School of Business.

The 2001–2003 bankruptcies were massive! Indeed, there were 100 Chapter 11 bankruptcy filings in that three-year period where the filing company had at least $1 billion in liabilities—and 12 of them had at least $5 billion! The number of billion-dollar liability companies dropped to 10 in 2004—still an impressive number. Bankrupt liabilities were over $330 billion in 2002 alone, followed by $110 billion in 2003 and $66 billion in 2004 (see Figure 7.7 in the prior chapter). These liabilities, in all of their forms—bonds, loans, leases, trade debt, and other claims—are the ingredients in this distressed debt investing industry.

Our measure of the distressed debt market's size includes public bonds and private debt, mostly bank loans, mortgages, and trade debt. We include those liabilities that have already defaulted as well as those not defaulted but in distress. The latter are bonds selling at a yield to maturity (YTM) at least 1,000 basis points over 10-year Treasuries and bank loans selling at below 90 cents on the dollar.

Table 8.1 shows our estimate of the size of the defaulted and distressed, public and private market at year-ends 2003 and 2004. We have followed the *public* market's size for many years, and the numbers, while large, are based on hard data. In order to estimate the size of the *private* market, we utilize a sampling technique of bankrupt entities in order to assess the ratio of private to public debt and then use this ratio to arrive at our private debt figures. For example, the most current sampling of over 150 bankruptcies from 2002 to 2004 showed that the average ratio of private to public debt is 2.2. In prior years' samples over the period 1990–2002, we have used ratios as high as 2.4 and as low as 1.4, and these ratios help to estimate the market size time series found in Figure 8.1. (Note that size estimates for certain years are not available.) As we will discuss shortly, the size of the market declined to about $600 billion (face value) and $400 billion (market value) at year-end 2004, as the latest benign credit cycle was in full bloom. Based on our forecast at year-end 2004 for an increase in the default rate and distressed securities from the lows of 2004, we expected the size of the distressed debt market to resume its growth in 2005.

Figure 8.2 shows the aggregate *public* bond market's distressed and defaulted bonds as a proportion of the high yield plus defaulted bond market from 1990 to 2004. Note, for example, the huge proportion of distressed debt (31 percent) at year-end 2000 prior to 2002's record default rate. While a good barometer of future defaults, the distressed debt proportion can be misleading if the credit market turns quickly as it did following the end of the last benign credit cycle in 1998, and nondistressed securities become distressed and default within a 12-month period. Note the proportion of distressed bonds was only 3.3 percent at year-end 2004.

TABLE 8.1 Estimated Face and Market Values of Defaulted and Distressed Debt, 2003–2004 ($Billions)

| | Face Value | | Market Value | | | | |
	12/31/2003	12/31/2004	12/31/2003	×Face Value	12/31/2004	×Face Value
Public Debt						
Defaulted	193.58	152.00[a]	87.11	0.45	76.00	0.50
Distressed	50.51	36.60[b]	32.83	0.65	23.79	0.65
Total Public	244.09	188.60	119.94		99.79	
Private Debt						
Defaulted	425.88	334.41[c]	298.11	0.70	234.09[c]	0.70
Distressed	111.12	80.60[c]	94.45	0.85	68.51[c]	0.85
Total Private	536.99	415.01	392.56		302.60	
Total Public and Private Debt	781.08	603.61	512.50		402.39	

[a]Calculated using (2003 defaulted population) + (2004 defaults − 2004 emergences).
[b]Based on 3.9% of size of high yield market ($940 billion).
[c]For 12/31/03 and 12/31/04, we use a private/public ratio of 2.2.
Sources: Estimated by Edward Altman, NYU Stern School of Business, from NYU Salomon Center Defaulted Bond and Bank Loan Databases.

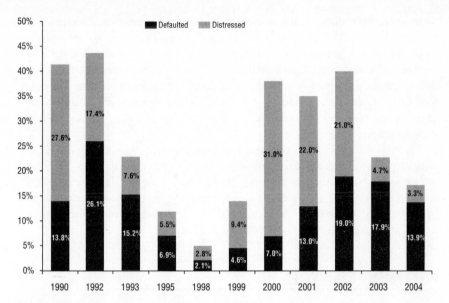

FIGURE 8.2 Distressed and Defaulted Debt as a Percentage of Total High Yield Plus Defaulted Public Debt Market, 1990–2004
Source: NYU Salomon Center Default Database.

DISTRESSED SECURITIES INVESTORS

We observed that the number of distressed debt investors grew impressively following the massive defaults of 1990–1991, and our 1992 estimate was that perhaps as much as $10 billion was under dedicated management in this sector. Most of these investors were very focused and specialized only in distressed debt and, in some cases, the equities of companies emerging from Chapter 11. We published (in Appendix A, Altman 1991) our first list of distressed investors, and there were more than 50 on the list. At the end of 2004 our list numbers about 150 strong in the United States (Appendix 8.1) and about 22 in Europe (Appendix 8.2). They range from small, specialized "shops" of two to five persons with under $50 million in assets to mega-firms with scores of portfolio managers and analysts and as much as $10 billion to $15 billion under management.

There is no one definitive estimate of the total funds under distressed securities management, but an educated guess was about $150 billion at the start of 2005. Periodically, large investors and private equity firms may become interested in these securities and possibly the control of distressed or bankrupt companies, but we are not including them (e.g., Warren Buffett's Berkshire Hathaway when it bought control of Finovia) in our distressed investor list and size estimates. Our list does include a growing number of hedge funds and private equity groups with significant assets in distressed debt as part of a number of different investment strategy portfolios. An example is Concordia Advisors with about $350 million dedicated to distressed debt and emerged equities out of over $2 billion under management.

So, from a supply and demand aspect, the market has matured in 2004 whereby the huge disequilibrium of the early 1990s and again in 2002 has narrowed considerably as demand catches up to supply. It is for this reason, among others, as we discuss in Chapter 9, that the performance has been so good of late (in 2003 and 2004). The near-term future, we believed, was likely to be more challenging, however.

INVESTMENT STRATEGIES

In conjunction with the impressive growth in the distressed debt market's size and diversity, another source of interest in these debt and emerging equity securities has been the stories about some spectacular vulture-investor successes (Rosenberg 1992 and 2000). Despite these unique episodes, usually involving large bets on corporate turnarounds, and the recent increase in new investors and capital, the formula for successful investing will continue to be a difficult set of skills involving fundamental valuation of debt and equity assets and technical, legal, and fixed income knowledge, complemented by a patient, disciplined, and, at times, highly proactive approach to asset management. We always tell our students that in order to be successful in distressed investing, one should not consider this field solely as a fixed income credit or an equity play, but rather as a combination of both with a number of credit-related substrategies that provide a more modern, rigorous risk-return framework. In addition, the attraction of this asset class is not only in its stand-alone individual security performance but also, very importantly, in its extremely low return correlation with other asset classes. We explore this important aspect at a later point in this chapter.

With respect to investment strategies, Figure 8.3 illustrates three major types, and several additional substrategies, as well as target returns for distressed debt investors. The portfolios of these investors typically consist of public defaulted bonds, private loans, high yield bonds and leveraged loans that are distressed, and residual cash and its equivalent. In addition, investors may hold other instruments for hedging purposes, such as credit derivatives or short-sale positions.

Active Control	Active/Noncontrol	Passive
Requires one-third minimum to block and one-half to control; may require partner(s)	Senior secured, senior unsecured	Invest in undervalued securities trading at distressed levels
Take control of company through debt/equity swap	Active participation in restructuring process; influence process	Substrategies: trading/buy-hold/senior or senior secured/sub debt/"busted converts"/capital structure arbitrage/long-short, value
Restructure or even purchase related businesses; roll-up	Exit via debt or equity (post–Chapter 11) markets	
Equity infusion; run company	Generally do not control	
Exit two to three years	Holding period of one to two years	Trading oriented; sometimes get restricted
Larger or mid-cap focus	Larger or mid-cap focus	Holding period of six months to one year generally; longer sometimes
Target return: 20% to 25%	Target return: 15% to 20%	Target return: 12% to 20%

FIGURE 8.3 Investment Styles and Target Returns in Distressed and Debt Investing

Active Control

The active control strategy involves mainly the "big boys and girls" of the distressed debt buying industry. The strategy requires a significant capital investment in specific company securities so that the distressed investor can possibly get control of the entire entity. In a sense, this is basically a private-equity strategy except the initial vehicle for getting involved, and eventually gaining control, is usually bank loans and/or public bonds. In addition, control often requires a subsequent injection of equity capital to help ensure the successful rehabilitation and turnaround of the firm. There have been some spectacular successes of late of distressed firms control in such industries as movie cinemas, steel, and retailing.

A related strategy to active control investing involves the purchase of several companies in the same industrial segment, leading to a combined roll-up strategy and eventual running of or sale of the combined company. An example of this is W. L. Ross's roll-up of the U.S. steel industry in the early 2000s, which took over two years, involving such major firms as LTV Corporation, Acme Steel, Bethlehem Steel, Weirton, and Georgetown Steel, and the eventual sale of the roll-up, International Steel Group (ISG), to another entity. This sale is being negotiated as we are writing this chapter, involving the purchase of ISG by an Indian firm, the Mittal Steel Group. Other examples are Philip Anschutz' efforts in the cinema industry and Eddie Lampert's purchase of Kmart and then adding Sears. The objectives of these bankruptcy acquisitions are to unlock dormant earning power, restructure the firms' liabilities, and reduce costs dramatically. The resulting success, if any, usually shows up in the aftermarket of the emerging equity, which was exchanged for the debt purchased earlier at a significant discount to par value.

One of the primary motivations of these distressed asset purchases is the concept that focused new management, with sufficient equity capital and capital market credibility, can turn around the struggling entity or entities. In the case of the steel industry, a critical factor was the shedding of some or all of the huge legacy costs involving retired employee pension and health care benefits—almost impossible to do except under the more flexible negotiating environment of the bankruptcy courts. The recent pension environment following LTV's Chapter 22 filing in 2000 has been even more accommodating than during LTV's first bankruptcy in 1986. The latter took seven years to consummate after a heated battle between LTV and the government's Pension Benefit Guarantee Corporation, which eventually took over most of the pension liabilities of the firm.

The essential valuation situation is that LTV was worth more as a going concern than it was in liquidation if and only if the firm did not need to assume most of its past legacy costs. The jobs, assets, and expected profits preserved in reorganization are presumably worth more to society at large than liquidation values. And since the distressed investor, in this case W. L. Ross & Co., controls the process by owning at least one-third of the liabilities in one or more of the impaired liability classes, the creditors were clearly motivated to vote for this plan. With the increase in the price of steel in the ensuing period after the sale of LTV and Bethlehem Steel to Ross, the strategy appears to be a huge success. A similar strategy is now being followed by Ross in the textile industry.

As indicated in Figure 8.3, the active control strategy through distressed security acquisition usually requires ownership of at least one-third in amount and one-half in number of the debt in one or more of the major impaired liability classes (e.g., unsecured bonds and/or loans), and usually requires an equity infusion by the distressed debt investor or a strategic partner, assuming control of the company via an equity-for-debt swap or exchange after the firm emerges from Chapter 11 and either managing the company for an indefinite period of time or selling the hopefully now rehabilitated company in two to three years, with a target return on investment of at least 20 to 25 percent per year. In most cases, the focus is on larger or mid-cap companies. Indeed, a number of prominent private-equity firms entered or planned to enter the distressed debt market after the huge growth years of 2001 and 2002. Typically, either a new fund is organized within the investment firm or a new unit is first organized to gain experience.

Active/Noncontrol

A second strategy that also involves active involvement by the distressed investor does not typically require controlling the entity after the reorganization period. The investor will actively participate in the restructuring process by being a member of the creditors' committee and/or by arranging for postfiling financing. The investor will often retain the equity for a period of perhaps six months to two years after the firm emerges and even place a member of its firm on the board of directors of the emerged company. Since the capital requirement is less than the control strategy, the target return is lower, perhaps 15 to 20 percent per year. Again, the focus is typically on larger or mid-cap companies—at least in terms of sales and liabilities—and usually involves several active/noncontrol investors.

Passive Investors

A fairly common type of strategy followed by distressed investors is to purchase a distressed company's bonds or loans expecting that the firm will turn around and not go bankrupt. The upside potential is from a heavily discounted price, say 50 to 60 percent of par, either to par value or to at least a significant increase in price before the firm may accomplish a distressed restructuring or acquire sufficient capital to engineer a tender offer at a smaller discount from par than the original purchase price paid by the distressed investor. Such was the case of Level 3 Communications in 2004 when it tendered for some of its outstanding public bonds at about a 15 percent discount. On the news of the tender offer, the bonds immediately responded favorably, rising to the mid 80 percents of par value—or higher for some issues. A similar situation involved Charter Communications in 2005.

Related to the distressed, but not defaulted, debt strategy is the ability to forecast whether the firm will go bankrupt. Such techniques as our Z-Score models, KMV's EDF model, CreditSights' BondScore model, or perhaps other failure prediction methods could be used to assess default probability (these models are discussed in Chapter 11). The prospect of an increase of value from a distressed state to par value in a relatively short period of time (e.g., 6 to 12 months) was achieved in many cases by both active and passive investors in recent years, especially in 2003. In that year, the rate of return to the lowest rating class of nondefaulted investors (triple C class) achieved an average return of as much as 60 percent! Indeed, investors in our defaulted bond index realized returns of over 80 percent in 2003 and almost 19 percent in 2004 (see the discussion in the next chapter).

Passive investors also invest in the securities of defaulted and bankrupt companies, waiting until the condition of the company is so drastic that a formal reorganization structure is necessary. The prospect of an increase in value after reaching some price nadir, as shown in Figure 8.4, is the motivating factor. Figure 8.4 is a stylized graph of the time-series price dynamics of a senior unsecured bond from one year prior to default, when the bond is in a fairly deep distress position and selling at a significant discount to par, proceeding to default after an unsuccessful restructuring attempt, and then defaulting. In our typical bond time line, the formal bankruptcy petition is filed several months after the firm has missed an interest payment and defaulted. Indeed, in perhaps 40 percent of the cases that we have studied, the Chapter 11 petition follows the default date rather than both occurring simultaneously.

After bankruptcy the firm's prospects become clearer, many times assisted by debtor-in-possession (DIP) financing, and then the price starts to rise based on the anticipated valuation of the reorganized firm. After a plan is submitted and confirmed by the court, based either on the affirmation of the creditors or, in some cases, by a "cram-down" by the bankruptcy judge, the firm emerges usually one to three months after confirmation. New securities are exchanged for the old debt and, in some cases, the old equity, which may participate in the newly emerged entity. Upon emer-

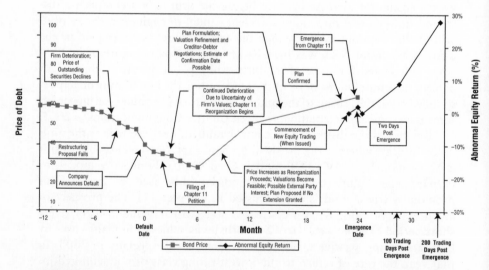

FIGURE 8.4 Stylized Security Value Time Line: Defaulted Unsecured Senior Debt and New Equity of Firms in Bankruptcy

gence, those still holding the debt securities will usually receive new debt and/or new equity. The key decision will then be whether to hold or sell the new equity. A study by Eberhart, Aggarwal, and Altman (1999) found that these new equities, a type of initial public offering (IPO), did extremely well in the postemergence 240-day period (also see Altman 1969 and Altman and Eberhart 1994). The Eberhart et al. (1999) study, based on data through 1993 and originally circulated in 1995, was followed by new interest by distressed investors in these equities. The performance of these equities was mediocre at best during the benign credit cycle years of 1993–1999 and they only performed really well in the post-2002 period. Indeed, in 2003 and 2004 emerging equities had amazing returns, probably averaging well over 100 percent annual returns. No further academic empirical study has documented this but several less scholarly analyses—for example, ones by Jefferies & Company (2003) and J. P. Morgan (2004)—also showed exceptional results.

The passive investor is basically a trader in specific distressed securities with an investment time horizon of less than one year in many cases. Hedging techniques are often utilized to protect against positions moving dramatically against the investor. These may include a short sale of the underlying equity of the company following the purchase of a distressed bond or loan that is thought to have a good chance for improvement but could default instead. The hedge can also be achieved by purchasing credit insurance, usually via the credit derivative market, whereby the distressed investor will receive par plus interest if the firm defaults on one or more companies' securities. Of course, all of these hedging instruments are costly and may not need to be exercised. We now proceed to analyze one of the newer hedging strategies called capital structure arbitrage.

CAPITAL STRUCTURE ARBITRAGE[2]

Capital structure arbitrage can loosely be defined as having simultaneous positions in two or more of a particular issuer's debt or equity securities. In the formal sense of the word, an investor may be attempting to capture price anomalies that may exist temporarily between different securities. In a broader sense, capital structure arbitrage may be used to tailor the risk-reward parameters of a particular trade to desired levels. The hedging nature of this strategy is particularly attractive to the hedge fund industry.

---

[2]This discussion is provided by Allan Brown, portfolio manager for the distressed debt funds at Concordia Advisors.

Consider the simplest possible two-tiered capital, that of a company that has one issue of zero coupon debt outstanding and then common equity below it. Structural models would say that the equity could be modeled as a call option on the firm's assets. Put-call parity would imply that the debt could be modeled as a risk-free zero coupon bond plus a put option with a strike price equal to the amount of debt outstanding. In this simple case, if we know the value of the firm, then the implied volatilities of both the put option and the call option should be equal. To the extent that they are different, an arbitrage profit opportunity exists.

Unfortunately, the application of pure structural models to identify capital structure opportunities in practice is complicated by the fact that capital structures are much more complex than the simple two-tiered model mentioned earlier, and certain variables are not clear. First, firm value is not readily observable. Many companies often segment their capital structures in a variety of ways in order to balance their need for financial flexibility and liquidity against the objective of minimizing the weighted average cost of this capital. Thus a company may have a number of outstanding securities including secured floating-rate bank debt, fixed-rate senior debt, subordinated debt, convertible bonds, and preferred stock in addition to common equity. Since there are likely to be various debt maturities, cash-pay instruments, imbedded options, and guarantees combined, modeling of the capital structure and applying arbitrage techniques in practice is a challenge.

Notwithstanding these factors, some investors attempt to capture anomalies that they believe are present. It may be the case that two securities' prices imply radically different default probabilities. For instance, even without knowing much about the fundamentals of the issuer, if one saw 10 percent senior notes of XYZ Corporation maturing in a year trading at a discount from par while the 11 percent subordinated notes of the same issuer and maturing on the same date were trading at 108, one would likely surmise that a pricing anomaly existed. While unfortunately such disparities rarely exist, the example does illustrate one way in which capital structure arbitrage can be employed. Here is a more realistic example:

10% senior notes due in five years trading at 100 (10.00% YTM).

11% senior subordinated notes due in six years trading at 98 (11.47% YTM).

The relative spread difference between the two of 147 basis points has to be considered in the context of the probability of default of the issuer over time and the relative recovery rates of each issue. For instance, if we are relatively confident that default probability is extremely low and that in the unlikely event of default the firm value is likely to cover the claims of both senior and subordinated debt by a wide margin, such a yield spread might be considered appropriate. If, however, the firm is a likely default candidate and fundamental analysis indicates recovery on the seniors to ultimately be worth par, while the subs are projected to recover only 50 cents on the dollar, then the yield spread between the two issues is likely too small. In that case an investor could create an effective putlike option by *buying* the senior bonds and *shorting* the subordinated bonds. Such a trade would result in a profit if the spread widened, as it would if the issuer fell into distress. Bonds can be shorted in much the same way that stocks can be shorted. The investor must first locate the bond (i.e., find a bondholder willing to lend the security to the investors wanting to short it). Such service is typically provided by the securities-lending operations of prime brokers. Although margin requirements will apply, bond traders do not have to announce to their broker they are shorting (they just sell), nor are they subject to any uptick rule. The trader who is short bonds must pay the equivalent coupon income to the lender of the security, much like a trader who is short stock must pay dividends, if applicable.

For simplicity, let us consider a binary outcome over a one-year horizon: Either the issuer defaults or it does not (see Table 8.2). In the

TABLE 8.2 Capital Structure Arbitrage Example: Different Seniority Bonds of Same Company

	Today	One Year from Today			
	Price	Price ($)	Yield	Income ($)	Total Return ($)
State of Nature: Nondefault					
10% Senior Bonds	100	100	10.00%	10	10
11% Subordinated Bonds	98	98.25	11.47%	−11	−11.25
					−1.25
State of Nature: Default					
10% Senior Bonds	100	85	n/a[a]	5	−10
11% Subordinated Bonds	98	40	n/a[a]	−5.5	52.5
					42.5

[a]We assume that the second semiannual coupon is not paid due to the company's default.

latter case, we will assume that yields stay constant, again for simplicity. In the nondefault case, we would have a small net negative carry over the course of the year and in addition lose one-quarter of a point on our short position as the subordinated bond accretes toward par and its price increases.

In the default case, we assume that the *ultimate* recovery of senior and subordinated bonds was 100 and 50, respectively. Given that the ultimate recovery will be a function of how long the Chapter 11 reorganization process takes, we would expect that, at default, the senior bonds would trade at some discount to that ultimate recovery (e.g., at 85—see Figure 8.3). Even though we would expect both bonds to decline significantly upon default, the thesis behind capital structure arbitrage is that the subordinated issue will fall further in price (e.g., to 40); thus profits on the short position would more than offset any losses incurred on the long position.

For the original bonds to be considered fairly priced today, the expected percentage return on this trade would have to be equal to the one-year risk-free rate. Using a one-year risk-free rate of 3 percent implies that the probability of default would have to be just under 10 percent for that to be the case. If the trader suspects the probability of default to be substantially higher than 10 percent, he or she would put this trade on. (Alternatively, if the probability of default is suspected to be closer to 0 percent, the trader might consider putting the reverse trade on: buying the subs and shorting the seniors). In that case, the probability of the "tail risk" (i.e., the risk of default) is small.

The reader should recognize that binary outcomes at specific points in time, while useful for illustrative purposes, do not often reflect reality. Defaults can occur continuously over time. As such, cumulative default probability functions are necessary to model the outcomes accurately. Similarly, recovery rates, as a function of time, might be influenced by future operating cash flows, asset depreciation, potential future changes to the capital structure of the company, and supply-demand conditions in the distressed debt market (see Chapter 15's discussion on recovery rates and Altman et al. 2002 and 2005), among a myriad of other reasons. From today's price, future states of nature would form a continuum along a number of different mathematical dimensions rather than just two discrete outcomes.

Capital structure arbitrage strategies based on seniority differences can similarly be arranged between secured bank debt and unsecured bonds as well as between bonds and common stock. These trades can be structured in a bearish or bullish fashion. Hedge ratios can be determined by optimizing a variety of parameters. For example, a trader might determine a hedge ratio so that expected return is maximized (on a defined amount of capital) subject to constraints on the maximum loss he or she would incur in any one state of nature.

Capital structure arbitrage trades can also be structured with two pari passu seniority securities that have different maturities. In this case, one knows that the recovery rates in a default scenario will be equal. That the prices and yields of the two securities are different today implies something about the perceived cumulative default probability curve to the issuer and, in some cases, the securities' relative coupon rates.

For an issuer that has various pari passu bonds outstanding (with many different maturities), one can construct a term structure of yields—a yield curve. For a nondistressed credit, this yield curve will usually be normal, that is, monotonically increasing as a function of maturity. However, as the issuer's credit quality deteriorates into distress, the yield curve will invert—shorter-dated bonds will have higher yields (to maturity). Longer-dated bonds, while trading with lower yields than their shorter-maturity brethren, will also have lower dollar prices and be trading closer to expected ultimate default recovery rates. One can understand this phenomenon if one realizes that the shorter-dated paper is subject to a smaller aggregate default probability than the longer-dated paper. The shorter-dated paper may have some reasonable chance of getting paid off at par in the near term, while the longer-dated bonds will just have to stick it out and take whatever comes their way. While the one-year bonds come with a greater yield (high reward), they also come with a higher dollar price and have further to fall in the event of default (higher dollar loss potential).

An inverted term structure of rates is unsustainable for any company. In general, conditions will either get better (price recovery) or get worse (default). As an example, consider the case of a distressed issuer that has the following two bonds outstanding:

8% notes due in 1 year trading at $80 (33.1% YTM).

8% notes due in 20 years trading at $45 (18.5% YTM).

Fundamental analysis on the credit might imply that if the bonds default they should trade at about $35 (i.e., imply a final, ultimate recovery of $45 to $50). The trader may also assume that in the case the company recovers and is able to pay off the one-year notes, the long-dated notes may also rally somewhat and perhaps trade up 10 points to yield 15.4 percent. If the trader were to short one of the one-year notes and buy one of the 20-year notes, the net profit in each state of nature would be as indicated in Table 8.3.

The reader can see that the trade makes money in the case of a default, but loses money if the company recovers. If, however, we change the

TABLE 8.3 Capital Structure Arbitrage Example: Pari Passu Bonds of the Same Company with Different Maturities

	Today	One Year from Today			
	Price ($)	Price ($)	Yield %	Income ($)	Total Return ($)
State of Nature: Recovery					
8% 1-Year Notes	80	100	matures	−8	−28
8% 20-year Notes	45	55	15.40%	8	18
					−10
State of Nature: Default					
8% 1-year Notes	80	35	n/a[a]	−4	41
8% 20-year Notes	45	35	n/a[a]	4	−6
					35

[a]We assume that the second semiannual coupon is not paid due to the company's default.

hedge ratio by buying two of the long-dated notes for every one of the one-year notes we short, the payoffs become positive in both states of nature. Indeed, for any hedge ratio above 1.55 and less than 6.8, the net payoffs in both states of nature are positive. (The reader should verify this.) Again, the hedge ratio can be structured to optimize the particular parameters the trader is interested in, be it maximizing return, minimizing risk, or otherwise.

One should recognize that an obvious shortcoming of this trade example is that it doesn't contemplate a third, and often viable, outcome. Should the issuing company be able to refinance the one-year notes by, for example, issuing four-year secured notes, the existing longer-dated notes would find themselves effectively subordinated to the new securities. In such a situation, the 20-year unsecured notes may suffer in price to reflect the lower pro forma default price for their now subordinated to the new debt situation (i.e., no longer a pari passu structure).

While we have described two relatively simple capital structure arbitrage examples, it should be clear to the reader that the number of possible combinations of trades and hedge ratios is very large. As corporate capital structures get more complex and the number and types of derivative securities continue to grow, opportunities for successful capital structure arbitrage trading strategies should be abundant. Indeed, instead of shorting the actual security, an investor today can usually purchase a credit derivative on the company (i.e., buy protection in case of a default).

Our examples do not consider transaction costs, which can be considerable, especially for longer-duration hedges, such as in short positions. One must therefore carefully consider the profit advantages of capital structure arbitrage opportunity situations net of those transaction costs and other uncertainties, such as counterparty risks. The latter is especially a factor in derivative transactions, where the payoff, given a default, will also be a function of the counterparty's default risk and recovery correlation with the underlying issuer's risk.

BONDS VERSUS LOANS

Related to the capital structure arbitrage strategy, it is quite interesting to observe the relative price movements of bonds and loans of the same company as default approaches, as well as just after default. A recent study by Altman, Gande, and Saunders (2004) found that the loan prices moved down earlier than did the bond prices of companies as they approached default. We concluded that the informational efficiency of securities' prices, based on daily secondary market prices, was greater for loans than bonds.

APPENDIX 8.1   U.S. Distressed Debt and Equity Managers in 2005

Abrams Capital	Carl Marks
AEG	Carlyle Strategic Partners
Angelo, Gordon & Company	Catlock Capital
Apollo Management	Cerebrus Partners
Appaloosa Management	Citadel Investments
Ares Corporate Opportunities Fund	Cohanzick Management
Ashmore Asian Recovery	Commonwealth
Avenue Capital Partners	Concordia Advisors
Basso Asset Management	Contrarian Capital Management
The Baupost Group	Corsair
Bay Harbour Advisors	Cypress Management
Bayside Capital	D. B. Zwirn Partners
Beltway Capital	D. E. Shaw
Bennett Management Company	Davidson/Kempner (MH Davidson)
Black Diamond	DDJ Capital Management
Blackport Capital Fund, LTD	Deephaven Capital Management
The Broe Companies	Delaware Street Capital
Buckeye Capital Partners	Deltec Recovery Fund
Canyon Capital	Durham Asset Management
Cardinal Capital	Eagle Rock Capital
Cargill Value Investment	

(Continued)

Elliott Advisors	Marathon Capital LLC
Endurance Capital	Mariner Investment Group
EOS Partners	Mason Capital Management
Epic Asset Management	MatlinPatterson Global Advisors
Fairfield Greenwich	Mellon HBV Capital Management
Farallon Partners	MHR
Forest Investment Management	Millenium
Fortress Capital	MJ Whitman Management Co.
Franklin Mutual Recovery	Moore Asian Recovery Fund
GE Finance	MSD Capital
Glenview Capital Management	Murray Capital
Golden Capital	MW Post
Golden Tree LLC	New Generation Advisers
Gracie Capital	Oakhill
Gramercy Capital	Oaktree Capital
Greenwich Capital	Och Ziff Friedheim
Greywolf Capital	Owl Creek Capital
Gruss Asset Management L.P.	Pacholder Associates, Inc.
GSC Capital	Pacific Alternative Asset Management
H.I.G.	Patriarch
Halcyon/Slika (Alan B.) Management	Pegasus Investors
Harvest Capital	Pequot Capital
Helios Advisors	Perry Partners
Highbridge	Peter Schoenfeld Asset Management
Highland Capital	Pine Creek
Ivory Investment Management	Pinewood Capital Partners LLC
JLL Partners	Plainfield Asset Management
JMB Capital	PMI
John A. Levin & Co.	PPM America
K Capital Partners	Proprietary Trading of Market Makers
KD Distressed Capital	Quadrangle Group LLC
King Street Advisors	Questor Management
KPS Special Stuations Fund	Radius Equity Partners
KS Distressed Debt	Redwood Capital
Lampe Conway	Republic
Langley Management	Resolution Partner
Laurel Ridge Asset Management	Restoration Capital Management
Leucadia National Corporations	Resurgence Corporate Fund
Levco Debt Opportunities	Salisbury
Litespeed Partners	Sandell Asset Management
Loeb Partners	Satellite Asset Management
Lonestar Partners	Schultze Asset Management
LongAcre Capital Partners	Scoggin Capital
Longroad Asset Management	Scott's Cove Capital Mgmt. LLC

APPENDIX 8.1 *(Continued)*

Seneca Capital Investment Partnership	Triage Capital
Signature Capital Partners	Trilogy Capital
Silvergang	Trust Company of the West
Silverpoint Capital	Turnberry Capital
Spring Street	Tyndall Partners
Stanfield Capital Management	Van Kampe
Stark Investments	Varde Partners, Inc.
Stonehill Capital	W. L. Ross & Co.
Strategic Value Partners	Wayland Fund
Summit Capital	Wellspring Capital Partners
Sun Capital Partners, Inc.	Wexford Capital
Sunrise Capital Partners	Whippoorwill Associates, Inc.
TA Mackay & Co.	William E. Simon & Sons
Taconic Capital Partners	Woodside Management
Third Avenue Value Fund	York Capital
Third Point Management	Xerion Partners

APPENDIX 8.2 Distressed Investors in Europe

U.S. Distressed Funds with European Offices in 2005	European Distressed Debt Managers in 2005
Cerebrus Partners	Argo Capital
Citadel Investments	Bluebay Asset Management
Elliott Advisors	Centaurus Capital
Fortress	Cognis Capital
Highbridge	Cyrus Capital
LoneStar	Orn Capital
Millenium	Picus Capital Management
Oaktree Capital	RAB Capital
Och Ziff Friedheim	Sisu Capital
Strategic Value Partners	Thames River
	Tisbury Capital
	Trafalgar Asset Managers

CHAPTER 9

Risk-Return Performance of Defaulted Bonds and Bank Loans

The prior chapter explored the anatomy of the distressed debt market, which includes investing in both distressed and defaulted securities. We discussed several elements of this market, including its size and growth, and the major players and their strategies. We now turn to the defaulted debt markets' performance attributes in terms of investment returns, risk parameters, and the correlation of its returns with those of several other relevant asset classes.

DEFAULTED CORPORATE BOND INDEX

The *Altman–NYU Salomon Center Defaulted Bond Index* was developed in 1990 for the purpose of measuring and monitoring the performance of defaulted debt securities.[1] At that time, there were no metrics of performance so we decided to construct one. The sample period of the index begins in January 1987, and as of December 31, 2004, included 104 issues from 54 firms. The index's market value in 2004 was $16.9 billion and its face value was $32.1 billion. The size of our index as measured by the face value of public defaulted bonds is about one and a half times the face value of the index and three times the market value levels during the early 1990s but about half the face value level of the record total in 2002. Because of the enormous increase in prices of existing bonds and in the prices of newly

---

[1]This index, originally developed in Altman's Foothill Report (1990), is maintained and published on a monthly basis at the NYU Salomon Center of the Leonard N. Stern School of Business. It is available, by subscription, along with data and reports on high yield debt default rates and performance, from the Center (212-998-0701 or 212-998-0709).

TABLE 9.1   Size of the Altman–NYU Salomon Center Defaulted Bond Index, 1987–2004

Year-End	Number of Issues	Number of Firms	Face Value ($Billions)	Market Value ($Billions)	Market/Face Ratio
1987	53	18	5.7	4.2	0.74
1988	91	34	5.2	2.7	0.52
1989	111	35	8.7	3.4	0.39
1990	173	68	18.7	5.1	0.27
1991	207	80	19.6	6.1	0.31
1992	231	90	21.7	11.1	0.51
1993	151	77	11.8	5.8	0.49
1994	93	35	6.3	3.3	0.52
1995	50	27	5.0	2.3	0.46
1996	39	28	5.3	2.4	0.45
1997	37	26	5.9	2.7	0.46
1998	36	30	5.5	1.4	0.25
1999	83	60	16.3	4.1	0.25
2000	129	72	27.8	4.3	0.15
2001	202	86	56.2	11.8	0.21
2002	166	113	61.6	10.4	0.17
2003	128	63	36.9	17.7	0.48
2004	104	54	32.1	16.9	0.53

Source: Altman–NYU Salomon Center Defaulted Bond Index Database.

defaulted bonds in 2003 and 2004, the market value level of the index at year-end 2004 was actually greater than the level in 2002. Table 9.1 exhibits various measures of our index's size since its 1987 inception. The variability in the number of issues, with a low of 36 in 1998 and a high of 231 in 1992, continues to be notable. The huge new-issue supply of non-investment-grade debt in the years 1996–1999 (see Chapter 7) resulted in an increase of default amounts during subsequent years until 2002. With the drop in default rates in 2003 and 2004 and a culling of issues that do not trade regularly, we observe a marked reduction in the number of issues and the face value of the index to $32.1 billion as of year-end 2004.

DEFAULTED CORPORATE BANK LOAN INDEX

Managers of distressed securities routinely arbitrage their portfolios in the distressed bonds and the private debt (particularly bank debt) of defaulting

TABLE 9.2   Size of the Altman–NYU Salomon Center Defaulted Bank Loan Index, 1995–2004

Year-End	Number of Issues	Number of Firms	Face Value ($Billions)	Market Value ($Billions)	Market/ Face Ratio
1995	17	14	2.9	2.0	0.69
1996	23	22	4.2	3.3	0.79
1997	18	15	3.4	2.4	0.71
1998	15	13	3.0	1.9	0.63
1999	45	23	12.9	6.8	0.53
2000	100	39	26.9	13.6	0.51
2001	141	56	44.7	23.8	0.53
2002	64	51	37.7	17.4	0.46
2003	76	43	39.0	23.9	0.61
2004	45	26	22.9	18.2	0.80

Source: Altman–NYU Salomon Center Defaulted Bank Loan Index Database.

companies. The size and liquidity of the distressed loan market have increased as market makers have devoted considerable resources to bank loan trading. Over the period 2003–2004, there was considerable trading in distressed bank debt (loans trading at or below 90 cents on the dollar), according to Loan Pricing Corporation data. Indeed, about 40 percent of the trading was in distressed and defaulted loans in 2003 and 37 percent in 2004.[2] We responded to this increased level of emphasis on bank loans by introducing an Index of Defaulted Bank Debt Facilities, as well as a Combined Index of bonds and bank loans in 1996.

The Altman–NYU Salomon Center Defaulted Bank Loan Index, like the Defaulted Bond Index, is a market-weighted, monthly total return index composed of U.S. and Canadian companies. The index contained 17 facilities at its inception in December 1995 and grew to a high of 141 facilities from 56 borrowers as of December 31, 2001. It has since shrunk to 45 facilities from 26 borrowers at the end of 2004 (see Table 9.2). The market value of this index was $18.2 billion at the end of 2004, with a face value of $22.9 billion. The reduced number of bankruptcies and their liabilities in 2004 and significant emergence from bankruptcy over the

---

[2]From Loan Pricing Corporation (LPC). The 2004 percentage is not exactly comparable to 2003 due to a change in the calculation methodology by LPC. The 2004 figure is an extrapolation.

year by firms already in bankruptcy accounted for the reason for the market's size decrease.

MARKET/FACE VALUE RATIOS

We consider the ratio of the aggregate market value to face value of the component securities that comprise our indexes to be an important measure of the defaulted debt markets' current relative health and potential future returns. This ratio for defaulted *bonds* has ranged, at year-end, from a maximum level of 0.74 in 1987 to a minimum of 0.15 in 2000 (see Figure 9.1). While the Defaulted Bond Index market/face value ratio has varied within a fairly narrow range of 0.30 to 0.55 during a majority of years in our 18-year sample period (1987–2004), abnormal annual returns for the index have resulted in a number of market/face value ratio observations well outside of this range. Indeed, the ratio was 0.25 or below for the five-year period 1998–2002 and ended 2002 at 0.17. In 2003, the ratio almost tripled to 0.47 and then increased further in 2004 to the near record 0.53. Note also that the Defaulted Bank Loan Index dropped to its all-time low in 2002 of 0.46, but rebounded sharply to 0.61 one year later and reached a record level of 0.80 as of year-end 2004.

From Figure 9.1, we can observe that the level of the market/face value ratios at the end of 2004 were somewhat above the mean and median level

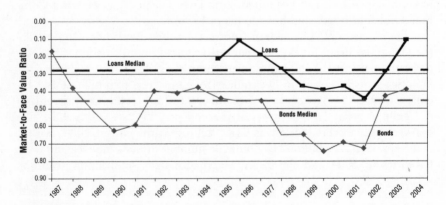

FIGURE 9.1   Defaulted Debt Indexes: Market-to-Face Value Ratios (Annual 1987–2004)
Loans median market-to-face value is 0.62 and average market-to-face value is 0.63. Bonds median market-to-face value is 0.45 and average market-to-face value is 0.39.

for the period 1987–2004 for defaulted bonds (0.53 vs. 0.45 median) and considerably above (0.80) the mean (0.63) and median (0.62) levels for defaulted bank loans. One can conclude that if there is movement in the average price level of both defaulted bonds and bank loans that resembles a regression to the mean, then both indexes should decrease after 2004, or at least not rise very much.

Our indexes are based on long-only investment strategy portfolios. Of course, many distressed debt investors now do not follow a long-only strategy, but hedge their portfolios through various arbitrage strategies using shorting techniques such as capital structure arbitrage and credit default swaps. And distressed investors can also invest in other instruments, such as the equity of firms emerging from bankruptcy, high yield bonds and loans, as well as holding cash.

PERFORMANCE MEASUREMENT

Our indexes include the securities of firms at various stages of reorganization in either bankruptcy or restructuring. We calculate the returns for the index using data compiled from just after default to the point when the bankrupt firm emerges from Chapter 11 or is liquidated, or until the default is "cured" or resolved through an exchange. The securities of distressed, restructured companies are also included in the index until the restructuring is completed. The Defaulted Bond Index includes issues of all seniorities, from senior secured to junior unsecured debt. A study by Altman and Eberhart (1994), updated by Standard & Poor's (Brand and Behar 2000), measures the performance of defaulted debt from the time of original issuance through default and then to emergence from bankruptcy. These studies conclude that the seniority of the issue is an extremely important characteristic of the performance of defaulted securities over specific periods, whether from issuance to emergence or from default to emergence. In both studies, the senior debt securities outperformed the more junior ones.

Our indexes do not include convertible or non-U.S. and Canadian company and non-dollar-denominated issues, nor do they include distressed, but not defaulted, securities. And, as noted, the performance measure is based on a fully invested, long-only strategy. Returns are calculated from individual bond and bank loan security movements; they are not based on some average performance by managers. Returns are gross returns and do not reflect manager fees and expenses. A manager performance index of distressed debt investors can also be found in the *Wall Street Journal*, on a daily basis.

PERFORMANCE OF DEFAULTED BONDS, 2004

The Altman–NYU Salomon Center Defaulted Bond Index continued its impressive performance in 2004, increasing by 18.93 percent. This marks the index's 12th positive annual return in our 18-year period (Table 9.3). The index experienced positive returns in 7 of the 12 months in 2004. The positive results are not surprising as the supply of newly defaulted bond issues decreased throughout the year, helping to drive up prices. The level of the index increased from 337.5 at the end of 2003 to 401.3 at the end of 2004 (December 1986 = 100).

The S&P 500 index finished 2004 with an annual return of 10.88 percent (assuming reinvestment of dividends) in 2004. Defaulted bond securities outperformed the total return on the S&P 500 index for the fourth year in a row. The Defaulted Bond Index also outperformed the Citigroup High Yield Bond Market Index, which itself returned an impressive 10.79 percent. Ten-year government bonds underperformed all of our risky security indexes, posting a positive return of only 4.87 percent. We will analyze the correlations of these different asset class returns shortly.

EIGHTEEN-YEAR COMPARATIVE PERFORMANCE

Table 9.3 exhibits the return on defaulted bonds, common stocks, and high yield bonds over the entire 18-year sample period, 1987–2004. The arithmetic annual average for the Altman–NYU Salomon Center Defaulted Bond Index increased to 11.34 percent, up by 0.45 percent from one year ago. This arithmetic average annual return is now about 2 percent below that of the S&P 500 index (13.38 percent per year). And the Defaulted Bond Index has an annual average return above that of the Citigroup High Yield Bond Market Index (9.77 percent per year) for the sample period. In 8 of the 18 years, defaulted bonds performed better than both of the other two indexes, and in 7 years the Defaulted Bond Index was the lowest performer.

The standard deviation of annual returns for the Defaulted Bond Index decreased somewhat in 2004, but for the second year in a row it remained the highest by far of the three indexes. Comparing volatility on a monthly basis, however, the standard deviation of monthly returns for defaulted bond issues (4.35 percent) is, in fact, slightly lower than that of the S&P 500 index (4.49 percent), while each of these indexes is considerably more volatile than the High Yield Bond Market Index (2.12 percent). The discrepancy between the relatively low standard deviation of high yield bonds

TABLE 9.3 Altman–NYU Salomon Center Defaulted Bond Index: Comparison of Returns, 1987–2004

Year	Altman–NYU Salomon Center Defaulted Bond Index	S&P 500 Index	Citigroup High Yield Bond Market Index
1987	37.85%	5.26%	3.63%
1988	26.49	16.61	13.47
1989	−22.78	31.68	2.75
1990	−17.08	−3.12	−7.04
1991	43.11	30.48	39.93
1992	15.39	7.62	17.86
1993	27.91	10.08	17.36
1994	6.66	1.32	−1.25
1995	11.26	37.56	19.71
1996	10.21	22.96	11.29
1997	−1.58	34.36	13.18
1998	−26.91	28.58	3.60
1999	11.34	20.98	1.74
2000	−33.09	−9.11	−5.68
2001	17.47	−11.87	5.44
2002	−5.98	−22.08	−1.53
2003	84.87	28.70	30.62
2004	18.93	10.88	10.79
1987–2004 Arithmetic Average (Annual) Rate	11.34%	13.38%	9.77%
Standard Deviation	28.32%	17.51%	12.30%
1987–2004 Compounded Average (Annual) Rate	8.03%	12.03%	9.15%
1987–2004 Arithmetic Average (Monthly) Rate	0.74%	1.04%	0.76%
Standard Deviation	4.35%	4.49%	2.12%
1987–2004 Compounded Average (Monthly) Rate	0.60%	0.91%	0.73%

Source: NYU Salomon Center, S&P, and Citigroup.

and the higher figure of defaulted bonds is expected, because high yield bonds pay a steady fixed interest component while defaulted bonds typically do not pay any interest at all.

DEFAULTED BANK LOAN PERFORMANCE

It is typical that managers of distressed securities invest in both the distressed bonds and the private debt (particularly bank debt) of defaulting companies. As noted, the increase in defaulted private debt investment has developed as the bank loan market has increased in size and liquidity. The comparative informational efficiency of the bank loan versus public bond daily prices of defaulting companies has been recently analyzed in Altman, Gande, and Saunders (2004). They found that bank loan prices fall earlier than bond prices as the firm migrates toward default, at least for the period 1999–2001.

In 2004, our Defaulted Bank Loan Index performed fairly well compared to most asset classes, returning 11.70 percent for the year and closing at 171.4 (December 1995 = 100). This index did not perform as well as our Defaulted Bond Index, but did slightly better than the Citigroup High Yield Bond Market Index and the S&P 500 index (see Table 9.4). Over the 1996–2004 period, defaulted bank loans have underperformed common stocks and high yield bonds, but the time series is quite short. The index was the top performer in three years of our nine-year sample period and was also the poorest performer in three years. Our Bank Loan Index logged eight positive return months in 2004. The average annual return of the Defaulted Bank Loan Index since its inception in 1996 rose to 6.81 percent from 6.20 percent at the end of 2003. The arithmetic average annual return is slightly below that of the Citigroup High Yield Bond Market Index (7.72 percent) over the comparable period. Returns on defaulted bank loans are considerably less volatile than defaulted bonds and also less volatile than stocks. And they are only slightly more volatile than high yield bonds.

COMBINED BOND AND BANK LOAN INDEX

Our Combined Defaulted Securities Index is calculated based on the relative market values and total returns of defaulted public bonds and pri-

TABLE 9.4 Altman–NYU Salomon Center Defaulted Bank Loan Index: Comparison of Returns, 1996–2004

Year	Altman–NYU Salomon Center Defaulted Bank Loan Index	S&P 500 Index	Citigroup High Yield Bond Market Index
1996	19.56%	22.96%	11.29%
1997	1.75	34.36	13.18
1998	−10.22	28.58	3.60
1999	0.65	20.98	1.74
2000	−6.59	−9.11	−5.68
2001	13.94	−11.87	5.44
2002	3.03	−22.08	−1.53
2003	27.48	28.70	30.62
2004	11.70	10.88	10.79
1996–2004 Arithmetic Average (Annual) Rate	6.81%	11.49%	7.72%
Standard Deviation	12.31%	20.71%	10.60%
1996–2004 Compounded Average (Annual) Rate	6.19%	9.64%	7.28%
1996–2004 Arithmetic Average (Monthly) Rate	0.56%	0.88%	0.62%
Standard Deviation	2.76%	4.69%	2.36%
1996–2004 Compounded Average (Monthly) Rate	0.53%	0.71%	0.56%

Source: NYU Salomon Center, S&P, and Citigroup.

vate bank loans. Returns for the index, from its inception in 1996 through 2004, are displayed in Table 9.5. The annual return for the Combined Index was up 15.14 percent for 2004. The cumulative index level closed out the year at 166.3, up from 144.4 at year-end 2003 (December 1995 = 100). The Combined Index enables us to benchmark performance criteria for a more broadly defined defaulted securities market. At the end of 2004, the market values of the bond versus bank loan indexes were very close to each other at $16.9 billion for bonds and $18.2 billion for loans.

TABLE 9.5 Combined Altman–NYU Salomon Center Defaulted Public Bond and Bank Loan Index: Comparison of Returns, 1996–2004

Year	Altman–NYU Salomon Center Combined Defaulted Securities Index	S&P 500 Index	Citigroup High Yield Bond Market Inded
1996	15.62%	22.96%	11.29%
1997	0.44	34.36	13.18
1998	–17.55	28.58	3.60
1999	4.45	20.98	1.74
2000	–15.84	–9.11	–5.68
2001	15.53	–11.87	5.44
2002	–0.53	–22.08	–1.53
2003	49.30	28.70	30.62
2004	15.14	10.88	10.79
1996–2004 Arithmetic Average (Annual) Rate	7.40%	11.49%	7.72%
Standard Deviation	20.10%	20.71%	10.60%
1996–2004 Compounded Average (Annual) Rate	5.81%	9.64%	7.28%
1996–2004 Arithmetic Average (Monthly) Rate	0.52%	0.88%	0.62%
Standard Deviation	3.26%	4.69%	2.36%
1996–2004 Compounded Average (Monthly) Rate	0.41%	0.71%	0.56%

Source: NYU Salomon Center, S&P, and Citigroup.

DIVERSIFICATION: MANAGEMENT STYLES AND RETURN CORRELATIONS

We now explore the risk dimensions of defaulted debt investing as well as the different investment strategies demonstrated by investors.

Return Correlations

Our analysis suggests that an effective strategy is to include defaulted debt in a larger portfolio of risky securities. Several domestic pension funds and foreign portfolios have effectively used this strategy by allocating a portion of their total investments to distressed debt money managers. And, of course, this is the primary strategy of certain funds of funds. The principal idea behind this strategy is that the returns from investing in distressed debt securities have relatively low correlations with returns for most other major asset classes, and, in the case of funds of funds, different investor styles complement each other. The former can be clearly seen from the data on the correlation of returns that we have been tracking for many years and from our listing of investment strategies in Figure 8.3 of the preceding chapter.

Table 9.6 exhibits the correlations between the Altman–NYU Defaulted Bond Index and the two other risky asset classes—common stocks and high yield bonds—as well as the 10-year U.S. Treasury bond for the period 1987–2004. As of December 31, 2004, the monthly return correlation between defaulted bonds and the S&P 500 for the period 1987–2004 was only 28.84 percent. The correlation between defaulted bonds and S&P equities in 2004 was slightly above the correlation between these two asset classes in 2003 (28.64). It is noteworthy that the correlation was weak, because holders of defaulted bonds usually exchange their debt for the equity of the emerged Chapter 11 entity, unless they sell the debt just prior to emergence. However, we do not yet have an index of emerging equity performance. Incidentally, the performance of emerging equities in 2004 was again, like in 2003, quite impressive (we do not have precise results). See Eberhart, Aggarwal, and Altman (1999) and J. P. Morgan (2004) for an analysis of the equity performance of firms emerging from Chapter 11.

The correlation between defaulted bonds and high yield bonds is comparatively strong. The monthly correlation of returns is 61.35 percent, while the quarterly correlation between these two asset classes is slightly

TABLE 9.6 Correlation of Altman–NYU Salomon Center Defaulted Bond Index with Other Securities Indexes, 1987–2004: Bond Index Correlations—Monthly

	Correlation of Monthly Returns January 1987 to December 2004			
	Altman Defaulted Bond Index	S&P 500 Index	Citigroup High Yield Bond Index	10-Year T-Bond
Altman Defaulted Bond Index	100.00%	28.84%	61.35%	−19.07%
S&P 500 Index		100.00%	50.13%	3.90%
Cititgroup High Yield Bond Index			100.00%	10.61%
10-Year T-Bond				100.00%

Source: NYU Salomon Center, S&P, and Citigroup.

higher. Both are down slightly from 2003. As was the case in the past, the correlation between high yield bonds and the Defaulted Bank Loan Index is weaker than that between defaulted bonds and high yield bonds, at 44.69 percent (see Table 9.7) versus 61.35 percent (Table 9.6). The returns for defaulted bank loans have a negative relationship with the S&P 500 (−0.90 percent) and an even more negative correlation (−19.64 percent) with 10-year U.S. Treasuries. Finally, the monthly returns correlation between our two defaulted debt indexes (bonds and bank loans) was "only" 61.09 percent. A somewhat higher correlation might have been expected, but the reality perhaps reflects the trading strategies of distressed investors, such as capital structure arbitrage, where bonds may be invested long and loans shorted or vice versa, as well as negotiated changes in the relative claims of loans versus bonds during the bankruptcy process. Indeed, in some months we observe quite dramatic increases in one security (e.g., the bank loans of Owens Corning in February 2005) and significant declines in the bonds of the same company, or vice versa.

Tables 9.7 and 9.8 also show our correlation results for subsample periods within the 18-year period. The correlations of defaulted bonds with other asset classes were weakest during the six-year benign credit cycle, 1993–1998, when default rates were extremely low. As we discussed in Chapter 7, the credit market was in a benign credit phase for the 15 months prior to year-end 2004 (and this condition persisted through at least the first half of 2005).

Diversification by Manager Style

Almost all portfolio managers involved in the distressed market are specialists in the sector, rather than investors in distressed securities within broader-based portfolios. (Some hedge funds, however, provide a multi-asset alternative to investors.) Therefore, the avenue of diversification appears to be primarily through the use of different investment managers. There are some rare exceptions where a mutual fund offers investments in more traditional debt and equity securities combined with distressed securities (e.g., Franklin Mutual Recovery Fund). Some funds of funds and foreign closed-end funds have adopted the strategy of selecting managers of distressed securities with different styles. In addition to diversifying across asset classes, these funds have a strategy of investing with managers of distressed securities who practice different strategies (e.g., active, passive, control, long-short, senior vs. subordinate). We discussed the three major types of strategies and their substrategies in Chapter 8. There were about 150 investment institutions that specialized in

TABLE 9.7 Correlation of Altman–NYU Salomon Center Index of Bank Loans with Other Securities Indexes, 1996–2004 Loan Index Correlations—Monthly

Correlation of Monthly Returns January 1996 to December 2004					
	Altman Loan Index	S&P 500 Index	Citigroup High Yield Bond Index	10-Year T-Bond	Altman Bond Index
Altman Loan Index	100.00%	–0.90%	44.69%	–19.64%	61.09%
S&P 500 Index		100.00	49.48	–16.67	24.18
Citigroup High Yield Bond Index			100.00	–6.49	63.69
10-Year T-Bond				100.00	–25.57
Altman Bond Index					100.00

Correlation of Monthly Returns January 1996 to December 2000					
	Altman Loan Index	S&P 500 Index	Citigroup High Yield Bond Index	10-Year T-Bond	Altman Bond Index
Altman Loan Index	100.00%	–7.41%	39.51%	–30.73%	58.68%
S&P 500 Index		100.00	56.12	16.55	18.53
Citigroup High Yield			100.00	2.97	56.16
10-Year T-Bond				100.00	–44.65
Altman Bond Index					100.00

Correlation of Monthly Returns January 2001 to December 2004					
	Altman Loan Index	S&P 500 Index	Citigroup High Yield Bond Index	10-Year T-Bond	Altman Bond Index
Altman Loan Index	100.00%	14.74%	50.95%	–10.27%	60.16%
S&P 500 Index		100.00	52.50	–47.92	45.72
Citigroup High Yield			100.00	–11.83	75.59
10-Year T-Bond				100.00	–9.69
Altman Bond Index					100.00

Source: NYU Salomon Center, S&P, and Citigroup.

TABLE 9.8   Correlation of Altman–NYU Salomon Center Index of Defaulted Bonds with Other Securities Indexes, 1987–2004 (Subperiods)

Correlation of Monthly Returns January 1987 to December 1992				
	Altman Bond Index	S&P 500 Index	Citigroup High Yield Bond Index	10-Year T-Bond
Altman Bond Index	100.00%	37.62%	60.28%	−18.64%
S&P 500 Index		100.00	49.25	21.52
Citigroup High Yield Bond Index			100.00	21.40
10-Year T-Bond				100.00

Correlation of Monthly Returns January 1993 to December 1998				
	Altman Bond Index	S&P 500 Index	Citigroup High Yield Bond Index	10-Year T-Bond
Altman Bond Index	100.00%	14.59%	50.49%	−25.18%
S&P 500 Index		100.00	61.45	26.74
Citigroup High Yield Bond Index			100.00	33.92
10-Year T-Bond				100.00

Correlation of Monthly Returns January 1999 to December 2004				
	Altman Bond Index	S&P 500 Index	Citigroup High Yield Bond Index	10-Year T-Bond
Altman Bond Index	100.00%	32.69%	68.92%	−15.06%
S&P 500 Index		100.00	46.76	−31.53
Citigroup High Yield Bond Index			100.00	−8.80
10-Year T-Bond				100.00

Source: NYU Salomon Center, S&P, and Citigroup.

distressed debt as of year-end 2004. Our estimate is that these investment enterprises had combined assets of about $150 billion under management at year-end 2004 dedicated to distressed debt and equity investments of emerging companies.

PROPORTION AND SIZE OF THE DISTRESSED AND DEFAULTED PUBLIC AND PRIVATE DEBT MARKETS

The distressed and defaulted public debt proportion of the straight (nonconvertible) high yield and defaulted corporate debt markets in the United States at year-end 2004 comprised about 17.2% percent of the combined total high yield and defaulted debt markets (about $1.1 trillion), down considerably from the 22.6 percent proportion in 2003 (see Figure 8.2). The distressed proportion of bonds yielding at least 1,000 basis points over 10-year Treasuries was 3.3 percent (3.9 percent of just the high yield market) in 2004. This level is lower than the 4.7 percent proportion in 2003 and the lowest since 1998 when the share was 2.8 percent. While such a low proportion generally bodes for very low future one-year default rates, observe that the 1999 default rate rose significantly to 4.15 percent (Table 7.1), despite the very low distressed proportion in 1998 (Figure 8.2).

The defaulted debt proportion also dropped in 2004, falling to 13.9 percent from 17.9 percent one year earlier. This reflects the relatively small size of new 2004 defaults ($11.7 billion) compared with emerging bonds from reorganization of more than $53 billion.

The total of defaulted and distressed public and private debt decreased in 2004 to just over $600 billion (face value) and about $400 billion (market value) (see Figure 8.1 and Table 8.1). This includes $152 billion (face value) of defaulted bonds still outstanding, down by more than $40 billion from one year earlier, as emergences continued to dominate new defaults. Indeed, at least 30 firms with a minimum of $100 million in liabilities and with public debt emerged from Chapter 11 in 2004. These include MCI/WorldCom's giant bankruptcy in April 2004, leading a group of seven emerged firms with public liabilities greater than $1 billion. Our distressed total dropped to slightly less than $37 billion (face value) as of year-end 2004. The market values of public and private defaulting securities fell to a bit over $400 billion—a drop of more than $100 billion in just one year. We have observed, however, that the size of the distressed and defaulted debt population increased again in the first half of 2005.

CONCLUSION

It is fair to say, we believe, that the distressed debt market has evolved to the point that it can be considered a legitimate investment asset class, with its own set of performance attributes, dedicated investors and relevant correlations with other asset classes. While the size of this market will vary over time, it is now clear that it will persevere as an asset class that deserves its own special analytics and attention.

CHAPTER 10

Corporate Governance in Distressed Firms

Almost every aspect of a firm's governance is affected in some way when firms enter financial distress and bankruptcy. To start, it is generally accepted that the fiduciary duties of managers and directors, normally owed only to the corporation and its shareholders, expand to include creditors when a firm is in the so-called zone of insolvency. Given that the interests of various parties in a reorganization including creditors and shareholders often conflict, this can create difficulties in determining managers' responsibilities. Further, both management and board of directors positions are likely to experience high turnover, particularly when the firm files for Chapter 11. Accompanying those changes, compensation contracts will be revised over the course of a restructuring. Finally, most significant restructurings lead to large changes in ownership, with the former creditors often emerging as the new owners of the company. As a result, changes in control are common, though the mechanisms through which this occurs can be quite different than for nondistressed firms. This chapter discusses these aspects of governance and their impact on the incentives of managers and other participants in the restructuring process.

Except in rare cases in which creditors or other parties successfully petition the court to appoint a trustee, the debtor's management continues to operate the business of a firm in Chapter 11. Management has an exclusive right to propose a reorganization plan during the first 120 days of bankruptcy, and during additional periods as approved by the court. These pro-debtor features of the Bankruptcy Code yield to the incumbent management considerable influence over the course of the restructuring and development of the plan. Given the number of creditors, shareholders, and other constituencies that may be involved, the Bankruptcy Code provides for appointments of committees for other groups. These committees are represented by professional advisers, and their costs are paid by the debtor (ultimately from distributions under the plan). For large public companies, an unsecured creditors committee is frequently appointed, but other committees must be approved by the court and appointed by the U.S. Trustee's office, making their influence on the negotiation process less certain. For example, Betker (1995) finds that an equity committee is formed in only 37.3 percent of a sample of 75 Chapter 11 cases between 1982 and 1990. The governance structure of the firm in bankruptcy will have an important influence on the permitted roles of the parties involved and the development of a reorganization plan.

FIDUCIARY DUTIES OF MANAGERS AND DIRECTORS

When a corporation is solvent, the managers and directors have fiduciary duties to the corporation and its shareholders. Creditors are entitled to protection only as provided in the terms of their original contracts. This relationship changes, however, when the firm becomes insolvent. The predominant view among legal scholars is that the directors and officers of an insolvent corporation owe fiduciary duties to both creditors and shareholders (Branch 2000).

The trigger point for this expansion of duties occurs not at an easily observable event, such as the filing of a Chapter 11 petition, but rather at the point when the corporation is in the zone of insolvency.[1] This presents some obvious difficulties in measuring when the company is insolvent, and makes valuation of the distressed firm a key issue. The expansion of duties also creates potential conflicts, as the shareholders and various creditors often have opposing interests. For example, senior creditors may prefer the liquidation of assets to avoid the loss of value of their collateral. Equity holders, on the other hand, hold an out-of-the-money option; they may prefer that the firm continue to operate, hoping that events will occur that will increase firm value and restore some residual value to equity.

The 1989 bankruptcy of Eastern Airlines, which is described by Weiss and Wruck (1998), provides a clear illustration of the potential magnitude

---

[1]The seminal case related to these issues is *Credit Lyonnais Bank Nederland, N.V. v. Pathe Communications Corp.*, 1991 Del. Ch. Lexis 215 (1991). Numerous decisions have discussed the zone of insolvency generally including, without limitation, the following: *Hechinger Investment Co. of Delaware, et al. v. Fleet Retail Finance Group, et al.*, 280 B.R. 90 (D. Del. 2002); *In re Kingston Square Assocs.*, 214 B.R. 713 (Bankr. S.D.N.Y. 1997); and *Geyer v. Ingersoll Publications Co.*, 621 A.2d 784 (Del. Ch. 1992).

of these conflicts. Weiss and Wruck estimate that at the time of filing, fixed claims against Eastern totaled more than $3.7 billion, but that, based on an offer to purchase the company, Eastern's equity was worth approximately $1.2 billion. Though Eastern would have been insolvent had it liquidated at the time of filing, based on the perceived going-concern value, creditor and other groups were initially supportive of attempts to reorganize. As the case progressed, however, Eastern continued to experience severe operating losses. In order for the airline to be able to continue flying, the bankruptcy court (Southern District of New York) granted Eastern's managers the right to use proceeds of asset sales to fund operations.

Ultimately, these attempts to preserve the airline failed and Eastern ceased operations on January 19, 1991. Weiss and Wruck estimate that during the 22-month period in bankruptcy, Eastern's value declined by more than $2 billion, and the company was clearly insolvent well prior to its liquidation. If management's goal was to promote the interests of shareholders, the best strategy was to continue to operate the airline and hope for an economic recovery. Once the firm was insolvent, however, creditors would have been better served if the proceeds of asset sales had been used to pay their claims rather than funding unprofitable operations. While the Eastern Airlines case is an extreme example of the tensions between liquidation and reorganization, conflicts between claimants and the accompanying difficulties in representing interests of both creditors and shareholders, or even representing various creditor groups with conflicting interests, are clear in many reorganization cases.

FREQUENCY AND TIMING OF MANAGEMENT AND BOARD CHANGES

The likelihood that managers, in particular the CEO, will be replaced in the event of financial distress will have an important impact on operating decisions both before and during distress. Further, critics of the Chapter 11 process have suggested that the process is too protective of incumbent management. For example, Bradley and Rosenzweig (1992) argue that even when performance is so poor as to render firms insolvent, incumbent managers go relatively unpunished because bankruptcy law allows them to retain control over corporate assets.

A number of academic studies have examined whether distress, and in particular Chapter 11, is costly to managers in the sense that they are likely to lose their jobs. Several of these studies are described in Table 10.1. The first study to systematically examine management turnover for distressed firms following the Bankruptcy Reform Act of 1978 is Gilson (1989).

TABLE 10.1   Studies of Management Changes for Financially Distressed Firms

Study	Sample	Turnover Rate
Gilson (1989)	Firms entering financial distress 1979 to 1984, including 69 Chapter 11 and 57 workouts; turnover of CEO, chairman, or president in four-year period beginning two years before debt restructuring or bankruptcy filing	Workouts: 60% by two years after debt restructuring Chapter 11: 71% by two years after filing
Betker (1995)	75 Chapter 11 firms 1982 to 1990; turnover of CEO in office two years prior to default	51% by time of filing 75% prior to emergence 91% at emergence
LoPucki & Whitford (1993)	43 large Chapter 11 cases 1979 to 1988; turnover of CEO in office 18 months before filing	91% by six months after confirmation
Hotchkiss (1995)	197 firms filing Chapter 11 1979 to 1988; turnover of CEO in office two years prior to filing	41% by time of filing 55% by time plan proposed 70% at emergence
Hotchkiss & Mooradian (1997)	288 firms defaulting on public debt 1980 to 1993, including 77 workouts and 197 Chapter 11 cases; turnover of CEO in office two years prior to default or filing	Workouts: 19.5% by time of default 36.4% by completion of workout Chapter 11: 18.8% by time of default 54.9% by time plan proposed 81.2% at emergence

Gilson examines turnover of "senior managers," which he defines as individuals with the title of CEO, chairman, or president in a four-year period beginning two years before filing. For the 69 bankruptcy cases he examines, 71 percent of these individuals are replaced as of two years after filing. The replacement rate for firms in bankruptcy is also significantly higher than for financially distressed firms that successfully restructure their debt out of court. Interestingly, Gilson finds that none of the executives who lose their positions are employed by another exchange-listed firm over a three-year period following their departure, suggesting large personal losses to these individuals. There is also likely a loss of personal income from reduced salary and loss in value of equity holdings as the firm's financial condition deteriorates, and potentially a loss of firm-specific human capital when managers leave their firms.

More recent studies of management turnover for Chapter 11 firms show a similar pattern of extremely high turnover. For example, Betker (1995) tracks a sample of Chapter 11 cases from two years prior to default to one year after confirmation, and finds a 91 percent turnover rate for the CEO by the time the firm emerges from bankruptcy. For comparison, several academic studies have documented CEO turnover rates in nondistressed firms. Weisbach (1988) finds a mean annualized resignation rate of 8 percent per firm year for a sample of firms listed on the New York Stock Exchange (NYSE). Warner, Watts, and Wruck (1988) find that the mean annual turnover rate is 0.12 changes per firm for a random sample of NYSE and American Stock Exchange (AMEX) firms. Both studies show that the rate of turnover is sensitive to firm performance, but it is clear that the turnover rates reported for the worst-performing firms in their samples are not nearly as high as observed for firms in financial distress or bankruptcy.

While it is clear that turnover is abnormally high for distressed firms, there is also evidence that incumbent management is more likely to be overly optimistic about prospects for the reorganized firm. As described in Chapter 3, several studies show that cash flow forecasts included in disclosure statements are on average overly optimistic relative to realized performance after firms emerge from Chapter 11. Hotchkiss (1995) shows that this bias is stronger when the prebankruptcy management is still in place at the time the cash flow forecasts are made. Further, there has been some discussion that pro-debtor biases are stronger in certain bankruptcy courts. For example, Hotchkiss (1995) also shows that firms that emerge from Chapter 11 after filing in the Southern District of New York are more likely to find themselves in a subsequent distressed restructuring. LoPucki (2004) strongly argues that the more recent influx of cases to Delaware is a result of its relatively pro-debtor stance. He suggests that this leads to "venue shopping," meaning that managers choose to file bankruptcy cases in districts where they expect to receive rulings that will help them to retain control of the process. The high turnover of managers runs counter to the notion that they are overly protected by the process. The studies described show, however, that a significant fraction of managers are able to stay in place at least until a plan is proposed, though it is more likely they will not remain at emergence from bankruptcy.

In addition to changes in management, there are also often significant changes in the membership and composition of boards when firms renegotiate their debt contracts. As firms become financially distressed, a substantial commitment of time and attention is required of managers and directors to address the firm's operating problems and develop a restructuring plan. Further, directors and officers have increasing concerns about personal liability. Certain parties, however, such as those making investments in the distressed firm or groups concerned about protecting their interests in the restructuring, may desire to take board seats. In some cases, though, even these individuals are unwilling to take board seats until the reorganization is complete because doing so would potentially impair their ability to trade claims in the distressed firm.[2]

Academic research has provided evidence consistent with these ideas. Gilson (1990) finds that when firms become financially distressed, the average board size declines and more directors are appointed who possess some special skill or interest in managing troubled companies, including investment bankers and workout specialists. He further finds that, on average, only 46 percent of directors who sit on the board prior to financial distress, and 43 percent of the CEOs, are still present when their firms emerge from bankruptcy or settle privately with creditors less than two years later. Hotchkiss and Mooradian (1997) focus on board and other governance activities of vulture investors specializing in investing in distressed firms. They show that for a large sample of firms defaulting on public debt, these investors are frequently active in the governance of the restructured firms. Vultures ultimately join the board of directors for 27.8 percent of the firms they study, and more than half of the time they maintain these positions for at least one year after emergence from bankruptcy. In some recent cases, however, including MCI (formerly WorldCom), distressed debt investors declined to join the board of the reorganized firm because simultaneous fiduciary responsibilities to shareholders of the reorganized firm and to investors in their own funds would have created a conflict of interest for these investors.[3]

MANAGEMENT COMPENSATION

Even when the firm's managers have been replaced, it is not always clear where managers' loyalties lie. Compensation policy is often an impor-

---

[2]Board members and creditor committee members have access to information such as financial projections that is not available to the public. See Chapter 8 for discussion of issues related to trading of claims in bankruptcy.

[3]Mitchell, Pacelle, and Shawn Young. "Carrion Call: As MCI Tries for a Second Act, 'Vultures' Add to the Drama—How Soon Will Big Investors Cash Out After Company Emerges from Chapter 11?—Refusing to Join the Board." *Wall Street Journal* (April 16, 2004).

tant part of firms' overall strategy for dealing with financial distress, through provisions that change managers' incentives or facilitate negotiations with creditors.

As a firm becomes financially distressed, it is often necessary to replace incumbent management involved in the decisions leading to poor performance. However, in order to preserve the firm's value it is also sometimes important to provide incentives to retain key employees. Cash bonuses to retain pivotal employees are routinely approved during bankruptcy proceedings, but it is sometimes not clear whether these payments are in the best interests of creditors or shareholders. Several recent examples highlight these concerns. In the days before its bankruptcy filing in January 2002, Kmart gave more than $30 million in retention and relocation loans to senior officers to try to keep them from leaving the company. Included in that amount was over $18 million paid to nine top executives, all of whom left the firm anyway by the following spring.[4] Prior to filing for Chapter 11 in 1996, Fruehauf Trailer Corporation approved bonuses to retain about 40 key employees. However, the company's plants and distribution centers were immediately liquidated in bankruptcy. Officials of the liquidating company argued that management had improperly taken assets for themselves instead of using the funds to pay creditors.[5]

Gilson and Vetsuypens (1993) provide a systematic study of distressed firms' compensation policies, examining both managers in place as the firms enter financial distress and the managers who replace them. They find that in addition to the high turnover rate previously documented, managers who remain often take substantial cuts in their salaries and bonuses. CEO pay also typically falls when the outgoing CEO is replaced by another incumbent manager; the median inside replacement CEO earns 35 percent less than his or her predecessor. In contrast, the median outside replacement CEO earns 35 percent more than the CEO he or she replaces.

An important aspect of the change in compensation contracts is that for the CEO of the emerging firm, the sensitivity of the CEO wealth to firms' stock price performance is very high. Gilson and Vetsuypens show that outside replacements typically receive large grants of stock options as

---

[4]Burton, Thomas M. "Departing CEO at Kmart Is Set to Get Big Payoff." *Wall Street Journal* (October 20, 2004).
[5]Schroeder, Michael. "Court Rules Against Pension Bonus—Fruehauf Plan to Award Special Benefits to Staff Is Considered Excessive." *Wall Street Journal* (January 25, 2005).

part of their compensation. Further, Gilson, Hotchkiss, and Ruback (2000), in their study of valuation issues for bankrupt firms, find that for 32 of the 63 Chapter 11 cases they study (50.8 percent), managers receive stock and/or options in the reorganized firm as incentive compensation. This may produce biases in determining the value of the reorganized firm, since a low value will benefit managers if the exercise price of options is set to that low value, or the percentage of stock they are allocated is higher based on that value. As described in Chapter 5, this produces a windfall for managers if the stock performs well after emerging from bankruptcy. Regardless, the high sensitivity of compensation to performance will have important incentive effects for the reorganized firm.

During Chapter 11, however, such long-term performance-based compensation may not be effective if the management during bankruptcy will not remain when the firm emerges. This is particularly likely if turnaround professionals have been brought in to lead the firm through its restructuring. In these cases, Gilson and Vetsuypens find that compensation for the current management is often tied to short-term goals, such as the successful resolution of the firm's bankruptcy or debt restructuring or the value of payoffs to creditors. In recent cases where a substantial portion of the firm's assets are sold through Section 363 sales, bonuses are often tied to completion of these sales.

A related issue that has received considerable recent attention is the repricing of out-of-the-money executive options for firms that have performed poorly. Repricing refers to the practice of lowering the strike prices of previously issued employee stock options. This is usually done after a significant stock price decline has left the options out-of-the-money. Critics argue that repricing rewards management following a period of poor performance, while proponents argue that it is necessary to provide proper incentives for management at that point. Chidambaran and Prabhala (2004) show that a majority of repricing firms attach a new vesting period or impose exercise restrictions relating to employment continuation for the repriced options, supporting the view that repricing is an important aspect of key employee retention. Regardless, the Financial Accounting Standards Board (FASB) ruled in 1998 that repriced options should be expensed, thus discouraging this practice. More recently, firms make new refresher option grants without canceling old underwater options or use a practice known as rescission. In a rescission, shares received by the employee from the exercise of options are returned to the company in exchange for a refund of the strike price. Similar to repricing, this practice has been criticized as symptomatic of poor governance, yet may be necessary to restore incentive structures for distressed firms.

CHANGES IN OWNERSHIP AND CONTROL

When distressed firms restructure their debt, there are often significant changes in the ownership structure of the firms' residual claims. This occurs for several reasons. The primary reason is that in a bankruptcy restructuring, the original equity holders often receive little or no shares in the reorganized firm. Most of the stock is distributed to former creditors, who become the new owners of the company. Further, investors who specialize in investments in distressed firms frequently purchase claims from numerous creditors, and may convert these consolidated claims into sizable equity positions. The size of these equity stakes is often sufficient to give the investor control of the reorganized firm. Finally, there is sometimes an infusion of equity to the reorganized firm from an investor as part of the restructuring plan.

The earliest studies of ownership changes for distressed firms after the 1978 Bankruptcy Reform Act did not find a great deal of control activity for the firms studied. A possible interpretation is that the structure of Chapter 11, under which incumbent management remains in control, discouraged acquisitions. Unlike acquisitions outside of bankruptcy, an acquisition that is part of a reorganization plan requires creditor approval, making hostile acquisitions of firms in Chapter 11 more difficult. Further, other firms in the same industry that would be likely bidders may be distressed themselves at the same time. Hotchkiss and Mooradian (1998) examine these issues for a sample of 55 transactions in which firms in Chapter 11 are acquired by another public company. They find that bankrupt targets are in fact most often acquired by firms in the same industry. The bidding firm often has some prior relationship with the bankrupt firm. For example, they may have previously purchased some assets of the target. There are often multiple bidders involved—18 out of 55 cases, which is at least as high as has been found for studies of nondistressed firms. Prices paid, however, are lower than those received for nonbankrupt targets in the same industry—this study finds discounts of 45 percent relative to prices paid for nonbankrupt targets in the same industry. However, these acquisitions do appear to lead to successful restructurings, in that the postmerger cash flow for the combined firm increases relative to the prebankruptcy levels, and the increase is greater than is observed for acquisitions of similar nonbankrupt companies.

Though changes in control were less common during the early life of Chapter 11, equity distributions under reorganization plans still lead to a concentration of the firm's ownership in the hands of prior creditors. Gilson (1990) studies 111 publicly traded companies that experienced severe financial distress between 1979 and 1985, 61 of which filed for Chapter 11. For the 61 bankruptcies, on average 80 percent of the common stock in the reorganized firm was distributed to creditors. Federal and state banking laws provide U.S. banks with the authority to hold common stock received in loan restructurings. In approximately three out of four firms in Gilson's sample, bank lenders and other creditors received significant blocks of voting stock under the firms' debt restructuring and Chapter 11 reorganization plans. On average, banks received 36 percent of firms' common stock, and in a number of cases banks appointed their representatives to the board of directors. James (1995) discusses the participation of banks in distressed restructurings. He studies a sample of 102 bank debt restructurings occurring between 1981 and 1990, and finds that banks took equity positions in 31 percent of these transactions. Moreover, the banks typically maintained a substantial stake for at least two years following the restructuring. More recently, the rise in the market for trading claims of distressed firms, including bank loans, has provided banks with an earlier opportunity to exit the process, with the new investors taking the banks' place in the negotiation of a restructuring plan. Hotchkiss and Mooradian (1997) find that vultures become blockholders (owning more than 5 percent of the reorganized firm's stock) in 49 percent of the sample of defaulting firms they study.

With the increase in the number of large public companies in financial distress in the 1980s and early 1990s, the market for trading claims of distressed companies has grown dramatically (see Chapter 8). This development had a dramatic effect on the incidence of control activity for distressed firms. A common strategy for an investor who specifically seeks control of the distressed firm is to purchase a large block of debt. With a large enough stake to potentially block a plan of reorganization, the investor gains influence over the course of the restructuring. Depending on the final negotiated terms of the plan, the stake potentially can be converted into a controlling ownership position.[6] Studying a large sample of 288 firms defaulting on their debt, Hotchkiss and Mooradian (1997) find that vultures gain control of 16.3 percent of the sample firms.

This activity provides an interesting contrast to control contests for nondistressed firms. Typically, when an investor acquires more than 5 percent of the firm's stock, it must file a 13-D statement with the Securities and Exchange Commission (SEC) disclosing its holdings and future intentions with respect to the company. For debt purchases, however, there is no such requirement. Therefore, for distressed companies, an investor seeking con-

---

[6]According to Wilbur L. Ross, an investor in a number of large bankruptcy cases, "Virtually every bankruptcy situation we're in involves a change-in-control issue; five years ago, it would have been a rarity." ("Debt Raiders See Bull Market in Bankruptcy," *Los Angeles Times*, October 21, 1990.)

trol can purchase a block of debt, which when converted to equity in a restructuring would leave them with a controlling stake in the company. Certain investors have, in fact, developed a reputation for using this strategy to gain control of firms in bankruptcy, and as a result manage a portfolio of investments in the equity of firms that have emerged from Chapter 11. Table 10.2 describes several recent examples of this type of control activity.

TABLE 10.2 Recent Examples of Control Activity for Firms in Chapter 11

Firm	Investor	Description of Activity
Kmart Emerged May 6, 2003	Edward S. Lampert	Purchases bonds and then bank loans during Chapter 11; converts debt into shares and makes additional investment in reorganized firm. Emerges as Kmart's largest shareholder, owning 48% of the equity, and becomes chairman.
XO Communications Emerged January 16, 2003	Carl Icahn	Purchases about 85% of the firm's senior secured debt and over $1.3 billion face amount senior notes. Receives 85% of the reorganized firm's stock and most of the firm's $500 million junior pay-in-kind preferred notes.
Burlington Industries Plan Confirmed October 30, 2003 Acquisition Completed November 2003	Wilbur Ross	Head of the unsecured creditors committee, Ross owns $82 million unsecured bonds and $7 million bank debt. Successfully purchases the firm's assets in bankruptcy-court-supervised auction.
Regal Cinemas Emerged January 30, 2002	Philip Anschutz and Oaktree Capital Management	Anschutz and Oaktree purchase 82% of Regal's bank debt and 93% of its bonds. Anschutz owns 60% and Oaktree owns 15% of the reorganized firm's equity.

Sources: News articles, company 10-Ks, and disclosure statements.

There are also a number of Chapter 11 cases in which there is a change in control based on an equity infusion from an outside investor. Gilson, Hotchkiss, and Ruback (2000) find 12 out of 63 cases (17.5 percent) they study have such an investment: The median percentage of equity acquired is 54.2 percent, and the investments range in size from 13.6 percent to 82.4 percent. Unlike acquisitions outside Chapter 11, in nine cases the CEO in office when the plan is proposed remains in office following emergence from bankruptcy, and these cases are characterized by the press as being friendly to the debtor management. Overall, this type of control activity, along with high management and board turnover, contributes to the significant changes in the governance of distressed firms.

Techniques for the Classification and Prediction of Corporate Financial Distress and Their Applications

CHAPTER 11

Corporate Credit Scoring– Insolvency Risk Models

This chapter discusses several of the primary motivating influences on the recent developments and revisions of corporate credit scoring models. There are at least two recent important factors stimulating these developments. These include the implications of Basel II's proposed capital requirements on credit assets and the enormous amounts and rates of defaults and bankruptcies in the United States in the years just following the turn of the twenty-first century. Despite the fact that we have moved from a tumultuous and difficult credit environment in 2001–2002 to a historically mild and benign one in 2004/2005, research on credit risk models has continued unabated. The evolution of credit risk models is reviewed with particular emphasis on two of the more prominent credit scoring techniques, our Z-Score model and Moody's Investors Service/KMV Corporation's expected default frequency (EDF) models. Both models are assessed with respect to default probabilities in general and to the infamous Enron and WorldCom debacles in particular. In order to be effective, these and other credit risk models should be utilized by firms with a sincere credit risk culture, observant of the fact that they are best used as additional tools, not the sole decision-making criteria, in the credit and security analyst process.

Around the turn of the most recent century, credit scoring models were given unprecedented significance by the stunning pronouncements of the new Basel Accord on credit risk capital adequacy—the so-called Basel II Accord; see Basel Commission on Banking Supervision (1999, 2001, and 2004). Banks, in particular, and most other financial institutions worldwide, have recently either developed or modified existing internal credit risk systems and are currently developing methods to conform with best practice systems and processes for assessing the probability of default (PD) and, possibly, loss given default (LGD) on credit assets of all types. Both inputs are necessary to qualify for the so-called advanced internal rating based (IRB) approach under Basel II. Coincidentally, defaults and bankruptcies reached unprecedented levels in the United States in 2001 and continued to even higher levels in 2002.

Credit scoring models for the repayment-risk assessment of corporate credit assets, mainly bonds, loans, and the accounts receivable of companies, have been used by financial institutions and other lenders for at least 150 years in the United States (see Figure 11.1 for an evolutionary listing of corporate credit scoring techniques). Early models included the qualitative assessment of companies and their personal owners going back to the 1850s, when institutions like the predecessor to Dun & Bradstreet and commercial banks provided opinions as to the creditworthiness of firms that sought to finance the growth of the U.S. economy. Perhaps the first corporate bond sold to private and institutional investors was issued by

---

- Qualitative (Subjective)
- Univariate (Accounting/Market Measures)
- Multivariate (Accounting/Market Measures)
  Discriminant, Logit, Probit Models (Linear, Quadratic)
  Nonlinear Models—for example, Recursive Participating Analysis (RPA) and Neural Networks (NN)
- Discriminant and Logit Models in Use
  Consumer Models (e.g., Fair Isaacs)
  Z-Score—Manufacturing
  ZETA Score—Industrials
  Private Firm Models (e.g., Risk Calc [Moody's], Z″-Score)
  EM Score—Emerging Markets, Industrial
  Other—Bank Specialized Systems
- Artificial Intelligence Systems
  Expert Systems
  Neural Networks (e.g., Credit Model [S&P], Central dei Bilanci [CBI], Italy)
- Option/Contingent Claims Models
  Risk of Ruin
  KMV Credit Monitor Model
- Blended Ratio/Market Value Models
  Moody's Risk Calc
  BondScore (CreditSights)
  Z-Score (Market Value Model)

FIGURE 11.1 Evolution of Scoring Systems
Source: Author compilation.

firms like the Schuylkill Permanent Bridge Company of Philadelphia in the first decade of the nineteenth century or larger firms like the First National City Bank in 1820. These qualitative type variable assessments (e.g., industrial segment, personal guarantees, collateral, experience of management) were soon supplemented by univariate ratio and other financial statement data in the early twentieth century. The beginnings of the formal rating agency industry occurred in 1909 with the formation of Moody's, followed soon by Standard & Poor's (1916). We reviewed these agencies' standard nomenclature of credit ratings in Chapter 7.

We built the first multivariate credit scoring model (Altman 1968), called Z-Score, which combined a number of financial statement and market value measures. The resulting score was then used to classify the observation (firm) into either a distressed (bankrupt) or nondistressed category. The statistical classification technique we utilized was discriminant analysis, which is one of a family of statistical techniques available to separate or predict the health of companies. Subsequent techniques used for similar purposes were logistic regression; probit (e.g., Ohlson 1980); recursive partitioning (e.g., Frydman, Altman, and Kao 1985); quadratic-discriminant (Altman, Haldeman, and Narayanan 1977); neural networks—for example, Altman, Marco, and Varetto (1994) and several studies found in Trippi and Turban (1996)—and a number of highly sophisticated techniques such as genetic algorithms—for example, McKee and Lensbergn (2002). In our opinion, many of these techniques, discussed in this chapter, are variations on the same theme—the rigorous treatment of firm indicators to classify/predict corporate distress. These techniques have been applied to manufacturers, other industrials, emerging market firms, financial institutions, and so on. Similar constructs have been in use for decades, assessing the creditworthiness of retail customers of financial institutions and corporations (e.g., retailers, oil organizations, especially for credit cards, and mortgages).

More recent techniques used to classify corporate health include artificial intelligence systems, option/contingent claims (e.g., Moody's/KMV's EDF model), and hybrid models (e.g., CreditSights' BondScore). We now will proceed to describe the most recent increase in the urgency to develop credit scoring models and the specifics of a few of the most popular models.

THE ENORMOUS INCREASE IN LARGE CORPORATE FAILURES

As noted earlier in this chapter and described in Chapter 1, large firm corporate defaults and bankruptcies in the United States are now fairly common occurrences. Indeed, companies that filed for bankruptcy/reorganization under Chapter 11 with greater than $100 million in liabilities amounted to at least $240 billion in liabilities in 2001 and $337 billion in 2002 (see Table 1.1 in Chapter 1). These liability levels tumbled to $110 billion and $66 billion in 2003 and 2004, respectively. And there were 100 firms in the three-year period 2001–2003 that filed for protection under the U.S. bankruptcy code with liabilities greater than $1 billion! A list of these billion-dollar babies can be found in the appendix to Chapter 1 of this volume. In the public bond arena, over $63 billion of U.S. domestic public, high yield (below investment grade) bonds defaulted in 2001, and the default rate on high yield bonds reached a near-record 9.8 percent (dollar weighted). These totals ballooned to almost $100 billion of defaults in 2002 and the default rate reached an unprecedented 12.8 percent level, including the $30 billion WorldCom bankruptcy in July 2002 (see Chapter 7).[1] These lofty totals plummeted in 2003 and fell even more so in 2004, when the high yield bond default rate registered just 1.25 percent.

Adding to the urgency to assess firm PDs, on June 26, 2004, after five years of debate, the final version of Basel II was submitted (Basel Commission on Banking Supervision 2004) and soon adopted in principal by many countries. Despite the cooling-off of defaults and bankruptcies of late, heralding a benign credit cycle,[2] and the removal of any further uncertainty about Basel II's recommendations, research into credit risk models and the application of scoring models to derive PDs and development of databases to determine loss given default (LGD) have continued unabated with major conferences on the subjects held on a frequent basis.[3]

We now discuss a model developed by one of the authors 38 years ago, the so-called Z-Score model, and its relevance to these recent developments. In doing so, we provide some updated material on the Z-Score model's tests and applications over time as well as a few modifications for greater applicability. We also discuss another widely used credit risk

---

[1] Data is derived from the NYU Salomon Center corporate bond default and bankruptcy databases. See Altman and Aguiar (2005) for results through 2004.

[2] Indeed, the U.S. Office of the Controller of Currency reported that nonperforming loans in the U.S. national banks fell to the lowest level in the past 20 years in November 2004 (0.97% of all loans 90 days or more past due).

[3] For example, Moody's/KMV and the NYU Salomon Center held an important conference on "Recent Advances in Credit Risk Research," May 19–20, 2004; for more information log on to both the Moody's and NYU Salomon Center (www.stern.nyu.edu/salomon) web sites. A following conference was held at the London Business School, May 26–27, 2005. Also, see Altman, Resti, and Sironi's review article on LGD (2005a) and book on recovery risk (2005b).

model, known as the Moody's/KMV approach, and compare both KMV and Z-Score in the now infamous Enron (2001) and WorldCom (2002) bankruptcy debacles. This material is not meant to be a comparison of all of the well-known and available credit scoring models, including other models, such as Moody's RiskCalc, CreditSights' BondScore, the Kamakura approach, Hillegeist et al.'s (2003) H-models, or the ZETA scoring model (Altman et al. 1977).

A major theme is that the assignment of appropriate default probabilities on corporate credit assets is a three-step process involving the sequential use of:

1. Credit scoring models.
2. Capital market risk equivalents—usually bond ratings.
3. Assignment of PDs and possibly LGDs on the credit portfolio.[4]

Our emphasis will be on step 1 and how the Z-Score model (Altman 1968) has become the prototype model for one of the three primary frameworks for determining PDs. The other two credit scoring structures involve either the bond rating process itself or option pricing capital market valuation techniques, typified by the Moody's/KMV expected default frequency (EDF) approach (McQuown 1993; KMV 2000; Kealhofer 2000). These techniques are also the backbone of most credit asset value at risk (VaR) models (e.g., CreditMetrics, 1997). In essence, we feel strongly that if the initial credit scoring model is sound and based on comprehensive and representative data, then the credit VaR model has a chance to be accurate and helpful for both regulatory and economic capital assignment and, of course, for distress prediction. If it is not, no amount of quantitative sophistication or portfolio analytic structures can achieve valid credit risk results.

CREDIT SCORING MODELS

Almost all of the statistical credit scoring models that are in use today are variations on a similar theme. They involve the combination of a set of quantifiable financial indicators of firm performance with, perhaps, a small

---

[4]Some might argue that a statistical methodology can combine steps 1 and 2 where the output from step 1 automatically provides estimates of PD. This is one of the reasons that many modelers of late and major consulting firms prefer the logit-regression approach, rather than the discriminant model that we prefer.

number of additional variables that attempt to capture some qualitative elements of the credit process. Then the model, whether a structural approach relating asset values to perceived liability obligations, a statistical-multivariate model, or an exogenous reduced-form approach, is assessed relative to a large database of past defaults to determine the models' PDs. Although we will concentrate on the quantitative measures, mainly financial ratios and capital market values, one should not underestimate the importance of qualitative measures in the process.[5]

Starting in the 1960s, some practitioners, and certainly many academicians, had been moving toward the possible elimination of ratio analysis as an analytical technique in assessing firm performance. Theorists had downgraded arbitrary rules of thumb (such as company ratio comparisons) that were widely used by practitioners. Since attacks on the relevance of ratio analysis emanated from many esteemed members of the scholarly world, does this mean that ratio analysis is limited to the world of nuts and bolts? Or has the significance of such an approach been unattractively garbed and therefore unfairly handicapped? Can we bridge the gap, rather than sever the link, between traditional ratio analysis and the more rigorous statistical techniques that became popular among academicians? Indeed, Scott (1981) explored the conceptual link between structural models and multivariate approaches, like the Z-Score and ZETA model, and concluded that the theoretical and empirical models had a great deal in common.

TRADITIONAL RATIO ANALYSIS

The detection of company operating and financial difficulties is a subject that has been particularly amenable to analysis with financial ratios. Prior to the development of quantitative measures of company performance, agencies had been established to supply a qualitative type of information assessing the creditworthiness of particular merchants. Classic works in the area of ratio analysis and bankruptcy classification were produced by Beaver (1966, 1968). His univariate analysis of a number of bankruptcy predictors set the stage for the multivariate attempts by one of the authors and others that followed. Beaver found that a number of indicators could discriminate between matched samples of failed and nonfailed firms for as long as five years prior to failure. However, he questioned the use of multi-

---

[5]Banking practitioners have reported that these so-called qualitative elements, which involve judgment on the part of the risk officer, can provide as much as 30 to 50 percent of the explanatory power of the scoring model.

variate analysis. The Z-Score model, developed by this author at the same time, has shown that Beaver's early concerns were not problematic.

The aforementioned studies imply a definite potential of ratios as predictors of bankruptcy to improve upon traditional ratio techniques in order to supply a multivariate profile of companies, one that is based on objective weights for each variable, where the results are clear, unambiguous, and (hopefully) not misleading. In general, ratios measuring profitability, liquidity, leverage, and solvency, and multidimensional measures, like earnings and cash flow coverage, prevailed as the most significant indicators. The order of their importance is not clear since almost every study cited a different ratio as being the most effective indication of impending problems. An appropriate extension of the previously cited studies, therefore, was to build upon their findings and to combine several measures into a meaningful predictive model.

DISCRIMINANT ANALYSIS

After careful consideration of the nature of the problem and of the purpose of this analysis, we chose multiple discriminant analysis (MDA) as the appropriate statistical technique in our original (Altman 1968) construction. Although not as popular as regression analysis, MDA had been utilized in a variety of disciplines since its first application in the biological sciences in the 1930s. MDA is a statistical technique used to classify an observation into one of several a priori groupings dependent upon the observation's individual characteristics. It is primarily used to classify or make predictions in problems where the dependent variable appears in qualitative form—for example, male or female, bankrupt or nonbankrupt. Therefore, the first step is to establish explicit group classifications. The number of original groups can be two or more. After the groups are established, data are collected for the objects in the groups. The technique has the advantage of considering an entire profile of characteristics common to the relevant firms, as well as the interaction of these properties. See Figure 11.2 for a description of the linear discriminant structure and an example involving the discrimination between healthy (O) and sick (X) companies by a simple two-variable (profitability and leverage measures) structure.

Subsequent to our earlier use of discriminant analysis, an alternative multivariate approach, logistic analysis, has also become popular (e.g., Ohlson 1980; Zavgren 1985), particularly used by consulting firms in assisting banks, especially when the analyst wants to consider the specific contribution of each variable and receive as an output a direct measure of the probability of default.

Linear Form

$$Z = a_1 x_1 + a_2 x_2 + a_3 x_3 + \ldots + a_n x_n$$

Z = Discriminant Score (Z-Score)

$a_1 \longrightarrow a_n$ = Discriminant Coefficients (Weights)

$x_1 \longrightarrow x_n$ = Discriminant Variables (e.g., Ratios)

Example

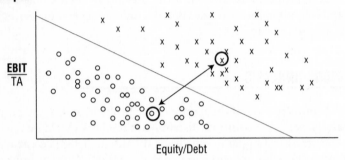

FIGURE 11.2   Forecasting Distress with Discriminant Analysis
Source: Author drawing.

DEVELOPMENT OF THE Z-SCORE MODEL

Sample Selection

The initial sample was composed of a matched sample of bankrupt and non-bankrupt firms. The bankrupt (distressed) group was all manufacturers that filed bankruptcy petitions under Chapter X from 1946 through 1965. A 20-year sample period is not the best choice since average ratios do shift over time. Ideally, we would prefer to examine a list of ratios in time period t in order to make predictions about other firms in the following period $(t + 1)$. Unfortunately, because of data limitations at that time, it was not possible to do this. Recent heavy activity of bankruptcies now presents a more fertile environment. Recognizing that this group is not completely homogeneous (due to industry and size differences), we made a careful selection of nonbankrupt (nondistressed) control firms. This group consisted of a paired sample of manufacturing firms chosen on a stratified random basis. The firms were

$$Z = 1.2\ X_1 + 1.4\ X_2 + 3.3\ X_3 + 0.6\ X_4 + 1.0\ X_5$$

X_1 = Working Capital/Total Assets

X_2 = Retained Earnings/Total Assets

X_3 = Earnings before Interest and Taxes/Total Assets

X_4 = Market Value of Equity/Book Value of Total Liabilities

X_5 = Sales/Total Assets

Z = Overall Index or Score

FIGURE 11.3 The Z-Score Model
Source: Altman (1968).

stratified by industry and by size, with the asset size range between $1 million and $25 million. Yes, in those days $25 million was considered a very large bankruptcy! The data collected were from the same years as those compiled for the bankrupt firms. For the initial sample test, the data are derived from financial statements that are dated one annual reporting period prior to bankruptcy. Some analyses (e.g., Shumway 2002) have criticized this static type of analysis, but we have found that the one-financial-statement-prior-to-distress structure yields the most accurate post-model-building test results.

Variable Selection and Weightings

After the initial groups were defined and firms selected, balance sheet and income statement data were collected. Because of the large number of variables that are potentially significant indicators of corporate problems, a list of 22 potentially helpful variables (ratios) was compiled for evaluation. From the original list, five were selected as doing the best overall job together in the prediction of corporate bankruptcy. The contribution of the entire profile is evaluated and, since this process is essentially iterative, there is no claim regarding the optimality of the resulting discriminant function.

The final discriminant function is given in Figure 11.3. Note that the model does not contain a constant term.[6] One of the most frequently asked

---

[6]This is due to the particular software utilized and, as a result, the relevant cutoff score between the two groups is not zero. Many statistical software programs now have a constant term, which standardizes the cutoff score at zero if the sample sizes of the two groups are equal.

questions is: "How did you determine the coefficients or weights?" These weights are objectively determined by the computer algorithm and not by the analyst. As such, they will be different if the sample changes or if new variables are utilized.

X_1, **Working Capital/Total Assets (WC/TA)**   The working capital/total assets ratio is a measure of the net liquid assets of the firm relative to the total capitalization. Working capital is defined as the difference between current assets and current liabilities. Liquidity and size characteristics are explicitly considered. This ratio was the least important contributor to discrimination between the two groups. In all cases, tangible assets, not including intangibles, are used.

X_2, **Retained Earnings/Total Assets (RE/TA)**   Retained earnings (RE) is the total amount of reinvested earnings and/or losses of a firm over its entire life. The account is also referred to as earned surplus. This is a measure of cumulative profitability over the life of the company. The age of a firm is implicitly considered in this ratio. It is likely that a bias would be created by a substantial reorganization or stock dividend, and appropriate readjustments should, in the event of this happening, be made to the accounts.

In addition, the RE/TA ratio measures the leverage of a firm. Those firms with high RE relative to TA have financed their assets through retention of profits and have not utilized as much debt. This ratio highlights the use of either internally generated funds for growth (low-risk capital) or OPM (other people's money)—higher-risk capital.

This variable has shown a marked deterioration in the average values of nondistressed firms in the past 20 years and, in subsequent model updates, we utilized a transformation structure in order to make its negative impact less dramatic on current Z-Scores. See our discussion (later in this chapter) for a partial description of this update modification, especially in assessing the bond rating equivalent of Z-Scores.

X_3, **Earnings before Interest and Taxes/Total Assets (EBIT/TA)**   This is a measure of the productivity of the firm's assets, independent of any tax or leverage factors. Since a firm's ultimate existence is based on the earning power of its assets, this ratio appears to be particularly appropriate for studies dealing with credit risk. We have found that this profitability measure, despite its reliance on earnings, which are subject to manipulation, consistently is at least as predictive as cash flow measures (see ZETA model results in Altman, Haldeman, and Narayanan 1977 and Altman 1993).

X_4, Market Value of Equity/Book Value of Total Liabilities (MVE/TL) Equity is measured by the combined market value of all shares of stock, preferred and common, while liabilities include both current and long-term obligations. The measure shows how much the firm's assets can decline in value (measured by market value of equity plus debt) before the liabilities exceed the assets and the firm becomes insolvent. We discussed this comparison long before the advent of the KMV approach (which I will discuss shortly)—that is, before Merton (1974) put these relationships into an option-theoretic structural model, to value corporate risky debt.

This ratio adds a market value dimension that most other failure studies did not consider. At a later point, we will substitute the book value of net worth for the market value in order to derive a discriminant function for privately held firms (Z') and for nonmanufacturers (Z").

X_5, Sales/Total Assets (S/TA) The capital turnover ratio is a standard financial ratio illustrating the sales-generating ability of the firm's assets. This final ratio is unique because it is the least significant ratio, and on a univariate statistical significance test basis it would not be selected at all. However, because of its relationship to other variables in the model, the sales/total assets (S/TA) ratio ranks high in its contribution to the overall discriminating ability of the model. Still, there is a wide variation among industries and across countries in asset turnover, and we will specify an alternative model (Z"), without X_5, at a later point.

Variables and their averages were measured at one financial statement prior to bankruptcy and the resulting F-statistics were observed; variables X_1 through X_4 are all significant at the 0.001 level, indicating extremely significant differences between groups. Variable X_5 does not show a significant difference between groups and the reason for its inclusion in the variable profile is not apparent as yet. On a strictly univariate level, all of the ratios indicate higher values for the nonbankrupt firms and the discriminant coefficients display positive signs, which is what one would expect. Therefore, the greater a firm's distress potential, the lower its discriminant score. Although it was clear that four of the five variables displayed significant differences between groups, the importance of MDA is its ability to separate groups using multivariate measures.

Once the values of the discriminant coefficients are estimated, it is possible to calculate discriminant scores for each observation in the samples, or any firm, and to assign the observations to one of the groups based on this score. The essence of the procedure is to compare the profile of an individual firm with those of the alternative groupings (distressed or nondistressed).

Testing the Model on Subsequent Distressed Firm Samples

In three tests performed subsequent to the development of the Z-Score model, we examined 86 distressed companies from 1969 to 1975, 110 bankrupts from 1976 to 1995, and 120 bankrupts from 1997 to 1999 (see Table 11.1). We found that the Z-Score model, using a cutoff score of 2.675, was between 82 percent and 94 percent accurate. In repeated tests, the accuracy of the Z-Score model on samples of distressed firms has been in the vicinity of 80 to 90 percent, based on data from one financial reporting period prior to bankruptcy. The Type II error (classifying the firm as distressed when it does not go bankrupt or default on its obligations), however, has increased substantially with as much as 25 percent of all firms having Z-Scores below 1.81. Using the lower bound of the zone of ignorance (1.81) gives a more realistic cutoff Z-Score than the 2.675, although the latter resulted in the lowest overall error in the original tests. An alternative technique for classifying companies will be presented shortly, which will also provide a probability of default (PD) estimate. This method utilizes a bond rating equivalent (BRE) of each firm's score.

Recalibrating the Model

We have continually observed the accuracy and relevance of the original Z-Score model over the almost four decades since its original development. While the Type I accuracy continues to be quite acceptable (i.e., greater than 80 percent prediction of default within one year of the default date), the Type II error has become quite high. As noted earlier, perhaps as many as 25 percent of U.S. firms have a financial profile more similar to bank-

TABLE 11.1   Classification and Prediction Accuracy Z-Score (1968) Failure Model[a]

Year Prior to Failure	Original Sample (25)	Holdout Sample (33)	1969–1975 Predictive Sample (86)	1976–1995 Predictive Sample (110)	1997–1999 Predictive Sample (120)
1	94% (88%)	96% (72%)	82% (75%)	85% (78%)	94% (84%)
2	72	80	68	75	74
3	48	—	—	—	—
4	29	—	—	—	—
5	36	—	—	—	—

[a]Using 2.67 as cutoff score (1.81 cutoff accuracy in parentheses).
Source: Author compilation.

rupt companies than to healthy entities. The main reason for this high error rate is that U.S. firms, in general, are far more risky than in the past. This higher risk is manifest in the deterioration of a number of financial indicators in the Z-Score model, particularly the retained earnings/total assets and equity/debt ratios. By specifying log transformations on this measure, we have both increased the Type I accuracy and reduced the Type II error. See our discussion in Altman and Rijken (2004) for more details.

Adaptation for Private Firms' Application

Another frequent inquiry that we receive is: "What should we do to apply the model to firms in the private sector?" Credit analysts, private placement dealers, accounting auditors, and firms themselves are concerned that the original model is applicable only to publicly traded entities (since X_4 requires stock price data). And, to be perfectly correct, the Z-Score model is a publicly traded firm model and *ad hoc* adjustments are not scientifically valid. For example, the most obvious modification is to substitute the book value of equity for the market value.

Rather than simply insert a proxy variable into an existing model to accommodate private firms, we advocate a complete reestimation of the model, substituting the book values of equity for the market value in X_4. One expects that all of the coefficients will change (not only the new variable's parameter) and that the classification criterion and related cutoff scores would also change. That is exactly what happens.

The result of our revised Z-Score model with a new X_4 variable is given in Figure 11.4. The equation now looks somewhat different than the earlier model. Note, for instance, that the coefficient for X_1 went from 1.2 to 0.7. But, in total, the model still looks quite similar to the one using market value of equity.

Bond Rating Equivalents

One of the main reasons for building a credit scoring model is to estimate the probability of default given a certain level of risk estimation. Indeed, Basel II's "foundation" and "advanced" internal rating based (IRB) approaches require that these estimates be made based on the bank's or capital market experience. Although we are aware that all of the rating agencies (Moody's, S&P, Fitch, and Dominion Bond Rating Service [DBRS]) are certainly not perfect in their credit risk assessments, in general it is felt that they do provide important and consistent estimates of default—mainly through their ratings. In addition, since there has been a long history and fairly large number of defaults that had ratings attached

$$Z' = 0.717\ X_1 + 0.847\ X_2 + 3.107\ X_3 + 0.420\ X_4 + 0.998\ X_5$$

$$X_1 = \frac{\text{Current Assets} - \text{Current Liabilities}}{\text{Total Assets}}$$

$$X_2 = \frac{\text{Retained Earnings}}{\text{Total Assets}}$$

$$X_3 = \frac{\text{Earnings before Interest and Taxes}}{\text{Total Assets}}$$

$$X_4 = \frac{\text{Book Value of Equity}}{\text{Total Equity}}$$

$$X_5 = \frac{\text{Sales}}{\text{Total Assets}}$$

$Z' > 2.90$: Safe Zone
$1.23 < Z' < 2.90$: Gray Zone
$Z' < 1.23$: Distress Zone

FIGURE 11.4 Z'-Score Private Firm Model
Source: Altman (1993).

to their securities, especially in the United States, we can profit from this history by linking our credit scores with these ratings and thereby deriving expected and unexpected PDs and perhaps LGDs. These estimates can be made for a fixed period of time from the rating date (e.g., one year) or on a cumulative basis over some investment horizon (e.g., five years). They can be derived from the rating agencies' calculations—that is, from the so-called "static pool" (S&P) or "dynamic cohort" (Moody's) approaches. An alternative is to use Altman's (1989) mortality rate approach (updated annually), which is based on the expected default *from the original issuance date* and its associated rating. A comparison of these results was discussed in Chapter 7 of this volume.

With respect to nonrated entities, one can calculate a score, based on some available model, and perhaps link it to a bond rating equivalent. The latter then can lead to the estimate of PD. For example, Table 11.2 lists the bond rating equivalents for various Z-Score intervals based on average Z-Scores for bonds rated in their respective categories. One observes that in the period 1996–2001, triple-A bonds had an average Z-Score of 6.2, while single-B bonds have an average score of 1.8. Recall that a score of 1.8 was the upper bound of our original Z-Score's distressed zone. We also indicate that the median score of firms that went bankrupt was just below zero (–0.2) based on data from the last financial statement prior to filing. This "bankrupt score" was derived from a sample of 244 bankrupt firms in the 2000–2004 period.

TABLE 11.2 Average Z-Scores by S&P Bond Rating, 1996–2001

	Average Annual Number of Firms	Average Z-Score	Standard Deviation
AAA	66	6.2	2.06
AA	194	4.73	2.36
A	519	3.74	2.29
BBB	530	2.81	1.48
BB	538	2.38	1.85
B	390	1.8	1.91
CCC	10	0.33	1.16
D[a]	244	−0.20	n.a.

[a]Median, based on data from 2000 to 2004.
Source: Compustat data tapes, 1996–2001, author compilation.

The analyst can then observe the average one-year PD from Moody's, S&P, or Fitch for B-rated bonds and find that it is in the 6 percent range or that the average PD *one year after issuance* is 2.85 percent (based on mortality rates discussed in Chapter 7). Note that our mortality rate's first year's PD is considerably lower than the PD derived from a basket of Moody's/S&P B-rated bonds, which contain securities of many different ages and maturities. We caution the analyst to apply the correct PD estimate based on the qualities of the relevant portfolio of credit assets.

A Further Revision—Adapting the Model for Nonmanufacturers and Emerging Markets

The next modification of the Z-Score model assesses the characteristics and accuracy of a model without X_5—sales/total assets. We do this in order to minimize the potential industry effect that is more likely to take place when such an industry-sensitive variable as asset turnover is included. In addition, we have used this model to assess the financial health of non-U.S. corporates. In particular, Altman, Hartzell, and Peck (1995a, 1997) have applied this enhanced Z″-Score model to emerging markets corporates, specifically Mexican firms that had issued Eurobonds denominated in U.S. dollars (see our in-depth discussion of this model in Chapter 12). The book value of equity was used for X_4 in this case.

The classification accuracy results are identical to the revised (Z'-Score) five-variable model. The new Z''-Score model is:

$$Z'' = 3.25 + 6.56 \ (X_1) + 3.26 \ (X_2) + 6.72 \ (X_3) + 1.05 \ (X_4)$$

where Z''-Scores below 0 indicate a distressed condition.

All of the coefficients for variables X_1 to X_4 are different from our original Z-Score model, as are the group means and cutoff scores. In the emerging market (EM) model, discussed in depth in Chapter 12, we added a constant term of +3.25 so as to standardize the scores with a score of zero equated to a D (default) rated bond. See Table 11.3 for the bond rating equivalents of the scores in this model. We believe this model is more

TABLE 11.3 U.S. Bond Rating Equivalent Based on Emerging Market (EM) Score

$Z'' = 3.25 + 6.56 \ (X_1) + 3.26 \ (X_2) \ 6.72 \ (X_3) + 1.05 \ (X_4)$	
U.S. Equivalent Rating	**Average EM Score**
AAA	8.15
AA+	7.60
AA	7.30
AA–	7.00
A+	6.85
A	6.65
A–	6.40
BBB+	6.25
BBB	5.85
BBB–	5.65
BB+	5.25
BB	4.95
BB–	4.75
B+	4.50
B	4.15
B–	3.75
CCC+	3.20
CCC	2.50
CCC–	1.75
D	0.00

Source: In-Depth Data Corp.: Average based on over 750 U.S. corporates with rated debt outstanding; 1995 data.

appropriate for nonmanufacturers than is the original Z-Score model. Of course, models developed for specific industries (e.g., retailers, telecoms, airlines, etc.) are an even better method for assessing distress potential of like-industry firms.

ESTIMATING THE PROBABILITY OF DEFAULT: BOND RATING EQUIVALENT METHOD

Earlier in this chapter, and also in Chapter 7, we mentioned an extension of credit scoring models for the purpose of specifying the probability of default of an enterprise. While the Z-Score models, just discussed, provide a continuous metric for assessing corporate health, we cannot derive a precise estimate of default probability directly from the score. And although some statistical classification techniques, such as logit or probit models, do provide an estimate of default between 0 and 1 (see note 4), we prefer to rely on the bond rating equivalent (BRE) method, which is based on the experience of over 2,000 defaulting firms over the past 35 years. In addition, we are unsure whether the specific logistic function is the correct one for modeling precise default estimates. Indeed, our experience with logit models is that an unusual proportion of the test samples have default estimates of either extremely high or low magnitudes.

As noted earlier, the BRE method is a three-step approach involving:

1. The calculation of credit scores on new or existing credits in the portfolio.
2. Mapping the credit score to a bond rating equivalent.
3. Utilizing mortality rates for new issues, or cumulative default probabilities for seasonal issuers, in order to specify a precise estimate of default probability for some time horizon in the future.

Earlier, in Tables 11.2 and 11.3, we specified the BREs for the Z-Score and Z″-Score models, respectively. These were based on recent samples of average scores for the various major bond rating classes. Drawing upon 35 years of default experience, calibrated to the original bond rating of an issue (mortality rate) or the rating as of the beginning of some measurement period (Moody's and S&P cumulative default rates), we can observe the historic likelihood that an issue with a certain score and BRE has defaulted over 1 to 10 years after the scoring period. The mortality rate metric for the period 1971–2004 is given in Table 11.4, while the comparison of mortality rates and the rating agencies' cumulative default rates (e.g., in Moody's and S&P's annual studies) was shown earlier in Chapter 7.

TABLE 11.4 Mortality Rates by Original Rating: All Rated Corporate Bonds,[a] 1971–2004

		1	2	3	4	5	6	7	8	9	10
AAA	Marginal	0.00%	0.00%	0.00%	0.00%	0.03%	0.00%	0.00%	0.00%	0.00%	0.00%
	Cumulative	0.00	0.00	0.00	0.00	0.03	0.03	0.03	0.03	0.03	0.03
AA	Marginal	0.00	0.00	0.32	0.16	0.03	0.03	0.00	0.00	0.03	0.02
	Cumulative	0.00	0.00	0.32	0.48	0.51	0.54	0.54	0.59	0.57	0.59
A	Marginal	0.01	0.10	0.02	0.09	0.06	0.11	0.06	0.21	0.11	0.06
	Cumulative	0.01	0.11	0.13	0.22	0.28	0.39	0.45	0.65	0.76	0.82
BBB	Marginal	0.36	3.22	1.43	1.28	0.77	0.45	0.20	0.20	0.14	0.40
	Cumulative	0.36	3.56	4.49	6.16	6.89	7.31	7.50	7.68	7.87	8.18
BB	Marginal	1.19	2.48	4.40	2.01	2.51	1.16	1.60	0.88	1.70	3.60
	Cumulative	1.19	3.64	7.88	9.74	12.00	12.93	14.36	15.07	16.52	19.60
B	Marginal	2.85	6.85	7.40	8.55	6.00	4.16	3.72	2.28	1.96	0.86
	Cumulative	2.85	9.51	16.20	23.37	27.94	30.96	33.46	34.97	36.25	36.80
CCC	Marginal	7.98	15.57	19.55	12.10	4.26	9.45	5.60	3.15	0.00	4.28
	Cumulative	7.98	22.31	37.50	45.06	47.37	52.35	55.01	56.43	56.43	58.30

[a]Rated by S&P at issuance.

Based on 1,796 defaulted issues.

Source: Standard & Poor's; Altman and Fanjul (2004).

We can observe that a newly issued security with a Z-Score of 1.8 has a BRE of B (Table 11.2) and a probability of default in the first year after issuance of 2.85 percent, while a seasoned B has a one-year probability of default of 5.71 percent (from Table 7.14, Chapter 7) based on S&P estimates and 5.81 percent based on Moody's estimates.

These PD estimates are critical to the Basel II inputs for internal or external determined IRB approaches and any credit asset (e.g., bond) valuation calculation. The promised cash flows from a bond issue can then be adjusted for default (and recovery) estimates in order to determine the *expected* cash flows. The discount rate in the present value calculation can then be assessed as a function of the risk-free rate plus a premium based on the *unexpected* loss of bonds in that specific BRE class.

COMPARISON OF BANKRUPTCY MODELS

A number of studies have analyzed the relative accuracies of different statistical techniques to predict bankruptcy (e.g., Zmijewski 1984). In addition, Mossman et al. (1998) compared four different, but restrictive, types of bankruptcy models (ratio variables only, cash flow variables only, rate of return variables only, and variance of return variables only) as to their bankruptcy prediction accuracy from various periods prior to failure. They found that during the last fiscal year preceding bankruptcy, none of the individual models may be excluded without a loss in explanatory power. This finding is consistent with our argument that a multivariate model can improve upon any univariate or single-variable type model. They also found that while cash flow variables dominated from two to three years prior to bankruptcy, ratio variables did the best job from the year immediately preceding bankruptcy.

LOSS GIVEN DEFAULT ESTIMATES (DEFAULT RECOVERIES)

Most modern credit risk models and all of the VaR models (e.g., CreditMetrics) assume independence between PD and the recovery rate on defaulted debt. Altman, Brady, Resti, and Sironi (2002, 2005), however, show that this is an incorrect assumption and simulate the impact on capital requirements when you factor in a significant negative correlation between PD and recovery rates over time. In particular, the authors found that in periods of high default rates on bonds, the recovery rate is low relative to the historical average and losses can be expected to be greater—for example, in 2001 and

2002 when bond recoveries (prices just after default) were 26.4 percent and 25.5 percent, respectively. And the reverse takes place when default rates are relatively low (e.g., in 2003 and 2004 when recovery rates climbed to between 45 and 57 percent). Hu and Perraudin (2002) find similar results and Frye (2001) specifies a systematic macroeconomic influence on recovery rates. This has caused serious concern among some central bankers regarding the potential procyclicality of a rating based approach, which is the approach being recommended by Basel II. Indeed, the Basel Committee recently (in 2004) initiated a study to analyze "LGD in downturns" in order to assess this correlation effect. In addition, investors in risky corporate debt and collateralized debt obligations (CDOs) need to be aware that recoveries will usually be lower in high-default periods. Other LGD studies include Moody's (1996); Fitch (2001); Gupten, Gates, and Carty (2000); and many in Altman, Resti, and Sironi (2005). We will explore the estimation of LGD in much greater depth in Chapter 15 of this volume.

Basel II, however, has made a real contribution by motivating an enormous amount of effort on the part of banks (and regulators) to build and evaluate credit risk models that involve scoring techniques, default and loss estimates, and portfolio approaches to the credit risk problem. This motivating force has perhaps been blunted somewhat in the United States since only the largest 10 banks, and perhaps another 10 to 20 banks, will opt for the advanced IRB approach. Others will remain Basel I banks! We now turn to an alternative approach to the Z-Score type models.

EXPECTED DEFAULT FREQUENCY (EDF) MODEL

KMV Corporation, purchased by Moody's in 2002, developed a procedure for estimating the default probability of a firm that is based conceptually on Merton's (1974) option-theoretic, zero coupon, corporate bond valuation approach. The starting point of the KMV model is the proposition that when the market value of a firm drops below a certain liability level, the firm will default on its obligations. In the KMV conceptual framework (see Caouette et al. 1998) the value of the firm, projected to a given future date (e.g., one year), has a probability distribution characterized by its expected value and standard deviation (see Figure 11.5). The area under the distribution that is below the book liabilities of the firm is the PD, called the EDF. In three steps, the model determines an EDF for a company. In the first step, the market value and volatility of the firm are estimated from the market value of its common stock, the volatility of its stock, and the book value of its liabilities. In the second step, the firm's default point is calculated relative to the firm's liabilities coming due over time. A measure is

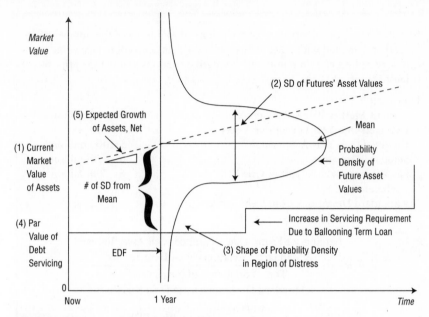

FIGURE 11.5   Moody's/KMV EDF Model
Source: Copyright by Caouette, Altman, and Narayanan (1998). Reprinted with permission of John Wiley & Sons, Inc.

constructed that represents the number of standard deviations from the expected firm value to the default point (the distance to default). Finally, a mapping is determined between a firm's distance to default and the default rate probability based on the historical default experience of companies with similar distance-to-default values.

For example, in Figure 11.6 we show that a firm with a current market value of assets of $910 million might be expected to grow by 10 percent to $1 billion in one year, and that value will be two standard deviations from the level of liabilities needed to be serviced ($700 million). In this hypothetical calculation, the calculation of the EDF is based on the proportion of firms in the Moody's/KMV database that indeed defaulted with the same characteristics (5 percent). Note that the EDF calculation based on the database is not the same estimate as would be derived from a theoretical two standard deviation distance to default (2.5 percent). So, while the EDF model is derived from Merton's conceptual model, the actual calculation is very much an empirical estimate, similar to the basis of our Z-Score and mortality rate BRE basis for estimating PDs. Indeed, both models utilize BREs, as shown earlier in Tables 11.2 and 11.3. An EDF of 20 percent is equivalent to a D rating in the Moody's/KMV model.

Based on empirical observation of the historical frequency of the number of firms that defaulted with asset values (equity + debt) exceeding face value of debt service by a certain number of standard deviations at one year prior to default.

For example:

Current Market Value of Assets	$ 910 million
Expected One-Year Growth in Assets	10%
Expected One-Year Asset Value	$1,000 million
Standard Deviation	$ 150 million
Par Value of Debt Service in One Year	$ 700 million

Therefore:

# Standard Deviations from Debt Service	2
Expected Default Frequency (EDF)	

$$EDF = \frac{\text{Number of Firms That Defaulted with Asset Values}}{\text{Total Population of Firms with}}$$
$$\frac{\text{2 Standard Deviations from Debt Service}}{\text{2 Standard Deviations from Debt Service}}$$

$$\text{e.g.,} \quad = \frac{50 \text{ Defaults}}{1,000 \text{ Population}} = .05 = EDF$$

FIGURE 11.6 KMV's Expected Default Frequency (EDF)
Source: Author example.

In the case of private companies, for which stock price and default data are generally unavailable, KMV estimates the market value and volatility of the private firm directly from its observed characteristics and values based on market comparables, in lieu of market values on the firm's securities.

For a firm with publicly traded shares, the market value of equity may be observed. Next, the expected asset value at the horizon and the default point are determined. An investor holding the asset would expect to get a payout plus a capital gain equal to the expected return. Using a measure of the asset's systematic risk, KMV determines an expected return based on historic asset market returns. This is reduced by the payout rate determined from the firm's interest and dividend payments. The result is the expected appreciation rate, which when applied to the current asset value gives the expected future value of the assets. It was assumed that the firm would default when its total market value falls below the book value of its liabilities. Based on empirical analysis of defaults, KMV has found that the most frequent default point is at a firm value approximately equal to current liabilities plus 50 percent of long-term liabilities (25 percent was first tried but it did not work well).

Given the firm's expected value and its default point at the horizon, KMV determines the percentage drop in the firm value that would bring it to the default point. By dividing the percentage drop by the volatility, KMV controls for the effect of different volatilities. The number of standard deviations that the asset value must drop in order to reach the default point is called the distance to default.

The distance to default metric is a normalized measure and thus may be used for comparing one company with another. A key assumption of the KMV approach is that all the relevant information for determining relative default risk is contained in the expected market value of assets, the default point, and the asset volatility. Differences because of industry, national location, size, and so forth are assumed to be included in these measures, notably the asset volatility.

Distance to default is also an ordinal measure akin to a bond rating, but it still does not tell you what the default probability is. To extend this risk measure to a cardinal or a probability measure, as noted earlier, KMV uses historical default experience to determine an expected default frequency as a function of distance to default. It does this by comparing the calculated distances to default and the observed actual default rate for a large number of firms from KMV's proprietary database. A smoothed curve fitted to this data yields the EDF as a function of the distance to default. While the Type I accuracy is reported to be quite impressive by KMV and its advocates, we have never observed or seen documentation on the Type II error discussed earlier for Z-Scores.

THE ENRON EXAMPLE: MODELS VERSUS RATINGS

We have examined two credit scoring models—the Z-Score model and KMV's EDF—and in both cases a bond rating equivalent could be assigned to Enron. Many commentators have noted that quantitative credit risk measurement tools can save banks and other investors from losing substantial amounts or at least reducing their risk exposures. A prime example is the recent Enron debacle, whereby billions of dollars of equity and debt capital have been lost. The following illustrates the potential savings involved from a disciplined credit risk procedure.

On December 2, 2001, Enron Corporation filed for protection under Chapter 11 and became the largest corporate bankruptcy in U.S. history—with reported liabilities at the filing of over $31 billion and off-balance-sheet liabilities bringing the total to more than $60 billion! Using data that was available to investors over the period 1997–2001, Figure 11.7, from Saunders and Allen (2002), shows the following: KMV's EDF, with its heavy emphasis on Enron's stock price, rated Enron AAA or AA as of year-end 1999, but then indicated a fairly consistent rating equivalent deterioration resulting in a BBB rating one year later and then a B– to CCC+ rating just prior to the filing. Our Z″-Score model (the four-variable model for nonmanufacturers) had Enron as BBB as of year-end 1999—the same as the rating agencies— but then showed a steady deterioration to B as of June 2001. So, both quantitative tools were issuing a warning long before the bad news hit the market.

Although neither model actually predicted the bankruptcy with the bogus data, these tools certainly could have provided an unambiguous early warning that the rating agencies were not providing (their rating remained at BBB/Baa until just before the bankruptcy). Both models were using a vast underestimate of the true liabilities of the firm. If we use the true liabilities of about $60 billion, both models would have predicted severe distress. To be fair, the rating agencies were constrained in that a downgrading from BBB could have been the death knell for a firm like Enron, which relied on its all-important investment grade rating in its vast counterparty trading

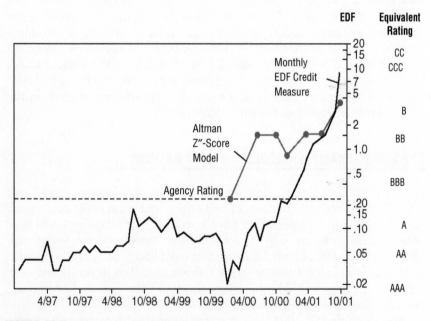

FIGURE 11.7 Enron Credit Risk Measures
Source: Copyright by Saunders and Allen (2002). Reprinted with permission of John Wiley & Sons, Inc.

and structured finance transactions. An objective model, based solely on publicly available accounting and market information, is not constrained in that the analyst is free to follow the signal and to be motivated to dig deeper into what, on the surface, may appear to be a benign situation.

WORLDCOM: A CASE OF HUGE INDIRECT BANKRUPTCY COSTS

A second high-profile bankruptcy that we have applied the two credit scoring models to is WorldCom—vying with Enron to be the largest Chapter 11 bankruptcy in our nation's history, with more than $43 billion of liabilities at the time of filing. WorldCom, one of the many high-flying telecommunications firms that have succumbed to bankruptcy in the past few years, but one with substantial real assets, was downgraded from its A– rating to BBB+ in 2001 and then to junk bond status in May 2002, finally succumbing shortly thereafter and filing for bankruptcy protection in mid-July.

We performed several tests on WorldCom, including the Z″-Score four-variable model, which is more appropriate for nonmanufacturers, and the KMV EDF risk measure. The Z-Score tests were done on the basis of three sets of financial scenarios: (1) the unadjusted statements available to the public before the revelations of massive overstatements of earnings and the write-offs of goodwill; (2) statements adjusted for the first acknowledgment of $3.85 billion of inflated profits in 2001 and the first quarter of 2002; and (3) statements adjusted for a further write-off of $3.3 billion and a massive write-off of $50 billion in assets (goodwill). These results are shown in Figure 11.8.

Our results show that the Z″-Score (using unadjusted data) was 1.50, or 4.75 with the constant term of 3.25 added to get our bond equivalent score at the end of 2000. This translates to a BB– rating. The EDF measure as of year-end 2000 was equivalent to BBB–/BB+. At that time, the actual S&P rating was A–. The BRE remained essentially the same, or even improved a bit throughout 2001, as did the EDF, when the rating agencies began to downgrade the company to BBB+. At the end of the first quarter of 2002, the last financials available before its bankruptcy, WorldCom's Z″-Score was 1.66 (4.91 with the 3.25 construct) and it remained a BB– bond equivalent.

The EDF rose and WorldCom's rating equivalent fell to about BB– by March 2002 and continued to drop to CCC/CC by June, when the S&P rating dropped to BB and then to CCC just before default. So, while both models were indicating a non-investment-grade company as much as 18 months before the actual downgrade to below investment grade and its

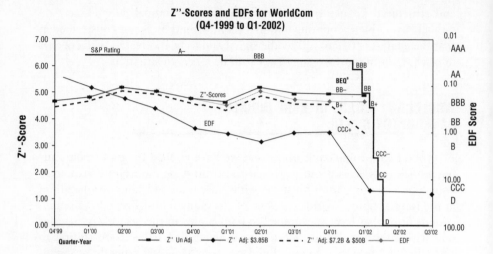

FIGURE 11.8   WorldCom Credit Risk Measures
[a]Z″-Score bond equivalent rating.
Source: Compilation by Edward Altman (NYU Stern School of Business), the KMV (Moody's) web site, and Standard & Poor's Corporation.

eventful bankruptcy, we would not have predicted its total demise based on the available financials. But it did go under, primarily because of the fraud revelations and the attendant costs due to the loss of credit availability. We refer to these costs as indirect bankruptcy costs, usually associated with the public's awareness of a substantial increase in default probability (see Altman 1984). This is a classic case of the potential enormous impact of these hard-to-quantify costs and is a clear example of where the expected costs of bankruptcy overwhelm the expected tax benefits from the debt.

Under the second scenario, we reduce earnings, assets, and net worth by $3.85 billion over the five quarters ending in the first quarter of 2002. The resulting Z″-Score is 1.36 (4.61 BRE) as of year-end 2001—a B+ bond equivalent—and 4.55 as of the first quarter of 2002—again a B+ equivalent. WorldCom's Z-Score (original five-variable model) is 1.7 as of the first quarter of 2002, a B rating equivalent, but in the distress zone. While the revised rating equivalent is lower, we still would not have predicted World-Com to go bankrupt, even with the adjusted financials. Indeed, after adjusting for the "second installment" of improper accounting of profits and a massive write-off of goodwill, the resulting bond rating equivalent is now lower (CCC+), but still not in the default zone.

CONCLUSION

In the Enron and WorldCom cases, and several other fraud cases that we are aware of, although tools like Z-Score and EDF were available, losses were still incurred by even the most sophisticated investors and financial institutions. Having the models is simply not enough! What is needed is a credit culture within these financial institutions, whereby credit risk tools are listened to and evaluated in good times as well as in difficult situations. And, to repeat an important caveat, credit scoring models should not be the only analytical process used in credit decisions. The analyst will, however, be motivated to consider or reevaluate a situation when traditional techniques have not clearly indicated a distressed situation but default prediction models indicate a potential corporate failure.

APPENDIX 11.1   Distress Classification and Prediction Models for Non-U.S. Companies (A Bibliography)

This book concentrates on corporate distress and bankruptcy in the United States. We do list and compare the bankruptcy codes in many other major countries in Chapter 2, and in this chapter we discussed, in detail, models that have been built to classify and predict corporate distress with primary emphasis on data and tests using U.S. data. In the next chapter, we explore one of these models in an emerging market context. With the problems in Latin America and Asia in the 1990s and with the periodic macro- and microeconomics crises all over the globe, distress prediction models would seem to be relevant just about everywhere.

We have always argued that the fundamentals of financial distress are really the same no matter where the corporation is located. As it turns out, there has been a fairly large number of studies conducted and published in journals about efforts to classify and predict corporate financial distress. Most of these attempts utilize the combination of accounting and market data with statistical classification methodologies, similar to our Z-Score approaches. In this appendix, we merely list a representative bibliography of these studies. They involve research on firms in about 20 countries outside the United States. We apologize if we have neglected to list any studies and ask that readers inform us so that we can update our files in the future.

For commentary on most of the studies listed in the bibliography, see Altman and Narayanan (1997).

An International Bibliography

We do not have space to review the numerous studies done throughout the world on failure classification and prediction. A large number of these studies have been published in two special issues of the *Journal of Banking & Finance* (Vol. 8, No. 2, 1984, and that journal's "Special Studies in Finance," Vol. 7, 1988). At least 20 countries are included, showing the interest and importance of such models. The following is a bibliography of most, but not all, of the international distress models.

Bibliography

Argentina

Swanson, E., and J. Tybout. 1988. "Industrial Bankruptcy Determinants in Argentina." *Journal of Banking and Finance* 7: 1–15.

Australia

Altman, E. I., and H. Y. Izan. 1983. "Identifying Corporate Distress in Australia: An Industry Relative Analysis." Australian Graduate School of Management, Sydney.

Castagna, A. D., and Z. P. Matolesy. 1977. "An Examination of Company Deaths: A Comparative Study of the Financial Profits of Acquired and Failed Companies." Research Paper #1, Center for Securities Industries Studies, Kuringai College of Advanced Education, Sydney.

Castagna, A. D., and Z. P. Matolcsy. 1982. "The Prediction of Corporate Failure: Testing the Australian Experience." *Australian Journal of Management* (June).

Izan, H. 1984. "Corporate Distress in Australia." *Journal of Banking and Finance* 8, No. 2 (June): 303.

Lincoln, M. 1984. "An Empirical Study of the Usefulness of Accounting Ratios to Describe Levels of Insolvency Risk." *Journal of Banking & Finance* 8, No. 2 (June): 321.

Webb, L. 1980. "Predicting Australian Corporate Failures." *Chartered Accountant in Australia* (September).

Brazil

Altman, E. I., T. Baidya, and L. M. Riberio-Dias. 1979. "Assessing Potential Financial Problems of Firms in Brazil." *Journal of International Business Studies* (Fall).

Kanitz, S. 1974. "*Como Prever y Falencia de Empresas.*" *Exame* (December).

Canada

Altman, E. I., and M. Lavalle. 1981. "Business Failure Classification in Canada." *Journal of Business Administration* (Summer).

Knight, R. M. 1979. "The Determination of Failure in Canadian Firms." ASA Meetings of Canada, Saskatoon, May 28–30; University of Western Ontario working paper (May).

Finland
Laitinen, T., and N. Kankaanpaa. 1999. "Comparative Analysis of Failure Prediction Methods: The Finnish Case." *The European Accounting Review* 8, No. 1: 67.
Prihti, Aalto. 1990. *"Konkunssin Ennustaminen Kaseinforrnation Avulla"* (with English summary: "The Prediction of Bankruptcy with Published Financial Data"). *Acta Academiae Oeconomica Heisingiensis* A, No. 13 (Helsinki).
Suominen, S. I. 1988. "The Prediction of Bankruptcy in Finland." *Studies in Banking and Finance* 7: 27.

France
Altman, E. I., M. Margaine, M. Schlosser, and P. Vernimmen. 1974. "Statistical Credit Analysis in the Textile Industry: A French Experience." *Journal of Financial and Quantitative Analysis* (March).
Collongues, Y. 1979. *"Ratios Financiers et Prevision des Faillites des Petites et Moyennes Enterprises"* ("Financial Ratios and Forecasting of Small and Medium Size Enterprises"). *Review Banque* No. 365.
Ghesquiere, S., and B. Micha. 1983. *"L'analyse des Defaillances d'Enterprises."* *Rapport de la Journee d'etude des Centrales de Bilans.*
Mader, F. 1975. *"Les Ratios et l'Analyse du Risqué"* ("Ratios and Analysis of Risk"). *Analyse Financiere*, Zeme trimestre.
Mader, F. 1979. *"Un Enchantillon d'Enterprises en Difficulte"* ("A Sample of Enterprises in Difficulty"). *Journee des Centrales der Bilans.*
Micha, B. 1984. "Analysis of Business Failures in France." *Journal of Banking & Finance* 8, No. 2 (June): 281.

Germany
Baetge, J., M. Huss, and H. J. Niehaus. 1988. "The Use of Statistical Analysis to Identify the Financial Strength of Corporations in Germany." *Studies in Banking and Finance* 7: 183.
Gebhardt, G. 1980. "Insolvency Prediction Based on Annual Financial Statements According to the Company Law—An Assessment of the Reform of Annual Statements by the Law of 1965 from the View of External Addresses." In H. Besters et al., eds., *Bochumer Beitrage Zur Untennehmungs und Unternedhmens-forschung*, Vol. 22, Wiesbaden.
Schmidt, R. 1984. "Early Warning of Debt Rescheduling." *Journal of Banking & Finance* 8, No. 2 (June): 357.
Von Stein, J. H. 1981. "Identifying Endangered Firms." Hohenheim University, Stuttgart-Hohenheim.
Von Stein, J. H., and W. Ziegler. 1984. "The Prognosis and Surveillance of Risk from Commercial Credit Borrowers." *Journal of Banking & Finance* 8, No. 2 (June): 249.

Weibel, P. F. 1973. "The Value of Criteria to Judge Credit Worthiness in the Lending of Banks." Bern/Stuttgart.

Weinrich, G. 1978. *Predicting Credit Worthiness, Directions of Credit Operations by Risk Classes.* Weisbaden: Galder.

Greece

Gloubos, G., and T. Grammatikos. 1988. "The Success of Bankruptcy Prediction Models in Greece." *Studies in Banking and Finance* 7: 37.

Grammatikos, T., and O. Gloubos. "Predicting Bankruptcy in Industrial Firms in Greece." *Spoudai* 33, Nos. 3–4: 421.

Papoulias, C., and P. Theodossiou. 1987. "Corporate Failure Prediction Models for Greece." Working paper, Fordham University.

Theodossiou, P., and C. Papoulias. 1988. "Problematic Firms in Greece: An Evaluation Using Corporate Failure Prediction Models." *Studies in Banking and Finance* 7: 47.

India

Bhatia, U. 1988. "Redicting Corporate Sickness in India." *Studies in Banking and Finance* 7: 57.

Satyanarayana, P. V., and P. K. Sen. n.d. "An Empirical Model to Predict Corporate Sickness." In S. K. Chakraborty and P. K. Sen, eds. *Industrial Sickness and Revival in India.* n.p.

Israel

Tamari, M. 1966. "Financial Ratios as a Means of Forecasting Bankruptcy." *Management International Review* 4.

Italy

Altman, E. I., G. Marco, and F. Varetto. 1994. "Corporate Distress Diagnosis: Comparisons Using Discriminant Analysis and Neural Networks; the Italian Experience." *Journal of Banking & Finance* 18: 505–529.

Appetti, S. 1984. "Identifying Unsound Firms in Italy." *Journal of Banking and Finance* 8: 269.

Cifarelli, D. M., F. Corielli, and G. Forestieri. 1988. "Business Failure Analysis, a Bayesian Approach with Italian Firm Data." *Studies in Banking and Finance* 7: 73.

Japan

Ko, C. J. 1982. "A Delineation of Corporate Appraisal Models and Classification of Bankruptcy Firms in Japan." Thesis (New York University).

Takahashi, K., and E. Altman. 1981. Conference on the State of the Art in Bankruptcy Classification Models, June 25 (Keio Graduate School of Business, Yokohama).

Takahashi, K., K. Kurokawa, and K. Watese. 1979. "Predicting Corporate Bankruptcy Through Financial Statements." Society of Management Science of Keio University (November).

Yoshimura, K. 1979. "Z-Score—There Are 90 Corporations Whose Score Was Below 1.0." *Nikkei-Business* (June 5).

Malaysia

Bidin, A. R. 1988. "The Development of a Predictive Model (PNB Score) for Evaluating Performance of Companies Owned by the Government of Malaysia." Studies in Banking and Finance, *Journal of Banking & Finance* 7: 91.

Mexico

Altman, E. I., J. Hartzell, and M. Peck. 1995. "Emerging Markets Corporate Bonds: A Scoring System." Salomon Brothers. Reprinted in *The Future of Emerging Market Flows*, edited by R. Levich and J. Mei. Holland: Kluwer, 1997.

Netherlands

Abrahams, A., and R. A. L. van Frederikslust. 1976. "Discriminant Analysis and the Prediction of Corporate Failure." *European Finance Association 1975 Proceedings*, R. Brealey and G. Rankine, eds. Amsterdam: North Holland.

Bilderbeek, J. 1979. "An Empirical Study of the Predictive Ability of Financial Ratios in the Netherlands. *Zeitschrift fur Betriebswirtschaft* No. 5 (May).

Van Frederikslust, R. A. L. 1978. "Predictability of Corporate Failure." Leiden: Martinus Nijhoff Social Science Division.

Norway

Lensberg, T., A. Eilifsen, and T. McKee. 2005. "Bankruptcy Theory Development and Classification via Genetic Programming." *European Journal of Operations Research*, in press.

Singapore

Ta, H. D., and L. H. Seah. 1988. "Business Failure Prediction in Singapore." *Studies in Banking and Finance* 7: 105.

South Korea

Altman, E. I., Y. H. Eom, and D.W. Kim. 1995. "Failure Prediction: Evidence from Korea." *Journal of Financial Management and Accounting* 6, No. 3: 230–249.

Spain

Briones, J. L., J. L. Martin, and M. J. V. Cueto. 1988. "Forecasting Bank Failures: The Spanish Case." *Studies in Banking and Finance* 7: 127.

Fernandez, A. I. 1988. "A Spanish Model for Credit Risk Classification." *Studies in Banking and Finance* 7: 115.

Turkey

Unal, T. 1988. "An Early Warning Model for Predicting Firm Failure and Bankruptcy." *Studies in Banking and Finance* 7: 141.

United Kingdom

Argenti, J. 1983. "Predicting Corporate Failure, Institute of Chartered Accountants in English and Wales." *Accountants Digest*, No. 138.

Ashton, R. H. 1979. "Some Implications of Parameter Sensitivity Research for Judgement Modelling in Accounting." *Accounting Review* 54, No. 1: 170–179.

Bank of England. 1982. "Techniques for Assessing Corporate Financial Strength." *Bank of England Quarterly Bulletin* (June): 221–223.

Betts, J. 1983. "The Identification of Companies at Risk of Financial Failure." Working Environment Research Group Report no. 5, University of Bradford, Bradford.

Earl, M. J., and D. Marais. 1982. "Predicting Corporate Failure in the U.K. Using Discriminant Analysis." *Accounting and Business Research*.

Marais, D. A. J. 1979. "A Method of Quantifying Companies' Relative Financial Strength." Working Paper No. 4, Bank of England, London.

Taffler, R. J. 1982. "Forecasting Company Failure in the U.K. Using Discriminant Analysis and Financial Ratios Data." *Journal of Royal Statistical Society*.

Taffler, R. J. 1984. "Empirical Models for the Monitoring of U.K. Corporations." *Journal of Banking and Finance* 8, No. 2 (June): 199.

Taffler, R. J., and H. Tisshaw. 1979. "Going, Going, Going—Four Factors Which Predict." *Accountancy*: 50.

Uruguay

Pascale, R. 1988. "A Multivariate Model to Predict Firm Financial Problems: The Case of Uruguay." *Studies in Banking and Finance* 7: 171.

International Survey

Altman, E., and P. Narayanan. 1997. "Business Failure Classification Models: An International Survey." In F. D. S. Choi, editor, *International Accounting and Finance Handbook*, 2nd ed. New York: John Wiley & Sons, Chapter 35.

An Emerging Market Credit Scoring System for Corporates

In the prior chapter, we explained the development and testing of several corporate credit scoring models based, essentially, on U.S. data. While there is no reason why these models cannot be applied to companies throughout the rest of the world, we recognize that each environment has its own peculiarities; hence, local models could be expected to perhaps outperform U.S. models, at least in their testing phase. Indeed, in Chapter 11, we presented a bibliography of numerous models built in over 20 countries throughout the world over the past 30 years. Still, we believe that generic credit risk models are applicable in most environments since the fundamentals of corporate insolvency analysis are relevant everywhere. What does differ is local bankruptcy laws (see Chapter 2), and therefore the expected and unexpected default *loss* function will be impacted.

In this chapter, we explore the application of one of our Z-Score approaches for credit rating purposes in emerging markets. We developed this model first in the mid-1990s (Altman et al. 1995) to provide an analytical framework for the then growing, but still nascent, corporate market for emerging market companies issuing bonds in nonlocal currency (usually U.S. dollars). Since this Eurobond market was launched in the early 1990s, there was little history and no defaults to facilitate the construction of models based on local data.

THE EMERGING MARKET SCORE MODEL (EMS MODEL)

The emerging market scoring system (EMS) model for rating emerging market credits is based first on a fundamental financial review derived from a quantitative risk model, and second, on our assessments of specific credit risks in the emerging market in order to arrive at a final modified rating. This rating can then be utilized by the investor, after considering the appropriate sovereign yield spread, to assess equivalent bond ratings and intrinsic values.

The foundation of the EMS model is an enhancement of our Z″-Score model, resulting in an EM score and its associated bond rating equivalent (BRE). The EM score's rating equivalent is then modified based on three critical factors: (1) the firm's vulnerability to currency devaluation, (2) its industry affiliation, and (3) its competitive position in the industry. Unique features of the specific bond issue should also be considered. These subjective modifications are an important complement to the EM score. The resulting analyst modified rating is compared to the actual bond rating (if any). Where no agency rating exists, our analyst modified rating is a means to assess credit quality and relative value both to credits within a country and to U.S. corporates. The implied yield spread based on the analyst modified rating can be observed from the U.S. corporate bond market. Steps 1 through 6 (next) outline the process by which we use the EM score to reach an analyst modified rating. You will note that our analyst modified rating is not constrained in any manner by the so-called sovereign ceiling. A sovereign ceiling is a standard rating protocol that usually limits an individual corporate issuer to receive an international rating no higher than the sovereign in which it is located. The reasoning is that the sovereign can usually expropriate resources from the corporation should there be a crisis of some sort. We do advocate, however, in most cases, to factor in the appropriate current sovereign yield spread differential between the emerging market country and comparable-duration U.S. Treasuries, when arriving at a required rate of return on the emerging market corporate.

Step 1: U.S. Bond Rating Equivalent

In developing our emerging market scoring system (EMS), we proceeded based on a series of steps. We scored each bond by its EM score and classified it relative to its stand-alone U.S. bond rating equivalent. Emerging market corporate credits should initially be analyzed in a manner similar to traditional analysis of U.S. corporates. This involves the examination of measures of performance in such a manner as to establish a rating equivalent of the particular issuer. Instead of using a new ad hoc system, which may not be based on a rigorous analytical examination of creditworthiness, we will use an established and well-tested system. Since it was not yet possible to build such a model from a sample of emerging market credits, we suggest testing the applicability of a modified version of the original Z-Score model. This Z″-Score model is based on a comparative profile of bankrupt and nonbankrupt U.S. manufacturers. Our modifications, we hope, could be applied to nonmanufacturing, industrial firms and to private and public entities.

The original Z-Score model is based on at least two data sources that make it inappropriate to use for all emerging markets corporates: (1) it requires the firm to have publicly traded equity and (2) it is primarily for manufacturers. In more than 35 years of experience in building, testing, and using credit scoring models for a variety of purposes, the original model has been enhanced to make it applicable for private companies and nonmanufacturers. The resulting model, which is the foundation for our EMS model approach, is of the form:

$$\text{EM Score} = 6.56\,(X_1) + 3.26\,(X_2) + 6.72\,(X_3) + 1.05\,(X_4) + 3.25$$

where X_1 = working capital/total assets
$\quad\ X_2$ = retained earnings/total assets
$\quad\ X_3$ = operating income/total assets
$\quad\ X_4$ = book value of equity/total liabilities

The constant term in the model (3.25), which is derived from the median Z″-Score for bankrupt U.S. entities, enables us to standardize the analysis so that a default equivalent rating (D) is consistent with a score below zero (actually scores below 1.75 are rated D).

Major accounting differences between the emerging market country and the United States must be factored into the data used in the calculations of our measures. For example, our calculation of retained earnings is based on the sum of past retained earnings plus the value of stock issuance plus the capital reserve, the surplus (or deficiency) on restatement of assets, and finally, the net income (or loss) for the current period.

The original Z″-Score model was tested on samples of both nonmanufacturers and manufacturers in the United States, and its accuracy and reliability have remained high. We have also carefully calibrated the variables and the resulting score with U.S. bond rating equivalents. These equivalents, given in Figure 12.1, are based on a sample of more than 750 U.S. firms with rated bonds outstanding.

	Z"-Score		Rating		Z"-Score		Rating	
Safe Zone	8.15	>8.15	AAA		5.65	5.85	BBB−	Gray Zone
	7.60	8.15	AA+		5.25	5.65	BB+	
	7.30	7.60	AA		4.95	5.25	BB	
	7.00	7.30	AA−		4.75	4.95	BB−	
	6.85	7.00	A+		4.50	4.75	B+	
	6.65	6.85	A		4.15	4.50	B	
	6.40	6.65	A−		3.75	4.15	B−	
	6.25	6.40	BBB+		3.20	3.75	CCC+	Distress Zone
	5.85	6.25	BBB		2.50	3.20	CCC	
					1.75	2.50	CCC−	
					<1.75	1.75	D	

FIGURE 12.1 Z"-Score and Bond Rating Equivalent
Source: E. Altman, J. Hartzell, and M. Peck, "A Scoring System for Emerging Market Corporate Bonds," Salomon Brothers, May 1995.

Step 2: Adjusted Bond Rating for Foreign Currency Devaluation Vulnerability

Each bond is then analyzed as to the issuing firm's vulnerability to problems in servicing its foreign-currency-denominated debt. Vulnerability is assessed based on the relationship between nonlocal currency revenues minus costs compared to nonlocal currency interest expense, and nonlocal currency revenues versus nonlocal currency debt. Finally, the level of cash is compared with the debt coming due in the next year.

If the firm has high vulnerability (is weak), that is, it has low or zero nonlocal currency revenues and/or low or zero revenues/debt, and/or a substantial amount of foreign currency debt coming due with little cash liquidity, then the bond rating equivalent in Step 1 is lowered by a full rating class, such as BB+ to B+. There is a one-notch (BB+ to BB) reduction for a neutral vulnerability assessment, but no change in rating for a low (strong) risk of a currency devaluation. This is so because we are interested in a U.S. BRE.

Step 3: Adjusted for Industry

The original (Step 1) bond rating equivalent is compared to a U.S. generic industry safety rating equivalent, as shown in Table 12.1. For up to each full-letter grade difference between the two ratings, Step 2's bond rating equivalent is adjusted up or down by one notch. For example, if the rating from Step 1 is BBB and the industry's rating is BBB–, BB+, or BB, then the adjustment is one notch down; if the difference is more than one full rating class but less than two full ratings, there is a two-notch adjustment. Finally, the industry environment in the specific emerging market country is factored into the analysis. For example, the Mexican construction industry's weakness in the post–peso crisis period was a consideration and its industry risk rating was adjusted lower than its U.S. counterpart.

Step 4: Adjusted for Competitive Position

Step 3's rating is adjusted up (or down) one notch depending on whether (or not) the firm is a dominant company in its industry or a domestic power in terms of size, political influence, and quality of management. It is also possible that the consensus competitive position result is neutral (no change in rating).

Step 5: Special Debt Issue Features

If the particular debt issue has unique features, such as collateral or a bona fide, high-quality guarantor, then the issue should be upgraded accordingly.

TABLE 12.1 Average Credit Safety of Industry Groups

Sector	Average Sector Credit Safety
Telecommunications	High A
Independent Finance	High A
Natural Gas Utilities	High A
Beverages	High A
High-Quality Electric Utilities	High A
Railroads	High A
Food Processing	Mid A
Bottling	Mid A
Domestic Bank Holding	Low A
Tobacco	Low A
Medium-Quality Electric Utilities	Low A
Consumer Products Industry	Low A
High Grade Diversified Mfg./Conglomerates	Low A
Leasing	Low A
Auto Manufacturers	Low A
Chemicals	Low A
Energy	Low A
Natural Gas Pipelines	High BBB
Paper/Forest Products	Mid BBB
Retail	Mid BBB
Property and Casualty Insurance	Mid BBB
Aerospace/Defense	Mid BBB
Information/Data Technology	Mid BBB
Supermarkets	High BB
Cable and Media	High BB
Vehicle Parts	High BB
Textile/Apparel	High BB
Low-Quality Electric Utilities	Mid BB
Gaming	Mid BB
Restaurants	Mid BB
Construction	Mid BB
Hotel/Leisure	Mid BB
Low-Quality Manufacturing	Mid BB
Airlines	Low BB
Metals	High B

Source: Salomon Brothers (June 1995).

We advocate that, if there is a high-quality guarantor, it be a legal guarantee and not an informal one. Such was the case in Argentina when an affiliate of a Pepsi-Cola bottler (Baesa, S.A.) did, indeed, default.

Step 6: Comparison to the Sovereign Spread

The analyst modified rating is then compared to what U.S. corporate bonds of the same rating are currently selling for. The U.S. corporate credit quality spread is then added to the appropriate option-adjusted spread of the sovereign bond. For example, if the modified rating of the bond is BBB and such quality bonds are trading in the United States at 100 basis points over U.S. Treasuries (e.g., 10-year T-bonds in early 2005 of 4.5 percent) and the Mexican comparable-duration treasuries are trading at 200 basis points over their U.S. counterparts, then the required return will be 7.5 percent (4.5% + 100bp + 200bp).

The analyst would then evaluate the actual yield on the particular emerging market corporate bond and compare it to the required yield based on the EM scoring model (e.g., in this case 7.5 percent). If the actual yield is greater than 7.5 percent, then the bond would be considered to be an attractive potential purchase, and vice versa.

Figure 12.2 summarizes the six-step process we have just outlined. While the last step illustrates our model's applicability to the investment process in choosing, or not, an individual bond, the generic process is a method to assess the relative credit quality of any corporation in the emerging market environment, regardless of whether it has an international bond outstanding. We now move to a few modifications and tests that we made based on an analysis of the model in the period just after we built it. Before observing these tests, however, we would like to suggest that the analyst who does not have the information, or the time, to make the adjustments suggested in Steps 2 through 6 still is able to apply the initial Step 1 calculation.

APPLYING THE EMS MODEL TO MEXICAN CORPORATES

In Table 12.2 we calculate the EM scores for almost 30 Mexican corporations that had issued corporate bonds in the Eurobond market. Note that only 13 had received a rating from at least one of the three rating agencies as of year-end 1994. Also, you can observe that the scores range across the full spectrum of bond rating equivalents from AAA to D. Indeed, only one firm, Aeromexico, was rated as D at the time of the peso crisis (December 1994), and that firm had already filed for bankruptcy in an experimental

- Step 1—Calculate the EM score and its bond rating equivalent (BRE) compared to the U.S. bond market.
- Step 2—Adjust (modify) the bond rating equivalent for foreign currency revaluation vulnerability:
  High vulnerability = −1 rating class (3 notches)
  Neutral vulnerability = −1 notch
  Low vulnerability = No change
- Step 3—Adjust BRE for risk of industry in the emerging market vs. risk of industry in the United States:
  ± 1 or 2 notches
- Step 4—Adjust BRE for competitive position:
  Dominant firm in industry = +1 notch
  Average firm in industry = No change
  Poor competitive position = −1 notch
- Step 5—Assess impact of special collateral or guarantees on BRE.
- Step 6—Assess the yield in the U.S. market on the modified BRE of the emerging market credit, then add the sovereign yield spread. Finally, compare the resulting required yield with the yield in the market.

FIGURE 12.2   An Emerging Market Credit Scoring System

test of the bankruptcy court system. We will later examine the profile of Aeromexico subsequent to its emergence from bankruptcy.

Four Mexican firms received the highest BRE, and many had ratings above the Mexican sovereign ceiling (BB). The modified ratings are also shown, and most firms received lower ratings than the original EMS rating from Step 1.

MODIFICATION AND TESTS OF THE EMERGING MARKET MODEL

After the initial testing of the emerging market model, we decided to make one further important modification dealing with the market value of the firms' equity.

Equity Market Value Consideration and Impact

When we first modified our U.S. Z″-Score model to adapt it to the emerging market bond sector, we decided to use a model with the book value of equity,

TABLE 12.2   Mexican Corporate Issuers—EM Scores and Modified Ratings, December 1994

Company	Industry	EM Score	Bond Rating Equivalent	Modified Rating	Ratings M/S&P/D&P
Aeromexico	Airlines	−4.42	D	D	NR/NR/NR
Apasco	Cement	8.48	AAA	A	Ba/NR/NR
CCM	Supermarkets	4.78	BB−	B+	NR/NR/NR
Cemex	Cement	5.67	BBB−	BBB−	Ba3/BB/BB
Cydsa	Chemicals	4.67	BB−	B+	NR/NR/NR
DESC	Conglomerate	4.23	B	BB+	NR/NR/NR
Empresas ICA	Construction	5.96	BBB	BB	B1/BB−/B+
Femsa	Bottling	6.37	A−	BBB+	NR/NR/NR
Gemex	Bottling	5.4	BB+	BB+	Ba3/NR/NR
GIDUSA (Durango)	Paper and Forest Products	4.61	B+	BB	B1/BB−/NR
GMD	Construction	4.85	BB	B−	B3/NR/NR
Gruma	Food Processing	5.56	BBB−	BBB+	NR/NR/NR
Grupo Dina	Auto Manufacturing	5.54	BBB−	BB+	NR/NR/B
Grupo Sidek	Conglomerate	4.68	BB−	B	NR/NR/CCC
Grupo Simec	Steel	4.42	B+	B−	NR/NR/CCC
Grupo Situr	Hotel & Tourism	5.17	BB+	B	NR/NR/CCC
Hylsamex	Steel	5.51	BBB−	BB−	NR/NR/NR
IMSA	Steel	5.45	BBB−	BB−	NR/NR/NR
Kimberly-Clark de Mexico	Paper and Forest Products	8.96	AAA	AA	NR/NR/NR
Liverpool	Retail	9.85	AAA	A+	NR/NR/NR
Moderna	Conglomerate	5.28	BB+	BB+	NR/NR/NR
Ponderosa	Paper and Forest Products	6.64	A	BB	NR/NR/NR
San Luis	Auto Parts	2.69	CCC	CCC−	NR/NR/NR
Synkro	Textile/Apparel	1.59	CCC−	CCC	NR/NR/NR
TAMSA	Steel Pipes	3.34	CCC+	B	NR/NR/NR
Televisa	Cable and Media	7.29	AA	BBB+	Ba2/NR/NR
TELMEX	Telecommunications	9.57	AAA	AA−	NR/NR/NR
TMM	Shipping	5.34	BB+	BB+	Ba2/BB−/NR
Vitro	Glass	5.18	BB+	BB	Ba2/NR/NR

M = Moody's
S&P = Standard & Poor's
D&P = Duff & Phelps
Source: Altman et al. (1995).

not the market value, as the fourth variable. This was done for several reasons, including the concern that emerging equity markets were not very liquid and possibly seriously inefficient. Also, we were not sure if we could even find continuous equity prices for some of our sample companies. We since discovered that equity prices were consistently available for many companies, especially the ones large enough to issue corporate bonds in the international bond market and that there could, indeed, be some valuable information content in the equity numbers and their changes over time.

Despite the inefficiencies in emerging market equity valuations, a company whose stock is valued highly by the financial community can usually borrow more easily and raise new equity or sell assets at better prices than one that is being discounted by investors. Since the corporate bonds of emerging market companies are, by rating agency definitions, almost all non–investment grade, their yield and volatility patterns at times are more correlated with equity market activity than are investment-grade corporates. The same could be argued for firms issuing bonds in the U.S. high yield bond market.

There are two ways that we can introduce a market value of equity factor into our system. First, a new variable reflecting the market to book value of equity, or some similar measure, could be added to the existing four variables. Since the original database used to construct the emerging market scoring system did not contain that variable, it is impractical to reestimate the equation using a new database. The second approach is to add an additional phase to our modified equivalent bond rating process—one that incorporates a comparison of the bond rating equivalent using the ratio of book value of equity to total liabilities (X_4 in the model) versus the same variable with the market value of equity (number of shares outstanding times the stock price) substituted for the book value.

The second approach is what we actually have done in this iteration of the EMS model. The procedure we followed is to calculate the bond rating equivalent in the traditional manner, which involves (1) the initial bond rating based on the multivariate model and (2) modifications based on currency devaluation vulnerability, industry affiliation, and competitive position. The final phase now is to compare the bond rating equivalent using book equity to the rating equivalent using the market value of equity.

If the two systems give the identical rating or are different by only one notch, then the modified rating is unchanged. If, however, the two versions result in a two-notch differential, then we increase or decrease the final modified rating by one notch. Finally, if the difference is a full rating class (three notches) or more, the modified rating is changed by two notches.

Testing the EMS Model

As an example of the application of this new adjustment, based on six months ended June 1996 data, there were 14 firms with higher bond rating equivalents when using the market value compared to the book value equity. Of the 14 firms, six had the same modified rating since the difference was only one notch; one had a one-notch upgrade, and seven had a two-notch upgrade. Six firms in total had lower EM scores using market value compared to book value of equity, with four resulting in a one-notch downgrade and the other two not changed. Nine firms had the identical rating using the book and market value of equity measures. The actual comparisons are not shown for each firm.

The impact of using the market value of equity versus the book value can be considerable in the final modified rating for a company. Such an impact could, however, reflect the often inefficient market for Mexican companies' equity. The volatility of the Mexican peso and its impact on the Mexican equity market can mask the intrinsic values of Mexican equities. In addition, inflation accounting can distort the book value of equity of Mexican firms because of income statement noncash charges and the consequent changes in retained earnings and stockholders' equity. We believe that despite these inefficiencies, the Mexican equity market had rallied sufficiently and was efficient and comprehensive enough to add value to our model in the postcrisis period.

PERFORMANCE OF THE EMS MODEL FOR MEXICAN FIRMS IN POST–PESO CRISIS PERIOD

We continued to monitor the emerging market scoring system model, which was used first to assess the creditworthiness of Mexican firms as of year-end 1994, just at the time that the peso crisis hit that country (Table 12.2). Subsequent bond equivalent modified ratings were calculated and evaluated for most of the same firms as of the third quarter of 1995 and through the second quarter (midyear) of 1996. We paid close attention to those firms, which the model classified as extremely risky (CCC or worse) or as likely near-term defaults (D). As noted earlier, we added the market to book value equity modified rating to the bond rating equivalent modified rating.

The emerging market model clearly illustrated the difficult economic and corporate environment in Mexico in the immediate period after the crisis and was a fairly accurate predictor of deteriorating credit quality in 1995 and then the recovering economy in 1996. More importantly, the model predicted accurately every defaulting firm's debt in the postcrisis period while also indicating the successful restructuring of a few entities. Table 12.3 updates the EM scores of 29 (out of the 31 companies listed) Mexican companies for two postcrisis periods, Q3-1995 and June 1996 (Q2), as well as their ratings at the time of the crisis in December 1994.

The EMS ratings were very accurate in assessing credit risk migration in the 18 months after the crisis. For example, we first rated Vitro Corporation BB in December 1994, downgraded it to B as of Q3-1995 and to B– in June 1996. Our adjustments were based on data reflecting Vitro's struggling U.S. subsidiary, Anchor Glass, and its progressive cash flow problems, as well as the resultant impact on Vitro's credit standing. Anchor Glass had represented over 40 percent of Vitro's consolidated revenues in previous years. In July 1996, both Moody's and S&P downgraded Anchor Glass to Caa from B2, and CC+ from B, respectively. In September 1996, Anchor Glass (U.S.) filed for bankruptcy through a prepackaged Chapter 11 reorganization. In other examples, Grupo Sidek and its subsidiaries, Grupo Situr and Grupo Simec, continued to struggle through a restructuring, which began in early 1995. As a result of the ongoing restructuring and uncertainty about the financial independence of these companies, we assigned a rating of D in June 1996 for all three companies. Grupo Sidek, Grupo Situr, and Grupo Simec had been rated CCC–, B+ and CCC–, respectively, in our December 1995 rating analysis. All three firms missed interest payments on their debt subsequent to our D rating.

Rating Transitions and Default Prediction

Table 12.3 lists 31 companies and their rating transitions. Between December 1994 and June 1996, our analysis generated 13 upgrades and 12 downgrades, with 6 ratings remaining unchanged. This was a reversal in the initial postcrisis (1995) upgrade/downgrade ratio, consistent with the turnaround in the Mexican economy. The Mexican economy had rebounded significantly since the beginning of 1996 with second-quarter year-to-year gross domestic product (GDP) comparisons showing a 7.2 percent increase. We similarly began to see the signs of renewed domestic growth in the private sector with margin and volume increases for many of the domestic focused industries in the third quarter ending September 1996. It also reflects the impact of our addition of a market/book value of equity factor to our modified rating system.

Eight firms experienced significant improvements in their modified ratings of at least three notches, including: CCM, DESC, Femsa, Gemex, Gruma, San Luis, Televisa, and TMM. These firms represent a cross section of domestic focused industries which enjoyed recovering demand for their products. Only two firms, Grupo Carso (not shown in Table 12.3)

TABLE 12.3   Mexican Corporate Issuers—Modified Ratings, 1994–1996

Company	Industry	Q4-1994	Q3-1995	Q2-1996	Ratings M/S&P/D&P
Aeromexico	Airlines	D	CCC+	B	NR/NR/NR
Apasco	Cement	A	BBB–	BBB	Ba2/NR/NR
CCM	Supermarkets	B+	B	BB+	NR/NR/NR
Cemex	Cement	BBB–	BB+	BB	B1/BB/BB
Cydsa	Chemicals	B+	BBB–	BB+	NR/NR/NR
Condumex	Steel	NR	BBB+	BBB+	NR/NR/BB
DESC	Conglomerate	BB+	BB	BBB	NR/NR/NR
Durango	Paper and Forest Products	BB	BBB	BB+	B1/BB–/NR
Elektra	Retail	NR	NR	A+	NR/B/BB+
Empaques Ponderosa	Paper and Forest Products	BB	A+	A	NR/NR/NR
Empresas ICA	Construction	BB	B+	B	B1/BB–/B+
Femsa	Bottling	BBB+	BB+	BBB+	NR/NR/NR
Gemex	Bottling	BB+	B+	BBB+	Ba3/NR/NR
GMD	Construction	B–	CCC	D	B3/NR/NR
Gruma	Food Processing	BBB+	BBB–	A–	NR/NR/NR
Grupo Dina	Auto Manufacturing	BB+	B+	B+	NR/NR/B–
Grupo Sidek	Conglomerate	B	CCC–	D	NR/NR/DD
Grupo Simec	Steel	B–	B+	D	NR/NR/DD
Grupo Situr	Hotel and Tourism	B	CCC–	D	NR/NR/DD
Hylsamex	Steel	BB–	BBB+	BBB	NR/NR/NR
Kimberly-Clark de Mexico	Paper and Forest Products	AA	A+	AA–	NR/NR/NR
Liverpool	Retail	A+	A+	A+	NR/NR/NR
Moderna	Conglomerate	BB+	BBB–	BB	NR/NR/NR
San Luis	Auto Parts	CCC–	B–	BB–	NR/NR/NR
Synkro	Textile/Apparel	CCC–	D	D	NR/NR/NR
TAMSA	Steel Pipes	B	B+	BB	NR/NR/NR
Televisa	Cable and Media	BBB+	BBB–	A+	Ba3/BB/NR
TELMEX	Telecommunications	AA–	AA–	AA–	NR/NR/NR
TMM	Shipping	BB+	BBB	A+	Ba2/BB–/NR
Tribasa	Construction	NR	CCC	CCC+	Caa/B+/B
Vitro	Glass	BB	B	B–	NR/NR/NR

M = Moody's
S&P = Standard & Poor's
D&P = Duff & Phelps
Source: Author computations, Moody's, S&P, Fitch Ratings (formerly Duff & Phelps).

and GMD, experienced significant downgrades of two or three notches. Carso still had a very respectable A– modified rating. GMD, however, had significant liquidity problems and dropped to D (default outlook). All the other downgrades were one-notch although Sidek, Situr, and Synkro were firmly entrenched in the D rating category.

Defaulted, D-Rated, and Low-Rated Bonds

As just noted, we ascribed a D rating to GMD. It was the only entity to receive this rating that had not yet defaulted. The three other firms with D ratings, Sidek, Situr, and Synkro, were all in restructuring on some of their outstanding indebtedness. All three had received either a CCC– or D rating prior to their defaults. And GMD did subsequently default.

Other low-rated entities were Grupo Tribasa (CCC+) and Vitro (B–). As mentioned, Vitro's U.S. subsidiary defaulted on its own U.S. bonds in September 1996. It should also be noted that the one firm with a D rating as of December 1994 (Aeromexico) recovered to a B rating after emerging from bankruptcy in a rare Mexican corporate court-orchestrated reorganization.

Rating Agency Comparisons

Of the 29 Mexican companies that we originally analyzed (Table 12.2), only 13 were rated at that time by at least one of the major rating agencies (Duff & Phelps, Moody's, and S&P). In this section, we compare our modified EMS rating for these firms to the three agencies' evaluations. Our ratings were not constrained by the sovereign ceiling (Ba2/BB). Our ratings were unconstrained in order to assign a stand-alone fundamental credit view of a company and its securities.

Our EM score's modified ratings in the second quarter of 1996 were higher than the rating agencies' for 7 of the 13 firms (Apasco, Cemex, Dina, Durango, Gemex, TMM, and Televisa). The EMS model assigned lower ratings for three firms, GMD, Tribasa, and ICA, than the ratings assigned by the rating agencies. In the case of GMD, we gave the firm our lowest rating (D), indicating a highly risky situation and distinct default possibility. GMD was rated B3 by Moody's and unrated by the other two agencies. ICA's B rating was slightly lower than all three of the agency ratings. Our modified rating for Tribasa was CCC+ versus a Caa from Moody's, a B+ from S&P, and a B from Duff & Phelps. Finally, our ratings were the same as S&P and Duff & Phelps and different by only one notch from Moody's for Cemex (modified rating: BB) and two others.

Some Time Series Examples and Risk Comparisons

Figures 12.3a and 12.3b demonstrate the EMS scores (Step 1) for two important Mexican companies over the period 1998–2002. Cemex, the

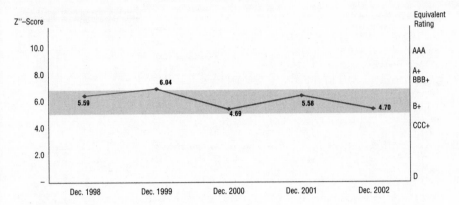

FIGURE 12.3a EMS for Cemex SA de CV (*Production, Distribution, Marketing, and Sale of Cement*)
Source: Bloomberg and author calculations.

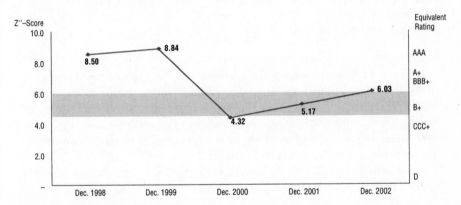

FIGURE 12.3b EMS for Telefonos de Mexico SA de CV (*Telecommunications Services [TELMEX]*)
Source: Bloomberg and author calculations.

perennial benchmark Mexican credit and the world's second largest cement company, shows a fairly stable EMS and BRE. The more recent (2002) score of 4.70 reflects Cemex's heightened leveraged condition as it pursued an aggressive acquisition strategy.

Telefonos de Mexico demonstrates the typical global telecom experience for major firms with established markets and subscriber bases. Scores were extremely high in the later 1990s, fell considerably in 2000 and 2001, and rebounded in 2002.

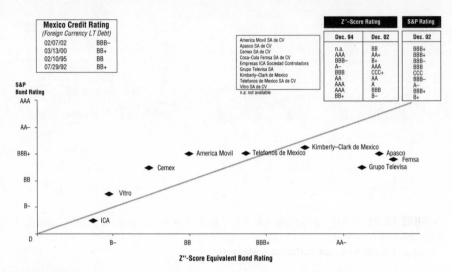

FIGURE 12.4 EM Scores, Bond Rating Equivalents, and S&P Ratings (as of December 31, 2002)
Source: Bloomberg and author calculations.

Figure 12.4 demonstrates the comparisons between our EMS model's BREs and those comparable company ratings from a major rating agency (S&P). The firms indicated above the diagonal are ones where the S&P rating was higher than the EMS rating equivalent, and vice versa for those below the line. Again, our model and its BREs are not impacted by the sovereign ceiling. The two firms' bonds shown in Figures 12.3a and 12.3b are both rated as somewhat more risky by the EMS model than by S&P. Note that we have not applied the quantitative modifications discussed earlier in Steps 2 to 6.

CONCLUDING REMARKS

Since 1996, we have, from time to time, applied the EMS model to emerging market companies other than Mexico. The results, too numerous to discuss here, were particularly robust in such countries as Brazil and Argentina in the late 1990s and also in many of the Southeast Asian countries in the pre- and post-1997 Asian crisis. While we are impressed and frankly a bit surprised by our modified U.S. model's successful application in non-U.S. environments, we still advocate building and testing models derived from the country's own data and experience, if possible.

Application of Distress Prediction Models

This chapter explores a number of direct and indirect applications of corporate distress prediction models for users of all types. While a fairly long list of potential applications will be identified, the list is probably not exhaustive. Space does not permit a complete treatment of each item in our list, but we hope that the reader can easily identify the essence of our intention. The list of applications is specified in Figure 13.1. The last application, "Managers of Distressed Firms," will be referred to in detail in the next chapter (14). This application on managing a financial turnaround is also an example of an interactive application.

- Lending Specialists
- Accounts Receivable Managers
- Investors
- Security Analysts
- Regulators
- Auditors
- Bankruptcy Lawyers
- Legal Direction (e.g., Deepening Insolvency)
- Bond Raters
- Risk Management Consultants
- Restructuring Advisers and Turnaround Managers
- Government Agencies and Other Purchasers
- Mergers and Acquisitions Analysts
- Managers of Distressed Firms

FIGURE 13.1   Financial Distress Prediction Users
Source: Author compilation.

LENDERS

Perhaps the most obvious application of distress prediction/credit scoring models is in the lending function. Banks and other credit institutions are continuously involved in the assessment of credit risk of corporate counterparties. The importance of credit scoring models for specifying the probability of default (PD) has been heightened and motivated immensely by the requirements of Basel II and the necessity for banks to develop and implement internal rating based (IRB) models. We hope that the decision of U.S. regulators (e.g., the Federal Reserve Board) *not* to require most banks in the United States to conform to Basel II will not serve to demotivate banks from developing these models—but we fear that it will, in many cases. On the other hand, banks in many other parts of the world, particularly Europe, have been encouraged, with great success, to modernize their credit risk systems by the requirements under Basel II.

One of the important dimensions of the lending function is to specify the "price" of credit (i.e., the appropriate interest rate). The use of credit scoring models permits the specification of the PD in the determination of LGD in the pricing algorithm. For example, in Figure 13.2, we use a loan rated as BBB by a scoring model to begin the LGD process (see our discussion in the prior chapter) and the pricing decision. The PD and recovery

---

Given: Five-Year Senior Unsecured Loan
 Risk Rating = BBB
 Expected Default Rate = 0.3% per year (30 b.p.)
 Expected Recovery Rate = 70%
 Unexpected Loss (σ) 50 b.p. (0.5%) per year
 BIS Capital Allocation = 8%
 Cost of Equity Capital = 15%
 Overhead + Operations Risk Charge = 40 b.p. (0.4%) per year
 Cost of Funds = 6%

Loan Price$_{(1)}$ = 6.0% + (0.3% × [1 − .7]) + (6[0.5%] × 15%) + 0.4% = 6.94%

Or

Loan Price$_{(2)}$ = 6.0% + (0.3% × [1 − .7]) + (8.0% × 15%) + 0.4% = 7.69%

FIGURE 13.2   Risk-Based Pricing: An Example
(1) Internal Model for Capital Allocation
(2) BIS Capital Allocation Method
Source: Author example.

rate assumption is given (0.3 percent per year and 70.0 percent respectively) and the *expected* loss of 0.09 percent per year is quantified.

The next step is to add the required amount to the price based on the unexpected loss. We can do this in two ways—based on either *economic capital* criteria or *regulatory capital* requirements. Economic capital requires an additional cost in making the loan for unanticipated losses based on the degree of conservatism of the lending institution (i.e., its own risk preference). For example, a bank with a high risk avoidance preference—that is, one that wants to attain a high credit rating for itself—will require a very high confidence interval for not exceeding a particular loss. In our example, we utilize a six-standard deviation requirement sometimes referred to in the required average return on capital (RAROC) approach of that of an AA bank. The estimated standard deviation of 50 basis points per year (given) is then multiplied by 6 to arrive at the required amount of capital for this lending institution for this counterparty rating (BBB). Finally, the resulting capital requirement (300bp) is multiplied by the bank's net opportunity cost for not investing of 300 basis points, and this product is added to the expected loss and other costs to arrive at the required economic capital. We suggest using the net cost of equity (cost of equity minus the risk-free rate) for the calculation. We also factor (add) in an estimated 40 basis points per year to cover such noncredit items as overhead and operating risk changes (the latter will be required under Basel II).

So, for the economic capital computation, in our example, the result is a required price, or interest rate, of 6.9 percent. This compares to the current regulatory capital requirement calculation based on a flat 8 percent instead of the 3 percent economic capital. The regulatory capital interest rate is higher, at 7.7 percent. One can now see why most banks will prefer the Basel II framework. Again, accurate scoring models are critical to the modern pricing structure. Even if a bank, or nonregulated institution, does not use or cannot use economic capital pricing criteria due to competitive conditions, the Basel II framework, in determining capital requirements and pricing, is helpful to ascertain how far from the actual price the one based on economic pricing is. Note that our example does not incorporate correlation and concentration issues in the pricing function. Such factors add to the complexity of credit decisions and should be considered by the portfolio management group of the financial institution.

ACCOUNTS RECEIVABLE MANAGEMENT

The wholesale banking application discussed in the preceding section has a similar analogue for corporate entities that have a risky customer portfolio and that sell their goods and services on credit. Just as banks use PD models to estimate the amount of nonperforming loans, accounts receivable managers need to evaluate the repayment potential of customers and specify an estimated "bad debts" account. Scoring models are widely used by these managers, and the industry is serviced by the National Association of Credit Managers (NACM) and its affiliated Credit Research Foundation.[1] The emphasis for these managers is primarily the accept/reject decision and the amount of exposure to allow.

INVESTORS

Beyond the financial institution investor in commercial loans, all sorts of financial institutions and individuals can profit from a well-tested and appropriate credit scoring system in their fixed income (and equity, too) strategies. Perhaps the most obvious application is to determine whether to invest in a debt instrument selling at, or near, par value. The determination of PDs is important for investment-grade bonds and loans as well as the more speculative non-investment-grade or junk bonds, discussed earlier in Chapter 7. Indeed, about one-quarter of all defaulting issues were originally rated as investment grade by the professional rating agencies! So the professional manager should include default risk analysis, as well as yield and concentration considerations, in his or her deliberations.

If the investment-grade company has a financial profile of a lower-rated entity, the required rate of return should reflect that. Consider the long-term debt obligations of General Motors Corporation (GM) in the first few months of 2005 (at the time we were writing this chapter). GM's bonds were still rated investment grade at that time by all of the rating agencies but its yield to maturity (or yield to worst) was selling more like a single-B security than a BBB one. The market was assessing its default risk as equivalent to about 600 basis points over U.S. Treasury bonds on April 15, 2005, considerably above the historical average of high yield bonds and, at least, 450 to 500 basis points higher than what BBB bonds were selling for at that time. And the Z-Score and Z″-Score models were rating GM's bonds as somewhere between CCC+ and B+ as early as 2003/2004! As we now know, GM's bonds were downgraded by S&P on May 2, 2005, to BB, followed by a downgrading by Fitch in June 2005 and Moody's in August.

---

[1]The research institute, www.crfonline.org (located in Columbia, Maryland), publishes a quarterly magazine called the *Credit and Financial Management Review* as well as periodic reports and conferences.

For bonds selling in a distressed condition (i.e., 1,000 basis points or more above Treasuries), the key question to ask is whether the company will continue to migrate to an even lower credit quality (or, in fact, default) or whether its PD is sufficiently low to assess that its price will return to par (assuming it had already migrated down, perhaps even in a "fallen angel" downgraded condition). The upside potential, from distressed to par, provides equity-type returns that are far greater than returns expected from a typical debt portfolio. Indeed, the average return on a portfolio of CCC-rated bonds in 2003 was about 60 percent, as a large proportion of those corporate bonds that were distressed as of the end of 2002 returned to par or above-par value in just one year. Probably the onset of the benign (forgiving) credit cycle had more to do with this incredible run than did credit default analysis, but one's conviction to select securities that are selling at "deep junk" or distressed yield levels can be heightened when the credit model ascribes a higher bond rating equivalent to the security than the one implied from the market.

The Type II error—that of selling, or not buying, the distressed security when in fact its price returns to par—is always possible but the cost involved is not an important one for most traditional debt investors. Where it does matter, however, is in the case of a distressed debt or highly leveraged hedge fund investor. We strongly believe that a disciplined investor will find credit scoring and default risk models of considerable benefit in the investment process.

SECURITY ANALYSTS

One of the fundamental axioms in finance is that the debt analyst is, and should be, far more focused on the downside possible movement of securities than is the common equity analyst. So, an obvious tool for the debt analyst is a default prediction model. Both traditional ratio analysis and one or more distressed prediction models would seem to be a prudent addition to the security analyst process.

The analyst should also consider a type of pro forma distressed prediction treatment of the entity, especially where a heavily leverage condition is likely to change through a series of steps expected from management. We have seen, in Chapter 6 of this volume, that highly risky capital structures can lead either to a healthy and high return scenario or to a default, depending on management's success in reducing debt and improving its rating equivalent status. The analyst earns his or her analytical status, in our opinion, by providing realistic expectations and forecasts about the likely success of management to achieve its target capital structure and cash flow goals. It is clear that highly leveraged companies, especially just after a major restructuring transaction, will be evaluated by most credit scoring techniques as a distressed situation. We advocate realistic pro forma scenario analysis as well as current financial statement criteria in the analysis process.

REGULATORS

Regulatory institutions, particularly bank examination department personnel, should be aware of and comfortable in evaluating the systems of credit risk used by constituent banks and other institutions. One of the challenges of the new Basel II framework is the role and expertise of the regulator, especially when evaluating the Pillar I capital requirement specifications of banks and in the Pillar II regulatory oversight function. Bank examiners need to be trained to evaluate the various credit scoring and probability of default/loss given default (PD/LGD) estimates used by banks. And, the various possible PD conclusions, on the same counterparty, from numerous banks will serve as useful inputs in this process.

In addition, it is quite common for a nation's central bank, like the Banque de France, Banca Italia, or the U.S. Federal Reserve, to utilize its own credit scoring evaluation system to assess the credit quality of bank portfolios and to monitor the assessments made by their individual bank customers.

AUDITORS

In a very early application of the original Z-Score model, we wrote an article (Altman and McGough 1974) about the potential use of credit scoring models to assist the accounting firm audit function to assess the going-concern qualification condition of customer accounts. We concluded, at that time, that while a reasonable proportion (about 40 percent) of bankrupt companies did receive a going-concern qualification in the year just prior to filing, the Z-Score approach predicted well over 80 percent of those entities as in the distress zone at the same time. This higher bankrupt prediction accuracy was not surprising since auditors are not in the distressed prediction business and their independent status does not necessarily mean a cautious model-driven approach to an entity's likelihood of failure. Indeed, the accounting profession is very sensitive to its responsibility and has argued that it should not be liable for not qualifying a firm's financials just because it is in a highly risky, low rating equivalent condition.

Despite the obvious potential conflict between a very conservative professional auditor posture and its desire to not cause problems for its customers and perhaps lose an account that it gives a going-concern qualification, it would seem that auditors should be aware of and, indeed, use credit scoring models and other failure assessment techniques. These approaches can add objective feedback in their own assessments as well as in their discussions with the clients about their financial condition and plans going forward.

BANKRUPTCY LAWYERS

One of the most prominent players in the bankruptcy and distressed firm arenas is the bankruptcy lawyer. The decision to take a firm into bankruptcy is a momentous one. While most bankruptcies are involuntary and decided on only as a last resort, whether to file and the timing of the filing are critical decisions. The longer a firm puts off the decision, the less likely, in most cases, it is that the reorganization will be successful. At the same time, if a successful turnaround can be managed out of court, then most likely the costs of financial distress will be lower than if the turnaround is achieved in bankruptcy (see Gilson, John, and Lang 1993). Usually, the bankruptcy lawyer is the prime adviser to the management of the firm as to whether to file and when to do so. Typically, the bankruptcy law firm will recommend to the ailing company potential consultants and paths of actions to take surrounding the bankruptcy or out-of-court restructuring decision. Such consultants, also discussed in this chapter, might be turnaround and other restructuring specialists, bankers for bailout financing or DIP financing, and so forth.

While there may be unmistakable signals of financial distress, lawyers can also productively use financial distress prediction models in their advisory work for clients. Whether the firm is mildly or deeply distressed is an important determinant. As we will explore in the next chapter of this book, management itself can use such models in its determination. Lawyers can benefit from the implications of a failure prediction model in such areas as the failing company doctrine and the increasingly important issue of deepening insolvency. We now turn to these topics.

LEGAL APPLICATIONS

Failure prediction models have had a number of direct applications in the legal arena over the years. These include such areas as (1) the failing company doctrine, (2) avoidance of pension obligations, and increasingly lately (3) the fiduciary responsibility of owners, managers, directors, and other corporate insiders like professional advisers. The last area relates to a concept and condition known as "deepening insolvency."

Failing Company Doctrine

One defense against an antitrust violation by firms attempting to merge is the argument that an otherwise illegal merger should be permitted to occur if one or both of the merging entities would have failed anyway and its market share would likely have been absorbed by the other entity. We wrote in detail about this so-called failing company doctrine in the first edition of this volume (1983) and in Altman and Goodman (1980, 2002), but space limitations in this edition preclude an exhaustive treatment.

Essentially, the failing company doctrine can be invoked if it can be shown that, while competitors that are trying to merge are unquestionably linked, either geographically or by market segment, at least one party was on the verge of bankruptcy and extinction. Examples might include two newspapers competing in a standard metropolitan area and one paper's demise would almost certainly result in its market share going to its closest competitor. This occurred in the antitrust dispute involving the *Detroit News* and *Detroit Free Press* in the early 1980s. Using several of the Z-Score models, one of the authors argued, in a deposition, that at least one of these entities would likely fail within a short period of time—both were in very bad shape. The court's solution was to permit the merger but to require the independence of the editorial staffs. Both entities remained in existence but the ownership with respect to revenues, costs, and profits was combined. Concerns about newspaper costs, labor relations, and other negative antitrust results were outweighed by the likely scenario of a single major newspaper for the city if the merger was not permitted.

Another example was the potential combination of two low-priced beer companies in the Northeast of the United States in the early 1970s—Schaefer Beer and Schmidt's of Philadelphia. Both firms competed for the low-end price customers of the beer market. We argued that Schaefer was a likely failing company and that while Schmidt's would surely absorb Schaefer's market share if the merger was permitted, that it would happen anyway if it wasn't. The plaintiff, in this case Schaefer itself, which did not want to be taken over by Schmidt's, argued that it was not failing since it was not receiving a going-concern qualification from its auditors (see earlier discussion) and its major creditor was not calling in its now long overdue loans, which had been nonperforming for almost two years. The judge agreed and essentially ruled that Schaefer was not failing because it had not failed—yet! Another beer company, Stroh's of Milwaukee, which did not compete directly with either company, soon purchased Schaefer. A related issue to this case is whether the firm was in a so-called zone of insolvency or not. We now turn to that issue.

Deepening Insolvency

The theory of deepening insolvency, as discussed in Kurth (2005), originated with two federal cases in the early 1980s, *In re Investors Funding Corporation* and *Schacht v. Brown*. The simple argument was made that a corporation is not a biological entity for which it can be assumed that any act that extends its existence is beneficial to it. This argument is in stark contrast to the fundamental premise of the turnaround management industry, and the principles underlying the Bankruptcy Code, that the estate, involving creditors, shareholders, and employees, typically benefits if a distressed company can be reorganized successfully. A deepening insolvency argument, on the other hand, argues that the efforts to save an obviously dying entity can benefit some at the considerable expense of others. For example, the managers, advisers, and others trying to save the entity receive payments during the failed turnaround period, which results in lower recoveries after bankruptcy to others, such as creditors.

Deepening insolvency is increasingly being recognized, Kurth observes, as an independent course of action. This action could argue that a bankrupt company, or its representatives, may recover damages caused by professionals, such as advisers, accountants, investment bankers, and attorneys, who have either facilitated the company's mismanagement or misrepresented its financial condition in such a way as to conceal its further deterioration from an insolvent condition into deepened insolvency. And one recognized method of calculating damages is to measure the extent of the company's deepening insolvency.

Several questions emerge around this legal argument. How do you know that a firm is in the zone of insolvency, and how do you measure its deepening condition? Is it enough to simply say that as long as a firm has not gone bankrupt or defaulted on its debt obligations or participated in a distressed restructuring (e.g., an equity-for-debt swap) it is not in the zone of insolvency? We do not believe so! A firm may be in an insolvent condition, but still not be defaulted.

The courts seem to be relying on a comparison between the fair market value of the firm's assets and the market value of its liabilities to determine whether it is insolvent. Recall that we discussed this as a basic definition of default (i.e., assets less than liabilities) when we described the KMV model in Chapter 11. Incidentally, we would argue that the appropriate comparison benchmark for assets is not the market value of debt, but its book value, since the latter is what needs to be repaid to creditors. This is especially true if you measure asset value as the sum of the market value of debt plus equity—as most financial economists do.

In any event, we would also argue that a reasonable test of whether a firm is in the insolvency zone is to calculate its bond rating equivalent or failure score using *several* statistical measures. In particular, we advocate using the Z-Score models and other techniques, such as the Moody's/KMV expected default frequency (EDF) approach. If both classify the firm as "in default" (e.g., a Z-Score below –0.20 and a KMV EDF of 20 or more) then its likely survival as a nonbankrupt or nondefaulted entity is seriously in doubt. Deteriorating scores will indicate a deepening condition, although we cannot argue that the deterioration is linear with respect to the change in score. Certainly, a firm with a Z-Score of –2.2 is in worse condition than one with a score of –0.2. The use of the Z-Score model in deepening insolvency cases and analyses was discussed by Appenzeller and Parker (2005).

A final note about the deepening insolvency legal claim. Most legal analysts point out that the original purpose of the argument was based on the bankruptcy that resulted after the insiders had perpetrated a type of Ponzi scheme or some other action that resulted in fraud or embezzlement, enriching its operators or advisers at the expense of unsuspecting creditors. And, it is argued, that the guilty parties knew, or should have known, that the firm's chance of survival was unlikely. So, while we can help to specify whether or not the firm has a failing company profile, we cannot say for sure whether some turnaround strategy could not be successful.

Certainly, if the firm's true condition was known, but not revealed by those who could profit from its continuing existence, then a legal cause for damages would seem to be valid. If, however, everything is revealed and best efforts are made to protect the remaining interests of owners, we would be reluctant to say that a firm's Z-Score in the distressed zone, or a rating equivalent of D, means that it could not be saved. What we are arguing for is a clear and unambiguous metric of a firm's financial condition rather than relying only upon an expert's fair valuation of the firm's assets.

The next chapter of this book shows how a manager, with the assistance of the Z-Score model, successfully used his business acumen and judgment to manage a financial turnaround. The essence of this case study is that all the indicators of financial distress were transparent and the strategy of simulating corrective actions with respect to a likely outcome on the firm's "health index" was not only appropriate, but also prudent. Even if these actions had failed, we do not believe that deepening insolvency would have been a legitimate argument in this case.

BOND RATERS

While bond rating agencies do not use failure prediction models to reach their rating conclusions, we would argue that the results of one or more well-tested and successful models could assist in the process. Obviously, Moody's saw great benefits in the output from the KMV EDF model (discussed in Chapter 11) since it paid a handsome sum to acquire KMV in 2002. Yet raters legitimately argue that such items as industry analysis, interviews with management, and a longer-perspective "through-the-cycle" approach will determine their rating designations and that a model's point-in-time perspective should not be the basis for rating decisions. See Loeffler (2002 and 2004) and Altman and Rijken (2004 and 2005) for discussions on rating stability, accuracy, and comparisons between through-the-cycle versus point-in-time models.

RISK MANAGEMENT AND STRATEGY CONSULTANTS

Basel II has also been an important catalyst for the growth in risk-management consulting firms. Entities such as Mercer-Oliver-Wyman, Algorithmics (purchased by Fitch Ratings in 2005), RiskMetrics, Kamakura, CreditSights, and the risk-management divisions of the other major rating agencies (e.g., KMV/Moody's, S&P's Risk Solutions, Fitch Risk) have prospered as the appetite for modern credit risk systems has grown. Most of these firms have developed credit risk tools that include scoring type, structural, or hybrid combinations of these two credit scoring models. In addition, smaller consulting entities, providing services related to valuation and portfolio management, might find that objective credit risk tools are helpful in their assessment of clients.

A related area of management consulting advice can be in mergers and acquisitions (M&A) strategies. A distressed firm could be encouraged to solicit a purchasing/strategic partner when its condition, assessed objectively, indicates going-concern problems. This would especially be helpful if potential acquirers do not share the same internal assessment. Obviously, the price of the acquisition will be reduced if it is generally known that the firm is in a highly distressed condition. Accurate early-warning models, however, can give a competitive advantage to users—whether they are the target or the acquiring firm.

RESTRUCTURING ADVISERS AND BANKERS, TURNAROUND CRISIS MANAGERS, AND ACCOUNTING FIRMS

Three of the most prominent types of consultants that have emerged as important players in the distressed firm industry are the restructuring specialists, usually from boutique investment banks, corporate turnaround or crisis managers from operations management consultants, and restructuring consultants from traditional accounting firms. Figure 13.3 illustrates their relationships and primary functions in the distressed firm industry. By 2005, the accounting firms' role had all but disappeared as their restructuring practices were sold or abandoned.

The competitive landscape in the turnaround consulting industry has evolved in the following way. In the mid to late 1980s, the market was led by accounting firms and the efforts by the larger investment banks that had issued large amounts of debt in the highly leveraged restructuring boom (primarily ill-fated leveraged buyouts and leveraged recapitalizations). For example, Drexel Burnham Lambert was a leading proponent of the out-of-court restructuring in the 1980s. In the early 1990s, with the huge increase in large Chapter 11 bankruptcies, some large investment banks, but in-

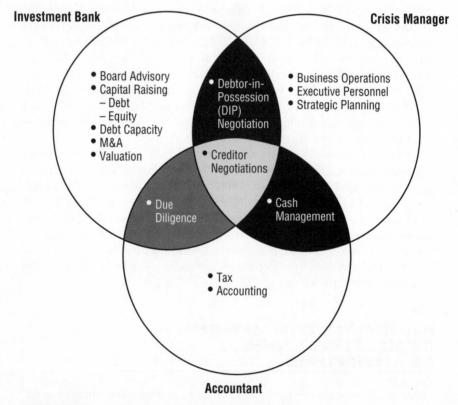

FIGURE 13.3 Comparison of Financial Advisers' Roles
Source: Lazard Freres, 2005.

creasingly new boutique divisions of smaller banks, sprung up to fill the void caused by conflicts of interest from the larger investment bank underwriting firms. Even more of these boutiques, sometimes as offshoots from the large accounting firms or investment banks, emerged in the 2001–2005 period, and the larger underwriters put resources into distressed refinancing, especially since M&A activity slackened.

In addition to these advisers and consultants, a fairly active banking market emerged to provide funding at the bankrupt stage, such as debtor-in-possession (DIP) financing, and exit at the financing stage. Many of the major commercial banks and also firms like GE Capital, Congress Finance, and CIT Finance became major players in this sector.

Although definitely not mutually exclusive, the turnaround consultants play a role as advisers for the restructuring of the firms' assets (operations consultants known as crisis managers) and liabilities (restructuring bankers and accountants). The number of specialists in these fields swelled to well over 20,000 globally in 2005, and many are members of the increasingly prominent Turnaround Management Association (TMA; web site: www.turnaround.org). This professional, educational, and networking organization, based in Chicago, Illinois, had 34 chapters globally (27 in the United States, one each in Australia, New Zealand, United Kingdom, Japan, and France, and two in Canada) and about 7,000 members as of mid-2005.[2]

Turnaround managers can be hired to assist a firm so as to avoid filing for bankruptcy or, once in a legal bankrupt condition, to assist in the reorganization of the firm's assets and liabilities. An example of a turnaround consulting firm that recently has worked in both capacities is Kroll, Zolfo-Cooper, which is assisting Krispy Kreme in its efforts "to stay alive" and avoid bankruptcy and also Enron as it liquidates assets and deals with creditors concluding its Chapter 11 in 2005. Other large turnaround management consulting companies are Alvarez and Marsal and AlixPartners. These firms also typically provide financial and capital structure advice. While these three firms are relatively large, each with more than 300 full-time employees, most turnaround management companies are quite small, with fewer than 10 full-time consultants.[3] Often, these professionals have

---

[2]Both authors serve the TMA as members of its Academic Advisory Council and contribute, along with market practitioners, to this organization's monthly publication, the *Journal of Corporate Renewal*, as well as periodic conferences, including ones devoted almost solely to education.

[3]There are also a number of relatively large turnaround management specialists in the 20- to 100-employee range that can provide a full spectrum of advisory services, including firms like Huron, XRoads, and BBK with at least 100 professionals each (see the TMA web site).

had prior experience as full-time corporate managers in such areas as finance, marketing, operations, human resources, and information systems and have chosen to work with ailing companies to assist in their corporate renewal. In addition to their primary operation functions, these firms often assist in such areas as creditor negotiations, cash, and even strategic management. In the past 10 years, a new position has been created to deal with the many complex reorganization issues of companies in crisis—the chief restructuring officer (CRO).

Corporate restructuring advisers from investment banks tend to specialize on the "left-hand side" of the balance sheet, with particular emphasis in assisting the management of distressed companies (or the turnaround specialist) to acquire needed capital during the restructuring period. One type of financing that has proven to be crucial to the early phase of the Chapter 11 process is debtor-in-possession (DIP) financing, whereby the new creditors typically have a superpriority status over all existing creditors. We discussed this financing mechanism earlier in Chapters 2 and 3. At the other end of the restructuring period is the so-called exit financing, whereby the firm needs to emerge from Chapter 11 with a capital structure that both is fiscally sound and provides the working capital to conduct business on a going-concern basis.

Some of the larger restructuring advisers that specialize in advising debtors are the boutique investment bankers like Lazard Freres, the Blackstone Group, Miller Buckfire, N. M. Rothschild & Sons, Evercore, and Greenhill, although there are also several smaller successful operations like Miller-Mathis. On the creditor advisory side, the largest advisers are Houlihan Lokey Howard & Zukin, Jefferies, Chanin, FTI, and Giuliani Partners. The last two are carve-outs or sales of divisions from accounting firms.

Bankruptcy Reform Bill

Leading up to the Bankruptcy Abuse Prevention and Consumer Protection Act of 2005 (BAPCPA), restrictions in the 1978 Bankruptcy Code had historically limited the participation of the larger investment banks in Chapter 11 restructuring work, especially if a bank was the underwriter of the debtor's securities within three years before the bankruptcy. While there were exceptions to this restriction and sometimes a formal appeal from one of the stakeholders groups was necessary to eliminate a major investment banking firm (e.g., the switch from UBS to Lazard as the debtor's adviser in the 2005 Trump Casinos & Entertainment Chapter 11), large underwriters were generally restricted under the premise that they were not disinterested professionals.

With the passage of BAPCPA the competitive landscape for distressed firm advisory work may change somewhat. Signed into law on April 17, 2005, and to take effect on October 17, 2005, this law impacts corporate bankruptcies, as well as consumer filings. It now permits heretofore excluded investment banks to be advisers as long as there is no clear conflict with the financing or other advisory work that helped cause the bankruptcy. Disinterestedness still requires that an entity not have an interest materially adverse to the interests of the estate or any class of creditors as equity security holders, by reason of any relationship or connection or interest in the debtor. So, while a current or former underwriter may be deemed not to still be disinterested, the prospect that other disinterested bulge-bracket firms will be eligible is very real. This will cause either a dilution in the market share of prominent distressed firm advisory boutiques or the outright purchase of these firms or individuals by the larger investment banks. Fees also may be more competitive, but don't bet on it!

We advocate that both the turnaround managers (who are trying to save the business either before filing for Chapter 11 or while in bankruptcy-reorganization) and the restructuring debtor advisers can effectively use distress-prediction credit scoring models as an early warning tool to assess the financial health of an enterprise or as a type of postrestructuring barometer of the health profile of an entity as it emerges. If the firm still looks like a distressed, failing entity upon emergence, then its chances for subsequent distress, indeed the Chapter 22 situation, would likely be higher than the renewal process should provide. Unfortunately, based on the frequent occurrence of Chapter 22 or other forms of continued distress (like distressed sales), it appears that the restructuring process is not always successful. Indeed, Gilson (1997), in a study of the success of Chapter 11s, found that too often firms emerge with excessive leverage or operating problems, and Hotchkiss (1995) found that emerging firms often do not perform as well as their industry counterparts. On the other hand, Eberhart, Altman, and Aggarwal (1999) found that emerging equities do extremely well in the post–Chapter 11 one-year trading period. And recent (2003–2004) evidence (e.g., J. P. Morgan 2004) supports that conclusion.

In conclusion, we advocate that firms be advised to emerge looking like going concerns and that equitylike securities, including options and warrants for junior creditors and old equity holders, be used wherever possible so as not to burden the "new" firm with too much fixed cost debt in the early years after emergence.

GOVERNMENT AGENCIES AND OTHER PURCHASERS

Many of the larger U.S. government agencies have a policy to screen their vendors as to their staying power and independence from government support should they become distressed. A related issue is whether the vendor will be able to deliver the goods and services that are contracted for. We have learned, over the years, that one of the screens used by government agencies and their auditing counterparts is the Z-Score model(s). For example, the U.S. Department of Defense had this policy, as did the government's Accounting Audit Agency. If an entity fares poorly by the Z-Score screen, then it will be screened even more closely and/or passed over as a possible vendor. As such, both the government and those firms seeking to become, or remain, suppliers to the federal or state government should understand the pros and cons of using an automated financial early-warning model, such as Z-Score. We would especially suggest that any agency using such an approach do so in conjunction with other screening tools—especially qualitative methods like interviews with existing customers of the vendor.

The use of financial screening models by purchasing agents should not be restricted to public agencies. Indeed, private enterprises should also be concerned about the health of their suppliers. This is especially true if the purchaser practices something like a just-in-time (JIT) inventory approach to its production process. For example, computer manufacturers, like IBM or Dell, want to be assured that the keyboards in their PC fabrications be available at the precise time that the rest of the computer is about ready to be shipped. Another industry where the health of vendors, and of the manufacturers themselves, is of vital concern is the U.S. auto industry in 2005. As its fragile condition became more obvious, going-concern and staying power probabilities were a pervasive issue. Indeed, a few medium to large auto-part suppliers already have succumbed (e.g., Intermet Corp., Tower Automotive, and Collins & Aikman) and filed for bankruptcy protection in 2004 and 2005.

A related issue to the manufacturer is the cost of supporting a vendor if the latter is sustaining continuing losses and is in jeopardy of failing and having to be bailed out. This was a common occurrence in Japan, and may still be.

We now turn, in Chapter 14, to the last of our distress-prediction credit scoring models applications—possible to be used by distressed firms themselves.

Distress Prediction Models: Catalysts for Constructive Change—Managing a Financial Turnaround

We have frequently been asked by managers and analysts the difficult question, "Now that your model has classified the entity as having a high probability of failure, what should be done to avoid this dismal fate?" Not being an operating manager or turnaround consultant, we had to throw up our hands and reluctantly reply, "Get yourself some new management or specialists in crisis management," or, even less satisfying, "That is your problem!" Needless to say, these answers were not accepted with applause, nor did the response capture the spirit of a true early-warning system. Such a system usually connotes prescribed rehabilitative action when the warnings are in other areas, such as medicine, weather, or military science. Unfortunately, management science applications of early warning systems are typically unique to the entity, and it is difficult to generalize rehabilitative prescriptions.

Our attitude toward this important and inevitable outgrowth of distress prediction has changed. One important incident has taught us a valuable lesson, one which is, we believe, transferable to other crisis situations. The lesson emanated not from a conceptual, academic analysis of the problem but from the application of the Z-score model (Chapter 11) to a real-world problem by a remarkably perceptive chief executive officer (CEO). Let us re-

---

This chapter has been derived and updated from an article by E. Altman and J. LaFleur, "Managing a Return to Financial Health," *Journal of Business Strategy* (Summer 1981). The story of GTI's turnaround was written for the popular press by Michael Ball (*Inc.*, December 1980).

view the case of GTI Corporation, a manufacturer of parts, subsystems, and processing equipment for the computer, automotive, and electronic industries. GTI Corporation was listed on the American Stock Exchange, and its CEO for many years was James LaFleur. Although this situation took place about 30 years ago, it is still as relevant in 2005 as it was in 1975.

ACTIVE VERSUS PASSIVE USE OF FINANCIAL MODELS

Statistically verified predictive models have long been used in the study of business. Generally, these models are developed by scientists and tested by observers who do not interact with or influence the measurements of the model. Consequently, the models, when valid, have predicted events with satisfactory accuracy, and business analysts regard them with a reasonable degree of confidence. As discussed briefly in prior chapters, this passive use of predictive models for credit analysis, investor analysis, and so on overlooks the possibility of using them actively. In the active use of a predictive model, the role of the observer is shifted to that of a participant. For example, a manager may use a predictive model that relates to business affairs of a company by deliberately attempting to influence the model's measurements. The manager makes decisions suggested by the parameters of the model in order to control its prediction.

In the specific case we will discuss, the Z-Score bankruptcy predictor model was used *actively* to manage the financial turnaround of a company, GTI Corporation, that was on the verge of bankruptcy. A series of management decisions was made to foil the model's prediction of bankruptcy. These decisions, many of which were specifically motivated by considering their effect on the financial ratios in the model, led directly to the recovery of the company and the establishment of a firm financial base.

Earlier in this book, we indicated that management could declare bankruptcy once the indication was that a firm was headed toward bankruptcy—in other words, that its overall financial profile was consistent with that of other firms that had gone bankrupt in the past. It took GTI Corporation, and specifically the management strategy formulated and implemented by Jim LaFleur, to turn the model inside out and show its ability to help shape business strategy to *avert* bankruptcy.

WHAT THE Z-SCORE TOLD GTI

Jim LaFleur, a Cal Tech graduate and successful entrepreneur and business executive, had recently retired but remained a director of several companies, one of which was the GTI Corporation. During the first six months of 1975, GTI had suffered the following financial results:

Working capital decreased by $6 million.

Retained earnings decreased by $2 million.

A $2 million loss was incurred.

Net worth decreased from $6.207 million to $4.370 million.

Market value of equity decreased by 50 percent.

Sales decreased by 50 percent.

Earlier in LaFleur's career, he had noticed an article in *Boardroom Reports* about the Z-Score. LaFleur immediately saw the potential application of the bankruptcy predictor to the problem at GTI. As we showed in Chapter 11, the original Z-Score model is of the form:

Factor	Definition	Weighting Factor
X_1	Working capital/Total assets	1.200
X_2	Retained earnings/Total assets	1.400
X_3	Earnings before interest and taxes/Total assets	3.300
X_4	Market value of equity/Book value of liabilities	0.600
X_5	Sales/Total assets	0.999

LaFleur, a member of the audit committee, was asked to replace the existing CEO. Plugging in the preliminary numbers for the five ratios, LaFleur put the Z-Score predictor to work for GTI; the resulting Z-Score was 0.7. At that level, the predictor indicates a condition of financial distress with a high probability of bankruptcy. When more accurate numbers were inserted into the Z-Score formula, it fell even lower, to 0.38, about half the earlier calculation. The prognosis was grave.

A TOOL FOR RECOVERY

Despite its portent of doom, the Z-Score was also seen as a management tool for recovery. The predictor's five financial ratios were the key to the Z-Score movement, either up or down. While the previous management had inadvertently followed a strategy that had decreased the ratios and caused the Z-Score to decline (see Figure 14.1), GTI's new management decided to reverse the plunge by deliberate management actions. But, before each decision, LaFleur and his team simulated the decision's impact on the model. Inherent in the Z-Score predictor was the message that *underutilized assets* could be a

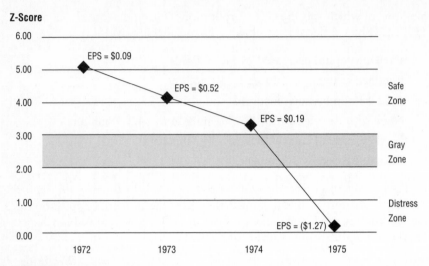

FIGURE 14.1   Z-Score Distressed Firm Predictor: Application to GTI Corporation, 1972–1975

major contributor to the deterioration of a company's financial condition. Such deterioration had taken place at GTI over several years. The company's total assets had grown out of proportion to other financial factors. We have found this to be the case in many business failures, particularly larger ones.

By using retrospective analysis, LaFleur concluded that the Z-Score could have predicted GTI's deterioration toward financial distress. For example, historical data in 1975 showed that GTI's Z-score started to dive precipitously at least two years prior to the spring of 1975.

TAKING QUICK ACTION

At year-end 1974, GTI's Z-Score approached the gray zone and its earnings per share (EPS) had fallen to $0.19. Thus, GTI's Z-Score had been falling for several years, even during periods when the company's profits were rising. That was further proof of the predictor's validity and suggested its ability to help set strategy to guide the company's recovery.

THE EFFECTS OF GROWTH FEVER

For more than two years, LaFleur had cautioned against what appeared to be overaggressive policies of debt and excessive expansion by GTI's operations. The warnings, unfortunately, had little effect. Along with most of the industry, GTI had succumbed through the 1960s to a highly competitive growth fever. During those years, many managers focused almost entirely on their profit and loss (P&L) statements. They were willing to borrow what was necessary to increase sales and profits. With stock values rising, they expected to obtain very favorable equity funding in the future to pay off the accumulated debt (does this sound like déjà vu in the late 1990s?). That strategy served them well until the economic downturn of 1972. Then, with profits falling, many companies had trouble servicing the debt that had looked so easy to handle a few years earlier. But GTI, like many others, continued pursuing the same strategy, despite changed economic conditions. That worked for a while. But early in 1975, GTI started losing money. Before that profit slide could be stopped, GTI's 1975 net loss accumulated to over $2.6 million on sales of $12 million, a loss of $1.27 per share.

Also, during the month of May, a member of the audit committee discovered information indicating that the figures for the first quarter of 1975 were reported incorrectly. As the evidence developed during the ensuing audit meetings, it was obvious that the company's problems were serious. GTI's auditing firm began a thorough reexamination of the company's first-quarter activities. The auditors quickly confirmed that there was, indeed, a material discrepancy in the figures and set to work revising first-quarter figures. As chairman of the audit committee, LaFleur contacted the Securities and Exchange Commission (SEC), disclosing the discrepancy and promising to define and correct it. He also asked the American Stock Exchange to halt trading of the company's stock. By finding and reporting the errors quickly, GTI had the stock back in trading in less than 10 days. No delisting of the stock ever occurred, and the company even received compliments from some observers on its rapid self-policing action.

At that point, GTI's board of directors chose a new executive team, asking LaFleur to become part of management and take over as chairman and chief executive officer. Having observed GTI going into debt to finance its operations over several prior years, even with record sales and profits on paper, LaFleur was determined to find the underlying problems. It didn't take long. Inventory, out of control, revealed itself as a major contributor to the company's ballooning assets. In many instances, returned goods had been set aside and not properly accounted for. Adding to that difficulty, work-in-process was grossly out of proportion to sales. Again, these symptoms seem to be common among corporations in crisis.

GENESIS OF STRATEGY

From this new evidence of excess assets, a recovery strategy began to emerge. It was to find ways to decrease GTI's total assets without seriously reducing the other factors in the numerators of the Z-Score's X ratios: working capital, retained earnings, earnings before interest and taxes, market value of equity, and sales. GTI started looking for assets that were not being employed effectively—that is, not earning money. When identified, such assets were sold and the proceeds used to reduce the company's debt. Having conceived the strategy, LaFleur began to implement the actions to eliminate GTI's excess assets. Excess inventory was sold as quickly as possible, even at scrap value in some cases. The effect was a decrease in the denominators of all five X ratios simultaneously. It is not enough simply to sell assets—the proceeds must be utilized as soon as possible. GTI's Z-Score rose accordingly.

While the bankruptcy predictor was originally designed for an observer's analysis of a company's condition, GTI used it as an aid to managing company affairs. The predictor actually became an element of active strategy to avoid GTI's impending bankruptcy.

STOPPING THE CASH BLEED

In quick order, GTI's cash bleed was stanched. The staffs at two unprofitable West Coast plants were sliced to a skeleton crew within 10 days, and the corporate staff at headquarters was pared from 32 to 6. A year earlier, with company's profits at $1.5 million, the corporate staff expense had been over $1 million! All capital programs were frozen. Only the most critical production needs, repair, and maintenance were authorized. GTI asked its creditors for additional short-term credit, then pushed strenuously ahead on its collections. Inventories were placed under strict control. Taking effect, these measures got cash and expenses under control and improved debt service capability. Reducing costs further took more analysis. A management function/location matrix, a "job versus cost" grid, was constructed for each of GTI's plants. The grid showed each executive's job, what work he or she performed, and how much that job cost the company. When overlaps or duplications were found, jobs were consolidated. The grid is illustrated in Figure 14.2 (actual dollars in each function/location not indicated). Where the revenues from different locations did not cover the identifiable costs, it was clear that a problem existed.

FINDING LOST PROFITS WITH EMPLOYEE ASSISTANCE

Employees were also involved in the turnaround. A simple questionnaire was handed out to the 250 employees of GTI's largest plant in Saegertown,

	Pennsylvania	Indiana	New York	California	West Germany	
Operations	$1	$1	$1	$1	$1	$ 5
Marketing	$1	$1	$1	$1	$1	$ 5
Engineering	$1	$1	$1	$1	$1	$ 5
Finance	$1	$1	$1	$1	$1	$ 5
	$4	$4	$4	$4	$4	$20

FIGURE 14.2   Function/Location Matrix

Pennsylvania, asking their opinions on why the plant was no longer profitable. The implied question was about the underutilized assets that had depressed GTI's Z-Score. The employees knew what was wrong! They were specific about how to improve the use of their machines. Many of the suggestions were implemented, and productivity improved. Eventually, however, this plant was sold and product lines moved elsewhere. Several weeks later, similar questions were asked at GTI's plant in Hadley, Pennsylvania. The employee responses resulted in changing the plant's organization from functional to product line, another move that more effectively employed the company's assets. Because they participated in the changes, the plant's employees really worked to make the reorganization succeed. After a few weeks, the plant began to return to profitability. In fact, profitable product lines were moved from Saegertown to Hadley.

Those profits were the forerunners of profits that would be produced in other parts of the company as time went on. The Z-Score, while it did not jump much as a result of those profits, did begin to react. By mid-1976, after slanting down for three years, the Z-Score bottomed out and started up. GTI began turning the corner.

SELLING OFF A PRODUCT LINE

Though cost reduction and increased profits had eased the problems, GTI needed stronger recovery actions. The function/location matrix analysis was extended to include products and was used to rate product profitability throughout the company. Plans were made to eliminate the losers and strengthen the winners. As a result, late in 1976, GTI sold one of its major underutilized assets. GTI's crystal base product line had appeared fairly strong, but the product matrix analysis presented a different view. Crystal bases were not complementary to GTI's other products, and though the line had been marginally profitable in the past, demand for its products was likely to decrease. The line also appeared to need a great deal of capital to be competitive in the future. The cash generated by the sale of the crystal base product line was used to reduce debt. The consequent simultaneous decrease of both total assets and debt produced a dramatic effect. The Z-Score leaped from under 1.0 to 2.95. In one transaction, GTI zoomed almost all the way into the Z-Score predictor's "safe" zone. Although to outside observers the company did not appear to turn around for another year and a half, LaFleur felt the firm was on the road to recovery with the sale of the crystal base product line. The company had come from almost certain bankruptcy to the stage where it could begin contemplating new products. In less than 18 months, the Z-Score had climbed from 0.38, in the near-death bankrupt zone, almost all the way to the Z-Score's safe zone (Figure 14.3). With heightened confidence in the model, GTI started working to put the Z-Score firmly in the safe zone. Since the company's improving stability and profitability were corroborating the Z-Score approach, GTI's headquarters staff began figuring how a proposed new product or financial transaction would affect the rising Z-Score. Further, GTI extended the product evaluation matrix from simple profit and loss to multiyear projections of return on assets. This involved taking a hard look at projected working capital and capital expenditure requirements, product by product. The analysis established what costs would be if the company attempted to expand within its current markets.

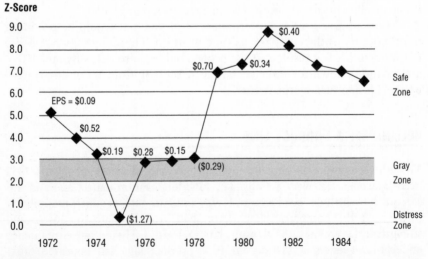

FIGURE 14.3   Z-Score Distressed Firm Predictor: Application to GTI Corporation, 1972–1984

PROGRESS IN OPERATIONS

While doing this planning, GTI continued to make progress on the operations side, finishing 1976 with $0.28 earnings per share and an increasing Z-Score as well. In 1977, earnings sagged to $0.15 per share and –$0.29 in 1978; but with an improving overall financial condition, GTI's Z-Score continued gradually to rise. The company even bought out a competitor's glass seal product line with notes secured by the acquired assets and with negligible adverse impact on the Z-Score.

Then in 1978, GTI boosted its Z-Score again by shutting down an entire division that made ceramic capacitors and selling its assets. That transaction, again based on the strategy of selling underutilized assets to pay off debt, occurred later than it should have. This was a case of emotion interfering with a rational, proven strategy. LaFleur had been swayed toward saving this technically interesting product line, though the Z-Score strategy consistently suggested disposal. Though delayed, the difficult disposal decision was made. As a result of the closing of the capacitor division and the sale of its assets, GTI's 1978 bottom line sustained a $0.29 per share loss, but the Z-Score increased as the company paid off more debt. As anticipated, operating profits continued to gain throughout the year, paving the way for a strong 1979. Once again, the asset-reduction strategy had worked.

INTO THE SAFE ZONE

After 1978, GTI's Z-Score continued climbing, rising through the safe zone as 1979 pretax profits reached $1.9 million and $0.70 per share on sales of $21 million. From a balance sheet viewpoint, in five years GTI's strategy had decreased the debt-to-equity ratio from 128 percent to 30 percent and increased stockholders' equity from $3.5 million to $4.7 million. The debt-to-equity (market equity) ratio improved even more in 1981, to just under 10 percent! During 1980 and 1981, GTI further consolidated its financial position and increased stockholders' equity. The company continued its policy of conservative financial management augmented by close attention to the Z-Score in business decision making. That spirit was reflected in actions taken in August 1980, when the company entered into an agreement with a research and development (R&D) limited partnership to investigate several new projects for the partnership. Further, to raise return on investment and to provide more funds for new growth in electronics, GTI disposed of a metal and plastics product line in early 1981. In July 1981, GTI negotiated a 10-year loan for $1 million at a fixed 16 percent to provide increased working capital. Yes, rates were that high in the early 1980s.

As a result of careful financial planning and continued profitability, GTI had attained positive flow from the net interest of its investment and loan portfolio. Essentially, the company had internalized control of the Z-Score, because it had sufficient funds available to pay off debt. In terms of the model, the firm could actively impact and control the financial ratio (X_4), the relation between its equity value and outstanding debt. GTI's Z-Score zoomed to 7.0 in 1979 and continued to rise to 8.8 as of year-end 1981, mainly as a result of improvement in X_4. This rise is all the more impressive in view of the recessionary period in the early 1980s, including a drop in earnings in 1980. GTI, before being purchased by a Scandinavian firm in 1992, was listed on the American Stock Exchange. GTI continued as a financially sound division pursuing new avenues with controlled growth. In major part, that success came about from implementing a financial strategy suggested by the Z-Score bankruptcy predictor model.

CONCLUSION TO THE GTI STORY AND USING Z-SCORES AS A BAROMETER OF A SUCCESSFUL TURNAROUND

We believe that certain predictive models offer opportunities to be used as management tools. Supporting that view, GTI's employment of the Z-Score bankruptcy predictor has been described as a specific illustration of how an ordinarily passive model can be used actively with substantial success. With emphasis made on prudent selection and use, managers are encouraged to search out and review predictive models that relate to their companies' activities. Improved business strategies could well result. It is quite conceivable that a large number of firms in a distressed situation at present can learn from and perhaps be put on the road to recovery by the strategies used by GTI Corporation.

In addition to the prescriptive use of a financial model in a turnaround strategy, we advocate the Z-Score model's use as a type of barometer to any restructuring. We often hear how turnaround managers use the model to indicate how distressed a firm has become. An additional use is to test the viability of the restructuring *before* sending the firm back into action. Not only is it important to avoid a Chapter 11, it is also important to reduce the chance of a Chapter 22!

CHAPTER 15

Estimating Recovery Rates
on Defaulted Debt

Earlier in this volume, especially in Chapters 7 and 11, we discussed models and procedures useful for estimating the probability of default of a counterparty in a credit transaction. Of equal importance for estimating the loss given default (LGD) of the transaction is the expected recovery rate (RR) on the defaulted security (e.g., on a bond or a loan). LGD, both expected and unexpected, was among the most important variables underlying the efforts of the Basel Commission when it finally completed its recommendations in 2004 for specifying capital requirements on credit assets held by banks throughout the world. The recovery rate, usually defined as the market price of the security just after default, is one of the two key variables analyzed by market practitioners in the pricing and other variables in the hugely important credit derivatives market.

Recoveries are also measured as of the end of the reorganization period, usually Chapter 11, where the rate or amount expected is referred to as the "ultimate recovery." This variable's importance was highlighted by the announcement by Standard & Poor's, in late 2003, that it would assign a "Recovery Rating" as an estimate of postdefault ultimate recovery of nominal principal on large commercial and institutional secured loans.[1]

The authors would like to thank the collaborative efforts of Brooks Brady (S&P), and Andrea Resti and Andrea Sironi, both of Luigi Bocconi University in Milan, for their contribution to this chapter. Various parts of the chapter are from Altman, Resti, and Seroni (2005a, b).
[1]S&P's recovery scale involves six categories of recovery risk from 1+ = the highest expectation (100%) of full recovery of principal to 5 = negligible recovery (0 to 25%) of principal. S&P will continue to provide its traditional credit rating, which reflects default risk and seniority elements. See Chew and Kerr (2005) in Altman, Resti, and Sironi (2005b).

Fitch Ratings followed soon after, in February 2005, announcing that it was considering introducing a new scheme of ratings involving a "Default Rating and Recovery Scale" on lower-rated speculative-grade securities.[2] In doing so, both agencies recognized the market's need for bifurcated information on the two main elements of credit risk (PD and RR). Moody's Investors Service has argued for many years that its credit ratings incorporate both PD and RR estimates and, for the time being (in 2004–2005), resisted separating out the two key elements. We expect, however, that Moody's will soon introduce its own version of recovery ratings.

RECOVERY RATE THEORY

Three main variables affect the credit risk of a financial asset: (1) the probability of default (PD); (2) the loss given default (LGD), which is equal to one minus the recovery rate in the event of default (RR); and (3) the exposure at default (EAD). While significant attention has been devoted by the credit risk literature on the estimation of the first component (PD), much less attention has been dedicated to the estimation of RR and to the relationship between PD and RR. This is mainly the consequence of two related factors. First, credit pricing models and risk management applications tend to focus on the systematic risk components of credit risk, as these are the only ones that attract risk premiums. Second, credit risk models traditionally have assumed RR to be dependent on individual features (e.g., collateral or seniority) that do not respond to systematic factors, and to be independent of PD.

This traditional focus on default analysis has been partly reversed by the recent increase in the number of studies dedicated to the subject of RR estimation and the relationship between the PD and RR (Fridson, Garman, and Okashima 2000; Gupton, Gates, and Carty 2000; Jokivuolle and Peura 2003; Altman, Resti and Sironi 2001 and with Brady 2003; Frye 2000a, 2000b, and 2000c; Hu and Perraudin 2002; and Jarrow 2001). This is partly the consequence of the parallel increase in default rates and decrease of recovery rates registered during the 1999–2002 period. More generally, evidence from many countries in recent years suggests that collateral values and recovery rates can be volatile (e.g., Franks and Sussman 2005) and, moreover, they tend to go down just when the number of de-

---

[2]Fitch's Ultimate Recovery Scale, if instituted, will rank securities on a scale from R1 (high recoveries) to R6 (low recoveries) and was proposed to be applied globally just to securities rated B or lower, including structured finance instruments.

faults goes up in economic downturns (Schleifer and Vishny 1992; Altman 2001; Hamilton, Gupton, and Berthault 2001).

This chapter first presents a detailed review of the way credit risk models, developed during the past 30 years, have treated the recovery rate and, more specifically, its relationship with the probability of default of an obligor. These models can be divided into two main categories: (1) credit pricing models and (2) portfolio credit value at risk (VaR) models. Credit pricing models can in turn be divided into three main approaches: (1) first-generation structural-form models, (2) second-generation structural-form models, and (3) reduced-form models. These three different approaches together with their basic assumptions, advantages, drawbacks, and empirical performance are reviewed and credit VaR models examined. The more recent studies explicitly modeling and empirically investigating the relationship between PD and RR are reviewed, and we assess some recent empirical evidence on recovery rates on both defaulted bonds and loans and also on the relationship between default and recovery rates.

CREDIT PRICING MODELS

First-Generation Structural-Form Models

The first category of credit risk models consists of the ones based on the original framework developed by Merton (1974) using the principles of option pricing (Black and Scholes 1973). In such a framework, the default process of a company is driven by the value of the company's assets, and the risk of a firm's default is therefore explicitly linked to the variability of the firm's asset value. As discussed in Chapter 11 of this book, the basic intuition behind the Merton model is relatively simple: Default occurs when the value of a firm's assets (the market value of the firm) is lower than that of its liabilities. The payment to the debt holders at the maturity of the debt is therefore the smaller of two quantities: the face value of the debt or the market value of the firm's assets. Assuming that the company's debt is entirely represented by a zero coupon bond, if the value of the firm at maturity is greater than the face value of the bond, then the bondholder gets back the face value of the bond. However, if the value of the firm is less than the face value of the bond, the shareholders get nothing and the bondholder gets back the market value of the firm. The payoff at maturity to the bondholder is therefore equivalent to the face value of the bond minus a put option on the value of the firm, with a strike price equal to the face value of the bond and a maturity equal to the maturity of the bond. Following this basic intuition, Merton derived an explicit formula for risky bonds, which can be used both to estimate the PD of a firm and to estimate the yield differential between a risky bond and a default-free bond.

In addition to Merton, first-generation structural-form models include Black and Cox (1976), Geske (1977), and Vasicek (1984). Each of these models tries to refine the original Merton framework by removing one or more of the unrealistic assumptions. Black and Cox introduce the possibility of more complex capital structures, with subordinated debt; Geske introduces interest-paying debt; Vasicek introduces the distinction between short- and long-term liabilities, which now represents a distinctive feature of the KMV model.[3]

Under these models, all the relevant credit risk elements, including default and recovery at default, are a function of the structural characteristics of the firm: asset levels, asset volatility (business risk), and leverage (financial risk). The RR is therefore an endogenous variable, as the creditors' payoff is a function of the residual value of the defaulted company's assets. More precisely, under Merton's theoretical framework, PD and RR tend to be inversely related. If, for example, the firm's value increases, then its PD tends to decrease while the expected RR at default increases (ceteris paribus). On the other side, if the firm's debt increases, its PD increases while the expected RR at default decreases. Finally, if the firm's asset volatility increases, its PD increases while the expected RR at default decreases, since the possible asset values can be quite low relative to liability levels.

Although the line of research that followed the Merton approach has proven very useful in addressing the qualitatively important aspects of pricing credit risks, it has been less successful in practical applications.[4] This lack of success has been attributed to different causes. First, under Merton's model the firm defaults only at maturity of the debt, a scenario that is at odds with reality. Second, for the model to be used in valuing default-risky debts of a firm with more than one class of debt in its capital structure (complex capital structures), the priority/seniority structures of various debts have to be specified. Also, this framework assumes that the absolute-priority rules are actually adhered to upon default in that debts are paid off in the order of their seniority. However, empirical evidence,

---

[3]In the KMV model, discussed in Chapter 11, default occurs when the firm's asset value goes below a threshold represented by the sum of the total amount of short-term liabilities and half of the amount of long-term liabilities.

[4]The standard reference is Jones, Mason, and Rosenfeld (1984), who found that, even for firms with very simple capital structures, a Merton-type model is unable to price investment-grade corporate bonds better than a naive model that assumes no risk of default.

such as in Weiss (1990) and in Franks and Torous (1994), indicate that the absolute-priority rules are often violated. Moreover, the use of a lognormal distribution in the basic Merton model (instead of a more fat-tailed distribution) tends to overstate recovery rates in the event of default.

Second-Generation Structural-Form Models

In response to such difficulties, an alternative approach has been developed that still adopts the original Merton framework as far as the default process is concerned but, at the same time, removes one of the unrealistic assumptions of the model, namely, that default can occur only at maturity of the debt when the firm's assets are no longer sufficient to cover debt obligations. Instead, it is assumed that default may occur anytime between the issuance and maturity of the debt and that default is triggered when the value of the firm's assets reaches a lower threshold level.[5] These models include Kim, Ramaswamy, and Sundaresan (1993); Hull and White (1995); Nielsen, Saà-Requejo, and Santa-Clara (1993); Longstaff and Schwartz (1995); and others.

Under these models, the RR in the event of default is exogenous and independent from the firm's asset value. It is generally defined as a fixed ratio of the outstanding debt value and is therefore independent from the PD. For example, Longstaff and Schwartz argue that, by looking at the history of defaults and the recovery rates for various classes of debt of comparable firms, one can form a reliable estimate of the RR. In their model, they allow for a stochastic term structure of interest rates and for some correlation between defaults and interest rates. They find that this correlation between default risk and the interest rate has a significant effect on the properties of the credit spread.[6] This approach simplifies the first class of models by both exogenously specifying the cash flows to risky debt in the event of bankruptcy and simplifying the bankruptcy process. The latter occurs when the value of the firm's underlying assets hits some exogenously specified boundary.

Despite these improvements with respect to Merton's original framework, second-generation structural-form models still suffer from three

---

[5]One of the earliest studies based on this framework is Black and Cox (1976). However, this is not included in the second-generation models in terms of the treatment of the recovery rate.

[6]Using Moody's corporate bond yield data, they find that credit spreads are negatively related to interest rates and that durations of risky bonds depend on the correlation with interest rates.

main drawbacks, which represent the main reasons behind their relatively poor empirical performance.[7] First, they still require estimates for the parameters of the firm's asset value, which is nonobservable. Indeed, unlike the stock price in the Black-Scholes formula for valuing equity options, the current market value of a firm is not easily observable. Second, structural-form models cannot incorporate credit-rating changes that occur quite frequently for default-risky corporate debts. Most corporate bonds undergo credit downgrades before they actually default. As a consequence, any credit risk model should take into account the uncertainty associated with credit rating changes as well as the uncertainty concerning default. Finally, most structural-form models assume that the value of the firm is continuous in time. As a result, the time of default can be predicted just before it happens and hence, as argued by Duffie and Lando (2000), there are no "sudden surprises." In other words, without recurring to a so-called jump-diffusion process, the PD of a firm is known with certainty.

Reduced-Form Models

The attempt to overcome the aforementioned shortcomings of structural-form models gave rise to reduced-form models. These include Litterman and Iben (1991); Madan and Unal (1995); Jarrow and Turnbull (1995); Jarrow, Lando, and Turnbull (1997); Lando (1998); Duffie (1998); and Duffie and Singleton (1999). Unlike structural-form models, reduced-form models do not condition default on the value of the firm, and parameters related to the firm's value need not be estimated to implement them. In addition to that, reduced-form models introduce separate explicit assumptions on the dynamic of both PD and RR. These variables are modeled independently from the structural features of the firm, its asset volatility, and leverage. Generally, reduced-form models assume an exogenous RR that is independent from the PD. More specifically, reduced-form models take as primitives the behavior of default-free interest rates, the RR of defaultable bonds at default, as well as a stochastic process for default intensity. At each instant, there is some probability that a firm defaults on its obligations. Both this probability and the RR in the event of default may vary stochastically through time. Those stochastic processes determine the price of credit risk. Although these processes are not formally linked to the firm's asset value, there is presumably some underlying relation. Thus Duffie and Singleton describe these alternative approaches as reduced-form models.

---

[7]See Eom, Helwege, and Huang (2001) for an empirical analysis of structural-form models.

Reduced-form models fundamentally differ from typical structural-form models in the degree of predictability of the default, as they can accommodate defaults that are sudden surprises. A typical reduced-form model assumes that an exogenous random variable drives default and that the probability of default over any time interval is nonzero. Default occurs when the random variable undergoes a discrete shift in its level. These models treat defaults as unpredictable Poisson events. The time at which the discrete shift will occur cannot be foretold on the basis of information available today.

Reduced-form models differ somewhat by the manner in which the RR is parameterized. For example, Jarrow and Turnbull (1995) assumed that, at default, a bond would have a market value equal to an exogenously specified fraction of an otherwise equivalent default-free bond. Duffie and Singleton (1999) followed with a model that, when market value at default (i.e., RR) is exogenously specified, allows for closed-form solutions for the term structure of credit spreads. Their model also allows for a random RR that depends on the predefault value of the bond. While this model assumes an exogenous process for the expected loss at default, meaning that the RR does not depend on the value of the defaultable claim, it allows for correlation between the default hazard-rate process and RR. Indeed, in this model, the behavior of both PD and RR may be allowed to depend on firm-specific or macroeconomic variables, and therefore to be correlated with each other.

Other models assume that bonds of the same issuer, seniority, and face value have the same RR at default, regardless of the remaining maturity. For example, Duffie (1998) assumes that, at default, the holder of a bond of given face value receives a fixed payment, irrespective of the coupon level or maturity, and the same fraction of face value as any other bond of the same seniority. This allows the bondholder to use recovery parameters based on statistics provided by rating agencies such as Moody's. Jarrow, Lando, and Turnbull (1997) also allow for different debt seniorities to translate into different RRs for a given firm. Both Lando (1998) and Jarrow, Lando, and Turnbull (1997) use transition matrices (historical probabilities of credit rating changes) to price defaultable bonds.

Empirical evidence concerning reduced-form models is rather limited. Using the Duffie and Singleton (1999) framework, Duffee (1999) finds that these models have difficulty in explaining the observed term structure of credit spreads across firms of different credit risk qualities. In particular, such models have difficulty generating both relatively flat yield spreads when firms have low credit risk and steeper yield spreads when firms have higher credit risk.

A recent attempt to combine the advantages of structural-form models—a clear economic mechanism behind the default process—and the ones of reduced-form models—unpredictability of default—can be found in Zhou (2001). This is done by modeling the evolution of firm value as a jump-diffusion process. This model links RRs to the firm value at default so that the variation in RRs is endogenously generated and the correlation between RRs and credit ratings, reported first in Gupton, Gates, and Carty (2000) and also Altman, Resti, and Sironi (2001), is justified.

CREDIT VALUE AT RISK MODELS

During the second half of the 1990s, banks and consultants started developing credit risk models aimed at measuring the potential loss, with a predetermined confidence level, that a portfolio of credit exposures could suffer within a specified time horizon (generally one year). These were mostly motivated by the growing importance of credit risk management, especially since the now completed Basel II was originally proposed in 1999 and finalized five years later (Basel Commission on Banking Supervision 2004). These value at risk (VaR) models include, among others, J. P. Morgan's CreditMetrics (now RiskMetrics) (Gupton, Finger, and Bhatia 1997), Credit Suisse Financial Products' CreditRisk+ (1997), McKinsey's CreditPortfolioView (Wilson 1998), KMV's CreditPortfolioManager, and Kamakura's Risk Manager.

Credit VaR models can be classified into two main categories: (1) default mode (DM) models and (2) mark-to-market (MTM) models. In the former, credit risk is identified with default risk and a binomial approach is adopted. Therefore, only two possible events are taken into account: default and survival. The latter includes all possible changes of the borrower's creditworthiness, technically called credit migrations. In DM models, credit losses arise only when a default occurs. In contrast, MTM models are multinomial, as losses arise also when negative credit migrations occur. The two approaches basically differ in the amount of data necessary to feed them: limited in the case of default mode models, much wider in the case of mark-to-market ones.

The main output of a credit risk model is the probability density function (PDF) of the future losses on a credit portfolio. From the analysis of such a loss distribution, a financial institution can estimate both the expected loss and the unexpected loss on its credit portfolio. The expected loss equals the (unconditional) mean of the loss distribution; it represents the amount the investor can expect to lose within a specific period of time (usually one year). On the other side, the unexpected loss represents the deviation from expected loss and measures the actual portfolio risk. This can in turn be measured as the standard deviation of the loss distribution. Such a measure is relevant only in the case of a normal distribution and is therefore hardly useful for credit risk measurement; indeed, the distribution of credit losses is usually highly asymmetrical and fat-tailed. This implies that the probability of large losses is higher than the one associated with a normal distribution. Financial institutions typically apply credit risk models to evaluate the economic capital necessary to face the risk associated with their credit portfolios. In such a framework, provisions for credit losses should cover expected losses,[8] while economic capital is seen as a cushion for unexpected losses. Indeed, Basel II in its final iteration (June 2004) separated these two types of losses.

Credit VaR models can largely be seen as reduced-form models, where the RR is typically taken as an exogenous constant parameter or a stochastic variable independent from PD. Some of these models, such as CreditMetrics, treat the RR in the event of default as a stochastic variable—generally modeled through a beta distribution—independent from the PD. Others, such as CreditRisk+, treat it as a constant parameter that must be specified as an input for each single credit exposure. While a comprehensive analysis of these models goes beyond the aim of this review,[9] it is important to highlight that all credit VaR models treat RR and PD as two independent variables.

LATEST CONTRIBUTIONS ON THE PD-RR RELATIONSHIP

During the past three years, new approaches explicitly modeling and empirically investigating the relationship between PD and RR have been developed. These models include Frye (2000a and 2000b); Jarrow (2001); Hu and Perraudin (2002); Jokivuolle and Peura (2003); Carey and Gordy (2003); Bakshi et al. (2001); Altman, Resti, and Sironi (2001 and with Brady 2003); and Acharya, Bharath, and Srinivasan (2003).

The model proposed by Frye draws from the conditional approach suggested by Finger (1999) and Gordy (2000). In these models, defaults are driven by a single systematic factor—the state of the economy—rather than by a multitude of correlation parameters. These models are based on the assumption that the same economic conditions that cause defaults to rise might cause RRs to decline—that is, the distribution of recovery is

---

[8]As discussed in Jones and Mingo (1998), reserves are used to cover expected losses.

[9]For a comprehensive analysis of these models, see Crouhy, Galai, and Mark (2000) and Gordy (2000).

different in high-default periods from low-default ones. In Frye's model, both PD and RR depend on the state of the systematic factor. The correlation between these two variables therefore derives from their mutual dependence on the systematic factor.

The intuition behind Frye's theoretical model is relatively simple: If a borrower defaults on a loan, a bank's recovery may depend on the value of the loan collateral. The value of the collateral, like the value of other assets, depends on economic conditions. If the economy experiences a recession, RRs may decrease just as default rates tend to increase. This gives rise to a negative correlation between default rates and RRs.

While the model originally developed by Frye (2000a) implied recovery to be taken from an equation that determines collateral, Frye (2000b) modeled recovery directly. This allowed him to empirically test his model using data on defaults and recoveries from U.S. corporate bond data. More precisely, data from Moody's Default Risk Service database for the 1982–1997 period were used for the empirical analysis.[10] Results show a strong negative correlation between default rates and RRs for corporate bonds. This evidence is consistent with the most recent U.S. bond market data, indicating a simultaneous increase in default rates and LGDs for the 1999–2002 period.[11] Frye's (2000b and 2000c) empirical analysis allows him to conclude that in a severe economic downturn, bond recoveries might decline 20 to 25 percentage points from their normal-year average. Loan recoveries may decline by a similar amount, but from a higher level.

Jarrow (2001) presents a new methodology for estimating RRs and PDs implicit in both debt and equity prices. As in Frye, RRs and PDs are correlated and depend on the state of the macroeconomy. However, Jarrow's methodology explicitly incorporates equity prices in the estimation procedure, allowing the separate identification of RRs and PDs and the use of an expanded and relevant data set. In addition to that, the methodology explicitly incorporates a liquidity premium in the estimation procedure, which is considered essential in light of the high variability in the yield spreads between risky debt and U.S. Treasury securities.

Using four different data sets ranging from 1970 to 1999, Carey and Gordy (2003) analyze LGD measures and their correlation with default rates. Their preliminary results contrast with the findings of Frye (2000b):

---

[10]Data for the 1970–1981 period have been eliminated from the sample period because of the low number of default prices available for the computation of yearly recovery rates.

[11]Hamilton, Gupton, and Berthault (2001) and Altman, Brady, Resti, and Sironi (2003) provide clear empirical evidence of this phenomenon.

Estimates of simple default rate–LGD correlation are close to zero. They find, however, that limiting the sample period to 1988–1998, estimated correlations are more in line with Frye's results (0.45 for senior debt and 0.8 for subordinated debt). The authors postulate that during this short period, the correlation rises not so much because LGDs are low during the low-default years 1993–1996, but rather because LGDs are relatively high during the high-default years 1990 and 1991. They therefore conclude that the basic intuition behind Frye's model may not adequately characterize the relationship between default rates and LGDs. Indeed, a weak or asymmetric relationship suggests that default rates and LGDs may be influenced by different components of the economic cycle.

Using defaulted bonds data for the sample period 1982–2002, which includes the relatively high-default years of 2000–2002, Altman, Resti, and Sironi (2001) find empirical results that appear consistent with Frye's intuition: a negative correlation between default rates and RRs. However, they find that the single systematic risk factor—the performance of the economy—is less predictive than Frye's model would suggest. Their econometric univariate and multivariate models assign a key role to the supply of defaulted bonds (the default rate) and show that this variable, together with variables that proxy the size of the high yield bond market and the economic cycle, explain a substantial proportion (close to 90 percent) of the variance in bond recovery rates aggregated across all seniority and collateral levels. They conclude that a simple microeconomic mechanism based on supply and demand drives aggregate recovery rates more than a macroeconomic model based on the common dependence of default and recovery on the state of the cycle. In high-default years, the supply of defaulted securities tends to exceed demand,[12] thereby driving secondary market prices down. This in turn negatively affects RR estimates, as these are generally measured using bond prices shortly after default. We will return to this linkage between defaults and recovery rates shortly in the empirical section.

Using Moody's historical bond market data, Hu and Perraudin (2002) also examine the dependence between recovery rates and default rates. They first standardize the quarterly recovery data in order to filter out the volatility of recovery rates due to changes over time in the pool of rated borrowers. They find that correlations between quarterly recovery rates and default rates for bonds issued by U.S.-domiciled obligors are 0.22 for post-1982 data (1983–2000) and 0.19 for the 1971–2000 period. Using extreme value

---

[12]Demand mostly comes from niche investors called vultures, who intentionally purchase bonds in default. These investors represent a relatively small (perhaps $100 billion) and specialized segment of the fixed income market.

theory and other nonparametric techniques, they also examine the impact of this negative correlation on credit VaR measures and find that the increase is statistically significant when confidence levels exceed 99 percent.

Bakshi et al. (2001) enhance the reduced-form models presented earlier to allow for a flexible correlation among the risk-free rate, the default probability, and the recovery rate. Based on some evidence published by rating agencies, they assume recovery rates to be negatively associated with default probability. They find some strong support for this hypothesis through the analysis of a sample of BBB-rated corporate bonds: More precisely, their empirical results show that, on average, a 4 percent worsening in the (risk-neutral) hazard rate is associated with a 1 percent decline in (risk-neutral) recovery rates.

Gupton and Stein (2002, 2005) analyze the recovery rate on more than 3,000 corporate bond, loan, and preferred stock defaults, from more than 1,400 companies from 1981 to 2004, in order to specify and test Moody's LossCalc model for predicting loss given default (LGD). Their model estimates LGD at two points in time—immediately and in one year—adding a holding period dimension to the analysis. The authors find that their multifactor model, incorporating microeconomic variables (e.g., debt type, seniority), industry, and some macroeconomic factors (e.g., default rates, changes in leading indicators), outperforms traditional historic recovery average methods in predicting LGD.

A rather different approach is the one proposed by Jokivuolle and Peura (2003). The authors present a model for bank loans in which collateral value is correlated with the PD. They use the option-pricing framework for modeling risky debt: The borrowing firm's total asset value triggers the event of default. However, the firm's asset value does not determine the RR. Rather, the collateral value is in turn assumed to be the only stochastic element determining recovery. Because of this assumption, the model can be implemented using an exogenous PD, so that the firm's asset value parameters need not be estimated. In this respect, the model combines features of both structural-form and reduced-form models. Assuming a positive correlation between a firm's asset value and collateral value, the authors obtain a result similar to that of Frye (2000b), that realized default rates and recovery rates have an inverse relationship.

Using data on observed prices of defaulted securities in the United States over the period 1982–1999, Acharya, Bharath, and Srinivasan (2003) find that seniority and security are important determinants of recovery rates. While this result is not surprising and is in line with previous empirical studies on recoveries, their second main result is rather striking and concerns the effect of industry-specific and macroeconomic conditions in the default year. Indeed, industry conditions at the time of default are found to be robust and important determinants of recovery rates. This result is consistent with those of Altman et al. (2001, 2003) in that there is little effect of macroeconomic conditions over and above the industry conditions. Acharya et al. suggest that the linkage, again highlighted by Altman et al. (2003), between bond market aggregate variables and recoveries arising due to supply-side effects in segmented bond markets may be a manifestation of Shleifer and Vishny's (1992) industry equilibrium effect: Macroeconomic variables and bond market conditions appear to be picking up the effect of omitted industry conditions. The importance of the industry factor in determining LGD has been recently highlighted by Schuermann (2003) in a survey of the academic and practitioner literature.

Frye (2000a), Pykhtin (2003), and Dullmann and Trapp (2004) all propose models that account for the dependence of recoveries on systematic risk. They extend the single-factor model proposed by Gordy (2000) by assuming that the recovery rate follows a log-normal (Pykhtin, 2003) or a logitnormal (Dullmann and Trapp 2004) pattern. The latter study empirically compares the results obtained using the three alternative models. They use time series of default rates and recovery rates from Standard & Poor's Credit Pro database, including bond and loan default information in the time period from 1982 to 1999. They find that estimates of recovery rates based on market prices at default are significantly higher than the ones obtained using recovery rates at emergence from restructuring (usually bankruptcy). The findings of this study are in line with previous ones: Systematic risk is an important factor that influences recovery rates. The authors show that ignoring this risk component may lead to downward-biased estimates of economic capital.

Finally, a model that allows for the dependence between recovery rates and default events has recently been proposed by Chabane, Laurent, and Salomon (2004). They study, from a purely theoretical point of view, the loss distributions for large credit portfolios and show that both credit losses and standard risk measures such as credit VaR and "expected shortfall" tend to increase compared to that of the Basel II "averages" approach (also see Resti and Sironi 2005).

RECOVERY RATES AND PROCYCLICALITY

Altman et al. (2001, 2005 with Brady) also highlight the implications of their results for credit risk modeling and for the issue of procyclicality[13] of

---

[13]Procyclicality involves the sensitivity of regulatory capital requirements to economic and financial market cycles. Since ratings and default rates respond to the cycle, the new internal ratings based (IRB) approach proposed by the Basel Commission risks increasing capital charges and limiting credit supply when the economy is slowing (the reverse being true when the economy is growing at a fast rate).

capital requirements. In order to assess the impact of a negative correlation between default rates and recovery rates on credit risk models, they run Monte Carlo simulations on a sample portfolio of bank loans and compare the key risk measures (expected and unexpected losses). They show that both the expected loss and the unexpected loss are vastly understated if one assumes that PDs and RRs are uncorrelated. Therefore, credit models that do not carefully factor in the negative correlation between PDs and RRs might lead to insufficient bank reserves and cause unnecessary shocks to financial markets.

As far as procyclicality is concerned, Altman et al. show that this effect tends to be exacerbated by the correlation between DRs and RRs: Low recovery rates when defaults are high would amplify cyclical effects. This would especially be true under the so-called advanced IRB approach, where banks are free to estimate their own recovery rates and might tend to revise them downward when defaults increase and ratings worsen. The impact of such a mechanism was also assessed by Resti (2002), based on simulations over a 20-year period, using a standard portfolio of bank loans (the composition of which is adjusted through time according to S&P transition matrices). Two main results emerged from this simulation exercise: (1) the procyclicality effect is driven more by up- and downgrades, rather than by default rates; in other words, adjustments in credit supply needed to comply with capital requirements respond mainly to changes in the structure of weighted assets, and only to a lesser extent to actual credit losses (except in extremely high-default years); and (2) when RRs are permitted to fluctuate with default rates, the procyclicality effect increases significantly.

With this potential negative aspect in mind, the Basel II Commission assigned a task force in 2004 to analyze "Recoveries in Downturns" in order to assess the significance of a decrease in economic activity on LGD. The task force issued its report in 2005 with some guidelines (paragraph 468 of the Framework Document) for banks (Basel Commission on Bank Supervision 2005).

EMPIRICAL EVIDENCE ON RECOVERY RATES

This section focuses on different measurements and recent empirical evidence of default recovery rates. Most credit risk models utilize historical average empirical estimates, combined with their primary analytical specification of the probability of default, to arrive at the all-important loss given default (LGD) input. Since very few financial institutions have ample data on recovery rates by asset type and by type of collateral, model builders and analysts responsible for Basel II inputs for their internal rating based (IRB) models begin with estimates from public bond and private bank loan markets. Of course, some banks will research their own internal databases in order to conform with the requirements of the advanced IRB approach.

Early Empirical Evidence

Published data on default recovery rates generally, but not always, use secondary market bond or bank loan prices. The first empirical study (that we are aware of) that estimated default recovery rates was in Altman, Haldeman, and Narayanan's (1977) ZETA model's adjustment of the optimal cutoff score in their second-generation credit scoring model. Interestingly, these bank loan recovery estimates did not come from the secondary loan trading market—they did not exist then—but from a survey of bank workout department experience (1971–1975). The general conclusion from this early experience of these departments was a recovery rate on nonperforming, unsecured loans of only about 30 percent (undiscounted) of the loan amount plus accrued interest. We refer to this experience as the "ultimate recovery" since it utilizes postdefault recoveries, usually from the end of the restructuring period.

In later studies, ultimate recovery rates refer to the nominal or discounted value of bonds or loans based on either the price of the security at the end of the reorganization period (usually Chapter 11) or the value of the package of cash or securities upon emergence from restructuring. For example, Altman and Eberhart (1994) observed the return performance of defaulted bonds, stratified by seniority, at the time of the restructuring emergence as well as the discounted value of these prices. They concluded that the most senior bonds in the capital structure (senior secured and senior unsecured) did very well in the postdefault period (20 to 30 percent per annum returns) but the more junior bonds (senior subordinated and subordinated) did poorly, barely breaking even on a nominal basis and losing money on a discounted basis. Similar, but less extreme, results were found by Fridson, Garman, and Okashima (2001) when they updated (1994–2000) Altman and Eberhart's earlier study, which covered the period 1981–1993.

Other studies that analyzed bank loan recovery rates were by Asarnow and Edwards (1995) and by Eales and Bosworth (1998). The first study presents the results of an analysis of losses on bank loan defaults based on 24 years of data compiled by Citibank, whose database comprised 831 commercial and industrial (C&I) loans, as well as 89 structured loans (highly collateralized loans that contain many restrictive covenants). Their results (based on ultimate recoveries) indicate an LGD of about 35 percent for C&I loans (with larger loans, above $10 million, showing a somewhat lower loss rate of 29 percent); unsurprisingly, the LGD for structured loans is considerably more acceptable (13 percent), due to the role played by collateral and covenants in supporting the early default-detection and recovery processes. In the second study, the authors report the empirical results on recovery rates from a foreign bank operating in the United States—Westpac Banking Corporation. The study focuses on small business loans and larger consumer loans, such as home loans and investment property loans.

More recently, Neto de Carvalho and Dermine (2003) analyze the determinants of loss given default rates using a portfolio of credits given by the largest private Portuguese bank, Banco Comercial Portugues. Their study is based on a sample of 371 defaulted loans to small and medium-size companies, originally granted during the period June 1985 to December 2000. The estimates of recovery rates are based on the discounted cash flows recovered after the default event. The authors report three main empirical results, which are consistent with previous empirical evidence: (1) The frequency distribution of loan losses given default is bimodal, with many cases presenting a 0 percent recovery and other cases presenting a 100 percent recovery; (2) the size of the loan has a statistically significant negative impact on the recovery rate; (3) while the type of collateral is statistically significant in determining the recovery, this is not the case for the age of the bank-company relationship.

More Recent Evidence

Table 15.1 presents recent empirical evidence on bank loan recoveries (Emery, Cantor, and Avner 2004) and on corporate bonds by seniority (Altman and Aguiar 2005) based on the average prices of these securities just after the date of default. Not surprisingly, the highest median recovery rates were on senior secured bank loans (71.5 percent) followed by senior secured bonds (55.8 percent). Although the data from Emery et al. (Moody's) and Altman and Aguiar were from different periods and samples, it is interesting to note that the recovery on senior unsecured bonds (42.4 percent) was similar, but lower than senior unsecured bank loans (50.5 percent), with similar standard deviations (in the mid to upper 20 percents). Indeed, Emery et al. (2004) find that average loss rates on bonds are greater than similarly rated loans. The estimates of median recoveries on the senior subordinated and subordinated bonds were virtually the same at 31 to less than 33 percent. Similar recoveries on defaulted bonds can be found in Varma et al. (2003). For example, Altman and Aguiar's (2005) value-weighted mean recovery rate on almost 2,000 bond default

TABLE 15.1 Recovery at Default[a] on Public Corporate Bonds (1974–2004) and Bank Loans (1989–2003)

Loan/Bond Seniority	Number of Issues	Median %	Mean %	Standard Deviation %
Senior Secured Loans	163	71.50	67.50	24.40
Senior Unsecured Loans	32	50.50	54.60	28.40
Senior Secured Bonds	256	55.75	54.15	23.05
Senior Unsecured Bonds	947	42.54	35.77	26.62
Senior Subordinated Bonds	399	32.79	30.17	24.97
Subordinated Bonds	248	31.00	31.06	22.53
Discount Bonds	145	19.00	22.15	18.64
Total Sample Bonds	1,945	40.67	34.44	24.97

[a]Based on average bid prices from dealers just after default on bonds and 30 days after default on loans.
Source: Emery, Cantor, and Avner (2004) (bank loans) and Altman and Aguiar (2005) (bonds).

issues was 35.4 percent compared to Moody's value-weighted mean of 33.8 percent and issuer-weighted mean of 35.4 percent on 1,237 issues.

Altman and Fanjul (2004a and 2004b) further break down bond recoveries just after the default date by analyzing recoveries based on the original rating (fallen angels vs. original rating noninvestment ["junk"] bonds) of different seniorities. For example, in Table 15.2, we observe that senior secured bonds, which were originally rated investment grade, recovered a median rate of 50.5 percent versus just 33.5 percent (54.5 percent versus 36.6 percent for mean recoveries) for the same seniority bonds that were below investment grade when issued. These are dramatic statistically significant differences for similar seniority securities. As indicated, the mean recovery rate differential was even greater. Since fallen angel defaults were more prominent in some recent years in the United States (e.g., close to 50 percent in dollar amount of defaults in 2001 and 2002 were fallen angels prior to default), these statistics are quite meaningful. The median differential was almost as great (42.7 percent vs. 30.0 percent) for senior unsecured bonds. Note that for senior subordinated and subordinated bonds, however, the rating at issuance is of no consequence, although the sample size for investment grade, low-seniority bonds was very small. Varma et al. (2003) also conclude that the higher the rating prior to default, including the rating at issuance, the higher the average recovery rate at default. Apparently, the quality of assets and the structure of the defaulting company's balance sheets favor higher recoveries for higher-quality original issue bonds.

TABLE 15.2   Investment-Grade versus Non-Investment-Grade (Original Rating) Prices at Default on Public Bonds, 1974–2003

Loan/Bond Seniority	Number of Issues	Median Price %	Average Price %	Weighted Mean %	Standard Deviation %
Senior Secured					
Investment Grade	89	50.50	54.50	56.39	24.42
Non–Investment Grade	283	33.50	36.63	31.91	26.04
Senior Unsecured					
Investment Grade	299	42.75	46.37[a]	44.05[a]	23.57
Non–Investment Grade	598	30.00	33.41	31.83	23.65
Senior Subordinated					
Investment Grade	11	27.31	39.54	42.04	24.23
Non–Investment Grade	411	26.50	31.48	28.99	24.30
Subordinated					
Investment Grade	12	35.69	35.64	23.55	23.83
Non–Investment Grade	238	28.00	30.91	28.66	21.98
Discount					
Investment Grade	—	—	—	—	—
Non–Investment Grade	113	16.00	20.69	21.24	17.23
Total Sample	**2,054**	**30.04**	**34.76**	**30.78**	**24.38**

[a]Including WorldCom, the average and the weighted average were 43.53% and 30.45%. Nonrated issues were considered as non–investment grade.
Source: Altman and Fanjul (2004a).

In Table 15.3a and 15.3b, we again return to the data on ultimate recoveries, only this time the results are from Keisman's/Standard & Poor's (2004) assessment of bank loan and bond recoveries. These results show the nominal and discounted (by the loan's predefault interest rate) ultimate recovery at the end of the restructuring period for well over 2,000 defaulted loans and notes over the period 1988–2003. Several items are of interest. First, in Figure 15.3a, the recovery on senior bank debt, which is mainly secured, was quite high at 87.3 percent and 78.3 percent for nominal and discounted values respectively. Senior secured and senior unsecured notes, which include loans and bonds, had lower recoveries, and the more junior notes (almost all bonds) had, not surprisingly, the lowest recoveries. Note that the differentials between the nominal and discounted recovery rates diminish somewhat at the lower seniority levels.

In Table 15.3b, Keisman shows the difference between the nominal ultimate recovery rate compared to the trading price, approximately 30 days

TABLE 15.3a Ultimate Recovery Rates on Bank Loan and Bond Defaults—Nominal and Discounted Values, 1988–2003

	Observations	Ultimate Nominal Recovery	Ultimate Discounted Recovery	Standard Deviation
Senior Bank Debt	859	87.32%	78.3%	29.9%
Senior Secured Notes	283	76.03	64.9	32.9
Senior Unsecured Notes	486	59.29	42.2	34.6
Senior Subordinated Notes	390	38.41	30.4	32.7
Subordinated Notes	354	34.81	29.9	34.5

Source: Keisman (2004), "Recovery Trends and Analysis," Standard & Poor's LossStats Database; 2,365 defaulted loans and bond issues 1987–2003. Recoveries are discounted at each instruments' predefault interest rate.

TABLE 15.3b Nominal Ultimate Recovery and Trading Price Recovery 15 to 45 Days after Default, 1988–2003

	Normal Ultimate Recovery	Trading Price at Default
Bank Debt	69.1%	61.1%
Senior Secured Notes	58.6	55.2
Senior Unsecured Notes	41.5	34.5
Senior Subordinated Notes	32.3	29.3

Source: Keisman (2004), "Recovery Trends and Analysis," Standard & Poor's LossStats Database; data on 791 of the 2,365 bank loans and bond issues defaulting 1987–2003.

after default. These differences are surprisingly small, especially since returns in 2003 on defaulted securities were so high—see Chapter 9.

Standard & Poor's (Keisman 2004) also find, not shown in our figures, that during the most recent "extreme stress" default years of 1998 to 2002, the recovery rates on all seniorities declined compared to the longer 1988–2003 sample period in Table 15.3a and 15.3b. Since 1998 and 1999 were not really high-default years, the results of S&P for 2000–2002 are consistent with Altman, Resti, and Sironi's (2001) predictions of an inverse relationship between default and recovery rates. Indeed, recovery rates were a relatively low 25 percent in the corporate bond market for both 2001 and 2002 when default rates were in the double digits, but increased to about 45 percent in 2003 and 58 percent in 2004 when default rates on high yield bonds tumbled to below-average annual levels (Chapter 7).

Some recovery studies have concentrated on rates across different industries. Altman and Kishore (1996) and Verde (2003) report a fairly high variance across industrial sectors. For example, Verde reports that recovery rates in 2001 versus 2002 varied dramatically from one year to the next (e.g., gaming, lodging, and restaurants recovered 16 percent in 2001 and 77 percent in 2002, retail recovered 7 percent in 2001 and 48 percent in 2002, while transportation recovered 31 percent in 2001 and 19 percent in 2002) but returned to more normal levels in 2003.

Another issue highlighted in some studies, especially those from S&P (Van de Castle and Keisman 1999; Keisman 2004) is that an important determinant of ultimate recovery rates is the amount of junior liabilities that a given seniority has below its level; the greater the proportion of junior securities, the higher the recovery rate on the senior tranches—the theory being that the greater the equity cushion, the more likely there will be assets of value, which under absolute priority go first in liquidation or reorganization to the more senior tranches.

RECOVERY RATE/DEFAULT RATE ASSOCIATION

We now return to the updated empirical results from Altman, Brady, Resti, and Sironi (2003), to show the important relationship between the coincident results of linking the recovery rate (i.e., weighted average price at default) on corporate bonds with that year's default rate. Figure 15.1 shows the simple linear and nonlinear regression relationships between these two crucial variables for the sample period 1982–2004.[14] The graph shows the linear, log-linear, quadratic, and power function regressions and documents that from 53.6 percent (linear) to as much as 65.3 percent (power function) of the variance in recovery rates can be explained simply by the knowledge of (or the estimate of) the coincident year's weighted average default rate on U.S. high yield (below investment grade) bonds. Indeed, Varma et al.'s (Moody's) linear *issuer*-weighted correlation shows an explanatory power (R^2) of 59.6 percent on a similar regression.

The supply-demand theory's remarkable negative association between the weighted (by issue size) average recovery rate with the weighted default

---

[14]Note that the 2004 default rate is an estimated figure based on an extrapolation of the first-half result.

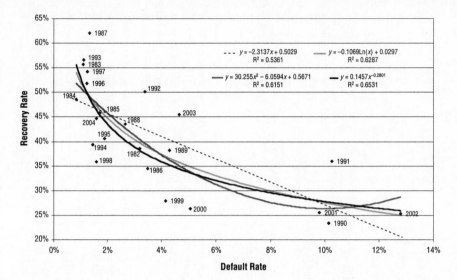

FIGURE 15.1 Recovery Rate/Default Rate Association: Dollar-Weighted Average Recovery Rates to Dollar-Weighted Average Default Rates, 1982–2004 (H-1)
Source: Altman and Fanjul (2004b).

rate has been discussed earlier, in Chapter 7. It is noteworthy to indicate that while default rates are also linked with aggregate economic performance, simply estimating the level or change in GDP does not come close to matching the explanatory power of the default rate, at least for explaining bond recovery rates.

CONCLUDING REMARKS

Table 15.4 summarizes the way RR and its relationship with PD are dealt with in the different credit models described in the previous sections of this chapter. While in the original Merton (1974) framework an inverse relationship between PD and RR exists, the credit risk models developed during the 1990s treat these two variables as independent. The currently available and most used credit pricing and credit VaR models are indeed based on this independence assumption and treat RR either as a constant parameter or as a stochastic variable independent from PD. In the latter case, RR volatility is assumed to represent an idiosyncratic risk, which can be eliminated through adequate portfolio diversification. This assumption strongly contrasts with the growing

TABLE 15.4 The Treatment of LGD and Default Rates within Different Credit Risk Models

	Main Models and Related Empirical Studies	Treatment of LGD	Relationship between RR and PD
Credit Pricing Models			
First-Generation Structural-Form Models	Merton (1974), Black and Cox (1977), Geske (1977), Vasicek (1984), Crouhy and Galai (1994), Mason and Rosenfeld (1984).	PD and RR are a function of the structural characteristics of the firm. RR is therefore an endogenous variable.	PD and RR are inversely related.
Second-Generation Structural-Form Models	Kim, Ramaswamy, and Sundaresan (1993), Nielsen, Saà-Requejo, and Santa Clara (1993), Hull and White (1995), Longstaff and Schwartz (1995).	RR is exogenous and independent from the firm's asset value.	RR is generally defined as a fixed ratio of the outstanding debt value and is therefore independent from PD.
Reduced-Form Models	Litterman and Iben (1991), Madan and Unal (1995), Jarrow and Turnbull (1995), Jarrow, Lando, and Turnbull (1997), Lando (1998), Duffie and Singleton (1999), Duffee (1998), and Duffee (1999).	Reduced-form models assume an exogenous RR that is either a constant or a stochastic variable independent from PD.	Reduced-form models introduce separate assumptions on the dynamic of PD and RR, which are modeled independently from the structural features of the firm.

Latest Contributions on the PD-RR Relationship	Frye (2000a and 2000b), Jarrow (2001), Carey and Gordy (2003), Altman, Resti, and Sironi (2001), Altman, Brady, Resti, and Sironi (2005).	Both PD and RR are stochastic variables that depend on a common systematic risk factor (the state of the economy).	PD and RR are negatively correlated. In the macroeconomic approach, this derives from the common dependence on one single systematic factor. In the microeconomic approach it derives from the supply and demand of defaulted securities.

Credit Value at Risk Models

CreditMetrics	Gupton, Finger, and Bhatia (1997)	Stochastic variable (beta distr.)	RR independent from PD
CreditPortfolioView	Wilson (1998)	Stochastic variable	RR independent from PD
CreditRisk+	Credit Suisse Financial Products (1997)	Constant	RR independent from PD
PortfolioManager	McQuown (1997), Crosbie (1999)	Stochastic variable	RR independent from PD

empirical evidence—showing a negative correlation between default and recovery rates—that has been reported in this chapter and in other empirical studies (e.g., Altman et al. 2001 and 2005a). This evidence indicates that recovery risk is a systematic risk component. As such, it should attract risk premiums and should adequately be considered in credit risk management applications. Finally, we feel that the microeconomic/financial attributes of an individual issuer of bonds or loans combined with the market's aggregate supply and demand conditions can best explain the recovery rate at default on a particular defaulting issue. An even greater challenge is to accurately estimate the ultimate recovery rate. This is the objective of the recovery ratings assigned by S&P on loans and possibly Fitch on speculative grade bonds.

References

CHAPTER 1 Corporate Distress: Introduction and Statistical Background

Altman, E. 1993. *Corporate Financial Distress and Bankruptcy*, 2nd ed., New York: John Wiley & Sons.

Walter, J. 1957. "Determination of Technical Insolvency." *Journal of Business* (January).

CHAPTER 2 Evolution of the Bankruptcy Process in the United States and International Comparisons

Acharya, V., R. Sundaram, and K. John. 2005. "Cross-Country Variations in Capital Structures: The Role of Bankruptcy Codes." Working paper, NYU and London Business School.

Altman, E. 1971. *Corporate Bankruptcy in America*. Lexington, MA: Heath-Lexington Books.

Altman, E. 1990 and 1992. *Altman-Foothill Reports on Distressed Bond Market and Distressed Bank Loan Markets*. Los Angeles: Foothill Corp.

Altman, E. 1991. *Distressed Securities*. Chicago: Probus; reprint, Frederick, MD: Beard Books, 1999.

Betker, B. 1991. "Management Changes, Equity's Bargaining Power and Deviations from Absolute Priority in Chapter 11 Bankruptcies." Working paper, School of Business, Ohio State University (October).

Cohen, J., H. Golden, J. Kennedy, J. Spiatto, and M. Cook. 1992. "Municipal Bankruptcies." *Turnarounds & Workouts* (January 15).

Damodaran, A. 2001. *Corporate Finance: Theory and Practice*, 2nd ed. New York: John Wiley & Sons.

Davydenko, S., and J. Franks. 2004. "Do Bankruptcy Codes Matter? A Study of Defaults in France, Germany and the UK." Working paper, London Business School.

Eberhart, A., T. Moore, and R. Roenfeldt. 1990. "Security Pricing and Deviation from Absolute Priority Sale in Bankruptcy Proceedings." *Journal of Finance* (December): 1457–1469.

Eckbo, E., and K. Thornburn. 2004. "Bidding in Mandatory Bankruptcy Auctions: Theory and Evidence." Working paper, Dartmouth University.

Flynn, E. 1989. "Statistical Analysis of Chapter 11." Administrative Office of the United States Courts, Washington, DC.

Fortgang, H., and T. Mayer. 1991. "Trading Claims and Taking Control of Corporations in Chapter 11." *Cardozo Law Review* 12 (October): 1, 13.

Franks, J., and W. Torous. 1989. "An Empirical Investigation of U.S. Firms in Reorganization." *Journal of Finance* 44: 747.

Franks, J., and W. Torous. 1992. "How Firms Fare in Workouts and Chapter 11 Reorganizations." In E. Altman (ed.), *Bankruptcy and Distressed Restructuring*. Homewood, IL: Dow Jones–Irwin.

Gilson, S. 1990. "Bankruptcy, Boards, Banks and Blockholders." *Journal of Financial Economics*: 27.

Rosenberg, H. 1992; rev. ed. 2000. *The Vulture Investors*. New York: John Wiley & Sons.

Salerno, T., and C. Hansen. 1991. "A Prepackaged Bankruptcy Strategy." *Journal of Business Strategy*.

Tilley, Allan. 2004. *A Matrix of Bankruptcy Codes*. London: Glass & Associates.

Weiss, L. 1990. "Bankruptcy Resolution: Direct Costs and Violation of Priority Claims." *Journal of Financial Economics* (December): 285–314.

CHAPTER 3 Post–Chapter 11 Performance

Alderson, Michael, and Brian L. Betker. 1999. "Assessing Postbankruptcy Performance: An Analysis of Reorganized Firms' Cash Flows." *Financial Management* 28: 68.

Betker, Brian L., Stephen P. Ferris, and Robert M. Lawless. 1999. "'Warm with Sunny Skies': Disclosure Statement Forecasts." *American Bankruptcy Law Journal* 73: 809.

Dahiya, Sandeep, Kose John, Manju Puri, and Gabriel Ramírez. 2003. "Debtor-in-Possession Financing and Bankruptcy Resolution: Empirical Evidence." *Journal of Financial Economics* 69, Issue 1 (July): 259–280.

Eberhart, Allan, Reena Aggarwal, and Edward Altman. 1999. "The Equity Performance of Firms Emerging from Bankruptcy." *Journal of Finance* 54: 1855.

Gilson, Stuart. 1997. "Transactions Costs and Capital Structure Choice: Evidence from Financially Distressed Firms." *Journal of Finance* 52: 161.

Goyal, Amit, Matthias Kahl, and Walter N. Torous. 2003. "The Long-Run Stock Performance of Financially Distressed Firms: An Empirical Investigation." Working paper, Emory University and UCLA.

Hotchkiss, Edith S. 1993. "Investment Decisions under Chapter 11 Bankruptcy." Ph.D. dissertation, New York University.

Hotchkiss, Edith S. 1995. "Postbankruptcy Performance and Management Turnover." *Journal of Finance* 50: 3.

Hotchkiss, Edith S., and Robert Mooradian. 1997. "Vulture Investors and the Market for Control of Distressed Firms." *Journal of Financial Economics* 43: 401.

Hotchkiss, Edith, and Robert Mooradian. 1998. "Acquisitions as a Means of Restructuring Firms in Chapter 11." *Journal of Financial Intermediation* 7: 240.

Hotchkiss, Edith, and Robert Mooradian. 2004. "Post-Bankruptcy Performance: Evidence from 25 Years of Chapter 11." Working paper, Boston College and Northeastern University.

Lee, J. 2004. "The Chapter After Chapter 11." New York: J.P. Morgan.

LoPucki, Lynn M., and William C. Whitford. 1993. "Patterns in the Bankruptcy Reorganization of Large, Publicly Held Companies." *Cornell Law Review* 78: 597.

Maksimovic, Vojislav, and Gordon Phillips. 1998. "Asset Efficiency and Reallocation Decisions of Bankrupt Firms." *Journal of Finance* 53: 1495.

McHugh, Christopher, Allen Michel, and Israel Shaked. 1998. "After Bankruptcy: Can Ugly Ducklings Turn into Swans?" *Financial Analysts Journal* 54, No. 3: 31.

Weiss, Lawrence A., and Karen H. Wruck. 1998. "Information Problems, Conflicts of Interest, and Asset Stripping: Chapter 11's Failure in the Case of Eastern Airlines." *Journal of Financial Economics* 48: 55.

CHAPTER 4   The Costs of Bankruptcy

Altman, Edward I. 1984. "A Further Empirical Investigation of the Bankruptcy Cost Question." *Journal of Finance* 39: 1067.

Andrade, Gregor, and Steven Kaplan. 1998. "How Costly Is Financial (Not Economic) Distress? Evidence from Highly Leveraged Transactions That Became Distressed." *Journal of Finance* 53: 1443.

Ang, James, Jess Chua, and John McConnell. 1982. "The Administrative Costs of Corporate Bankruptcy: A Note." *Journal of Finance* 34: 219.

Betker, Brian. 1997. "The Administrative Costs of Debt Restructurings: Some Recent Evidence." *Financial Management* 26: 56.

Bris, Arturo, Ivo Welch, and Ning Zhu. 2004. "The Costs of Bankruptcy." Yale ICF Working Paper No. 04-13.

Cutler, David M., and Lawrence H. Summers. 1988. "The Costs of Conflict Resolution and Financial Distress: Evidence from the Texaco-Pennzoil Litigation." *Rand Journal of Economics* 19: 157.

Franks, Julian R., and Walter N. Torous. 1989. "An Empirical Investigation of U.S. Firms in Reorganization." *Journal of Finance* 44: 747.

Gilson, Stuart, Kose John, and Lawrence Lang. 1990. "Troubled Debt Restructurings: An Empirical Study of Private Reorganization of Firms in Default." *Journal of Financial Economics* 27: 315.

Haugen, Robert, and Lemma Senbet. 1978. "The Insignificance of Bankruptcy Costs to the Theory of Optimal Capital Structure." *Journal of Finance* 33: 383.

Jensen, Michael. 1989. "Active Investors, LBOs, and the Privatization of Bankruptcy." *Journal of Applied Corporate Finance* 2: 35.

Jensen, Michael C. 1991. "Corporate Control and the Politics of Finance." *Journal of Applied Corporate Finance* 4, No. 2: 13.

Kaplan, Steven. 1989. "Campeau's Acquisition of Federated: Value Created or Value Destroyed?" *Journal of Financial Economics* 25: 191.

Kaplan, Steven. 1994. "Campeau's Acquisition of Federated: Post-Bankruptcy Results." *Journal of Financial Economics* 35: 123.

Lawless, Robert M., and Stephen P. Ferris. 1997. "Professional Fees and Other Direct Costs in Chapter 7 Bankruptcies." *Washington University Law Quarterly* 75: 1207.

LoPucki, Lynn M., and Joseph W. Doherty. 2004. "The Determinants of Professional Fees in Large Bankruptcy Reorganization Cases." *Journal of Empirical Legal Studies* 1.

Lubben, Stephen J. 2000. "The Direct Costs of Corporate Reorganization: An Empirical Examination of Professional Fees in Large Chapter 11 Cases." *American Bankruptcy Law Journal* 74: 509.

Maksimovic, Vojislav, and Gordon Phillips. 1998. "Asset Efficiency and Reallocation Decisions of Bankrupt Firms." *Journal of Finance* 53: 1495.

Opler, Tim, and Sheridan Titman. 1994. "Financial Distress and Corporate Performance." *Journal of Finance* 49: 1015.

Pulvino, Todd. 1998. "Do Asset Fire-Sales Exist? An Empirical Investigation of Commercial Aircraft Transactions." *Journal of Finance* 53: 939.

Pulvino, Todd. 1999. "Effects of Bankruptcy Court Protection on Asset Sales." *Journal of Financial Economics* 52: 151.

Tashjian, Elizabeth, Ronald C. Lease, and John J. McConnell. 1996. "An Empirical Analysis of Prepackaged Bankruptcies." *Journal of Financial Economics* 40: 135.

Warner, Jerold. 1977. "Bankruptcy Costs: Some Evidence." *Journal of Finance* 32: 71.

Weiss, Lawrence A. 1990. "Bankruptcy Resolution: Direct Costs and Violation of Priority of Claims." *Journal of Financial Economics* 27: 285.

CHAPTER 5   Distressed Firm Valuation

Alderson, Michael J., and Brian L. Betker. 1995. "Liquidation Costs and Capital Structure." *Journal of Financial Economics* 39: 45.

Bebchuk, L. 1988. "A New Approach to Corporate Reorganizations." *Harvard Law Review* 101: 775.

Bruner, Robert F. 2004. *Applied Mergers and Acquisitions*. Hoboken, NJ: John Wiley & Sons.

Cornell, B., and K. Green. 1991. "The Investment Performance of Low-Grade Bond Funds." *Journal of Finance* 46: 29.

Damodaran, Aswath. 1996. *Investment Valuation: Tools and Techniques for Determining the Value of Any Asset*. New York: John Wiley & Sons.

Damodaran, Aswath. 2002. *Investment Valuation: Tools and Techniques for Determining the Value of Any Asset*. 2nd ed. New York: John Wiley & Sons.

Fama, Eugene, and Kenneth French. 2002. "The Equity Premium." *Journal of Finance* 57: 637–659.

Gilson, S., E. Hotchkiss, and R. Ruback. 2000. "Valuation of Bankrupt Firms." *Review of Financial Studies* 13: 43.

Hausch, D., and J. Seward. 1995. "Mitigating the Corporate Valuation Problem in Chapter 11 Reorganizations: Transferable Put Rights and Contingent Value Rights." Working paper, University of Wisconsin–Madison.

Hotchkiss, Edith S. 1995. "Postbankruptcy Performance and Management Turnover." *Journal of Finance* 50: 3.

Hotchkiss, Edith S., and Robert Mooradian. 1997. "Vulture Investors and the Market for Control of Distressed Firms." *Journal of Financial Economics* 43: 401.

Hotchkiss, Edith, and Robert Mooradian. 1998. "Acquisitions as a Means of Restructuring Firms in Chapter 11." *Journal of Financial Intermediation* 7: 240.

Hotchkiss, E., and T. Ronen. 2002. "The Informational Efficiency of the Corporate Bond Market: An Intraday Analysis." *Review of Financial Studies* 15: 1325–1354.

Kaplan, S., and R. Ruback. 1995. "The Valuation of Cash Flow Forecasts: An Empirical Analysis." *Journal of Finance* 50: 1059–1093.

Lehavy, R. 1998. "Reliability of Financial Statements after Adoption of Fresh Start Reporting." Working paper, University of California at Berkeley.

McKinsey & Company. 2005. *Valuation: Measuring and Managing the Value of Companies.* New York: John Wiley & Sons.

Newton, G. 1994. *Bankruptcy & Insolvency Accounting.* New York: John Wiley & Sons.

Pantaleo, Peter V., and Barry W. Ridings. 2005. "Reorganization Value." *Business Lawyer* 60: 27.

Pulvino, Todd. 1999. "Effects of Bankruptcy Court Protection on Asset Sales." *Journal of Financial Economics* 52: 151.

Ruback, R. 1998 "Capital Cash Flows: A Simple Approach to Valuing Risky Cash Flows." Working paper, Harvard Business School.

Scarberry, M., K. Klee, G. Newton, and S. Nickles. 1996. *Business Reorganization in Bankruptcy: Cases and Materials.* St. Paul, MN: West Publishing Co.

CHAPTER 6   Firm Valuation and Corporate Leveraged Restructuring

Altman, E. 1984. "A Further Empirical Investigation of the Bankruptcy Cost Question." *Journal of Finance* (September).

Altman, E., and R. Smith. 1991a. "Firm Valuation and Leveraged Restructurings." In E. Altman, editor, *Corporate Bankruptcy and Distressed Restructurings,* Homewood, IL: Dow Jones–Irwin.

Altman, E., and R. Smith. 1991b. "Highly Leveraged Restructurings: A Valid Role for Europe." *Journal of International Securities Markets* (Winter): 347–357.

Amihud, Y. 1989. *Leveraged Management Buyouts: Causes and Consequences.* Homewood, IL: Dow Jones–Irwin.

Andrade, G., and S. Kaplan. 1998. "How Costly Is Financial (Not Economic) Distress: Evidence from Highly Leveraged Restructings That Become Distressed." *Journal of Finance* 21: 1721–1748.

Bulow, J., and J. Shoven. 1978. "The Bankruptcy Decision." *Bell Journal of Economics* (Autumn).

Chen, Y., J. F. Weston, and E. Altman. 1995. "Financial Distress and Restructuring Models." *Financial Management* 2 (Summer): 57–75.

Copeland, T., and W. H. Lee. 1990. "Exchange Offers and Stock Swaps—New Evidence." Working paper, UCLA.

Denis, D. and D. Denis. 1995. "Causes of Financial Distress Following Leveraged Recapitalizations." *Journal of Financial Economics* 37: 129–158.

Durand, D. 1959. "The Cost of Capital in an Imperfect Market: A Reply to Modigliani and Miller." *American Economic Review* (June).

Jensen, M. 1989. "Eclipse of the Public Corporation." *Harvard Business Review* (September–October).

Jensen, M., and W. Meckling. 1976. "Theory of the Firm: Managerial Behaviour, Agency Costs and Ownership Structure." *Journal of Financial Economics* (October): 305–360.

Kaplan, S. 1989. "Management Buyouts: Evidence on Taxes as a Source of Value." *Journal of Finance* (September).

Kaplan, S., and J. Stein. 1993. "The Evolution of Buyout Pricing and Financial Structure in the 1980's. *Quarterly Journal of Economics* 108: 2, 313–357.

McKinsey & Company. 2005. *Valuation: Measuring and Managing the Value of Companies.* New York: John Wiley & Sons.

Miller, M. 1989. "The Modigliani-Miller Theorems after 30 Years." *Journal of Applied Corporate Finance* (Spring).

Modigliani, F., and M. Miller. 1958. "The Cost of Capital, Corporation Finance and the Theory of Investment." *American Economic Review* (June).

Modigliani, F., and M. Miller. (1963). "Corporate Income Taxes and the Cost of Capital: A Correction." *American Economic Review* (June).

Moore, H. 1990. "Trends and Characteristics of Recent LBO Experience." Working paper, New York University (November).

Smith, R., and I. Walter. 1990. "Economic Restructuring in Europe and the Market for Corporate Control." *Journal of International Security Markets* (Winter).

Warner, J. 1977. "Bankruptcy Costs: Some Evidence." *Journal of Finance* (May).

Weston, J. F. 1963. "A Test of Cost of Capital Propositions." *Southern Economic Journal* (October).

Weston, J. F. 1989. "What MM Have Wrought." *Financial Management* (Summer).

CHAPTER 7 The High Yield Bond Market: Risks and and Returns for Investors and Analysts

Altman, E. 1988. *Corporate Bond Mortality and Performance.* New York: Merrill Lynch.

Altman, E. 1989. "Measuring Corporate Bond Mortality and Performance." *Journal of Finance* (September): 909–922.

Altman, E. 1993. *Corporate Financial Distress and Bankruptcy.* 2nd ed. New York: John Wiley & Sons.

Altman, E., and J. Bencivenga. 1995. "A Yield Premium Model for the High Yield Debt Market." *Financial Analysts Journal* (September–October).

Altman, E., B. Brady, A. Resti, and A. Sironi. 2005. "The Link Between Default and Recovery Rates." *Journal of Business* (November). Also ISDA web site, 2002.

Altman, E., A. Resti, and A. Sironi. 2005. *Recovery Risk*. London: Risk Books.

Asquith, P., D. Mullins, and E. D. Wolff. 1989. "Original Issue High Yield Bonds: Aging Analysis of Defaults, Exchanges and Calls." *Journal of Finance* (September): 923–952.

Fons, J., and D. Lucas. 1990. *Special Report on Corporate Bond Default and Default Rates 1970–1989*. New York: Moody's. Also 2005 update by D. Hamilton and S. Oh.

Standard & Poor's. 1991. "A Transition Matrix of Corporate Bond Defaults." *S&P Credit Week*. Also 2005 update by B. Brady, S&P.

CHAPTER 8   Investing in Distressed Securities

Altman, E. I. 1969. "Bankruptcy Firms' Equity Securities as an Investment Alternative." *Financial Analysts Journal* (July/August).

Altman, E. I. 1991. *Distressed Securities*. Chicago: Probus. Reprint, Frederick, MD: Beard Books, 1999.

Altman, E. I. 2002. *Bankruptcy, Credit Risk and High Yield Bonds*. Malden, MA: Blackwell Publishers.

Altman, E. I., B. Brady, A. Resti, and A. Sironi. 2002. "The Link between Default and Recovery Rates." NYU Salomon Center, Working Paper S-02-9. *ISDA* (January); *Journal of Business* (November 2005).

Altman, E. I., and A. Eberhart. 1994. "Do Seniority Provisions Protect Bondholders' Investments?" *Journal of Portfolio Management* (Summer).

Altman, E. I., A. Gande, and A. Saunders. 2004. "The Informational Efficiency of Loans versus Bonds: Evidence from Secondary Market Prices." Working paper, NYU Finance Department (March).

Altman, E. I., and R. Miranda. 2005. "The Investment Performance and Market Size of Defaulted Bonds and Bank Loans in 2004 and Market Outlook." NYU Salomon Center Special Report (February).

Altman Foothill Report. 1990. *Investing in Distressed Securities*. Los Angeles: Foothill Corporation.

Altman Foothill Report. 1992. *The Market for Distressed Securities and Bank Loans*. Los Angeles: Foothill Corporation.

Branch, B., and H. Ray. 1992. *Bankruptcy Investing*. Chicago: Dearborn Press.

Brand, L., and R. Behar. 2000. "Recoveries on Defaulted Bonds Tied to Security Ratings." *S&P's Credit Week* (February).

Carlson, J., and F. Fabozzi. 1992. *The Trading and Securitization of Senior Bank Loans*. Chicago: Probus.

Eberhart, A., R. Aggarwal, and E. I. Altman. 1999. "The Equity Performance of Firms Emerging from Chapter 11." *Journal of Finance* (October).

Jeffries & Company. 2003. "How to Perform a Post-Restructuring Equity Valuation." New York: Jeffries Recapitalization and Restructuring Group.

J. P. Morgan. 2004. *The Chapter After Chapter 11*. New York: J. P. Morgan.

Parker, V. R., ed. 2005. *Managing Hedge Fund Risk*. London: Risk Books.

Ramaswami, M., and S. Moeller. 1990. *Investing in Financially Distressed Firms*. New York: Quorum Books.

Rosenberg, H. 1992. *The Vulture Investors*. New York: HarperCollins. Rev. ed., New York: John Wiley & Sons, 2000.

CHAPTER 9   Risk-Return Performance of Defaulted Bonds and Bank Loans

Altman, E. I., and E. Eberhart. 1994. "Do Seniority Provisions Protect Bondholders' Investments?" *Journal of Portfolio Management* (Summer).

Altman Foothill Report. 1990. *Investing in Distressed Securities*. Los Angeles: Foothill Corporation.

Altman Foothill Report. 1992. *The Market for Distressed Securities and Bank Loans*. Los Angeles: Foothill Corporation.

Brand, L., and R. Behar. 2000. "Recoveries on Defaulted Bonds Tied to Security Rankings." *S&P's Credit Week* (February).

Eberhart, A., R. Aggarwal, and E. I. Altman. 1999. "The Equity Performance of Firms Emerging from Chapter 11." *Journal of Finance* (October).

Ramaswami, M., and S. Moeller. 1990. *Investing in Financially Distressed Firms*. New York: Quorum Books.

Rosenberg, H. 1992. *The Vulture Investors*. New York: HarperCollins. Rev. ed., New York: John Wiley & Sons, 2000.

CHAPTER 10   Corporate Governance in Distressed Firms

Betker, Brian L. 1995. "Management's Incentives, Equity's Bargaining Power, and Deviations from Absolute Priority in Chapter 11 Bankruptcies." *Journal of Business* 68: 161.

Bradley, Michael, and Michael Rosenzweig. 1992. "The Untenable Case for Chapter 11." *Yale Law Journal* 101: 1043.

Branch, Ben. 2000. "Fiduciary Duty: Shareholders versus Creditors." *Financial Practice and Education*: 339.

Chidambaran, N. K., and Nagpurnanand R. Prabhala. 2004. "Executive Stock Option Repricing: Creating a Mountain out of a Molehill?" EFA 2003 Annual Conference Paper No. 797.

Gilson, Stuart. 1989. "Management Turnover and Financial Distress." *Journal of Financial Economics* 25: 241.

Gilson, Stuart. 1990. "Bankruptcy, Boards, Banks and Blockholders." *Journal of Financial Economics* 26: 355.

Gilson, Stuart, Edith Hotchkiss, and Richard Ruback. 2000. "Valuation of Bankrupt Firms." *Review of Financial Studies* 13: 43.

Gilson, Stuart, and Michael Vetsuypens. 1993 "CEO Compensation in Financially Distressed Firms: An Empirical Analysis." *Journal of Finance* 43: 425.

Hotchkiss, Edith S. 1995. "Postbankruptcy Performance and Management Turnover." *Journal of Finance* 50: 3.

Hotchkiss, Edith S., and Robert Mooradian. 1997. "Vulture Investors and the Market for Control of Distressed Firms." *Journal of Financial Economics* 43: 401.

Hotchkiss, Edith, and Robert Mooradian. 1998. "Acquisitions as a Means of Restructuring Firms in Chapter 11." *Journal of Financial Intermediation* 7: 240.

James, Christopher. 1995. "When Do Banks Take Equity? An Analysis of Bank Loan Restructurings and the Role of Public Debt." *Review of Financial Studies* 8: 1209.

LoPucki, Lynn M. 2004. *Courting Failure: How Competition for Big Cases Is Corrupting the Bankruptcy Courts.* Ann Arbor: University of Michigan Press.

LoPucki, Lynn M., and William C. Whitford. 1993. "Corporate Governance in the Bankruptcy Reorganization of Large, Publicly Held Companies." *University of Pennsylvania Law Review* 141: 669.

Warner, Jerold B., Ross L. Watts, and Karen H. Wruck. 1988. "Stock Prices and Top Management Changes." *Journal of Financial Economics* 20: 461.

Weisbach, Michael S. 1988. "Outside Directors and CEO Turnover." *Journal of Financial Economics* 20: 431.

Weiss, Lawrence A., and Karen H. Wruck. 1998. "Information Problems, Conflicts of Interest, and Asset Stripping: Chapter 11's Failure in the Case of Eastern Airlines." *Journal of Financial Economics* 48: 55.

CHAPTER 11   Corporate Credit Scoring— Insolvency Risk Models

Altman, E. 1968. "Financial Ratios, Discriminant Analysis and the Prediction of Corporate Bankruptcy." *Journal of Finance* (September): 189–209.

Altman, E. 1984. "A Further Empirical Investigation of the Bankruptcy Cost Question." *Journal of Finance* 34, No. 4 (September): 1067–1089.

Altman, E. 1989. "Measuring Corporate Bond Mortality and Performance." *Journal of Finance* (September): 909–922.

Altman, E. 1993. *Corporate Financial Distress and Bankruptcy.* 2nd ed. New York: John Wiley & Sons.

Altman, E., P. Araman, and G. Fanjul. 2004. "Defaults and Returns in the High Yield Bond Market." *NYU Salomon Center Report and Journal of Applied Finance* (Spring–Summer): 98–112.

Altman, E., B. Brady, A. Resti, and A. Sironi. 2002. "The Link between Default Rates and Recovery Rates: Implications for Credit Risk Models and Procyclicality." NYU Salomon Center, Working Paper S-02-9.

Altman, E., R. Haldeman, and P. Narayanan. 1977. "ZETA Analysis: A New Model to Identify Bankruptcy Risk of Corporations." *Journal of Banking & Finance* 1, No. 1 (June): 29–54.

Altman, E., J. Hartzell, and M. Peck. 1995a. "Emerging Markets Corporate Bonds: A Scoring System." *The Future of Emerging Market Flows*, edited by R. Levich. Kluwer, Holland: J.P. Mei, 1997.

Altman, E., J. Hartzell, and M. Peck. 1995b. "A Scoring System for Emerging Market Corporate Bonds." Salomon Brothers (May).

Altman, E., G. Marco, and F. Varetto. 1994. "Corporate Distress Diagnosis: Comparisons Using Linear Discriminant Analysis and Neural Networks (the Italian Experience)." *Journal of Banking & Finance* 18, No. 3: 505–529.

Altman, E., A. Resti, and A. Sironi. 2002. "Analyzing and Explaining Default Recovery Rates." *ISDA* (January); and *Journal of Business* (November 2005).

Altman, E., A. Resti, and A. Sironi. 2005a. "Default Recovery Rates in Credit Risk Modeling: A Review of the Literature and Recent Evidence." *Journal of Financial Literature* 1 (Winter): 21–45.

Altman, E., A. Resti, and A. Sironi. 2005b. *Recovery Risk: The Next Challenge in Credit Risk Management*. London: Risk Books.

Altman, E., and H. Rijken. 2004. "How Rating Agencies Achieve Rating Stability." *Journal of Banking & Finance* 28: 2679–2714.

Basel Commission on Banking Supervision. 1999. "Credit Risk Modeling: Current Practices and Applications." *BIS* (June).

Basel Commission on Banking Supervision. 2001. "The Basel Capital Accord." Basel, Switzerland: Bank for International Settlements (January).

Basel Commission on Banking Supervision. 2004. "International Convergence of Capital Measurement and Capital Standards: A Revised Framework." Basel, Switzerland: Bank for International Settlements (June).

Beaver, W. 1966. "Financial Ratios as Predictors of Failures." In *Empirical Research in Accounting: Selected Studies*. Journal of Accounting Research 71–111.

Beaver, W. 1968. "Alternative Accounting Measures as Predictors of Failure." *Accounting Review* (January): 46–53.

Caouette, J., E. Altman, and P. Narayanan. 1998. *Managing Credit Risk*. New York: John Wiley & Sons.

Fitch. 2001. "Bank Loan and Bond Recovery Study: 1997–2001." New York: Fitch (March 19).

Frydman, H., E. Altman, and D. L. Kao. 1985. "Introducing Recursive Partitioning Analysis for Financial Classification." *Journal of Finance* 50, No. 1: 269–291.

Frye, J. 2000. "Collateral Damage." *Risk* (April).

Gupton, G., C. Gates, and L. Carty. 2000. "Bank Loan Loss Given Default." *Moody's* (November).

Hillegeist, S., D. Cram, E. Keating, and K. Lundstedt. 2003. "Assessing the Probability of Bankruptcy." Northwestern University, Kellogg School working paper (September).

Hu, Y. T., and W. Perraudin. 2002. "The Dependency of Recovery Rates of Corporate Bond Issues." Birkbeck College, Mimeo (February).

Kealhofer, S. 2000. "The Quantification of Credit Risk." San Francisco: KMV Corporation (January) (unpublished).

KMV. 2000. "The KMV EDF Credit Measure and Probabilities of Default." San Francisco: KMV Corporation.

McKee, T., and T. Lensbergn. 2002. "Genetic Programming and Roughsets: A Hybrid Approach to Bankruptcy Classification." *European Journal of Operations Research* 128, No. 2 (April): 436–451.

McQuown, J. A. 1993 "A Comment on Market vs. Accounting Based Measures of Default Risk." San Francisco: KMV Corporation.

Merton, R. C. 1974. "On the Pricing of Corporate Debt: The Risk Structure of Interest Rates." *Journal of Finance* (June): 449–470.

Moody's. Annually. "Corporate Bond Defaults and Default Rates." Special Report, *Moody's Investors Service* (January).

Moody's. 1996. "Defaulted Bank Loan Recoveries," Special Report, *Moody's Investors Service* (November; also June 1998 update).

Mossman, C. E., G. Bell, L. M. Swartz, and H. Turtle. 1998. "An Empirical Comparison of Bankruptcy Models." *Financial Review* 33, No. 2 (May): 35–54.

Ohlson, J. 1980. "Financial Ratios and the Probability Prediction of Bankruptcy." *Journal of Accounting Research* 18: 1.

Saunders, A., and L. Allen. 2002. *Credit Risk Measurement*, 2nd ed. New York: John Wiley & Sons.

Scott, J. 1981. "The Probability of Bankruptcy: A Comparison of Empirical Predictions and Theoretical Models." *Journal of Banking & Finance* (September): 317–344.

Shumway, T. 2002. "Forecasting Bankruptcy More Accurately: A Simple Hazard Model." TMA Advanced Education Workshop, Boston College, MA (June 21) from University of Michigan working paper, 1999.

Standard & Poor's. Annually. "Rating Performance: Stability and Transition." Special Report, updated annually. New York: S&P Corporation.

Trippi, R., and E. Turban, eds. 1996. *Neural Networks in Finance and Investing.* Chicago: Probus.

Zavgren, C. V. 1985. "Assessing the Vulnerability of Failure of American Industrial Firms: A Logistic Analysis." *Journal of Business, Finance and Accounting* 12, No. 1: 19–45.

Zmijewski, M. E. 1984. "Methodological Issues Related to the Estimation of Financial Distress Prediction Models." *Journal of Accounting Research* 22 (suppl.): 59–82.

CHAPTER 12   An Emerging Market Credit Scoring System for Corporates

Altman, E., J. Hartzell, and M. Peck. 1995. *Emerging Market Corporate Bonds: A Scoring System*. New York: Salomon Brothers.

CHAPTER 13   Application of Distress Prediction Models

Altman, Edward. 1983. *Corporate Financial Distress*. New York: John Wiley & Sons.

Altman, Edward, and Laurie Goodman. 1980. "An Economic and Statistical Analysis of the Failing Company Doctrine." NYU School of Business working paper. Reprinted in E. Altman. *Bankruptcy, Credit Risk and High Yield Bonds.* Malden, MA: Blackwell Publishers, 2002.

Altman, Edward, and Thomas McGough. 1974. "Evaluation of a Company as a Going Concern." *Journal of Accountancy* (December).

Altman, Edward, and Herbert Rijken. 2004. "How Rating Agencies Achieve Stability." *Journal of Banking & Finance* 28: 2679–2714.

Altman, Edward, and Herbert Rijken. 2005. "The Effect of Rating through the Cycle on Rating Stability, Rating Timeliness and Default Prediction Performance." *Financial Analysts Journal*, forthcoming in 2006.

Appenzeller, P., and R. Parker. 2005. "Deepening Insolvency Is a Liability Trap for the Unwary." *Journal of Corporate Renewal* (July).

Eberhart, Allan, Edward Altman, and Reena Aggarwal. 1999. "The Equity Performance of Firms Emerging from Chapter 11." *Journal of Finance* 54 (October): 1855–1868.

Gilson, Stuart. 1997. "Transaction Costs and Capital Structure Choice: Evidence from Financially Distressed Firms." *Journal of Finance* 52: 161–197.

Gilson, Stuart, Kose John, and Larry Lang. 1993. "Troubled Debt Restructuring: An Empirical Study of Private Reorganization of Firms and Default." In E. Altman, editor, *Bankruptcy and Distressed Restructurings*. Homewood, IL: Business One Irwin: 77–124.

Hotchkiss, Edith. 1995. "The Post-Emergence Performance of Firms Emerging from Chapter 11." *Journal of Finance* 50: 3–21.

J. P. Morgan. 2004. The Chapter After Chapter 11." New York (January).

Kurth, Mette. 2005. "List of Defendants Grows in Deepening Insolvency Cases." *Corporate Renewal* (January): 4–7.

Loeffler, G. 2002. "Avoiding the Rating Bounce: Why Agencies Are Slow to React to New Information." Working paper.

Loeffler, G. 2004. "An Anatomy of Rating through the Cycle." *Journal of Banking & Finance* 28: 695–720.

CHAPTER 15 Estimating Recovery Rates on Defaulted Debt

Acharya, Viral V., Sreedar T. Bharath, and Anand Srinivasan. 2003. "Understanding the Recovery Rates on Defaulted Securities." Working paper, London Business School.

Altman, Edward I. 2001. "Altman High Yield Bond and Default Study." Salomon Smith Barney, U.S. Fixed Income High Yield Report (July).

Altman, Edward I., and Juan Martin Aguiar. 2005. "Defaults and Returns in the High Yield Bond Market: 2004 in Review and Outlook." NYU Salomon Center Special Report (February).

Altman, Edward I., Brooks Brady, Andrea Resti, and Andrea Sironi. 2003. "The Link between Default and Recovery Rates: Theory, Empirical Evidence and Implications." NYU Salomon Center, Working Paper S-03-4; *Journal of Business* (November 2005).

Altman, E., and A. Eberhart. 1994. "Do Seniority Provisions Protect Bondholders' Investments?" *Journal of Portfolio Management* (Summer): 67–75.

Altman, E., and G. Fanjul. 2004a and 2004b. "Defaults and Returns in the High Yield Bond Market: Analysis Through 2003 and 2004." NYU Salomon Center Special Reports (January).

Altman, E., R. Haldeman, and P. Narayanan. 1977. "ZETA Analysis: A New Model to Identify Bankruptcy Risk of Corporations." *Journal of Banking & Finance* 1, No. 1 (July): 29–54.

Altman, Edward I., and Vellore M. Kishore. 1996. "Almost Everything You Wanted to Know About Recoveries on Defaulted Bonds." *Financial Analysts Journal* (November/December).

Altman, Edward I., Andrea Resti, and Andrea Sironi. 2001. *Analyzing and Explaining Default Recovery Rates*. ISDA Research Report, London (December).

Altman, Edward I., Andrea Resti, and Andrea Sironi. 2005a. "Default Recovery Rates in Credit Risk Modeling: A Review of the Literature and Recent Evidence." *Journal of Finance Literature* 1, No. 1.

Altman, Edward I., Andrea Resti, and Andrea Sironi. 2005b. *Recovery Risk: The Challenge in Credit Risk Management*. London: Risk Books.

"Altman High Yield Bond Default and Return Report: 2004." Citigroup (2005).

Asarnow, Elliot, and David Edwards. 1995. "Measuring Loss on Defaulted Bank Loans: A 24 Year Study." *Journal of Commercial Bank Lending* 77, No. 7: 11–23.

Bakshi, G., Dilip Madan, and Frank Zhang. 2001. "Understanding the Role of Recovery in Default Risk Models: Empirical Comparisons and Implied Recovery Rates." Finance and Economics Discussion Series, 2001-37, Federal Reserve Board of Governors, Washington, D.C.

Basel Commission on Banking Supervision. 2004. "International Convergence of Capital Measurement and Capital Standards—A Revised Framework." Basel, Switzerland: Bank for International Settlements (June).

Basel Commission on Banking Supervision. 2005. "Guidance on Paragraph 468 of the Framework Document." Basel, Switzerland: Bank for International Settlements (July).

Black, Fischer, and John C. Cox. 1976. "Valuing Corporate Securities: Some Effects of Bond Indenture Provisions." *Journal of Finance* 31: 351–367.

Black, Fischer, and Myron Scholes. 1973. "The Pricing of Options and Corporate Liabilities." *Journal of Political Economics* (May): 637–659.

Carey, Mark, and Michael Gordy. 2003. "Systematic Risk in Recoveries on Defaulted Debt." Mimeo, Federal Reserve Board, Washington, D.C.

Chabane, Ali, Jean-Paul Laurent, and Julien Salomon. 2004. "Double Impact: Credit Risk Assessment and Collateral Value." Mimeo.

Chew, William, and Steven Kerr. 2005. "Recovery Ratings: A New Window on Secured Loans." In E. Altman, A. Resti, and A. Sironi. *Recovery Risk: The Next Challenge in Credit Risk Management*. London: Risk Books.

Credit Suisse Financial Products. 1997. *CreditRisk+: A Credit Risk Management Framework*. Technical document.

Crosbie, Peter J. 1999. "Modeling Default Risk." Mimeo. San Francisco: KMV Corporation.

Crouhy, Michel, Dan Galai, and Robert Mark. 2000. "A Comparative Analysis of Current Credit Risk Models." *Journal of Banking & Finance* 24: 59–117.

Duffee, Gregory R. 1999. "Estimating the Price of Default Risk." *Review of Financial Studies* 12, No. 1 (Spring): 197–225.

Duffie, Darrell. 1998. "Defaultable Term Structure Models with Fractional Recovery of Par." Graduate School of Business, Stanford University.

Duffie, Darrell, and David Lando. 2000. "Term Structure of Credit Spreads with Incomplete Accounting Information." *Econometrica.*

Duffie, Darrell, and Kenneth J. Singleton. 1999. "Modeling the Term Structures of Defaultable Bonds." *Review of Financial Studies* 12: 687–720.

Dullmann, Klaus, and Monika Trapp. 2004. "Systematic Risk in Recovery Rates— An Empirical Analysis of U.S. Corporate Credit Exposures." Mimeo, University of Mannheim; updated in Altman, Resti, and Sironi (2005b).

Eales, Robert, and Edmund Bosworth. 1998. "Severity of Loss in the Event of Default in Small Business and Large Consumer Loans." *Journal of Lending and Credit Risk Management* (May): 58–65.

Emery, K., R. Cantor, and R. Avner. 2004. "Recovery Rates on North American Syndicated Bank Loans, 1989–2003." Moody's Investors Service (March).

Emery, Kenneth, R. Cantor, S. Oh, R. Solomon, and P. Stumpp. 2004. "Credit Loss Rates on Similarly Rated Loans and Bonds." *Moody's Special Comment* (December).

Eom, Young Ho, Jean Helwege, and Jing-zhi Huang. 2001. "Structural Models of Corporate Bond Pricing: An Empirical Analysis." Mimeo.

Finger, Chris. 1999. "Conditional Approaches for CreditMetrics Portfolio Distributions." *CreditMetrics Monitor* (April).

Franks, Julian, and O. Sussman. 2005. "Do Bankruptcy Codes Matter? A Study of Defaults in France, Germany and the U.K." Working paper, London Business School.

Franks, Julian, and Walter Torous. 1994. "A Comparison of Financial Recontracting in Distressed Exchanges and Chapter 11 Reorganizations." *Journal of Financial Economics* 35: 349–370.

Fridson, Martin S., Christopher M. Garman, and Kathryn Okashima. 2001. "Recovery Rates: The Search for Meaning." Merrill Lynch & Co., High Yield Strategy.

Frye, John. 2000a. "Collateral Damage." *Risk* (April): 91–94.

Frye, John. 2000b. "Collateral Damage Detected." Federal Reserve Bank of Chicago, working paper, Emerging Issues Series (October): 1–14.

Frye, John. 2000c. "Depressing Recoveries." *Risk* (November).

Geske, Robert. 1977. "The Valuation of Corporate Liabilities as Compound Options." *Journal of Financial and Quantitative Analysis* 12: 541–552.

Gordy, Michael. 2000. "A Comparative Anatomy of Credit Risk Models." *Journal of Banking and Finance* (January): 119–149.

Gupton, Gregory, Christopher Finger, and Mickey Bhatia. 1997. *CreditMetrics— Technical Document.* New York: J. P. Morgan & Co.

Gupton, Greg M., Daniel Gates, and Lea V. Carty. 2000. "Bank Loan Loss Given Default." Moody's Investors Service, Global Credit Research (November).

Gupton, Greg M., and Roger M. Stein. 2002. "LossCalc: Moody's Model for Predicting Loss Given Default (LGD)." Moody's/KMV, New York. Updated in 2005, "LossCalc V2, Dynamic Prediction of LGD." Moody's/KMV (January).

Hamilton, David T., Greg M. Gupton, and Alexandra Berthault. 2001. "Default and Recovery Rates of Corporate Bond Issuers: 2000." Moody's Investors Service (February).

Hu, Yen-Ting, and William Perraudin. 2002. "The Dependence of Recovery Rates and Defaults." Mimeo, Birkbeck College (February).

Hull, John, and Alan White. 1995. "The Impact of Default Risk on the Prices of Options and Other Derivative Securities." *Journal of Banking and Finance* 19: 299–322.

Jarrow, Robert A. 2001. "Default Parameter Estimation Using Market Prices." *Financial Analysts Journal* 57, No. 5: 75–92.

Jarrow, Robert A., David Lando, and Stuart M. Turnbull. 1997. "A Markov Model for the Term Structure of Credit Risk Spreads." *Review of Financial Studies* 10: 481–523.

Jarrow, Robert A., and Stuart M. Turnbull. 1995. "Pricing Derivatives on Financial Securities Subject to Credit Risk." *Journal of Finance* 50: 53–86.

Jones D., and J. Ming. 1998. "Bank Reserves and Expected Losses." Washington, D.C.: Federal Reserve Board.

Jones, E., S. Mason, and E. Rosenfeld. 1984. "Contingent Claims Analysis of Corporate Capital Structures: An Empirical Investigation." *Journal of Finance* 39: 611–627.

Jokivuolle, Esa, and Samu Peura. 2003. "A Model for Estimating Recovery Rates and Collateral Haircuts for Bank Loans." *European Financial Management* (Fall).

Keisman, D. 2004. "Recovery Trends and Analysis." Standard & Poor's, *Loss Stats Database*, New York.

Keisman, D. 2004. "Ultimate Recovery Rates on Bank Loan and Bond Defaults." S&P *Loss Stats*, New York.

Kim, I. J., K. Ramaswamy, and S. Sundaresan. 1993. "Does Default Risk in Coupons Affect the Valuation of Corporate Bonds? A Contingent Claims Model." *Financial Management* 22, No. 3: 117–131.

Lando, David. 1998. "On Cox Processes and Credit Risky Securities." *Review of Derivatives Research* 2: 99–120.

Litterman, Robert, and T. Iben. 1991. "Corporate Bond Valuation and the Term Structure of Credit Spreads." *Financial Analysts Journal* (Spring): 52–64.

Longstaff, Francis A., and Eduardo S. Schwartz. 1995. "A Simple Approach to Valuing Risky Fixed and Floating Rate Debt." *Journal of Finance* 50: 789–819.

Madan, Dileep, and Haluk Unal. 1995. "Pricing the Risks of Default." University of Maryland working paper.

Merton, Robert C. 1974. "On the Pricing of Corporate Debt: The Risk Structure of Interest Rates." *Journal of Finance* 2: 449–471.

Neto de Carvalho, A., and Jean Dermine. 2003. "Bank Loan Losses-Given-Default—Empirical Evidence." Working paper, INSEAD.

Nielsen, Lars T., Jesus Saà-Requejo, and Pedro Santa-Clara. 1993. "Default Risk and Interest Rate Risk: The Term Structure of Default Spreads." Working paper, INSEAD.

Pykhtin, M. 2003. "Unexpected Recovery Risk." *Risk* 16: 74–78.

Resti, Andrea. 2002. *The New Basel Capital Accord: Structure, Possible Changes, Micro- and Macroeconomic Effects.* Brussels: Centre for European Policy Studies.

Resti, Andrea, and Andrea Sironi. 2005. "Loss Given Default and Recovery Risk under Basel II." In E. Altman et al. *Recovery Risk.* London: Risk Books, 2005.

Schleifer, A., and R. Vishny. 1992. "Liquidation Values and Debt Capacity: A Market Equilibrium Approach." *Journal of Finance* 47: 1343–1366.

Schuermann, Til. 2004. "What Do We Know about Loss Given Default?" Working paper, Federal Reserve Bank of New York. Forthcoming in D. Shimko (ed.), *Credit Risk Models and Management,* 2nd ed. London: Risk Books.

Van de Castle, Karen, and David Keisman. 1999. "Suddenly Structure Mattered: Insights into Recoveries of Defaulted. " S&P *Corporate Ratings* (May 24).

Varma, P., R. Cantor, and D. Hamilton. 2003. "Recovery Rates on Defaulted Corporate Bonds and Preferred Stocks." *Moody's Investors Service* (December).

Vasicek, Oldrich A. 1984. *Credit Valuation.* San Francisco: KMV Corporation.

Verde, Mariarosa. 2003. "Recovery Rates Return to Historic Norms." *Fitch Ratings* (September).

Weiss, Lawrence. 1990. "Bankruptcy Resolution: Direct Costs and Violation of Absolute Priority." *Journal of Financial Economics* 27: 419–446.

Wilson, Thomas C. 1998. "Portfolio Credit Risk." Federal Reserve Board of New York, *Economic Policy Review* (October): 71–82.

Zhou, Chunsheng. 2001. "The Term Structure of Credit Spreads with Jump Risk." *Journal of Banking & Finance* 25: 2015–2040.

Author Index

Acharya, V., 56, 315, 318, 319
Aggarwal, R., 91, 193, 295
Aguiar, J.M., 322
Alderson, M., 86, 116
Allen, A., 256
Altman, E., 91, 97, 121, 123, 132, 139,
    163, 168, 183, 193, 199, 207, 235,
    242, 247, 251, 286, 288, 291, 295,
    297, 308, 315, 317, 319, 321, 322,
    323, 325, 326
Amihud, Y., 138
Andrade, G., 99, 132
Ang, J., 94
Appenzeller, P., 290
Asarnow, E., 321
Asquith, P., 168
Avner, R., 322

Bakshi, G., 318
Beaver, W., 238
Bebchuk, L., 119
Behar, R., 207
Berthault, A., 316
Betker, B., 34, 86, 97, 98, 116, 220
Bharath, S., 315, 318, 319
Bhatia, M., 314
Black, F., 309, 310, 311
Bosworth, E., 321
Bradley, M., 221
Brady, B., 163, 251, 317, 319, 326
Branch, B., 183
Brand, L., 207
Bris, A., 97
Brown, A., 193
Bruner, R., 113
Bulow, J., 132
Burton, T.M., 225

Cantor, R., 323, 326
Carey, M., 316
Carlson, J., 183
Carty, L., 252, 308, 314
Chabane, A., 319
Chen, Y., 132
Chew, W., 307
Chidambaran, N.K., 226

Chua, J., 94
Cohen, J., 28
Cook, M., 28
Copeland, T., 136
Cornell, B., 115
Cox, J., 310, 311
Crosbie, P., 329
Crouhy, M., 315
Cutler, D.M., 99

Dahiya, S., 82
Damodaran, A., 106, 111
Davydenko, S., 56
Denis, David, 128
Denis, Diane, 128
Dermine, J., 322
Doherty, J., 97
Duffee, G., 313
Duffie, D., 312, 313
Dullmann, K., 319
Durand, D., 131

Eales, R., 321
Eberhart, A., 91, 193, 207, 295, 321
Eckbo, E., 56
Edwards, D., 321
Emery, K., 322
Eom, Y.H., 312

Fabozzi, F., 183
Fama, E., 111
Fanjul, G., 323
Ferris, S., 97
Finger, C., 314, 315, 316
Flynn, E., 38
Fons, J., 168
Fortgang, H., 30
Franks, J., 34, 56, 98, 308
French, K., 111
Fridson, M., 308, 321
Frydman, H., 235
Frye, J., 308, 315, 319

Galai, D., 315
Gande, A., 199
Garman, C., 308, 321

Gates, C., 252, 308, 314
Geske, R., 310
Gilson, S., 89, 98, 109, 112, 117–118, 221, 224–227, 230, 287, 295
Golden, H., 28
Goodman, L., 288
Gordy, M., 315, 316
Goyal, A., 91
Green, K., 115
Gupton, G., 252, 308, 314, 316, 318

Haldeman, R., 242, 321
Hamilton, D., 316, 323, 326
Hansen, C., 52
Hartzell, J., 247
Haugen, R., 93
Hausch, D., 119
Helwege, J., 312
Hotchkiss, E., 81, 82, 84, 86–90, 103, 107, 109, 115, 117–119, 223, 224, 226, 227, 230, 295
Hu, Y.T., 252, 308, 317
Huang, J., 312
Hull, J., 311

Iben, T., 312

James, C., 228
Jarrow, R., 308, 312, 313, 316
Jensen, M., 93, 101, 132, 138
John, K., 56, 82, 98, 287
Jokivuolle, E., 308, 318
Jones, D., 315
Jones, E., 310

Kahl, M., 91
Kao, D.L., 235
Kaplan, S., 99, 117, 124, 128, 132
Kealhofer, S., 237
Keisman, D., 324–325, 326
Kennedy, J., 28
Kerr, S., 307
Kim, I., 311
Kishore, V., 326
Klee, K., 105
Kurth, M., 289

LaFleur, J., 279
Lando, D., 312, 313
Lang, L., 98, 287
Laurent, J.P., 319
Lawless, R., 97
Lease, R., 98
Lee, J., 91
Lee, W.H., 136
Lehavy, R., 115
Lensbergn, T., 235

Litterman, R., 312
Loeffler, G., 291
Longstaff, F., 311
LoPucki, L., 89, 97, 223
Lubben, S., 97
Lucas, D., 168

Madan, D., 312, 318
Maksimovic, V., 85, 100
Marco, G., 235
Mark, R., 315
Mason, S., 310
Mayer, T., 30
McConnell, J., 94, 98
McGough, T., 286
McHugh, C., 88
McKee, T., 235
McKinsey & Co., 112, 135
McQuown, J., 237
Meckling, W., 132
Merton, R., 243, 253, 309–311, 327
Michel, A., 88
Miller, M., 113, 129–132
Mingo, J., 315
Miranda, R., 183
Mitchell, P., 224
Modigliani, F., 113, 129–132
Moeller, S., 183
Mooradian, R., 81, 82, 84, 86, 90, 103, 107, 224, 227
Moore, H., 140
Mossman, C.E., 251
Mullins, D., 168

Narayanan, P., 242, 259, 321
Neto de Carvalho, A., 322
Newton, G., 105, 115
Nickles, S., 105
Nielsen, L., 311

Ohlson, J., 239
Okashima, K., 308, 321
Opler, T., 100

Pantaleo, P., 105
Parker, R., 290
Parker, V.R., 183
Peck, M., 247
Perraudin, W., 252, 308, 317
Peura, S., 308, 318
Phillips, G., 85, 100
Prabhala, N.R., 226
Pulvino, T., 100, 107
Puri, M., 82
Pykhtin, M., 319

Ramaswami M., 183
Ramaswamy, K., 311
Ramirez, G., 82

Ray, H., 183
Resti, A., 163, 251, 308, 315, 317, 320, 325, 326
Ridings, B., 105
Rijken, H., 291
Ronen, T., 115
Rosenberg, H., 30, 183
Rosenfeld, E., 310
Rosenzweig, M., 221
Ruback, R., 109, 112, 113, 117–118, 226, 230

Saà-Requejo, J., 311
Salerno, T., 52
Salomon, J., 319
Santa-Clara, P., 311
Saunders, A., 199, 256
Scarberry, M., 105
Scholes, M., 309
Schroeder, M., 225
Schuermann, T., 319
Schwartz, E., 311
Scott, J., 238
Senbet, L., 93
Seward, J., 119
Shaked, I., 88
Shleifer, A., 319
Shoven, J., 132
Shumway, T., 241
Singleton, K., 312, 313
Sironi, A., 163, 251, 308, 315, 317, 325, 326
Smith, R., 121, 123
Spiatto, J., 28
Srinivasan, A., 315, 318, 319
Stein, J., 128
Stein, R., 318
Summers, L., 99
Sundaram, R., 56
Sundaresan, S., 311
Sussman, O., 308

Tashjian, E., 98
Thornburn, K., 56
Tilly, A., 56
Titman, S., 100
Torous, W., 34, 91, 98
Trapp, M., 319
Trippi, R., 235
Turban, E., 235
Turnbull, S., 312, 313

Unal, H., 312

Van de Castle, K., 326
Varetto, F., 235
Varma, P., 322, 323, 326
Vasicek, O., 310
Verde, M., 326
Vetsuypens, M., 225, 226
Vishny, R., 319

Walter, I., 123
Walter, J., 5
Warner, J., 94, 132, 223
Watts, R., 223
Weisbach, M., 223
Weiss, L., 34, 94, 98, 220
Welch, I., 97
Weston, J.F., 132
White, A., 311
Whitford, W., 89
Wilson, T., 314
Wolff, E.D., 168
Wruck, K., 87, 220, 223

Young, S., 224

Zavgren, C.V., 239
Zhang, F., 318
Zhou, C., 314
Zhu, N., 97
Zmijewski, M.E., 251

Subject Index

Absolute priority:
  claims, 34
  doctrine, 26, 34
  violations of, 34
Adelphia Communications Corp., 184
Adjusted present value. *See* Valuation
Aeromexico, 271
Agency effects/costs, 35, 132, 133
A.H. Robins, 28
Algorithmics, 291
Allegheny International, 30, 31, 41–42
Allen, Judge William A., 43–44
Altman Foothill Reports, 184
Altman/NYU Salomon Center:
  Combined Defaulted Securities Index, 210
  Defaulted Bank Loan Index, 205, 206,
    210, 214
  Defaulted Bond Index, 179, 203, 206,
    208, 213
Analyst modified rating, 266
Apasco, S.A. de C.V., 278
Argentina, 260, 280
Asset sales, 127
Australia, 260
Automatic stay, 61

Baesa, S.A., 271
Banco Comercial Portugues, 322
Bank for International Settlements, 168
Bank setoffs, 31
Bankruptcy(ies), 4, 58
  costs of. *See* Costs of bankruptcy
  cram-down. *See* Cram-down provision
  direct costs, 1. *See also* Costs of bankruptcy
  employee claims, 29
  exclusivity period, 33, 49
  executory contracts, 29, 61
  filings, 8–11, 27
  industry, 11
  international, 55
  largest, 15
  leases, 29, 54
  legal, 14
  municipal, 28
  plan, 33, 37, 89
  plan confirmation rates, 78–81

preference(s), 53
prepackaged. *See* Prepackaged
  bankruptcy(ies)
priorities, 29, 35, 54
taxes, 39, 54
theory, 7
time in reorganization, 38, 98
trading claims, 30
Bankruptcy Abuse Prevention and
  Consumer Protection Act of 2005, 10,
  11, 45, 47, 294
Bankruptcy Act of 1898, 21
Bankruptcy Reform Act of 1978 (1978
  BankruptcyCode), 3, 21, 26–29, 31, 39
Bankruptcy Tax Bill of 1980, 40
Basel Accord on credit risk capital adequacy
  (Basel II Accord), 168, 233, 236, 252,
  286, 315
Basel II Commission, 320
Beaver, W., 238
Bethlehem Steel Corporation, 87, 189
Bond rating equivalent (BRE) method, 249
Brazil, 260, 280
Bright-line responsibility, 43
British Commonwealth system, 55
Burlington Industries, 229
Business failure(s), 4, 13

Campeau Corp., 127
Canada, 260
Capital cash flow(s). *See* Valuation
Capital structure arbitrage, 193
Cash flow(s), 87
Cemex, S.A. de C.V., 278
Chandler Act of 1938, 22, 25
Chapter 7, 3, 7, 9, 25, 81, 116
Chapter 9, 28
Chapter X, 14, 23, 24
Chapter XI, 22–24
Chapter 11, 32. *See also* Bankruptcy(ies)
"Chapter 22," 12, 88–90, 295
"Chapter 33," 12
"Chapter 44," 90
Chateaugay, 31
Chief restructuring officer (CRO), 294
CIT Finance, 293

Citigroup's High Yield Bond Index, 176, 177, 208, 210
Clark Pipe & Supply, 37
Collins & Aikman, 296
Congress Finance, 293
Conseco, 3
Continental Airlines, 28, 88
Controladora Comercial Mexicana (CCM), 276
Corporate governance, 219
Corporate restructuring(s), 122–126
    advisers, 294
Costs of bankruptcy, 93, 139, 140
    direct, 93, 94
    implications, 101
    indirect, 93, 95, 99, 132
Cram-down provision, 34, 38
Credit Lyonnais Bank Netherland, 44, 220
CreditMetrics, 237, 251
Credit pricing model(s):
    first-generation, 309
    reduced-form, 312
    second-generation, 311
Credit Research Foundation, 284
Credit risk. *See* Credit value at risk model(s)
CreditSights' BondScore, 191, 235, 291
Credit value at risk model(s), 314, 327
Creditors committee, 32
Cross-border bankruptcies. *See* United Nations Commission on International Trade Law (UNCITRAL)
Crystal Oil, 98

Debt-for-equity swaps, 135
Debt securities:
    default risk, 147
    illiquidity, 147
    paydown, 141, 143
    ratings, 146
Debtor-in-possession (DIP):
    financing, 44, 45, 82, 293
    lending, 46–47
Default(s), 4, 5, 148
    age, 156
    cumulative rate(s), 173
    fallen angel, 156
    industry, 153
    loss(es), 159
    loss rate, 159–163
    rate(s), 6, 7, 148, 151, 320, 328
    rate comparison, 179
    recovery. *See* Recovery rate(s)
    technical, 5
Deferred-payment interest bonds. *See* LBO financing
Deleveraging, 133
DESC, S.A. de C.V., 276
Detroit News, 288

Dina, S.A. de C.V., 278
Direct bankruptcy costs, 41. *See also* Costs of bankruptcy
Discharge of indebtedness, 40
Discriminant analysis, 239
Disinterestedness, 50, 51, 295
Distress prediction model(s):
    applications, 281, 297
    development, 233, 240
Distress restructuring, 5, 148
Distressed firm:
    costs, 139
    valuation. *See* Valuation
Distressed security(ies), 183
    investment strategies, 188
    investors, 187, 199–201
    market size, 183, 217
Drexel Burnham Lambert, 145, 292
Dun & Bradstreet, 4, 13, 234
Durango, S.A. de C.V., 278

E-II Holdings, 104
Eastern Airlines, 81, 87, 220
Economic value, 8
Emerging market score (EMS) model, 247, 248, 265
    application, 271
    modification, 272
    performance, 275
Employee claims. *See* Bankruptcy(ies)
Enron, 3, 184, 237, 255
Equitable subordination, 36
Equity receiverships, 21
Exchange offers, 88
Exclusivity period. *See* Bankruptcy(ies)
Exide Technologies, 104
Expected default frequency model, 191, 233, 235, 252, 290
Exposure at default (EAD), 308

Failing company doctrine, 288
Failure, economic, 4
Fallen angel(s), 147. *See also* Default(s)
Federal Reserve Board, 282
Femsa, S.A. de C.V., 276
Financial Accounting Standards Board (FASB), 226
Finland, 261
Finovia, 188
Fitch:
    Ratings, 308
    Risk, 291
Footstar Inc., 80
Ford Motor Company, 4, 147
Foster Wheeler Corp., 156
France, 261
Franklin Mutual Recovery Fund, 214
Fraudulent conveyance, 36

Free cash flow. *See* Valuation
Fresh Start Accounting, 41, 115
Fruehauf Trailer Corporation, 225
Function/location matrix, 302–303

"G" reorganization, 42, 43
Gateway Corporation, 127
GE Capital, 293
Gemex, S.A. de C.V., 276
General Motors Corporation, 4, 147, 284
Genetic algorithms, 235
Germany, 261
Global Crossing, 102, 184
GMD, S.A. de C.V., 278
Government's Accounting Audit Agency, 296
Greece, 262
Gruma, S.A. de C.V., 276
Grupo Sidek, 276
Grupo TMM, 276
Grupo Tribasa, 278
GTI Corporation, 298–306

High yield bond(s), 145, 274
  break-even yield, 178
  new issues, 178
  yield spread(s), 176
Hillsborough Holdings, 127

ICA (Empresas ICA S.A. de C.V.), 278
In re Investors Funding Corporation, 289
India, 262
Insolvency, 4, 5, 28
  deepening, 5, 289
  zone of, 43, 220
Interco Inc., 129
Intermet Corp., 296
Internal-rate-based (IRB) approach, 168
International bankruptcy(ies). *See* Bankruptcy(ies)
International distress models, 259–264
International Steel Group, 87, 189, 190
Interstate Bakeries, 156
Interstate Commerce Commission, 24
Investment strategy(ies), 188
  active control, 189
  active/noncontrol, 191
  passive investors, 191
Isosceles PLC, 127
Israel, 262
Italy, 262

J.P. Morgan, 193
Japan, 262
Japonica Partners, 30
Jefferies & Co., 193. *See also* Restructuring advisers
Johns Manville Corp., 28, 36

Junk bond(s), 125, 145
Just-in-time inventory, 296

Kamakura, 291
Key employee retention plans, 49
Kmart, 79, 87, 102, 225, 229
Kohlberg Kravis Roberts & Co. (KKR), 134
Krispy Kreme, 293

LaFleur, J., 298–302, 305
Law firms:
  Davis Polk & Wardwell LLP, 14, 47
  Kirkland & Ellis LLP, 14
  Skadden Arps, Slate, Meager & Flom LLP, 14, 47
  Strook, Strook & Lavan LLP, 14
  Weil Gotshal & Manges LLP, 14
  Wilkie-Farr & Gallagher LLP, 14
LBO financing:
  balcony financing, 125
  deferred-payment interest bonds, 126
  equity financing, 126
  mezzanine financing, 125
  orchestra financing, 126
  payment-in-kind bonds, 126
  preferred financing, 126
  reset notes, 126
  subordinated debt, 126
LBO restructuring, 136
Lease rejection(s), 54
Level 3 Communications, 148, 191
Leveraged buyout (LBO), 121, 124, 127–128, 131–134, 136, 140–143
  cash out, 127
  successful, 127, 141
Leveraged recapitalizations, 99, 123, 129, 135
Leveraged restructurings, 123
Linear discriminant structure, 239
Liquidation, 7, 25
  value, 86, 116
Loan(s):
  default, 204
  pricing, 282
  size, 205
Logistic analysis/regression, 235, 239
Long-Term Capital Management, 151
Loss given default (LGD), 251, 307, 316–317, 318, 321–322, 328
LTV Corporation, 30, 36, 87, 102, 189

Macy's, 134, 135
Malaysia, 263
Management buyouts (MBOs), 99, 124–125, 127
Management compensation, 224. *See also* Options
Mercer-Oliver-Wyman, 291

Mergers and acquisitions, 123
Merry-Go-Round, 81
MGM/UA Communications, 44
Milken, M., 145
Mirant, 104
Mittal Steel Group, 190
MNC Commercial Corp., 36
Modigliani, F., and Miller, M., 113, 129–132
Moody's, 168, 249, 278, 326
   debt ratings, 146
   Default Risk Service, 316
   High Yield Debt Market, 179
   Investors Service, 308
   LossCalc model, 318
Moody's/KMV's expected default frequency model. *See* Expected default frequency model
Mortality of corporate bonds:
   approach(es), 168
   cumulative rate, 169
   loss(es), 170, 172
   marginal rate, 169
   rate, generally, 168, 171, 250
   survival rate, 169
Multiple discriminant analysis (MDA), 239
Municipal bankruptcies, 28

National Association of Credit Managers (NACM), 284
National Bankruptcy Conference, 22
National Gypsum, 79, 103, 104, 127
Net operating loss (NOL) carryovers. *See* Tax loss carryforwards
Netherlands, 263
Neural networks, 235
New Generation Research, 81

Olympia & York Development Company, 55
Options:
   management compensation, 118, 226
   repricing/rescission, 226
Owens Corning, 214

Pacific Gas & Electric, 102
Parmalat, 55
Pathe Communications Corporation, 43, 44, 220
Pay-in-kind bonds (PIKs). *See* LBO financing
Pegasus Communications, 148
Penn Central, 4, 26
Pension Benefit Guarantee Corp., 190
Pillowtex, 90
Postbankruptcy performance, 79
   operating performance, 84
   stock performance, 90
Postpetition interest, 36

Prediction of corporate distress, 233
   emerging markets, 265. *See also* Emerging market score (EMS) model
Preferences. *See* Bankruptcy(ies)
Prepackaged bankruptcy(ies), 5, 48, 51–53, 98
Probit, 235
Procyclicality, 319

Quadratic-discriminant analysis, 235

Rating agency(ies):
   comparisons, 278
   Dominion Bond Rating Service, 245
   Duff & Phelps, LLC, 278
   Fitch, 245
   Moody's, 245, 246. *See also* Moody's
   Standard & Poor's, 245, 246. *See also* Standard & Poor's
Ratio analysis, 238
RCN Corp., 153
Recovery rate(s), 159, 163, 166, 307, 308, 319, 320
   default rate association, 326, 327
Recursive partitioning, 235
Regal Cinemas, 229
Reorganization process, 21–78
Required average return on capital (RAROC), 283
Restructuring advisers:
   Blackstone Group, 294
   Chanin Capital Partners, 294
   Evercore Partners, 294
   FTI Consulting Inc., 294
   Giuliani Partners, 294
   Greenhill & Co., 294
   Houlihan Lokey Howard & Zukin, 294
   Jefferies & Co., 294
   Lazard Freres, 294
   Miller Buckfire, 294
   Miller-Mathis & Co., 294
   N.M. Rothschild & Sons, 294
Revere Copper & Brass, 31
RiskMetrics, 291. *See also* CreditMetrics
RJR Nabisco, 125, 134
Ross, W.L., 189, 228

San Luis, S.A. de C.V., 276
Sarbanes-Oxley, 44
Schacht v. Brown, 289
Schaefer Beer, 288
Schuylkill Permanent Bridge Company, 235
Section 364, 44. *See also* Debtor-in-possession (DIP)
Securities and Exchange Commission (SEC), 22, 24, 33
Singapore, 263
South Korea, 263
Southland Corporation, 52, 98, 127

Spain, 263
Standard & Poor's, 168, 207, 249, 278, 307
   Credit Pro database, 319
   debt ratings, 146
   Risk Solutions, 291
Standard Industrial Classification codes, 105
Stelco, 153
Storage Technology, 104
SunGard, 125

Tax-free reorganization, 42, 43
Tax loss carryforwards, 42
Tax Reform Act of 1986, 43
Tax shields, 113
Telefonos de Mexico, 279
Televisa, S.A. de C.V., 276
Temporary debt, 140
Texaco, 28
Time in reorganization. *See*
   Bankruptcy(ies)
Total enterprise value, 106
Tower Air, 81
Tower Automotive, 296
Trade claims. *See* Bankruptcy(ies)
Tricom, 148
Trump Hotels & Casino Resorts, 148, 153,
   294
Turkey, 263
Turnaround consulting firm(s):
   AlixPartners, 293
   Alvarez and Marsal, 293
   BBK, Ltd., 293
   Huron Consulting, 293
   Kroll, Zolfo, Cooper, 293
   XRoads Solutions Group, 293
Turnaround Management Association, 293
Turnaround managers, 293–294, 295
Turnarounds & Workouts, 28
Type I accuracy, 244, 255
Type II error, 244, 255, 285

USAir, 148, 153
U.S. Trustee, 14, 32, 39, 49, 79, 220
United Kingdom, 264
United Merchants and Manufacturing
   (UMM), 26
United Nations Commission on
   International Trade Law (UNCITRAL),
   56–57
   Model Law on Cross-Border Insolvencies,
   56
Uruguay, 264

Valuation:
   adjusted present value, 109, 113
   beta, 111, 115
   capital asset pricing model, 110
   capital cash flow(s), 113
   capital structure, 121, 129
   "comparable company" approach,
      105–108
   "comparable M&A transaction"
      approach, 107, 109
   discounted cash flow method(s),
      109
   distressed firm, 103
   free cash flow, 109, 110
   liquidation, 116
   in reorganization, 33
   strategic use, 117
   terminal value, 111, 112
Vitro Corporation, 276
Vulture investing, 81, 188, 224, 228

WCI Steel Corporation, 104, 107, 111,
   113
Weighted average cost of capital (WACC),
   109
   unlevered, 115
Westpac Banking Corporation, 322
Wilson Foods, 36
WIND telecom, 125
WorldCom, 3, 102, 170, 184, 224, 233,
   236, 257
W.T. Grant, 4, 26

XO Communications, 229

Yields on high yield bond portfolios. *See*
   High yield bond(s)
Youngstown Sheet & Tube, 36
Yukos, 153

Z-Score(s), 235, 238
   bond rating equivalent, 245
   model, 191, 233, 236, 240, 249, 267,
      290
   vs. rating(s), 255
Z'-Score model, 245, 246, 248
Z"-Score, 243, 248, 257, 268
   emerging market(s). *See* Emerging market
      score (EMS) model
   model, 243, 248, 249
   vs. rating(s), 257
ZETA®, 238, 242